Communication Perspectives on
Popular Culture

Communication Perspectives in Popular Culture

Series Editors
Andrew F. Herrmann, East Tennessee State University
Art Herbig, Indiana University–Purdue University, Fort Wayne

The *Communication Perspectives in Popular Culture* series examines the integral role that popular culture plays in scholarship and teaching. We use it to critique culture and to exemplify theory. We use it to understand public discourse as well as help us to explain the role that those discourses play in our daily lives. The way popular culture helps construct, define, and impact everyday reality must be taken seriously, specifically because popular culture is, simply, popular. Rather than assuming that popular culture is an unimportant place of fantastical make-believe with no impact beyond the screen, this series studies popular culture and what it can tell us about identity, gender, organizations, power, relationships, and numerous other subjects. The goal of this series is to provide a glimpse into the differing relationships between academic research and a number of popular culture artifacts from a variety of perspectives to create a space for larger discussions.

Titles in Series

Communication Perspectives on Popular Culture, edited by Andrew F. Herrmann and Art Herbig

Communication Perspectives on Popular Culture

Edited by
Andrew F. Herrmann and Art Herbig

LEXINGTON BOOKS
Lanham • Boulder • New York • London

Published by Lexington Books
An imprint of The Rowman & Littlefield Publishing Group, Inc.
4501 Forbes Boulevard, Suite 200, Lanham, Maryland 20706
www.rowman.com

Unit A, Whitacre Mews, 26-34 Stannary Street, London SE11 4AB

British Library Cataloguing in Publication Information Available

Library of Congress Cataloging-in-Publication Data

Names: Herrmann, Andrew F., 1966- editor. | Herbig, Art, 1977- editor.
Title: Communication perspectives on popular culture / edited by Andrew F. Herrmann and Art
    Herbig.
Description: Lanham : Lexington Books, [2016] | Series: Communication perspectives on popular
    culture | Includes bibliographical references and index.
Identifiers: LCCN 2016034708 (print) | LCCN 2016044373 (ebook)
Subjects: LCSH: Popular culture. | Mass media and culture.
Classification: LCC HM621 .C6434 2016 (print) | LCC HM621 (ebook) | DDC 302.23--dc23
LC record available at https://lccn.loc.gov/2016034708

ISBN 9781498523929 (cloth : alk. paper)
ISBN 9781498523943 (pbk. : alk. paper)
ISBN 9781498523936 (electronic)

∞™ The paper used in this publication meets the minimum requirements of American
National Standard for Information Sciences Permanence of Paper for Printed Library
Materials, ANSI/NISO Z39.48-1992.

Printed in the United States of America

Contents

Acknowledgments

It would be a mistake to believe that this book is our production alone. There were many individuals, groups, and organizations that made the conversations that led to this book possible. Thanks to the members, officers, and volunteers of the Central States Communication Association, our "home base" for the conversations that led to this text. It seems as if all of our good ideas come from conversations at CSCA. We would also like to thank everyone who participated in the creation of this book, including the panel audience members that kept pushing us forward, the contributors, Nicolette Amstutz, Alison Pavan, and Kasey Beduhn.

I (Andrew) want to thank Art Bochner, Carolyn Ellis, Charles Guignon, Bob Krizek, Chris Poulos, and Paaige Turner. You were and are my mentors, so this is your fault. Unmitigated thanks to my Communication Studies colleagues at ETSU: Amber Kinser, Wesley Buerkle, and Kelly Dorgan, whose support is undying. Thanks also to my students who help me get my geek on, particularly Alana Claxton and Hailey Patrick; and my former students, Jeni Hunniecutt, Annalee Tull, and Michael Wallace. Besides the wonderful people in this, I must say thanks to the great people who through personal communication and conferencing have enlarged my thinking about pop culture: Jennifer C. Dunn, Stephanie L. Young, Michelle Calka, Megan Wood Gillette, Brian Johnston, Bobby Funk, and Kristen Blinne. A shout out to the authors waiting patiently for me to start working on the organizational autoethnography collection. Love to Mom, Charlie, Amy, and the Herrmann Men (Fred, Jim, and Garrett).

And I (Art) would like to start by thanking my partner Alix Watson for all of her help and support. My mentors include Rob Anderson, Bob Krizek, Paaige Turner, Robert Gaines, James F. Klumpp, Shawn Parry-Giles, and Trevor Parry-Giles, and I would like to thank each of them for all of the time they put in to get me to this point. I would also give a special thanks to Raymie McKerrow for being a wise and kind voice of reason to a scholar who he had no reason to help. I cannot thank him enough. I really appreciate all of the continued love and support from my family—Pat, Art, and Scott Herbig. Also, I would like to thank my colleagues at IPFW, especially Marcia Dixson and Irwin Mallin, for helping provide a space for me to learn and grow. As I continue to evolve, I have gotten to work with some excellent scholars. Special thanks to Andrew F. Herrmann, Adam W. Tyma, Danielle Stern, Kathy Denker, Jennifer C.

Dunn, Stephanie L. Young, Michelle Calka, Jimmie Manning, Tony E. Adams, Michaela D. E. Meyer, CarrieLynn D. Reinhard, and Aaron Hess for all of their pushes and collaborations. I have the great fortune to work with brilliant people and even greater fortune to call them friends.

Introduction

Not Another Pop Culture Series!
Studying the World(s) We Occupy

Andrew F. Herrmann and Art Herbig

It's hard to believe that as we near the third decade of the twenty-first century, there are still places where studying popular culture is frowned upon, not taken seriously, or used as a straw man in arguments about higher education.[1] Despite this, popular culture studies continue to develop and expand, and many "pop culturists" founded their own conferences, journals, and book series devoted to looking at the role popular culture plays in our lives. So, why another book series? Why more books? Why should we explore a topic with such diverse and creative insights already? In a word: evolution.

Unless you have been asleep for the last 25 years, you must have noticed that almost everything about popular culture changed: from its content to the way we (and here we mean creators, audiences, fans, and academics) participate with and through it, and to the way content is delivered. The dilemma is that while all those aspects of popular culture changed dramatically, research and scholarship—even the terminology we use—has barely kept up.[2] This is not surprising given the paradoxical nature of research, which simultaneously emphasizes the conservative and the innovative.[3] What this book series and this text as a primer take seriously is that the way we examine, study, and discuss popular culture needs to evolve just as the subject(s) we are studying evolves. So what do we mean?

For one, it means we must reevaluate and reframe the term "media," taking it back from those who seek to divorce it from its singular form: medium. Walter J. Ong theorized that a change in medium fundamentally changes us as well.[4] "Technologies are not mere exterior aids, but also interior transformations of consciousness, and never more than when they affect the word."[5] If that is true, then we exist in a time when what we mean by knowledge is changing, not just in the content as what "counts" as knowledge, but how knowledge comes to be in an era of changing media (in the plural). Studies of media, transmedia, and polymedia must be interwoven with studies of ontology, epistemology, axiology, and so on. These are areas where shifts can be identified and examined through our relationships to the popular.

Any artifact can be a form of mediation, yet when talking about media we are normally referring to the big five: print, radio, film, television, and the Internet. However, media simultaneously stay the same and change and blur. Newspapers are online and in print. Television is produced both by broadcast stations and by Netflix, in your living room and on your phone. Movies are made for theatres, for Instagram, for Snapchat. Even I Heart Radio. Henry Jenkins, Joshua Green, and Sam Ford tell us that "if it doesn't spread, it's dead."[6] While that is poetic, it begs two questions. Is that true? And if that is true, what does that mean for popular culture, and its relationship to communication and knowledge?

Secondly, when talking about popular culture's evolution, we are including more than merely what we experience through the media. We spread and communicate pop culture through the patches we attach to our messenger bags and in the action figures that we carefully store on our bookcases. Like a sports jersey or a cosplay costume, these popular culture artifacts have the power to create both identification and difference. The question, "So, you are into DC Comics?" can strike up a friendship or start an argument as easily as "So you're a Yankees fan?"

Thirdly, time and location also provide opportunities for these conversations. Place is an important factor in our experiences of popular culture. For instance, when Jon Stewart and Stephen Colbert took their particular brands of political comedy to the National Mall in Washington DC, I (Art) went with producer Alix Watson and colleague Aaron Hess to make a film and write an essay about what drew people to be a part of the story.[7] Places like Indio, California, are relatively unknown until someone mentions it is the home of the Coachella Music and Arts Festival. Matthew J. Smith shows us the experience, draw, and significance of places such as San Diego Comic-Con.[8] These are sites of popular culture where experiences and connections are created that can never be replicated, but can be continued and carried forward as memories. These cases are interesting because they are spread through interaction and experience, not through coaxial cables or satellite signals. In our discussions and research, we need to account for the vast experiences one can have through, with, about, around, and because of popular culture.

Finally, the words popular and culture suggest popular culture is a force of connection and conjunction. As such, this is a place to unpack this combination of terms, and what this connection says about us. Whether it is about the communities established through the brewing, tasting, and discussing of beer, or the ways in which we harken back to eight-bit video games, there is currency in popular culture that allows us the opportunity to examine how different aspects of our identities are constructed. Identity is important. Individuals get invested in popular culture. They take artifacts of popular culture when they leave important spaces, places, events, and moments. Popular culture is both a tool for memory and a means for expressing who we are in the present.

In fact, identification is one reason why we have heated discussions. Buffy Summers or Bella Swan?[9] Which band best encapsulated punk rock: The Sex Pistols, The Ramones, or The Clash?[10] Who was the better government agent on television: *Alias'* Sydney Bristow or *24's* Jack Bauer?[11] Did Humphrey Bogart, James Cagney, or Edward G. Robinson play the best gangster?[12] Who had the better disses: Ice Cube versus Dr. Dre versus Eazy-E?[13] Is your favorite Doctor Dr. Leonard "Bones" McCoy, Dr. Stephen Strange, or Dr. Who (and which iteration?)?[14] Are you on Team Cap or Team Ironman?[15] These questions appear trivial. However, "our identities and identifications with popular culture artifacts assist in our creation of self. Our identities and pop culture have a long-term recursive relationship."[16]

Let me (Andrew) give an example. Imagine you followed me around for a day. Here's some of what you'd see. In the morning when we go into the kitchen to make coffee, you'd notice the ceramic *Doctor Strange* statue. As I got dressed, you'd see my ever-growing collection of *Doctor Strange* t-shirts. When we went into my home office, you'd notice my *Doctor Strange* action figures, posters, and graphic novels. You'd watch me skip over anything on Facebook related to this autumn's upcoming *Doctor Strange* movie (no spoilers!). In the living room, you'd note the *Doctor Strange* animated movie. As I head out the door, you'd note I threw on a *Doctor Strange* baseball cap. Once we got to my office, you'd see a number of texts devoted to Marvel and *Doctor Strange*, while we listen to *Doctor Strange* mp3s downloaded on my Mac. When we got back home, I'd show you my *Doctor Strange #1* comic book, one that I've cherished for years. But what does this mean? To me it means popular culture activities are polymediated, are part of what Eric Eisenberg calls my "surround," and are significant to my identity.[17]

As I (Art) currently write, my eyes are drawn to a slow-moving countdown clock on the webpage ProphetsOfRage.com. On Tuesday, May 17, the web presence for the band Rage Against the Machine came back to life after the band broke up in 2011.[18] As a Rage Against the Machine fan, I was excited by the promise of a reunion. My excitement turned to disappointment when they revealed this was not a reunion. That disappointment turned into utter joy when I realized that three members of Rage Against the Machine would be teaming up with Public Enemy's Chuck D and Cypress Hill's B-Real to form the supergroup Prophets of Rage. As rumors began to leak about the potential of a summer tour or an anti-convention in Cleveland to coincide with the Republican National Convention, I am intrigued and delighted by the potential. The ticking clock, along with the rumors, has my attention. What was once Rage Against the Machine is becoming something else. It has a new web presence, new music to play, new messages to deliver, new spaces to play, and opportunities to become something connected to what it was, while developing into something it never could have been.

Like Rage Against the Machine, for those of us who study popular culture, it is time to evolve.

THE LIMITS OF PAST DILEMMAS IN
POPULAR CULTURE RESEARCH

As part of our exploration of future directions for communication studies of popular culture, we thought we would start with an examination of some of the past tensions and impasses. Many of these represent tensions that exist in writing *about* popular culture and not necessarily *in* popular culture. Others reverberate and need to be confronted through continued examination. Ultimately, these are places where we can start to understand the evolution process. Some of what we discuss will at first glance appear tangential. However, given that popular culture, communication, and polymediation are intermingled,[19] it is important to touch on dichotomies of the past, and interrogate what is happening now.

High versus Low

We live in a world where some of the wealthiest among us seek fame in the form of reality television stardom and infinite retweets, a time where a rich "outsider" candidate for US president conducts Twitter wars with politicians and entertainers alike. Technology has blurred, if not erased, the old lines between high culture and low culture. The wealthy and the non-wealthy use the same technologies to play in the same "sandbox" (We return to class issues below). For example, the wealthy now exploit themselves on what was once considered "trash" television. Regular people suddenly find themselves among the famous when they create social media accounts for their dogs.[20] Sometimes this is purposeful, as in the case of Rebecca Black, whose family paid thousands of dollars to produce her most watched and much-disparaged music video "Friday."[21] Sometimes it happens to them, as was the case with Kyle Craven, better known by the meme his friend created, "Bad Luck Brian."[22] These examples reflect the power of what Henry Jenkins referred to as convergence,[23] but convergence has not completely democratized discourse. While Doug the Pug, Rebecca Black, and Bad Luck Brian achieved fame, we can still see the influence of major media outlets on the web. We can also see the reach of large institutions and corporations such as Microsoft and Amazon. The web is not as much a place of equality as it is a space for opportunity. High and low are products of discourse in many of the same ways people say, "The book is better than the movie." Claiming "high" culture can be seen within comic book communities, Harry Potter fans, and *Dungeons & Dragons* players as a strategy to display ethos, originality, or status.

Consequently, there is a benefit to understanding the remnants of the high versus low dichotomy as a rhetoric. "The Academy" still tells us what the best movies are every year at the spectacle known as "The Oscars." National news still comes from places like the *New York Times* or the *Wall Street Journal*. Rather than seeing these examples as a sign of the legacy of the culture industry decried by Horkheimer and Adorno,[24] we need to examine the intersection of ethos and distribution. Certainly, there are big budget movies audiences avoid (*Ender's Game*, anyone?). There are upstart news agencies that do excellent journalism, and independent studios that make small successful films. Yet, there is credibility in the historicity and facticity and discursivity of the popular that keeps people coming back. The last vestiges of high culture point toward an ideological superstructure similar to that described by Raymond Williams as a totality steeped in repetition and hegemony, not affirmed by insight.[25] The popular begets the popular as a powerful position, especially when that position is connected to the idea of credibility, reinforcing the perception that certain institutions and events are high culture until those connections are questioned and broken. It is ideological, discursive, and impacts how we interact with the material.

Mass versus Public

Past research on popular culture theorized mass and public as dichotomous and oppositional. What we are learning is they are not. C. Wright Mills wrote that

> the public and mass may be most readily distinguished by their dominant modes of communications: in a community of publics, discussion is the ascendant mode of communication, and the mass media, if they exist, simply enlarge and animate discussion, linking one *primary public* with the discussions of another. (emphasis in original)[26]

What once seemed naïve or optimistic now seems problematic and prophetic. It is clear that modern media created a situation in which mass culture and publics are intimately intertwined. Whether through the comments section on a national news story, or the uproar by fans when creators choose to take their narratives or characters down certain paths,[27] people are involved in mass media in ways never envisioned. Mass media became the dominant form of information in the early twentieth-century with the advent and dissemination of technologies like radio, television, and film.[28] Those technologies still exist. However, now they are accompanied and extended by public technologies that have discussion boards and the "two-screen experience."[29]

We do not need to pronounce the death of mass media in order to examine or understand the role of public media such as social media in our lives. We now understand that what Mills understood as a "primary public" is actually an infinite amount of publics and counter-publics connected through the dissemination of information.[30] We also need to understand "mass" as a way of distributing information and as a constitutive force that defines *audiences*, rather than a singular *public*. Both mass and public exist, but how we understand and examine them is due for a change.

Pop versus Cult

The same dichotomy raises its head regarding popular versus cult. When I (Andrew) was growing up in the 1980s, I was interested in underground alt-Christian rock music.[31] At the time, rock music was publicly shunned in Christian culture, and listening to weird post-punk Christian music was the epitome of being an outcast.[32] While there was a little clique in my neighborhood with others interested in this music, we had to search each other out. Building this community took time. Now, however, I can visit a multitude of online sites to geek out with people from around the globe about Daniel Amos, The Choir, or the 77s. As Bob Batchelor inquired, now that online communities exist wherein people can discuss their particular passions, is there such a thing as *cult* pop culture?[33] There are now spaces dedicated to the intricate plot details of Joss Whedon's failed but popular television series *Firefly*, the bizarre guitar techniques of King Crimson's Robert Fripp, and the tiny details between the various cuts of *Bladerunner*.[34]

Technology allowed these underground or "geek" topics to go mainstream. The Internet and the social media that propagated along with it allow for what were once private and personal obsessions to be aired, discussed, and argued in public. Whether it is niche television networks, online discussion forums, or fan conventions, smaller communities of people have a much larger voice in modern culture. While some continue to worry about "going mainstream" or "selling out," there are more spaces for these communities to thrive. As we will discuss below, this is not necessarily a good thing. However, it is happening.

Private versus Public

Erving Goffman famously wrote about the *Presentation of Self in Everyday Life*, but Goffman never had to account for the complicated frontstage/backstage relationship posed by modern media.[35] Building on Goffman and others, Michelle Calka examined the impact digital technologies can have on identity:

> Our self is decentered but interconnected. All of our performances, online and offline, constitute the self. I problematize the notion of the self here, adapting the term to include multiple, equally valid performances of self. We could use the term "selves," but the idea of decentered but interconnected selves points to different aspects, not entirely different selves.[36]

Whether one believes the self is entirely a performance, an assembled narrative, a rhetorical construction, or a "core" individuality, the concept of identity is complicated by the growing and changing media used for expressing our "self."

Take, for instance, the growth of fringe militaristic groups. There was a time when their ideas were marginalized and bound by the disconnection of distance. Now these people can seek out others that share their political beliefs and perspectives in shared online spaces. They can find places to express their identity, and freely voice their hate and vitriol. These individuals often value the anonymity and secrecy that comes with a digital existence. It is the public-privateness of them that allows people to be both a conspirator and (probably unbeknownst to you) a co-worker. New technologies lead to a blend of the private and public in interesting ways. We all have simultaneous private public selves online. The same individual who trolls a YouTube video or Catfishes a potential victim, also maintains profiles and accounts in digital spaces he or she wishes to remain private. Online bank accounts, shopping accounts, and digital streaming platforms are all potential examples of public spaces in which people wish to maintain some form of privacy.

We have to manage the difference between public private selves and public selves. Goffman could not have imagined the intersection of being yourself in a public context engaged in a performance for people in that room, and then having that performance distributed to the world via social media. What happens when that private public performance becomes public-public? In 2015, Darryn King wrote about such a phenomenon in *Vanity Fair*.[37] Known to many as the "Ermahgerd Girl," Maggie Goldenberger was a 23–year-old travelling abroad when she found out her image had become "Internet famous." She became part of popular culture, although her role in popular culture was entirely divorced from her private existence.

Accessing various platforms is also a matter of navigating private and public. In a world where news stories are marked NSFW (Not Safe for Work) and pulling out your phone in a job interview is seen as uncouth, the medium *itself* becomes a negotiation of the public and private. This negotiation has become so important that in 2014 the US Supreme Court took the case *Riley v. California* to examine the roles mobile phones play in our lives.[38] How do we balance the need between privacy and security, which was the point of conflict between Apple and the Federal Bureau of Investigation regarding the San Bernardino shooter's iPhone?[39] Public and private, frontstage and backstage are areas in need of further interrogation.

We often reserve very important private spaces for interactions with popular culture commodities. Action figures from childhood have special shelves in our homes. I (Art) have sports memorabilia, film posters, and various tokens from events I attended prominently displayed in both my home and office. Some of us have the worn-out edition of a favorite book sitting on a nightstand. Although we already know every word, we binge watch our favorite television program one more time. It is better than comfort food. Our private spaces are filled with trinkets and markers of how popular culture is part of both our public and private lives.

The dichotomies posed when discussing the relationship between high or low, mass versus public, pop versus cult, or private versus public is woven deeply into the fabric of modern popular culture, but we need to move past seeing them as either/or relationships. New technologies provide us new forms of connection, to traverse great spaces to find those with whom we identify. However, we are simultaneously told these spaces are public spaces, to be wary of catfishing, phishing, and to manage our online existence as if we are public relations professionals. We are told using hashtags and Facebook pages to muster a larger, louder voice is "slacktivism." We are told celebrities who have their digital nude photos stolen "had it coming to them" for having the photos in the first place. What YouTube comment sections show us is we have not effectively mastered the use of digital spaces or modern polymediated discourse. Likewise, we have not figured out how these spaces function simultaneously as private and public. This is not merely a matter of keeping our accounts from being hacked; it is about our ability to tap into new understandings of both popular and culture.

RESEARCHING POSSIBILITIES IN NEW DIRECTIONS FOR POPULAR CULTURE RESEARCH

Conceptualizing Audiences and Participants

One of the prominent future directions for popular culture criticism is examining the dual roles of participant and audience. Ever since Janice Radway took us through the world of romance novel readership, and communication scholars examined soap opera viewership, we have been trying to understand the audience experience.[40] The office water cooler, where people discussed "Who killed Laura Palmer?" or "Who shot JR?" or "Is Buffy really dead?" moved online. As we noted in our examination of *Supernatural* as a polymediated television narrative, audiences "are blogging, Tweeting during broadcasts, Facebooking spoilers, writing fan/slash fiction, or being involved with participatory television talk shows."

They are "active participants, both consumers and producers simultaneously."[41]

Of course audiences exist. Nele Simons found many people are neither engaging online resources nor motivated to engage them while in the midst of watching television.[42] Similarly, the backlash against the AMC movie chain's proposal to allow social media use during films was so strong they backed away from the policy.[43] People still want to act as audiences, but that does not mean that members of an audience cannot change roles before, during, or after reading, listening, and/or viewing. Audiences have changed with the changes in popular culture and media. Being an audience member must now be considered a transitory state instead of a fixed position in relation to a mass culture.[44]

The Metaphor of the Consumer

What cannot get lost in any discussion of bottom-up participant-led popular culture is the role of class. In fact, the "bottom-up" metaphor ignores the ways in which people exist both inside and outside of media systems. The two most prominent words used to describe people in relation to media and pop culture have been audience (already covered) and consumer. As a metaphor for the purchasers of popular culture commodities, consumer suggests a top-down orientation to popular culture participation. Regarding class, it is important to remember not all people have the economic means to participate or consume in this way. Being a collector or a geek means having economic means to do so. As we wrote previously, we must acknowledge the inclusivity and exclusivity that exist in popular culture as an integral part of its discursive function.[45] In a word, we are talking about access.

For instance, we are big fans of HBO's *Game of Thrones*. To watch *Game of Thrones*, you must subscribe to cable, with the accompanying cable box and HBO add-on. Or you must have an Internet connection to a device with a subscription to HBONOW or Amazon Prime. Or you must have a place to access the Internet and a mobile device with a subscription to HBONOW or Amazon Prime. An Internet connection and a device bind even those who illegally pirate the episode. Not all of these are equal. The distinction between HBONOW and Amazon Prime is important. HBONOW hosts individual episodes right after they air. Amazon Prime gets seasons only after the whole season has aired (same with Netflix). Access to, and therefore "consumption," of *Game of Thrones*, is based on any number of factors including wealth, time, location, and opportunity.

The dilemmas posed by access are similar in some ways, and attendant to, the concept of spoilers. In the case of the spoiler, a consumer must regurgitate elements of what they consumed (and reactions are similar to being regurgitated on). However, the spoiler concept contradicts the notion of a person as a consumer in relation to popular culture.

It is not about *consuming*, but *experiencing, feeling*, and *sharing* their experience with others. An individual who reveals a spoiler believes accessing a text is both a shared opportunity and a shared experience. Neither is necessarily true, much to the chagrin of the person who just heard the huge reveal in a movie they have yet to see. The spoiler exists at the intersections of mass and public culture—and interpersonal communication—revealing that none fully articulates modern media interactions.

If we limit the metaphor of consumer to economic transactions, the metaphor still falls short. The metaphor of consumer presumes that you are taking something from "the mass" for your own consumption. Purchasing a shirt at Comic-Con or a ticket to a film is not an act of consumption. It is an act of participation. Even purchasing your groceries is an act of *participation* that leads to *consumption* rather than an *a priori* act of consumption. The inclusivity and exclusivity of a Whole Foods or a Fresh Market speaks to the importance of understanding how one is able to access and interact based on race, gender, class, location, or sexuality in a culture where what is popular will never be universal and open access is a myth in need of criticism.

Reality

When discussing online and polymediated forms of communication, we often talk about how those interactions are somehow "less real" than the ones we experience in "real" life. We tend to subordinate identification with celebrities into "parasocial" interactions. Robert Andrew Dunn subordinated online experiences to "polyreality."[46] However, it is worth trying to unpack the realness of our popular culture experiences. For instance, aren't the feelings of someone who has been catfished real?[47] What about the connections maintained through Facebook after distance has separated friends? Is a username on Twitch an identity? Does the IP address a hacker uses to have you "SWATed" become your reality identifier?[48] Or, how real are the "parasocial" relationships individuals have with their favorite characters from pop culture as a means for their own expressions about lived experiences and understandings, as we have with Xander Harris from *Buffy the Vampire Slayer*?[49] While some find themselves immersed in "reality television," online media have worked their way into our romantic relationships, friendships, credit reports, consumer habits, and political participation. Put simply, into our realities.

The key to language such as "parasocial" and "polyreality" is how it subordinates people's experiences into a modified version of the actual thing. For instance, I (Art) have a parasocial love/hate relationship with J. J. Abrams. I loved the new *Star Wars* film, but hated what he did to *Star Trek*. I learned his views about fandom, digital technology, storytelling, and many other topics in interviews and in print. I follow his Twitter account and Facebook threads at times and feel as though I know a bit about him as a public figure. Is this a "parasocial" relationship, a relationship at all, or is it something else?

For greater clarity, let me (Art) try this in reverse. I have a public figure Facebook page. I require students in my media and basic communication courses to follow the page and to interact with me. Sometimes students choose to continue to follow the page and comment long after their course officially ends. Am I in a "parasocial" relationship with my former students? When did it become "parasocial?" New technologies are creating different kinds of relationships no less "real" or "significant," but they do have different stakes and kinds of interactions. Relegating the reality of those relationships as "less than real" is not as productive to understanding their dynamics. "Hyperreal" knowledge does not make it "not" knowledge.[50] It makes it different. As a communicator in the twenty-first century, one cannot help but be aware of the role of communication contexts. Having a conversation on Facebook is distinct from Twitter is distinct from Yik Yak. The attention paid to texting and driving, as well as video of people bumping into walls while on social media on their phones, reveals to us the role of physical context in relation to digital spaces (Not to mention the people falling off cliffs, and so on, and actually dying while taking selfies).[51] Managing the physical world in relation to the digital is one of the great challenges of the polymediated age.

All of the above ideas, conceptualizations, theoretical musings, problemitizations, and questions lead us to the following tenet regarding communication studies of popular culture: Popular culture is communicative in nature. Therefore, popular culture is not only about artifacts, but also about our relationships with artifacts, and our relationships. It is about discourse, and narrative, and storytelling, and not just text. As communication, popular culture is social and studies of it are also studies of our intersubjective understandings. Popular culture research must take into consideration studies that include orientations that are both process and product oriented. Popular culture is simultaneously personal and political, public and private, and polymediated.

WHAT YOU WILL FIND IN THIS BOOK

We are proud to have worked with some of the finest scholars we know to discuss the role that popular culture plays across the communication discipline. The contributors represent numerous theoretical and methodological approaches to popular culture. Each chapter serves metaphorically as both a cornerstone and as a touchstone. As any child with a Lego set can tell you, the cornerstone is the most important part of the building, the foundation that can be built upon by others. A touchstone, in the Shakespearean tradition, is a controversial guide; the person who points out what should be obvious to everyone (but isn't). This text is by no means exhaustive; it is a primer, and as such it is designed to create jumping-off points for future research, provide insight, and evoke controversy. While each author comes at popular culture from a different lens, they are all attuned in various ways to popular culture as process and product, as personal and political, as public and private.

To begin, Tony E. Adams theorizes the varied ways by which popular culture can be approached and interpreted as queer. Delving into *The Golden Girls, The Leftovers,* and *Inside Out,* Adams elaborates on how queer readings of popular culture texts provide a critical response to harmful cultural assumptions and offer original conceptualizations about intimacy and relationships, promising a better and more inclusive future. Bob Batchelor also provides us with a theoretical approach to popular culture. Using DeLonge's Angels & Airwaves, Batchelor reinterprets popular culture theory through the Engage, Adapt, and Transform model. This model moves us away from studying an "object" of popular culture, instead bringing into focus how people convert objects into thoughts, feelings, ideas, and emotions.

For Andrew F. Herrmann, Eric M. Eisenberg, and Adam W. Tyma, organizations play a large role in popular culture. Things get scary as Herrmann considers the perils and promise (as well as the disciplinary politics) of studying pop culture as an organizational communication scholar through a study of the popular cult hit television series *Supernatural.* He interrogates the metaphor of the "family business," the discourses surrounding work-life balance, as well as the organizing processes of sensemaking and stigma used by Sam and Dean Winchester as they hunt phantastical creatures. Eisenberg explores how the researchers' and practitioners' conceptions of leadership changed over the past few decades, while simultaneously chronicling popular culture representations of organizational leadership in the popular police dramas *Hill Street Blues* and *NYPD Blue,* as well as in news coverage. He shows how popular notions of leadership reflect new realities, yet are also lacking in our world of ambiguity and equivocality. We travel to outer space with Tyma, where he employs both organizational and political economic concepts to identify the Ideological and Repressive State Apparati signified and enacted within Ridley Scott's sci-fi horror masterpiece *Alien.* Furthermore, he examines each *Nostromo* crewmember's fears and desires about power and identity within the organizational matrix of—and discourses provided by—"The Company." Importantly, all three chapters not only explore organizations within popular culture, but processes of organizing.

Back on Earth, Deanna Sellnow surveys her life's work on the rhetorical study of music. She argues we must study the "what, how, and why" music communicates to and for us in our daily lives, because as popular culture it is both pervasive and persuasive. Sellnow illuminates how music can be a powerful force for change, as it communicates to and for us deep within our souls, and can be more persuasive than talk. While music can be a force for change, it, as well as other forms of popular culture, are sometimes used for overt political means.

Politicians cultivate audiences for both campaigns and policies in places such as *The Tonight Show* as well as *Between Two Ferns*. Historically, candidates call on popular culture—and portrayals in popular culture—as examples of the best or worst of contemporary culture, from comic books as a cause of juvenile delinquency, to the Sex Pistols' demonization, to Dan Quayle's pronouncements about Murphy Brown, to *The West Wing, House of Cards*, and *Veep*. Using the graphic novel and subsequent movie *The Watchmen*, Trevor Parry-Giles, Will P. Howell, and Devin Scott explore the intricacies of political representation. They argue there are reflections and deflections of politics in popular culture we need to meaningfully examine for us to understand the role *depictions* of politics have on our *perceptions* of politics. Similarly, Cheryl Ann Lambert, Jessalynn Strauss, and Natalie T. J. Tindall examine the texts and portrayals of the television series *Scandal* and *Ray Donovan* for what they accurately and inaccurately tell us about public perceptions of public relations and public relations professionals.

Politics are not only portrayed on the screen, but also exist in the production of the scholarship on popular culture. Both Art Herbig and Michelle Kelsay Kearl examine process as well as product. Herbig is particularly interested in the role that critical rhetoric can play in public discourses about popular culture. When Raymie McKerrow wrote that critical rhetoric represents "the reversal of 'public address' to 'discourse which addresses publics' places the critic in the role of 'inventor,'"[52] he inspired critics to deeply consider their role in public discourses. As part of that enterprise, Herbig argues that critical rhetoricians have a responsibility to engage popular culture on its own terms. He contends it is necessary to build new outlets for the creation and dissemination of critical rhetoric that goes beyond the words on a page in academic journals (I, Andrew, agree with Art. I refer to the dissemination of our ideas as confined to academic texts, as "The International Journal of Two Readers," whereby we only talk to ourselves).[53] In her intertextual approach, Kearl analyzes the complex matrix of power and identity in *Orange Is the New Black*, paying close attention to the lived experiences of people of color in relationship to the prison industrial complex (PIC). She notes that *OITNB*, while critical of the PIC, does not fundamentally challenge the underlying economic, social, and structural dilemmas faced by communities of color, reifying the neo-liberal discourses of "individual responsibility."

Similarly, Danielle M. Stern and Krista Catalfamo examine how identity is expressed in Women Against Feminism (WAF) polymediated environments and its various problematics. They note WAF members operate within the neo-liberal discourses of individualism and American ethnocentrism. Coupled with anti-feminist discourse, these neo-liberal discourses in the hands of WAF risk dehistoricizing feminism in popular culture. Taking a broader look at our peculiar political moment, Lawrence Grossberg examines the Tea Party movement, noting the multiple paradoxes at its heart, which is why attempting to understand it from a strict ideological standpoint is impossible. He suggests the movement is the expression of widely felt fears, in a context of norms and hopes that are no longer possible to actualize in contemporary America.

Politics and political movements are important, and yet popular culture also provides the opportunity to interrogate and investigate points of relational connection. Given the importance of popular culture in our interpersonal lives, Jimmie Manning offers new approaches, methods, and theories for studying popular culture and people. Manning emphasizes the relational nature of popular culture in interpersonal communication, an important, necessary, and understudied aspect of popular culture's role in our lives. Moving from the general to the specific, Rob Anderson and Ken Cissna delve into one of the most important public dialogues of the twentieth century. Their analysis of the correspondence between Carl Rogers and B.F. Skinner portrays two cultural icons with conflicting visions working together privately to ensure more dialogic and less polarized public encounters. The detailed analysis of these iconic public intellectuals offers us an exemplar and one possible way out of our current political schisms.

In their examination of *The Family Hustle,* Siobhan E. Smith, Ryessia Jones, and Johnny Jones examine black masculinity and fatherhood on television. They note that while media depictions of black families can provide a progressive and lucrative place in television, more portrayals that challenge patriarchy, particularly normative black masculinity, would be beneficial for people of color. Robert Andrew Dunn also criticizes portrayals in media, by turning his journalist's eyes toward video games and gaming culture. Dunn challenges the demonization of gaming culture as exclusively aggressive and violent, which too often overlooks the positive and meaningful impact that video games play in people's lives. While these anti-social behaviors do exist, he provides a serious examination of video gaming culture as a place and a space for cooperation, social connectivity, cohesion, and community building.

In our final chapter, Kristen L. McCauliff and Katherine J. Denker examine how teaching with and through popular culture can allow teachers to connect material across all of these contexts with the lives and experiences of their students. Providing us with informative case studies, and looking at our own privilege as professors, McCauliff and Denker, take us into their classrooms. Their examples show us exactly how we can use popular culture to connect with our students, challenge our students, and be challenged by our students, creating a community of learner-teachers and teacher-learners.

Ultimately, these chapters look at popular culture, look at the field of communication, and look at the relationship between the two. Our goal is for you, the reader, to find something that helps inspire you to take the next step, author the next chapter, write the next book, and of course, argue with us and our contributors. In every instance, the authors were asked to provide a starting point. Where you go next will be up to you.

NOTES

1. Ivan Hewett, "Is it Time to End the Distinction between High and Low Art?" *The Telegraph,* January 30, 2015. www.telegraph.co.uk/culture/11378145/Is-it-time-to-end-the-distinction-between-high-and-low-art.html. (Accessed May 14, 2016.); Daniel Lametti, Aisha Harris, Natasha Geiling, and Natalie Matthews-Ramo, "Which Pop Culture Property Do Academics Study the Most?" *Slate,* June 11, 2012. www.slate.com/blogs/browbeat/2012/06/11/pop_culture_studies_why_do_academics_study_buffy_the_vampire_slayer_more_than_the_wire_the_matrix_alien_and_the_simpsons_.html. (Accessed May 14, 2016.); Elwood Watson and Marc W. Shaw, *Performing American Masculinities: The 21st-century Man in Popular Culture* (Bloomington, IN: Indiana State University Press, 2011.); Peter Wood, "Lily Bart vs. Lady Gaga." *The Chronicle of Higher Education,* March 1, 2011. chronicle.com/blogs/innovations/lily-bart-vs-lady-gaga/28742. (Accessed May 14, 2016.)

2. Adam Tyma, Andrew F. Herrmann, and Art Herbig, "Introduction: The Beginnings: #WeNeedaWord," in *Beyond New Media: Discourse and Critique in a Polymediated Age,* eds., Art Herbig, Andrew F. Herrmann, and Adam W. Tyma (Lanham, MD: Lexington Books, 2015): ix–xxiv; Art Herbig and Andrew F. Herrmann, "Polymediated Narrative: The Case of Supernatural's 'Fan Fiction,'" *International Journal of Communication* 10 (2016): 748–65.

3. Robert L. Krizek, "Lessons: What the Hell Are We Teaching the Next Generation Anyway?," in *Fiction and Social Research: By Ice or Fire,* eds., Anna Banks and Stephen P. Banks (Walnut Creek, CA: AltaMira Press, 1998): 89–114.

4. Walter J. Ong, *Orality and Literacy: The Technologizing of the Word* (1982; London: Routledge, 2001).

5. Ibid., 81.

6. Jenkins, Henry, Sam Ford, and Joshua Green, *Spreadable Media: Creating Value and Meaning in a Networked Culture* (New York, NY: NYU Press, 2013): 1.

7. Art Herbig and Aaron Hess, "Convergent Critical Rhetoric at the 'Rally to Restore Sanity': Exploring the Intersection of Rhetoric, Ethnography, and Documentary Production," *Communication Studies* 63.3 (2012): 269–89. doi: 10.1080/10510974.2012.674617.

8. Matthew J. Smith, "Introduction: The Pilgrimage to Comic-Con," in *It Happens at Comic-Con: Ethnographic Essays on a Pop Culture Phenomenon,* eds., Ben Bolling and Matthew J. Smith (Jefferson, NC: McFarland & Company, 2014): 9–14.

9. Christine Seifert, "Bite Me (Or Don't)," *Bitch Media,* December 15, 2008, bitchmedia.org/article/bite-me-or-dont. (Accessed May 22, 2016.)

10. Michael Enright, "The Birth of Punk," *Rewind with Michael Enright.* April 21, 2016. CBC-Radio Canada. www.cbc.ca/radio/rewind/the-birth-of-punk-1.3541039. (Accessed May 14, 2016.)

11. Bethan Jones, "Buffy vs. Bella: Gender, Relationships and the Modern Vampire," in *The Modern Vampire and Human Identity,* ed, Deborah Mutch (London, UK: Palgrave McMillan, 2013): 37–54.

12. Charles Rivers. *Hollywood's Gangster Icons: The Lives and Careers of Humphrey Bogart, James Cagney, and Edward G. Robinson.* Boston, MA: Charles Rivers Editors, 2014.

13. Tina Buckley, *The N.W.A. Handbook: Everything You Need to Know about N.W.A.* (Queensland, Australia: Emereo Publishing, 2016).

14. www.dorkly.com/toplist/60027/the-best-doctor-ever. (Accessed May 22, 2016.)

15. Betsy Cook and Riley Vasold, "Team Ironman vs. Team Captain America," *The Talon*, May 13, 2016. thetalon.news/6062/features/team-iron-man-vs-team-captain-america. (Accessed May 14, 2016.)

16. Jack Z. Bratich, "Spies Like Us: Secret Agency and Popular Occulture," in *Secret Agents: Beyond James Bond*, ed., Jeremy Packer (New York, NY: Peter Lang, 2009): 111–32.

17. Art Herbig, Andrew F. Herrmann, and Adam W. Tyma eds., *Beyond New Media: Discourse and Critique in a Polymediated Age* (Lanham, MD: Lexington Books, 2015); Eric M. Eisenberg, "Building a Mystery: Toward a New Theory of Communication and Identity," *Journal of Communication* 51 (2001): 534–52. doi: 10.1111/j.1460–2466.2001. tb02895.x

18. Chris Payne, "Rage Against the Machine, Public Enemy & Cypress Hill Members form Supergroup Prophets of Rage: Sources," *Billboard.com*, May 18, 2016. www. billboard.com/articles/news/7377487/rage-against-machine-public-enemy-cypress-hill-prophets-rage. (Accessed May 22, 2016.)

19. Tyma, Herrmann, and Herbig, xx.

20. Lesile Mosier, "Doug the Pug," *YouTube*. www.youtube.com/user/leslieanddoug. (Accessed June 8, 2015.)

21. Pamela Chelin, "Exclusive: Rebecca Black Fighting Ark Music Factory Over 'Friday.'" *Rolling Stone* April 1, 2011. www.rollingstone.com/music/news/exclusive-rebecca-black-fighting-ark-music-factory-over-friday-20110401. (Accessed May 22, 2016.)

22. Jessica Contrara, "Being Bad Luck Brian: When the Meme that Made You Famous Starts to Fade Away," *The Washington Post*, January 5, 2015. www. washingtonpost.com/lifestyle/style/being-bad-luck-brian-when-the-meme-that-made-you-famous-starts-to-fade-away/2015/01/05/07cbf6ac-907c-11e4–a412–4b735edc7175_story.html. (Accessed May 22, 2016.)

23. Henry Jenkins, *Convergence Culture: Where Old and New Media Collide* (New York, NY: New York University Press, 2006).

24. Max Horkheimer and Theodor W. Adorno, *Dialectic of Enlightenment: Philosophical Fragments*, ed. Gunzelin Schmid Noerr, trans. Edmund Jephcott (Stanford, CA: Stanford University Press, 2002).

25. Raymond Williams, "Base and Superstructure in Marxist Cultural Theory," in *Rethinking Popular Culture: Contemporary Perspectives in Cultural Studies*, eds. Chandra Mukerji and Michael Schudson (Berkeley, CA: University of California Press, 1991): 407–423.

26. C. Wright Mills, "Mass Society and Liberal Education," in *Power, Politics, and People: The Collected Essays of C. Wright Mills*, ed. Irving Louis Horowitz (New York, NY: Ballantine Books, 1963): 355.

27. Devin Faraci, "Fandom is Broken: Controversies and Entitlement Shine a Light on a Deeply Troubling Side of Fandom," *Birth. Movies. Death.*, May 30, 2016. birthmoviesdeath.com/2016/05/30/fandom-is-broken. (Accessed June 8, 2015.)

28. Adam W. Tyma, "I am you and you are we and we are all . . . me? Understanding Media and/as Context (The Road to Polymediation)," in *Beyond New Media: Discourse and Critique in a Polymediated Age*, eds. Art Herbig, Andrew F. Herrmann, and Adam W. Tyma (Lanham, MD: Lexington Books, 2015): 1–14.

29. Breeanna Hare, "Twice as much TV? How Networks are Adapting to the Second Screen," *CNN*, September 15, 2012. www.cnn.com/2012/09/15/showbiz/tv/second-screen-tv-our-mobile-society/. (Accessed June 8, 2015.)

30. See Michael Warner, *Publics and Counterpublics* (New York, NY: Zone Books, 2005).

31. Andrew F. *Herrmann*, "Daniel Amos and Me: The Power of Pop Culture and Autoethnography," *Popular Culture Studies Journal* 1 (2013): 6–17. mpcaaca.org/wp-

content/uploads/2013/10/PCSJ-V1–N12–Herrmann-Daniel-Amos-and-Me.pdf. (Accessed May 12, 2016.)

32. Mark Allan Powell, *Encyclopedia of Contemporary Christian Music* (Peabody, MA: Hendrickson Publishers, 2002): 698.

33. Bob Batchelor, *Cult Pop Culture: How the Fringe Became Mainstream* (ABC-CLIO, 2011): xvii.

34. Jeff Jensen, "Firefly: 'Browncoats Unite" Reunion Tonight: Why Joss Whedon's Cult Classic has Endured for a Decade," *Entertainment Weekly*, November 11, 2012.www.ew.com/article/2012/11/11/firefly-browncoats-reunion-joss-whedon. (Accessed May 22, 2016.); Ted Greenwald, "Q&A: Ridley Scott Has Finally Created the *Bladerunner* He Always Imagined," *Wired,* September 26, 2007.www.wired.com/2007/09/ff-bladerunner. (Accessed May 22, 2016.); John Diliberto, "Zen & the Art of Fripp's Guitar," *Electronic Musician,* January 19, 2006.www.emusician.com/artists/1333/zen--the-art-of-fripps-guitar/36105. (Accessed May 1, 2016.)

35. Erving Goffman, *The Presentation of Self in Everyday Life* (New York, NY: Doubleday, 1959).

36. Michelle Calka, "Polymediation: The Relationship between Self and Media," in *Beyond New Media: Discourse and Critique in a Polymediated Age*, eds. Art Herbig, Andrew F. Herrmann, and Adam W. Tyma (Lanham, MD: Lexington Books, 2015): 15–30.

37. Darryn King, "Ermahgerddon: The Untold Story of the Ermahgerd Girl," *Vanity Fair.* www.vanityfair.com/culture/2015/10/ermahgerd-girl-true-story. (Accessed May 1, 2016.)

38. *Riley v. California.* Bd., 573 U.S. __ (2013). www.supremecourt.gov/opinions/13pdf/13–132_8l9c.pdf. (Accessed May 22, 2016.)

39. Gordon Grovitz, "FBI vs. Apple Isn't Over," *Wall Street Journal*, March 27, 2016. www.wsj.com/articles/fbi-vs-apple-isnt-over-1459116064. (Accessed May 22, 2016.)

40. Janice Radway, *Reading the Romance: Women, Patriarchy, and Popular Culture* (Chapel Hill, NC: University of North Carolina Press, 1984); Marlene G. Fine, "Soap Opera Conversations: The Talk that Binds," *Journal of Communication* 31 (1981): 97–107; Nancy L. Buerkel-Rothfuss, and Sandra Mayes, "Soap Opera Viewing: The Cultivation Effect," *Journal of Communication* 31 (1981): 108–15.

41. While this is not to get into the complete concepts of polymedia and polymediated narrative, we note that "the worlds of *Supernatural* are not bound by the medium. It expands application conceptions of narrative as a story crafted to fit the larger narratives and discourses to which it is connected. It is more than a simple text; it is the intermingling of multiple textual threads, media, stories, and grammars. The episode is the result of, and shows the impact of, recursivity between producers and consumers via polymediation, while simultaneously incorporating fragments from previous episodes, genre conventions, grammars, and so forth. Yet, even with all of these influences and changes and variables, the episode "hangs together," and for those familiar with the series, the story is narratively fidelitous." Herbig and Herrmann, "Polymediated Narrative," *International Journal of Communication* 10 (2016): 761.

42. Nele Simons, "Audience Reception of Cross- and Transmedia TV Drama in the Age of Convergence," *International Journal of Communication*, 8 (2014): 2220–39, accessed June 8, 2016, ijoc.org/index.php/ijoc/article/view/2598/1207.

43. Brett Molina, "AMC Ditches Plan to Allow Texting in Theaters," *USA Today*, April 15, 2016, www.usatoday.com/story/tech/news/2016/04/15/amc-ditches-plan-allow-texting-theaters/83074118/. (Accessed June 8, 2016.)

44. Herbig and Herrmann, "Polymediated Narrative," 741.

45. Herbig and Herrmann, "Polymediated Narrative," 759–60.

46. Robert Andrew Dunn, "Polyreality," in *Beyond New Media: Discourse and Critique in a Polymediated Age*, eds, Art Herbig, Andrew F. Herrmann, and Adam Tyma (Lantham, MD: Lexington, 2015): 109–24.

47. Jimmie Manning, "Ipsedixitism, Ipseity, and Ipsilateral Identity: The Fear of Finding Ourselves in the Fissures between Phishing and *Catfish*," in *Beyond New Media:*

Discourse and Critique in a Polymediated Age, eds, Art Herbig, Andrew F. Herrmann, and Adam Tyma (Lanham, MD: Lexington Books, 2015): 83–107.

48. According to the Federal Bureau of Investigation, SWATting "is making a hoax call to 9-1-1 to draw a response from law enforcement, usually a SWAT team. The individuals who engage in this activity use technology to make it appear that the emergency call is coming from the victim's phone. Sometimes swatting is done for revenge, sometimes as a prank. Either way, it is a serious crime, and one that has potentially dangerous consequences." www.fbi.gov/news/stories/2013/september/the-crime-of-swatting-fake-9-1-1-calls-have-real-consequences. (Accessed May 19, 2016.)

49. Andrew F. Herrmann and Art Herbig, "All too Human: Xander Harris and the Embodiment of the Fully Human, *Popular Culture Studies Journal* 3 (2015): 85–111, mpcaaca.org/wp-content/uploads/2015/10/pcsj_vol3_no1-2.pdf (Accessed June 10, 2016.)

50. Jean Baudrillard, *Simulacra and Simulation*, trans. Sheila Faria Glaser (Ann Arbor, MI: University of Michigan Press, 1994).

51. John P. Pullen, "6 Times People Died While Taking Selfies," *Time*, March 14, 2016, time.com/4257429/selfie-deaths. (Accessed May 22, 2016.)

52. Raymie E. McKerrow, "Critical Rhetoric: Theory & Praxis," *Communication Monographs* 56, no. 2 (1989): 101. doi: 10.1080/03637758909390253.

53. As quoted in Bob Batchelor, "Creating Public Intellectuals: Popular Culture's Move from Nicheto Mainstream in the Twenty-First Century," in *Popular Culture in the Twenty-First Century*, eds, Myc Wiatrowski and Corey Baker (Newcastle upon Tyne: Cambridge Scholars Publishing, 2013): 2–13.

ONE

Queering Popular Culture

Tony E. Adams

Popular culture texts possessing "queer" characteristics and espousing "queer" messages are important. Such texts—such queer texts—can subvert, spoil, and promote transgressive ideas about culturally prevalent, false and insidious beliefs, practices, and expectations, especially those tied to same-sex attraction, heterosexuality, sexual desire, kinship, and family. Queer texts can acknowledge, reclaim, and celebrate affects commonly perceived to be peculiar, inappropriate, incoherent, or disgusting, and, in so doing, curb the shame associated with these affects. Queer texts can also offer innovative ideas about intimacy, relationships, and the future.

My purpose for this chapter is to demonstrate how to interpret popular culture texts in queer ways. I first define and describe various uses of "queer." I then discern queer characteristics of three popular culture texts: the television series *The Golden Girls* (1985–1992), the HBO television series *The Leftovers* (2014–2016), and the Disney/Pixar film *Inside Out* (2015). I conclude with additional insights about the queerness of popular culture texts.

DEFINING "QUEER"

"Queer" is a term with many uses. Queer can refer to same-sex attraction or be used synonymously with "homosexual," "lesbian," "gay," "bisexual," or "transgender."[1] Queer can also describe messages and actions that rebel against heterosexual—"heteronormative"—expectations of intimate relationships, including biases against being single, aspirations for marriage, norms about intimacy, desires for monogamy, and assumptions about the importance of biological reproduction, kinship, and family lineage.[2] Given these definitions, a queer popular culture text might subtly reference, or explicitly celebrate, same-sex attraction, homosexuality, lesbian, gay, bisexual, and transgender (LGBT) issues and identities; or the text might subtly avoid, or explicitly rebel against, heteronormative expectations of intimate relationships.

Other definitions of queer do not pertain to sexuality and heteronormativity. Queer can be used to describe messages and actions that rebel against culturally prevalent, false and insidious promises about optimism, happiness, and the future.[3] Queer can also describe affects commonly perceived to be peculiar, inappropriate, incoherent, or disgusting—affects such as undecidability, failure, depression, and melancholy.[4] Given these definitions, a queer popular culture text might subtly avoid, or explicitly rebel against, prevalent, false and insidious promises; or the text might subtly reference, or explicitly celebrate, affects commonly perceived to be peculiar, inappropriate, incoherent, or disgusting.

As I mentioned, queer popular culture texts—texts that espouse any of these queer definitions and that appeal to mass, everyday audiences—are important for numerous reasons. Queer texts can subvert, spoil, and promote transgressive ways to talk about culturally prevalent, false and insidious beliefs, practices, and expectations, especially those tied to same-sex attraction, heterosexuality, sexual desire, reproduction, kinship, and family.[5] Queer texts can acknowledge, reclaim, and celebrate affects commonly perceived to be peculiar, inappropriate, incoherent, or disgusting, and, in so doing, curb the shame associated with these affects.[6] Queer texts can also offer innovative ideas about intimacy, relationships, and the future.[7]

Next, in order to illustrate various queer interpretations, I discern queer characteristics of three popular culture texts. I first describe how the series *The Golden Girls* (1985–1992) promotes queer messages, especially regarding same-sex attraction, sexual desire, kinship, and family relationships. I then offer a queer interpretation of *The Leftovers* (2014–2016)—a series that does not espouse messages of same-sex attraction or foreground non-heterosexual assumptions or relationships, but instead promotes the recognition, and even celebration of, queer affects such as melancholy, despair, and prolonged grief. As a third example, I offer a queer analysis of the film *Inside Out* (2015), a film that is queer in its references to same-sex attraction and sexual desire, as well as queer in its celebration of "sadness," an affect often considered to be taboo.

STAYING GOLDEN

The television series *The Golden Girls* (1985–1992) foregrounds the lives of four women—Blanche, Dorothy, Rose, and Sophia—all of whom share a house in Miami, Florida. All of the women are White; Blanche, Dorothy, and Rose are in their late 50s/early 60s; Sophia is in her early 80s. Each episode focuses on comedic, though sometime serious, situations these women encounter. Even though the series ended in 1992, it has been in syndication for more than two decades on a variety of cable channels within the United States (US). As of this writing (2016), the series continues to air on two channels: Hallmark, a channel that foregrounds "family-friendly" programming; and Logo, a channel that offers programming for LGBT—that is, queer—audiences. But why might a series that ended in 1992 air on a channel that explicitly caters to queer audiences (Logo)? One explanation is that the show promotes queer beliefs, practices, and expectations, especially those tied to same-sex attraction, heterosexuality, sexual desire, reproduction, kinship, and family.

Numerous episodes of *The Golden Girls* explicitly address queer issues and demonstrate queer ways of living. Nearly every episode makes at least one reference to same-sex attraction, and some episodes foreground LGBT content. For example, in one episode, Dorothy's best friend, Jean, who identifies as a lesbian, struggles with her intimate attraction to Rose. In one episode, Blanche's brother, Clayton, worries about telling Blanche that he is gay; in a later episode, Clayton worries about telling Blanche that he plans to marry Doug, his (male) partner.

The content of the series—four unmarried women living together and who proudly discuss their desire to take care of each other—also disrupts traditional ideas about who constitutes a family.[8] In one episode, Rose has a heart attack and the hospital staff will not allow Blanche, Dorothy, and Sophia to visit because they are not Rose's "family." When Rose's daughter, Kirsten, arrives, she also will not allow the women to visit Rose as they are not (biological) family. Kirsten soon realizes the women are indeed Rose's family and arranges for them to visit. In another episode, a city official threatens to fine Blanche for renting her house to too many people (Dorothy, Rose, and Sophia). Blanche bypasses the fine by putting all of the women on the title to the house, as it belongs to, and thus should be owned by, all of them.

Other episodes of *The Golden Girls* offer representations of relationships that could be interpreted as queer—that is, as peculiar, absurd, and inappropriate. One episode foregrounds Blanche's conflict with her daughter, Rebecca, for pursuing artificial insemination and wanting to have a child as a single, unmarried mother. Another episode features Dorothy's conflict with her White son, Michael, and his desire to marry a Black woman who is nearly twice his age. Another episode shows Rose's struggle with dating a short person. Numerous episodes also unapologetically celebrate aging and foreground the women's sexual desires—another queer feat of the series, especially for people who frame these desires as peculiar and inappropriate.[9]

BEING LEFTOVER

Ten years ago, Brett—my friend and first significant boyfriend—died suddenly, either from committing suicide after coming out as gay to his father, or because of complications from diabetes.[10] I had never had someone so close to me die, especially someone who felt like my only family. I was estranged from my family of origin after telling them I identified as gay, and Brett comforted me through many tumultuous interactions. He was my security, someone who cared for me when no one else could/would. Brett was also the first relational partner with whom I ever lived. He served as my queer mentor who taught me to feel less shame about my sexuality, and the first person to show me how ex-boyfriends could remain loving and close.

I miss Brett every day. But I have learned not to tell many people that I still miss him. In moments when I have said that I do, some people—even friends and family members—have questioned me about his significance in my life, questions that indicated something peculiar and inappropriate—queer—about my grief: I should no longer miss Brett as I did, and I felt as though I was expected to improve my sadness, as it may be unhealthy. But why can't I miss Brett, often and publicly, without the risk of being questioned or evaluated? Why can't my grief be considered a lengthy, and possibly even permanent, temperament never to be absolved or wished away? Why can't I embrace, and even celebrate, being a melancholic queer?[11]

Others have made similar observations regarding the peculiarity and inappropriateness—the queerness—of prolonged grief. Blake Paxton uses queer theory to "convey alternative frameworks for long-term grief" and to subvert "feeling rules for emotional expression."[12] Carolyn Ellis critiques the tendency to view prolonged grief as pathological, as something from which to "move on." Instead, she argues, "it can be healthy to hold on to grief as a way to maintain a relationship with a person who has died."[13] And in writing about the continued mourning of his father's death, Jonathan Wyatt attempts to "trouble the received wisdom about bereavement," noting that his mourning "does not feel pathological" and that he does not envision or desire the process to end.[14]

My experiences with grieving Brett, coupled with this research on prolonged grief, inform my queer interpretation of *The Leftovers*, an HBO television series based on the book by the same name. *The Leftovers* primarily takes place in a small community—Mapleton, New York—and focuses on how members of the community cope with the mysterious disappearance of two percent of the population three years prior. Some community members grieve by joining the Guilty Remnant, a cult whose members wear white, constantly smoke, refuse to (verbally) speak, and believe that the disappearance was an act of/by God. Some community members grieve by committing crimes and harming others, including members of the Guilty Remnant. Some members try to better understand, and to establish effective ways to cope with the loss of their friends and family members such as by purchasing expensive, personalized mannequins that resemble the people who disappeared.

Although *The Leftovers* is not queer in terms of same-sex attraction, it is queer in its tone and content: It is melancholic, pessimistic, and unhappy, characteristics that others may consider to be peculiar and inappropriate—and maybe even disgusting. The soundtrack to *The Leftovers*, composed by Max Richter, is also brilliantly, and queerly, melancholic, pessimistic, and unhappy, each track tinted by grief and loss. For Mapleton residents, there is no forgetting or adequate ways to grieve and three years after the disappearance, their grief still exists. The sudden, catastrophic disappearance continues to tarnish community relationships, many of which are represented as eccentric, incoherent, and scarred by the past.

THE PROMISE OF SADNESS

In *The Promise of Happiness,* Sara Ahmed, a prominent queer theorist, writes against popular uses, conceptualizations of, and desires for happiness—an unattainable affect that she frames as prevalent, false, and insidious. Ahmed's writing encourages me to think about the ways in which sadness and depression continue to be stigmatized, at least when juxtaposed against ideas of joy and happiness. I think about depression being dismissed as weak or unimportant, as a temperament to cure, or how it may even be racially considered, as Boylorn experienced, a "white person's disease."[15]

These ideas inform my queer interpretation of the Disney/Pixar film *Inside Out*. The film tells the story of Riley, an eleven-year-old girl, and how five emotions—Anger, Sadness, Joy, Disgust, and Fear—guide her ideas and inter/actions. Throughout the first part of the film, Joy dominates Riley's emotional state; the other emotions matter much less and turn to Joy when Riley encounters disconcerting or stressful situations. Joy also aggressively curbs Sadness' influence on Riley by trying to distract Sadness with tasks such as reading cognitive operating manuals, asking Sadness to stay in a circle outlined in chalk on the floor, and even trying to encourage Sadness to become less sad.

Joy soon loses control of Sadness and both characters fall out of the emotional "control center." With the support of other minor characters, the goal of the rest of the film is to return Joy to the control center. The motivation to return Sadness is not as important because it is still perceived that Sadness is less necessary, and even unnecessary, for Riley's well-being. However, on their journey together, Joy not only experiences sadness, but also recognizes the importance of Sadness for Riley; Joy recognizes that all of Riley's joyful experiences have tinges of sadness, and, without Sadness, Joy could not exist.

Although Joy realizes that Sadness is one emotion Riley can use to garner attention from others—a realization that still frames sadness as an emotion that can/should motivate concern from others and, as such, may need to be improved (whereas joy cannot be used to garner attention nor does joy need to be improved)—Sadness is recognized as a necessary emotion; the character becomes important, and even celebrated, in the text. With this message, the film becomes increasingly queer as it rails against the culturally prevalent, false, and insidious promise of joy and happiness.

There are other queer characteristics of *Inside Out*, all of which relate to sexuality, same-sex attraction, and LGBT identities. For example, Riley wears a rainbow sweater when she first arrives in San Francisco—a possible reference to the rainbow typically associated with same-sex attraction, homosexuality, and LGBT identities, and a reference further enhanced by the setting of San Francisco, a city known for its queer spaces, histories, and sexual freedoms. Another queer instance happens when Disgust says, "There are no bears in San Francisco," to which Anger replies, "I saw a really hairy guy; he looked like a bear." Anger's comment offers an explicit, yet still coded, acknowledgment of "bear" subculture—that is, the community that celebrates large and hairy gay men.[16]

I interpret one of the minor characters, Rainbow Unicorn, in a queer way as well, not only because of the use of "Rainbow" in the character's name and the rainbow color of its mane, but also because of the character's subtle references to sex, desire, and the pornography film genre/industry. For example, when Joy first meets Rainbow Unicorn, Joy says, "I loved you in *Fairy Dream Adventure, Part Seven*." Mainstream films typically do not use seven sequels; porn films often do. Then, when Fear sees Rainbow Unicorn acting, Fear says that Unicorn should find a different plotline, a comment that suggests all of Unicorn's previous roles were similar—another common characteristic of porn actors/films. In the same scene, when Rainbow Unicorn begins to act, its flowing mane and demure posture resembles the classic image of Venus, the Roman goddess of love, sex, and desire.[17] Further, the "top definition" of "Unicorn" on Urban Dictionary.com refers to a bisexual person, often a woman, who becomes sexually, though not emotionally, involved with an "existing couple"—another instance of how a Unicorn can signify sex and desire.[18]

Taken together, all of the aforementioned queer characteristics queer *Inside Out* in two additional ways. First, children, a primary audience of the film and an audience often assumed to be asexual,[19] will be exposed to subtle and ambiguous references about porn, sex, and desire. Second, the film may even equip children with the ability to at least talk about five emotions and, further, be able to say, with less shame, that they feel sad and that feeling sad is ok.

MAKING QUEER TEXTS | READING TEXTS QUEERLY

A queer popular culture text might subtly reference, or explicitly celebrate, same-sex attraction, homosexuality, LGBT issues and identities; or the text might subtly avoid, or explicitly rebel against, heteronormative expectations of intimate relationships. Although I demonstrated how texts such as *The Golden Girls* and *Inside Out* illustrated such queer characteristics, many popular culture texts also possess these characteristics. Examples include songs such as Macklemore's "Same Love" or Kacey Musgrave's "Follow Your Arrow," television series such as *Modern Family*, *Looking*, or *The L Word*, or the rainbow photo filter that allowed Facebook users to add a rainbow tint to their profile photo in order to mark their support for the United States Supreme Court ruling in support of same-sex marriage.[20]

A queer popular culture text might also not reference sexuality at all. Instead, the text may subtly avoid, or explicitly rebel against, culturally prevalent, false and insidious promises; or it might subtly reference, or explicitly celebrate, affects commonly perceived to be peculiar, inappropriate, incoherent, or disgusting. Although I demonstrated how texts such as *The Golden Girls*, *The Leftovers*, and *Inside Out* illustrated such queer characteristics, many popular culture texts possess these characteristics as well. Examples include songs such as Radiohead's "Creep," Hozier's "Take Me to Church," or Rihanna's, "Diamonds," films such as *Requiem for a Dream*, *Amour*, *Blue Valentine*, *45 Years*, or *Who's Afraid of Virginia Woolf*, and television series such as *Lost* or *Six Feet Under*.

To conclude, I want to make two additional observations about queer popular culture texts. First, queer texts are contextual: They become queer in the moment they are interpreted as peculiar, inappropriate, incoherent, disgusting, or as not/anti-heterosexual. As such, texts may not always be queer—they may be perceived as peculiar and inappropriate in one context, but typical and appropriate in another time and place.[21] Further, when a text becomes less peculiar, inappropriate, incoherent, or disgusting, it becomes less queer.[22] For example, within the United States, the hula-hoop, a prominent toy of popular culture, may have been normal in the 1950s; however, the popularity of the hula-hoop has since diminished. If someone asked for a hula-hoop, or advocated for a hula-hoop competition, the person may now be perceived as peculiar—that is, as a bit queer. Or consider how cigarette smoking, especially in many

public contexts within the United States, has become increasingly peculiar, inappropriate, and even disgusting; in such contexts, smoking has
become a queer act.

As long as queer can be used as synonymous with same-sex attraction, homosexuality, and LGBT issues and identities, popular culture
texts such as the ones I reference will always be queer in these ways.
However, when heteronormative expectations of intimate relationships
lessen in importance (e.g., desires for biological reproduction), when culturally prevalent, false and insidious promises lessen in importance (e.g.,
the unwieldy praising of happiness), and when affects commonly perceived to be peculiar, inappropriate, incoherent, or disgusting (e.g., prolonged sadness or grief) become less peculiar and disgusting and more
appropriate and coherent, then the texts I've described may become less
queer. New queer characteristics might develop and may be illustrated in
these texts, but knowing these new characteristics means trying to predict
what future expectations, ideas, and affects will be considered peculiar,
inappropriate, incoherent, or disgusting.

Second, note that the study of popular culture could be considered a
queer area of study. Popular culture is still sometimes perceived as taboo,
referred to as a part of "low culture," considered to be of not much
importance and inappropriate for academic study; given that popular
culture consists of the "everyday experiences of ordinary folks," it lacks
seriousness and prestige, and is perceived to revel in "the informal, the
underside, the grotesque."[23] However, as I've argued, one way to be
queer is to acknowledge, reclaim, and celebrate inappropriate and disgusting—grotesque—texts through "love and identification,"[24] texts that
may never appear in, or be appreciated by, supposedly less disgusting
and more appropriate "high culture" contexts such as theatres, museums,
and even universities. By reading, and appreciating, this essay about
popular culture, you too have become increasingly queer.

As I have tried to illustrate, queer popular culture texts—texts that
possess queer characteristics and/or espouse queer messages and texts
that appeal to mass, everyday audiences—have numerous purposes:
They call attention to harmful cultural assumptions and expectations;
subvert, spoil, and promote transgressive ideas about same-sex attraction, heterosexuality, and kinship; acknowledge, reclaim, and celebrate
affects commonly perceived to be peculiar, inappropriate, incoherent, or
disgusting; and provide innovative ideas about intimacy, relationships,
and the future. Given these purposes, queer texts offer us different possibilities for relating with others, different ways to understand ourselves,
and different techniques for incorporating peculiar desires, attractions,
and affects into our lives.

NOTES

1. Authors who use queer synonymously with same-sex attraction, homosexuality, and/or lesbian, gay, bisexual, and transgender identity include Alexander Doty, *Making Things Perfectly Queer: Interpreting Mass Culture* (Minneapolis: University of Minnesota Press, 1993); Pamela Demory and Christopher Pullen, eds, *Queer Love in Film and Television: Critical Essays* (New York: Palgrave Macmillan, 2013); and Corey Creekmur and Alexander Doty, eds, *Out in Culture: Gay, Lesbian, and Queer Essays on Popular Culture* (Durham, NC: Duke University Press, 1995).

2. As Sara Ahmed writes, "to be 'in line' is to direct one's desires toward marriage and reproduction; to direct one's desires toward the reproduction of the family line." Conversely, Ahmed argues, to be queer is to be out of line with one's desires and against reproducing the family line. Sara Ahmed, *Queer Phenomenology: Orientations, Objects, Others* (Durham, NC: Duke University Press, 2006), 74. Julia Erhart associates queerness with donor conception as "donor conception is easily associated with sexual outlaws and practices: lesbians, infertile women and men, men who masturbate for money." Julia Erhart, "Donor Conception in Lesbian and Non-lesbian and Television Families," in *Queer Love in Film and Television: Critical Essays*, eds, Pamela Demory and Christopher Pullen (New York: Palgrave Macmillan, 2013), 83. Other authors who use queer to describe messages and actions that rebel against heteronormative expectations of intimate relationships include Michael Cobb, *Single: Arguments for the Uncoupled* (New York: New York University Press, 2012) and Anne M. Harris, "Ghost-child," in *On (Writing) Families: Autoethnographies of Presence and Absence, Love and Loss*, eds, Jonathan Wyatt and Tony E. Adams (Rotterdam, The Netherlands: Sense Publishers, 2014), 69–75.

3. Authors who refer to messages and actions that rebel against culturally prevalent, false and insidious promises about optimism, happiness, and the future as "queer" include Sara Ahmed, *The Promise of Happiness* (Durham, NC: Duke University Press, 2010); Lauren Berlant, *Cruel Optimism* (Durham, NC: Duke University Press, 2011); and Dustin Bradley Goltz, *Queer Temporalities in Gay Male Representation* (Routledge: New York, 2010).

4. Joseph Litvak writes, "Although it is hard to think of queer theory apart from a certain tonality of the euphoric and the outrageous, it now seems to me that what I have always secretly loved about it is its preternatural responsiveness to the rich modern repertoire of bad vibes, the verve with which it picks up on all the clammy emotions." Joseph Litvak, "Glad to be Unhappy," *South Atlantic Quarterly* 106, no. 3 (2007): 524. doi: 10.1215/00382876-2007-011. Other texts that refer to affects commonly perceived to be peculiar, inappropriate, incoherent, or disgusting as "queer" include Ann Cvetkovich, *Depression: A Public Feeling* (Durham, NC: Duke University Press, 2012); Judith Halberstam, *The Queer Art of Failure* (Durham, NC: Duke University Press, 2011); Stacy Holman Jones and Tony E. Adams. 2014. "Undoing the Alphabet: A Queer Fugue on Grief and Forgiveness," *Cultural Studies ↔ Critical Methodologies* 14, no. 2 (2014): 102–110. doi: 10.1177/1532708613512260. Blake Paxton, "Queerly Conversing with the Dead: Re-membering Mom," *Cultural Studies ↔ Critical Methodologies* 14, no. 2 (2014): 164–173. doi: 10.1177/1532708613512273.

5. Authors who describe how queer texts can subvert, spoil, and promote transgressive ways to talk about prevalent, false and insidious beliefs, practices, and expectations include Ahmed, *The Promise of Happiness*; Judith Butler, "Gender as Performance," in *A Critical Sense: Interviews With Intellectuals*, ed, Peter Osborne (New York: Routledge, 1996): 109–125; and Erin J. Rand, *Reclaiming Queer: Activist & Academic Rhetorics of Resistance* (Tuscaloosa: University of Alabama Press, 2014).

6. "Part of what I understand to be the exciting charge of the very word 'queer,'" Eve Sedgwick writes, "is that it embraces, instead of repudiating, what have for many of us been formative childhood experiences of difference and stigmatization." Eve Kosofsky Sedgwick, "How to Bring Your Kids up Gay," in *Fear of a Queer Planet: Queer*

Politics and Social Theory, ed, Michael Warner (Minneapolis: University of Minnesota Press, 1993): 80.

7. Stuart Hall, "What Is this "Black" in Black Popular Culture," *Social Justice* 20 (1993): 113.

8. Elizabeth Yuko writes, "The portrayal of these women as a family unit is comforting for those who found it difficult to identify with their biological family—including many LGBT individuals. It presented the possibility of finding a group of people to serve as a surrogate but very real family, even later in life. Living in a society with such an emphasis placed on heterosexual romantic relationships as the most authentic and the only basis for being considered a family, *The Golden Girls* emphasized the importance and legitimacy of a family falling outside those rigid parameters." Elizabeth Yuko, "Op-ed: Why *The Golden Girls* Never Lost Its Luster," *Advocate*, September 8, 2015, accessed September 15, 2015, www.advocate.com/commentary/2015/09/08/op-ed-why-golden-girls-never-lost-its-luster.

9. Judith C. Daniluk, *Women's Sexuality Across the Life Span: Challenging Myths, Creating Meanings* (New York: Guilford Press, 2003).

10. Tony E. Adams, *Narrating the Closet: An Autoethnography of Same-Sex Attraction* (Walnut Creek, CA: Left Coast Press, 2011); Holman Jones and Adams, "Undoing the Alphabet."

11. Ahmed, *The Promise of Happiness*.

12. Paxton, ""Queerly Conversing," 165.

13. Carolyn Ellis, "Seeking My Brother's Voice: Holding onto Long-term Grief through Photographs, Stories, and Reflections," in *Stories of Complicated Grief: A Critical Anthology*, ed., Eric D. Miller (Washington, DC: National Association of Social Workers, 2014): 4.

14. Wyatt, Jonathan. "What Kind of Mourning? Autoethnographic Fragments." *International Review of Qualitative Research* 2 (2010): 501.

15. Robin M. Boylorn, *Sweetwater: Black Women and Narratives of Resistance* (New York: Peter Lang, 2013): 89.

16. For discussion of the bear subculture, see Patrick Santoro, "Lather, Rinse, Reclaim: Cultural (Re)conditioning of the Gay (Bear) Body." In *Critical Autoethnography: Intersecting Cultural Identities in Everyday Life*, eds., Robin M. Boylorn and Mark P. Orbe (Walnut Creek, CA: Left Coast Press, 2014): 159–175.

17. I thank Kathy Denker for this observation.

18. I thank Chris Patti for this observation. "Unicorn," Urban Dictionary, accessed September 1, 2015, www.urbandictionary.com/define.php?term=Unicorn.

19. Steven Bruhm and Natasha Hurley, eds. *Curiouser: On the Queerness of Children* (Minneapolis: University of Minnesota Press, 2004).

20. As I mentioned, the rainbow has become a symbol often affiliated with same-sex attraction, homosexuality, and lesbian, gay, bisexual, and/or transgender identities and issues. After the June 2015 Supreme Court ruling in support of same-sex marriage, more than 26 million users added the rainbow tint to their photo. Associated Press, "Rainbow Facebook Photos: Armchair Activism or Shifting Tide?" *New York Times*, July 2, 2015, accessed September 15, 2015, www.nytimes.com/aponline/2015/07/02/technology/ap-us-tec-facebook-rainbows.html.

21. Kenji Yoshino notes, "an identity that is normal in one sphere will often be queer" in another context. For example, he refers to mothers as the "queers" of the corporate workplace (United States), as many have to avoid flaunting, and even discussing, their roles as mothers. In other contexts—e.g., working as a stay-at-home mom—mothers may be considered less queer and more normal. Kenji Yoshino, *Covering: The Hidden Assault on Our Civil Rights* (New York: Random House, 2006), 162. The act of hand-holding by people (perceived to be) of the same-sex is another example of the contextual characteristic of queerness, as same-sex hand-holding may be less queer in a LGBT-friendly space such as in a bar that caters to LGBT audiences, more queer if it happens in a rural grocery store. See Stephanie Rosenbloom, "A Simple Show of

Hands," *New York Times*, October 5, 2006, accessed September 15, 2015 from www. nytimes.com/2006/10/05/fashion/05hands.html?pagewanted=all&_r=0.

22. Judith Butler argues when acts become increasingly predictable and normalized, they begin to lose their queerness. Butler, "Gender as Performance."

23. Hall, "Black Popular Culture," 107–108.

24. Feil argues that camp—a characteristic of homosexual (queer) culture that acknowledges, reclaims, and celebrates inappropriate and disgusting texts through "love and identification"—"reinvests both queerness and low culture with value, as it simultaneously redefines what 'value' means." Ken Feil, "'Fearless Vulgarity': Camp Love as Queer Love for Jackie Susan and *Valley of the Dolls*," in *Queer Love in Film and Television: Critical Essays*, eds., Pamela Demory and Christopher Pullen (New York: Palgrave Macmillan, 2013): 142.

TWO

CultPopCulture

*Reconsidering the Popular Culture Framework via the
Engage, Adapt, and Transform (EAT) Model*

Bob Batchelor

In 2005, musician Tom DeLonge formed Angels & Airwaves (AvA) after his former band, multi-platinum selling punk rockers Blink-182, went on hiatus. The move seemed natural and organic. Music fans valued his work and the age-old notion of a successful singer going solo is commonplace. Yet, DeLonge visualized more than simply another rock group. He often characterized AvA as either alternatively an "art project" or "a multimedia project."[1] Clearly, the punk rocker had a larger agenda. Yet, his goal remained connecting to audiences: "Art is evoking a feeling out of somebody. So what you do with your instrument or what you do with your paintbrush, all it has to do is capture the attention and imagination of somebody else walking by."[2]

Realizing DeLonge's vision of what a band could become, Angels matured into a creative collective that mixed music, visual communications, publishing, and animation. While AvA continued to exist as a music group DeLonge fronted, both recording and selling music, the concept expanded to encompass a film production company, music studio to score film soundtracks, publishing house (print and web), fashion design company, and animation studio. DeLonge recruited specialists from across these industries to help him execute his goals for AvA.

Technology has basically eliminated barriers that at one time in entertainment history might have made it difficult for artists to "cross over" from one field to another. As a result, a musician/artist like DeLonge who creates something in its initial scope now seems like an obvious jumping off point to discuss a new model for popular culture studies theory. What DeLonge represents is the fusing of two essential parts of cultpopculture—first, that technological innovation has provided a wider array of tools for analyzing popular culture and, second, that what might be deemed *popular culture* has simultaneously entered a new phase. Technology has enabled us to move away from thinking that popular culture is an object or thing to something more akin to emotion, a mental equation, or kind of supercharged brainwave that tightly links a person to the things she treasures.

When DeLonge—an artist whose career centers on bringing joy to audiences via music, film, and writing—characterizes the feeling as "attention" or "imagination" with the goal of "evoking a feeling out of somebody," he is essentially moving popular culture studies to a territory that more closely resembles the pure connection people have with the exact idea of what popular culture now embodies. Technology enables consumers, fans, and audiences to connect with objects in a manner that has revolutionized the field itself.

Rather than offer a twist on the staid, pedantic popular culture theory arguments about whether an object's status is "high" or "low" or even whether these mass communications items warrant serious academic study, this essay suggests a complete overhaul based on the technology-based world we inhabit. The Engage, Adapt, and Transform model (EAT) is a dynamic reinterpretation of popular culture theory.

The EAT model transforms popular culture into a verb, from the way we view things to how people convert objects into thoughts, feelings, ideas, and emotions. As a result of this new model, popular culture is not simply labeling items on some mythical scale from common to elite, but rather the highly personalized manner that people experience objects as they move from things to thoughts that are then used to create and re-fashion one's worldviews. EAT engages with contemporary society and technology, unquestionably the most visual, textual, and filmic age in human history.

Cultpopculture is the outcome (or, perhaps the expression) of EAT. In an environment in which people are perpetually engaging, adapting, and transforming with objects within their everyday lives, their relationships to many of these items grows cult-like and brings about intense fandom. In other words, cultpopculture exists in the interaction with artifacts, not the artifacts themselves.

The EAT model moves us away from the impression that popular culture is a thing (like an Andy Warhol print) and instead centers on the emotion, feeling, assessment, and impression that I get when I take it in and it swirls around with all the things that makes me who I am and how I define myself both as an individual entity and part of larger groups.

Ironically, EAT is similar to the verb *eat*, like one's attraction to a piece of pecan pie: the intensity of the emotion surrounding it, the process of ingestion, and then the manner that the body turns it into other things, from energy to waste. From this example of actually eating a slice of pecan pie, one realizes that the tie to an object is not just emotional.

Cultpopculture takes us past merely enjoying or loving an object to absorbing it and simultaneously altering it, making it new. To be clear, this new conceptualization is not simply based on an emotional attachment or joyful reaction to an object. Rather, it is the entire process and broad consequences we constantly make in thinking our way through our daily lives.

People saw a similar phenomenon with the release of *Star Wars: The Force Awakens*.[3] From an EAT model perspective, the notion of giving away the film's contents via the generic term *spoilers*, turned Facebook and other social media sites into battlegrounds between friends and acquaintances over secrecy, details, and the film's plot points. Threats of *de-friending*—about as serious as one can be in today's social media-saturated and curated world—became the de facto pledge for anyone divulging secrets.

What people wanted to retain when viewing the new *Star Wars* film on their own terms centered on joy and delight. In other words, viewers hoped to see the film the way children and young people experience popular culture objects—pure, elated, and with a sense of wonder. This EAT notion—that we can feel objects, essentially taking them into our beings, and then having them transform us—mirrors the purity of a child's wonder, but energized by an adult's sense of employing technology to gain a deeper fulfillment.

What cultpopculture and the EAT model propose is divorcing popular culture studies from its *object versus object* past, and then intending a radical reworking of how we assess the field in the future. These initiatives also ask scholars and researchers to return to a time before we felt the need to find definitive *answers* or *labels*. Instead, we should allow the freedom to actually experience joyfulness—the bliss that children feel when they engage, adapt, and transform the objects that help them define themselves and their worlds.

Cultpopculture and the EAT model offer a new way of thinking about popular culture studies that suggests a framework built to encompass the pervasiveness of popular culture objects in the contemporary world.

ENGAGE

Few experiences depict what it means to engage with popular culture objects more intensely than being a parent to a tween. Little makes a hip parent feel his age than an afternoon surrounded by a pack of 10- to 12-

year-olds. You enter their world and it is a swirl of synthesized music, pounding beats, bright colors and styles, and even a stylized lingo that only they seem to fully understand. It is a machine-gun like cadence, more than a little difficult to follow.

The tween interface with popular culture is illuminating. First, their engagement is innocent and virtually unburdened by the life experiences that weigh down adults. Our wild pack of tweens lives with a much purer engagement with brands and products. However, tweens are also self-obsessed little monsters, placing themselves at the center of their own little universes and allowing entry based solely on emotion, impulse, and happiness. Almost intuitively, they engage with one another and pop culture in a highly personalized fashion, from choosing YouTube celebrities over television networks to creating avatars and virtual worlds in Minecraft. Rather than the age-old tenets of consumer marketers who launched campaigns that gave them control, tweens point to a new era where they not only want a voice, but actually demand it.

The rise of celebrity "YouTubers," for example, demonstrates how tweens are determining the way they interact. Certainly television shows and cable networks are not going away anytime soon, but the YouTube channels reveal the personalization that viewers demand. Two of my 10-year-old daughter Kassie's favorite personalities broadcast via the screen names stampylonghead and PopularMMOs.

Stampy, for example, ranks as the Minecraft YouTuber with the sixth most subscribers (7.1 million), while the latter comes in at seven (7.09 million). While these numbers might boggle the mind, the astonishing figures are that between the two, they have uploaded about 4,800 videos that have been viewed more than 9.6 billion times. One of her other favorites is TheDiamondMinecart, hosted by a chipper young man who uses the screen name DanTDM. He ranks third with more than 9.7 million followers and views surpassing 6 billion.[4]

For parents who hear (and/or watch) these channels, the energetic, and sometimes frantic babble is almost maddening. But, this is what young people are watching, with the kind of frequency that dwarfs Teen Disney on cable and the tween films being released. Technology, from iPads and other handheld devices to smart phones and laptops, has given the YouTubers an outlet for their specialized content and the tween audiences a way to determine authenticity and engagement. The ability to comment via the YouTube channel also plays a role in a purer experience for young people, since they can chat with like-minded gamers from around the world.

The adult version of Minecraft or YouTubers might be something like Spotify, which enables users to create music playlists based on personal tastes, but also to access other people's lists based on theme or type of music. The ability to swap and then build on playlists gives Spotify users the ultimate mix-tape experience, blending the old idea of total curation with the technological advances that enable virtually unlimited access to musicians and music.

Spotify solves the traditional challenge when it came to playing music—access. So, instead of worrying about the range of music or having enough, users can focus on interacting with the content. The main idea is that users are in control and simultaneously engaged with both the musicians and other curators, who might range from the guy in the cube next to yours to someone half a world away. The amalgamation of technology and interest is the first leg of cultpopculture, which is fueled in this example by almost unlimited access and the engagement that results.

ADAPT

If technology fuels engagement for contemporary users, then the ability to adapt the accumulation is amplified geometrically. Returning to Spotify momentarily, the power to transform content is revolutionized by innovation. A listener no longer needs to bother with the fourth song on a Pearl Jam CD that strikes her as off. She can remix her own version or cherry pick the exact songs she wants and play them as much as she wants. Similarly, people have used video editing programs to make their own videos, filmed themselves reenacting favorite movie scenes, and created what is akin to televised variety shows, all because technology provides the means for adaptation.

The remix culture dates far back into history, but one views its contemporary seeds in the 1980s and 1990s when marketers attempted to sell consumer goods by exploiting popular culture objects. For example, an advertising campaign for Calvin Klein's Obsession fragrance in 1990 employed filmmaker and television show creator David Lynch to reenact scenes based on F. Scott Fitzgerald's *The Great Gatsby* (1925).

The black and white spot opened with a close-up on the face of then-little known actor Benicio Del Toro with the familiar Obsession logo in large white letters. Romantic, yet melancholy, horns wailed. As the logo faded, "F. Scott Fitzgerald" appeared in smaller letters. As Del Toro turned his head, the narrator read a passage about the first kiss between Gatsby and Daisy: "He knew that when he kissed this girl, and forever wed his unutterable visions to her perishable breath, his mind would never romp again like the mind of God."[5]

Quickly, actress Heather Graham—also before she became famous—appeared as Daisy. Del Toro attempted smoldering intensity, but actually seemed frightened. As they bent toward each other, a sky full of stars was superimposed over the screen. Then, as they met (a super close-up of their lips touching), a blossoming white flower appeared. As the commercial ended, the word "Obsession" appeared, accompanied by a bottle of the fragrance. As cheesy as this commercial seems today, it paid off for

Calvin Klein—sales at the time rose to more than $100 million annually, making it one of the top-selling perfumes in the world.[6] Without technology and YouTube as a platform, the Lynch commercial would be lost forever, but instead, it is an early example of how corporations usurped the notion of adaptation.

It is no wonder that film and television are central facets when discussing cultpopculture topics. They define our national dialogue, essentially providing Americans with basic talking points across race, political ties, gender differences, or any other demographic features that usually separate people. The narratives, regardless of the reason they attract or repel us, give context and a way of interpreting society and culture.

As millions of Americans interact with mass media, whether watching the same movies and television shows or listening to radio programs, a common language develops that opens new lines of communications. The downside, however, is that the fascination with popular culture diverts attention from important challenges the nation confronts. In this light, popular culture serves as a kind of placebo. The obsessive, loving nature of cult objects intensifies this diversion critique of popular culture because the focus on a specific cult influence distracts people and, at the same time, enables them to feel good about the world without really forcing them to directly confront critical issues.

The technology foundation is blurring the lines between cult and non-cult, actually drawing the former into the mainstream. It is not possible to distinguish where one or the other stops or starts. At what point, for instance, does a film or person magically transform from something interesting to a phenomenon that creates obsessive, loving followers? A simple definition does not exist, so people are forced to draw their own conclusions.

What is clear, however, is that the ability to covet a cult topic individually is both shrinking and expanding as technology becomes more omnipresent. These contrasting forces enable one to be as completely obsessive as he or she wishes while simultaneously allowing that person to be fully public or private about it. A person can build an online shrine to his or her cult icons, potentially drawing an audience of many millions, or ferret out information alone with nothing but the ideas and a glowing computer screen in front of him or her.

In terms of cult topics, the connection between people may be deeper and stronger, based on a sense that enthusiasts share some tightly held meaning or feeling of ownership regarding the object. In some cases, such as fan fiction or cover bands, people are so intricately wrapped up in the meaning of a cult topic that they will participate in the creation of new or alternative meanings.

TRANSFORM

In 2013, Coca-cola launched the "Share a Coke" campaign, which featured personalized plastic bottles, first with people's names on them, then later with words identifying moods and emotions. In Great Britain, Coke replaced its iconic logo with 1,000 popular names and watched as consumers took over. The next year, the campaign resulted in 998 million Twitter impressions, 150 million personalized bottles sold, and 730,000 personalized glass bottles sold via the corporate e-commerce store. The global success Coke unleashed via the campaign underscores the EAT model. Rather than merely a brown, fizzy sugar-laden drink, Coke offered people a new way to engage with the product, and then the ability to transform it based on their own desires, from wall art to personalized gifts.[7]

Rather than look at the personalized bottles individually or even the campaign as a whole and declare: "this is popular culture!" what cultpopculture provides is a framework for moving beyond labels and objects to a deeper form of engagement and its consequences. And its use as a framework does not overcommit us to individual theorists, thus opening popular culture studies theory to a wider, pragmatic, and interdisciplinary worldview. Our new aspiration, then, is to explicate and interrogate, not solve a problem or cloud a topic with layer after layer of obscure thinking.

This last step in EAT is critical in contemplating the consequences of culture on people, families, communities, and societies. On one hand, people are transforming the objects they see, hear, read, and feel by entering them into the great vat of gumbo that makes up their personal worldview. However, the objects are likewise altering them. The change might be overt, implicit, or perhaps even subconscious, but change takes place.

The notion of *transformation* can transport us back in time, just like *adapt* returned us to childhood. Using actor Brad Pitt as an example, certainly one of the most recognizable people in the contemporary world, demonstrates how connected we are to the prehistoric times and the culture resonance that exists in people right down to a structural level. What Pitt reveals, as does the link to the origins of culture, is that transformation is about symbolism—how people manifest the ideas at the heart of culture.

Thinking about modern celebrity at the iconic level—say Pitt, his wife Angelina Jolie, and a small handful of others—we might speculate that these individuals are no longer really human. Surely they still breathe, at least we assume they do, but they exist at the idea or impulse level. Like a stock market ticker that moves figures up and down or the symbolic ideas represented by one's retirement savings, the numbers have little meaning as anything more than abstract representations. Brad Pitt and Angelina Jolie move the cultural needle in a similar fashion. It all has concrete value to someone, but one perceives the calibration as a feeling more than physical sensation. Pitt is an ephemeral impression on the global consciousness.

Leaping back in time to civilization about 40,000 years ago, ancient humans experienced the last mega–Ice Age blanketing most of the earth in snow and cold. For the next 15,000 years, people clung on the verge of extinction. Thankfully, enough survived to carry on humanity, perhaps as few as 10,000 exalted souls. It might be logical to assume that little culture existed in such a state of day-to-day survival. However, what remains from the Ice Age provides a record of astonishing artistic achievement. Historian David Christian explains, "In harsh environments, knowledge is as crucial as tools . . . knowledge was highly valued, and carefully codified and stored in stories, rituals, songs, paintings, and dances."[8]

Culture flourished, from human figurines found across Europe and Russia to cave paintings throughout Europe and Africa. Stephen Matthews and Sally Mallam suggest that Cro-Magnons used art to cope with the changing circumstances and stresses of life in such a severe environment.[9] Rob DeSalle and Ian Tattersall point to artworks found in the Vogelherd cave in southern Germany that contained animal figurines of a horse, mammoth, and lion. Although these ancient trinkets are more than 30,000 years old, they are not straightforward renditions. The horse, for example, they report, "is a perfect evocation of the abstract essence of all horses: symbolic in every sense of the term."[10]

Although early artwork and animal figurines demonstrate early humankind's symbolic reasoning, the link between their world and ours grows closer when examining the Venus figures found across Europe and into Russia. These include the Venus of Willendorf, one of the earliest images of the human body made by humans, which archaeologist Josef Szombathy discovered on the banks of the Danube River in Austria in 1908. The Venus of Willendorf is about four and a half inches tall and dates back approximately 25,000 to 30,000 years ago. The figurine and others similar to it are notable for having exaggerated female body parts, including large breasts and hips.

Since few women probably looked like the Venus of Willendorf in a nomadic period of foraging, and other Venus statuettes have similar body types, some researchers conclude that the figurine is of an idol or idealized female, maybe even a cultic idol. Here the comparison with Brad Pitt comes full circle, since Pitt himself is now more photographic or filmic image than real being and certainly idolized from many perspectives. In certain films, Pitt has exaggerated male features designed to accentuate his star quality, from the oversized physique of *Troy* to the sleek extreme of *Fight Club*.

Another interesting way to look at the Venus of Willendorf/Brad Pitt connection is that the actual image of the statuette and the celebrity image of Pitt are cultural constructs. In other words, certain people within the culture are using ideal images or, in the case of Willendorf and Pitt in certain films, as representations of adulation. We do not know for sure why specific characteristics of the Venus of Willendorf are exaggerated or even the rationale for the statuette, but considering the craftsmanship it took to sculpt it, the figurine had meaning. Conversely, we may think we understand why Pitt is super buff or beefed up for certain roles or even why he is presented as the ideal male, but I think this points to the foundational nature of culture. Maybe this notion will someday lead us to the existence of a culture gene.

What Pitt and Willendorf also demonstrate is the enduring power of symbolism and the way people make use of these iconic representations as they map their personal viewpoints. The transformation of an object from idea to object and then back to thought works on a constant loop, making the outcome that much more significant.

MAKING THE POPULAR CULTURE FRAMEWORK PRAGMATIC

The idea of making theory pragmatic might strike some as an odd goal. Yet, we can again gather clues from the way marketers operate. Recent marketing campaigns capitalize on the principles of cultpopculture by connecting with audiences via hyper-personalization and customized consumer goods, products, and services, like the Coke campaign discussed above.

What we learn from consumers—whether tweens or their octogenarian grandparents—is that they want a voice in determining how they engage with products and services. They also demand authentic conversations with organizations, which technology enables in an accessible way for the first time in history. It is the combination of technology and consumer culture that resides at the heart of the transformation in people as both consumers and creators within the capitalist environment.

Cultpopculture, with the EAT model as its engine, offers a meaningful discourse and opens the popular culture studies conversation to a broader, more interdisciplinary perspective. Perhaps we no longer even frame the dialogue around *theory*, but as Jeffrey J. Williams suggests, on *criticism*, which is both more inclusive and useful.[11]

The real value here, he suggests, is, basically, to make criticism pragmatic, to "inform and educate" versus the dominant theory regime that narrowed thinking. Williams explains:

> A good deal of contemporary criticism is circular, slavish to authority (isn't it odd that a criticism that puts all things in question relies so heavily on a fairly narrow set of authorities, who it intones with genuflections, "as Derrida says," "as Butler says," and so on?), and pretentiously ponderous . . . the goal of criticism seems to be to make endless

minor adjustments—we "complicate" and "problematize" texts, once
again—that have relevance only to a rarefied coterie and function
largely to keep the coterie going.[12]

Williams' plea for inclusion not only moves us past the staid battles over
theories and theorists, but also opens Humanities work to broader audiences as a means of overcoming the general public's disdain for intellec-
tualism and the public official's demand that a university education centers on job training.

Williams extends the argument a step further, explaining that criticism that is obscure or "difficult" is most likely due to "carelessness or
windiness."[13] These writers are playing a role as venerable thinker, rather than producing work that has meaning to anyone outside their small
tribe of likeminded thinkers. Williams concludes—and I heartily agree—
that the deliberate decision to be demanding and difficult turns our work
into "a self-interested hobby."[14]

The curious piece of theory formation is that more academics do not
seem to want to create their own theories. Instead, they simply fall back
on their intellectual "crutches," as Williams explains above. Does the
scholarly conversation really need another Derrida or Foucault quote,
particularly when they are strategically placed as a signpost to other
academic readers?

The argument against the preceding sentence will certainly be that
this is not the way scholars work, yet examples of this type of theorist/
object writing begins rearing up in graduate training and often continues
deep into careers, despite opposite claims. I am the first to admit this
preoccupation in a great deal of my own work, quoting Ray B. Browne as
if his name alone will wipe away decades of academics looking dubious-
ly at popular culture studies as a scholarly discipline. The duck-and-
cover mentality of constant censure at the heart of academe forces all but
the few at the highest echelons of intellectual reputation to play this
theorist shell game.

What results is intellectual toadyism—applying a theorist or theory to
an object or issue to *complicate* the thing, rather than the innovative thinking that enables one to *contemplate* what the object might mean or its
consequences. As writers, thinkers, and intellectuals, our objective is to
help society understand what is going on and perhaps even employ that
information to help us envision the future. We achieve these aspirations
not in silos meant to excite a handful of readers, but when our work cuts
across intellectual boundaries and opens us all to expanding the conversation.

Returning to Tom DeLonge and the Angels & Airwaves multimedia
project, one finds a pragmatic interpretation of the EAT model by an
artist/creator of popular culture objects, rather than simply a critic's favorite show pony. I suggest that it is this instinctual link to culture that

results in the chemical reaction that bursts in one's brain when encountering popular culture items. DeLonge provides a glimpse behind the Wizard's cloak, revealing his goals as he produces creative works across music, film, books, and graphic design. That rush can *feel* like or actually *be* chemistry, hatred, attraction, antipathy, or love. But it is also more than just emotion, because the person experiencing the object then does something with it that may actually remove it from its original condition.

Whether it is a favorite novel, poignant film, or rollicking music, we are chemically attuned to popular culture. Observers claim that the brain is *hard-wired* to comprehend many things, and popular culture is one of the most critical. Again, on an instinctual level then, popular culture is the manifestation of our physical desire for culture that we engage in via objects that comprise our daily lives. I hazard this is why a baby will dance and sway to music long before she realizes what music actually is and why people are attracted to certain actors, narratives, and situations. In a sea of objects, popular culture enables us to navigate our world and simultaneously connects us to one another through shared responses.

NOTES

1. Steve Forstneger, "Blink-182," *Illinois Entertainer*, August 1, 2011, illinois entertainer.com/2011/08/cover-story-blink-182.

2. Tom DeLonge, interview by Steven Rosen, *UltimateGuitar.com*, December 25, 2014, www.ultimate-guitar.com/interviews/interviews/tom_delonge_im_writing_songs_different_now_because_i_realized_how_bored_i_am_of_myself.html.

3. Lawrence Kasdan, J. J. Abrams, and Michael Arndt, *Star Wars: The Force Awakens*, directed by J. J. Abrams (Lucasfilm/Bad Robot, Walt Disney Studios, 2015).

4. The figures presented in the essay are as of March 2016, but will be woefully outdated by publication, which simply demonstrates how popular these figures are. For a ranking of Minecraft YouTubers, please see the *SeusCraft* website: seuscraft.com/youtubers.

5. F. Scott Fitzgerald, *The Great Gatsby*, ed. Matthew J. Bruccoli (New York: Cambridge University Press, 1991), 101.

6. Kim Foltz, "The Media Business: Advertising; A New Twist for Klein's Obsession," *New York Times*, 15 August 1990, www.nytimes.com/1990/08/15/business/the-media-business-advertising-a-new-twist-for-klein-s-obsession.html; The commercial can be viewed at YouTube, either searching via keywords or at www.youtube.com/watch?v=Lv_5sVCuXQ8.

7. Matthew Hepburn, "The Share a Coke Story," Coca-Cola UK, www.coca-cola.co.uk/stories/history/advertising/share-a-coke/#.

8. David Christian, *Maps of Time: An Introduction to Big History* (Berkeley: University of California Press, 2004), 197.

9. Stephen Matthews and Sally Mallam, eds., "Pre-Axial Thought: Paleolithic Beginnings." *The Human Journey*. The Institute for the Study of Human Knowledge, www.humanjourney.us/PaleolithicBeginnings.html.

10. Rob DeSalle and Ian Tattersall. *Human Origins: What Bones and Genomes Tell Us about Ourselves* (College Station, TX: Texas A&M University Press, 2008), 196.

11. Jeffrey J. Williams, *How to Be An Intellectual: Essays on Criticism, Culture, and the University* (New York: Fordham University Press, 2014), 2–3, 7.

12. Jeffrey J. Williams, "Long Island Intellectual," in *The Critical Pulse: Thirty-Six Credos by Contemporary Critics*, eds. Jeffrey J. Williams and Heather Steffen (New York: Columbia University Press, 2012), 55.

13. Ibid., 56.

14. Ibid.

THREE

"Saving People. Hunting Things. The Family Business"

Organizational Communication Approaches to Popular Culture

Andrew F. Herrmann

Organizational communication scholars are in a unique position to examine the portrayals of organizations and processes of organizing in popular culture artifacts. Despite multiple calls for organizational communication scholars to interrogate popular culture, few seriously consider doing so, and those that do are often considered out of the mainstream of the subdiscipline. In this chapter I outline a few reasons why this is the case. From there, I briefly interrogate the television show *Supernatural*, to present how organizational communication scholars can attend to important portrayals of organizing.

Popular culture and organizational communication sound like two separate spheres, despite the fact they can be considered interrelated. Popular culture research is the multifaceted manner by which scholars critically examine power and discourses in popular texts broadly defined, including movies, movie genres, video games, music scenes, phantastical folklore, television series, and other artifacts.[1] Likewise, organizational communication is a vast, complex, multi-theoretical examination of organizations and communication as the processes and practices of organizing, interrogating such topics as the creation of workplace identities, discourses of power, how narratives organize, problematic work-life issues, and organizational leadership, amongst others.[2]

Recently, Karen Lee Ashcraft and Dennis Mumby repeated the refrain that organizational communication scholars need to expand our inquiries beyond topics we are currently investigating, including examining popular culture.[3] Yet rarely are the interrogations of organizational communication and popular studies initiated from within the organizational communication subdiscipline. This need not be so. We are inundated with organizational portrayals in popular culture. Following this line of thought, I contend that organizational communication and popular culture studies need deeper and more nuanced conversations than are currently occurring, particularly from within the organizational communication subdiscipline.

Media portrayals of organizations have a long history. Think of some of the most popular or most culturally relevant television dramas. *Hill Street Blues. Daredevil. The West Wing. Marcus Welby, M.D.* Each takes place inside or around a particular organization: a police station, a law firm, the White House, a hospital. Organizational representations are also portrayed in television comedies: *Barney Miller* (a police station), *30 Rock* (a media conglomerate), *The Office* (an office!). Organizational portrayals are not limited to television. One need only think of *Casablanca, Clerks*, or *Alien*. These too portray various work places: a bar, a convenience store, on the Weyland-Yutani–owned spacecraft *Nostromo*. (See Adam Tyma's and Eric Eisenberg's chapters for more on *Alien* and *Hill Street Blues*, respectively.)

Regardless of the medium, however, these workplaces are generally dismissed as "the setting," the background, a place where action happens. However, numerous scholars point out these portrayals have effects beyond the screen, including influencing our conceptions of workplace roles, workplace gender identities, ideas about workplace professionalism, and so forth.[4] As Ashcraft and Mumby pointed out, organizational frameworks examining popular culture attends to how "society portrays and debates its institutions and the very nature of work."[5] Studying the portrayals of organizations on television and film (and comic books, music, theatre, et al) is one approach to integrate and interrogate popular culture through an organizational communication lens.

There's another approach beyond the portrayals of organizations in popular culture. We normatively think of organization as a noun, rather than as a verb: the activity of organizing.[6] Organizations are the *product* of the *processes* of *organizing* and *sensemaking* that occur through *communicating*.[7] Organizations are, in general, created through these processes as people come together to solve problems and make sense. The same organizing processes occur within popular culture artifacts. Consider, for example, the video game *Civilization* that asks players to create and organize an entire society, strategize war tactics, and develop varied technologies. Relatedly, *World of Warcraft* players often collaborate in guilds to complete important quests. (See Andrew Dunn's chapter on the overlooked research on collaborative activities in video gaming.) Or consider the reality show *Big Brother*, where the teams morph, change, and reform so contestants can endure another contest and survive another week. These teams continually organize for survival, based on cooperative, and eventually individualistic competition. Scholars in popular culture have criticized this reality television format as reinforcing the dominant narratives of neoliberalism, including the self-made man and social Darwinism, all topics within the purview of organizational communication.[8] So why are organizational scholars generally reluctant to tackle these and related aspects of popular culture?

There are a few reasons, related to organizational communication as a subdiscipline, for the lack of sustained interrogation of popular culture artifacts. First, there is an unspoken bias, the continued proclivity that popular culture is "low-brow" and "unserious." This leads to the neglect of studies at the intersection of organizational communication and popular culture from organizational perspectives. As Alf Rehn noted, "It is a telling conceit of organization studies that its relationship with popular culture is seen not as one between equals . . . but as one where the latter stands for a lesser or a more frivolous representation of reality."[9] However, the way popular culture portrays organizing processes must be taken seriously, specifically because popular culture is, in a word, popular. This does not suggest organizational communication scholars are completely ignoring this line of inquiry. However, given the breadth and depth of organizational scholarship in general, this line of inquiry is an exception.

Another dilemma affecting organizational communication researchers struggling to study popular culture is the idea that organizational communication is the study of communication that occurs *inside* organizations. Under this trope, superior-subordinate communication, organizational narratives, and organizational socialization, and so on "count" as proper lines of inquiry. However, forty years ago, with the introduction of systems theory and cultural/critical approaches, organizational scholars exploded the concept of the organization as a container in which communication occurs.[10] Our perceptions of work, organizations, and identity are shaped by discourses outside of organizations proper, including popular culture representations. This framework underscores "the organizing properties of public discourse as it shapes available institutions, as well as how we participate in them and come to understand 'work' endeavors."[11] Still, the old bias that organizational communication is the study of communication *inside* organizations persists.

Regrettably, our peers working at the intersection of popular culture and organizational communication find themselves "organized" out of organizational communication. Their work as organizational scholars studying pop culture is not considered serious because it supposedly lies outside the boundaries of our subdiscipline. Scholars sometimes find themselves stigmatized, positioned as outsiders within the subdiscipline.

(Ironically organizing and disciplining our subdiscipline.) As such, these organizational scholars drift toward media studies, popular culture studies, and mass communication, needing to find outlets for their work. The astute reader may note many endnotes for this chapter were not published in organizational journals, but in journals on media, popular culture, and various other outlets.[12]

We continue to reify the divide between high culture versus low culture, with "proper" organizational communication standing in high culture's stead. Again, this is problematic. Whether it is Donald Trump saying, "You're fired!," the remnant trying to survive the Cylon attack on the *Battlestar Galactica,* or *Buffy the Vampire Slayer's* Scooby Gang trying to evaluate an ethical dilemma, organizations and the process of organizing are important aspects in themselves. This will become apparent as we interrogate the supernatural drama *Supernatural.* (Spoilers!)

UNPACKING THE FAMILY BUSINESS METAPHOR

Supernatural, now in its eleventh season, is ostensibly about Sam and Dean Winchester, brothers travelling around the United States in a black 1967 Chevrolet Impala "saving people" and "hunting things" (ghosts, djinn, zombies, etc.). *Supernatural's* mythology is complex, including new takes on the traditions of heaven and hell, the lore of werewolves and shape-shifters, as well as urban legends and folktales.[13] They refer to being hunters as "the family business" which they learned from their father John. As such, *Supernatural's* mythology, like its predecessors in the supernatural drama genre, including *Buffy the Vampire Slayer* and *Twin Peaks,* is a text scholars continue to interrogate.[14] Scholarly inquiry on *Supernatural* includes gender, identit(ies), ethics, economics, the use of humor, music, and more.[15]

Given that hunting in the show is continually referred to as a "business," it is ripe for an investigation from an organizational communication perspective. As Dean tells Sam, "Killing things that need killing. It's kind of our job."[16] A place to start is with the concept of a "family business." Scholars have not yet agreed on a definition.[17] For our purposes, James Lea's definition proves useful.

> A business is a family business when it is an enterprise growing out of the family's needs, built on the family's abilities, worked by its hands and minds, and guided by its moral and spiritual values; when it is sustained by the family's commitment, and passed down to its sons and daughters as a legacy as precious as the family's name[18]

Family business scholars try to model the reciprocity between family and business systems, including "the development of functional families and profitable firms."[19]

While it is a certainty that Sam and Dean are guided by the values and skills instilled in them by their father John, and that he handed "the family business" down to them, hunting is no traditional business. Hunting is not a job, nor is it a career, nor does it make a profit. The Winchesters do not get paid for saving people. Rather, hunting is an avocation, a calling, with spiritual and religious overtones.[20] The Winchesters may have a mission, and they may refer to hunting as "the family business," but they are not running a normal family business, despite the use of the family metaphor.

Framing a business in terms of the family metaphor is problematic.[21] Metaphors frame reality in particular and partial ways, expressing specific values and belief systems.[22] The family metaphor has a long history, often used to create the idea that an organization is itself an intimate place, a safe dwelling, and a personal habitat. As such, the family metaphor is often utilized to influence organizational members to overlook other aspects of organizational life.[23] The worker-employer relationship, based upon the social contract, is replaced with the idea of a family and "the employer as a benevolent family caretaker" which "conceals what employers want in return."[24]

Whenever Sam expresses doubts or hesitations about their work, Dean retorts with a line about "family," or "being brothers," or "we're blood, Sammy," using the power of the family to get Sam back into line. This is definitely a power move, as Dean suggests all the interpersonal and avocational problems they face can be subsumed under the idea of family and brotherhood, and by doing so tries to maintain control over their relationship. This tactic works until Season Nine when Sam finally counteracts this use of metaphor.

> Dean: Okay, look. Whatever happened, we are family. OK?
> Sam: You say that like it's some sort of cure-all, like it can change the fact that everything that has ever gone wrong between us has been because we're family.
> Dean: So what—we're not family now?[25]

As Gibb Dyer and Wendy Handler noted, "The problems inherent in working with family members are a function of the intersection of two systems, the family and the firm."[26] The metaphor of "the family business" is a powerful one instituted originally in the first episode of *Supernatural*. It is continually used, and then finally challenged nine seasons later. Ultimately, however, this challenge does not work, given the Winchesters' struggle surrounding their calling as hunters and as the family continues in later seasons. While this is one example, popular culture is rife with metaphoric language that can be unpacked by organizational communication scholars.

PROBLEMATIZING WORK-LIFE BALANCE

Another important arena of study is the concept of work-life balance and boundaries.[27] The idea of work-life balance, a construct of the industrial revolution, proposed the public and the private are two separate domains. Annis Golden and Cheryl Geisler noted the public sphere includes "the workplace, associated with competitive individualism, rationality, and profit motive" while the private sphere is "the homespace, associated with relational concerns, emotions, and altruistic nurturance."[28] *Supernatural* provides a unique take on work-life balance.

For most of the series, the Winchesters don't work out of an office. Rather, they live on the road, working, eating, sleeping, collaborating, and arguing in grungy motel rooms or in Dean's Impala. From an organizational communication standpoint this portrayal of their working lives exemplifies the concept of work-life balance as outmoded. The opportunities for the Winchesters to create and perform work-life balance, and maintain these boundaries are extremely limited, similar to other populations living on social and economic margins.[29] For Sam and Dean, living and working on the road epitomizes not the blurred boundaries between what is considered home and what is considered work, but the *complete erasure* of those boundaries. They live in the same spaces where they work, sharing these locations without the possibility of separation or distance (unless one of them decides to leave, which happens, but never lasts long). The locations in which they find themselves are simultaneously workspaces and intimate spaces.

Dean and Sam are always "at work." When they confront familial and personal issues, they deal with them in the context of their work as hunters. As Dean said, "I mean, our family's so screwed to hell, maybe we can help some others. Makes things a little bit more bearable. And I'll tell you what else helps. Killing as many evil sons-of-bitches as I possibly can."[30] The Winchesters have no lives outside of their work, and it costs them their lives and their souls, actually and figuratively. Scholarship on work-family boundaries generally suggests that these spheres are managed along a continuum from segmentation to integration.[31] However, as people on the margins, Sam and Dean exist in a liminal space where "the presupposed border is no longer exclusive of one domain or the other, but blends both work and family, creating a borderland which cannot be exclusively called either domain."[32] In this borderland they are the ultimate mobile-workers, continually telecommuting, transient, and constantly researching cases or on-site hunting. They live to work, and considering the phantasmagoric creatures they encounter often want to kill them, they must work to live. For Dean and Sam there is no respite from work or each other. The brothers live within the borderland of the domains of family and work within the construct of their mission of "saving people, hunting things." Home life is work life and work life is home life. There is no difference.

However, there is another work life–private life border within *Supernatural* that the Winchesters strictly manage. There is the world of the hunters who know about the phantasmagorical, and there is the world of everyone else. When either brother meets a possible intimate other, those relationships are doomed to failure, due to the nature of their work. Dean finds his relationship with Lisa and her son Ben is incompatible with his life as a hunter. Similarly, Sam realizes (too late) that the demon Ruby is using him as a pawn to start the apocalypse. When Sam realizes Dean told Cassie about the business, he yelled, "We do what we do and we shut up about it!"[33] There are numerous other examples in which a possible relationship ends with danger, horror, and sometimes death. Nothing good comes from crossing over the border or blurring the lines of the work-life dichotomy when it comes to intimate others and those on the outside.

In the world of *Supernatural*, the brothers Winchester are always on the job, and relationships are often ended by the brothers themselves, in order to protect the private lives, and actual lives, of those they care about. While *internally* their work-life divide is erased within the auspices of "the family business," the portrayals of the Winchesters' *external* relationships reify the work-life divide. The simultaneity of both blurred work-life boundaries and the strict demarcation of work-life issues provided by *Supernatural* and other popular culture artifacts provides a unique perspective on work-life issues to which organizational communication scholars can attend.

SENSEMAKING AND STIGMATIZATION

Another ongoing organizing process in *Supernatural* is how creatures are defined, categorized, and stigmatized. In almost every episode ambiguous and equivocal situations confront the Winchesters. As such, they immediately employ communication as sensemaking to reduce equivocal situations.[34] Sensemaking "is the reduction of message equivocality— that is, messages with too many possible meanings, accomplished through communicative action."[35] For Karl Weick, sensemaking includes making sense of one's own identity, because "people learn about their identities by projecting them into an environment and observing the consequences."[36] Similar to Weick, Erving Goffman indicates that stigmatization is framed though "our subjective involvement."[37] The stigmatized is no longer identified as an individual, but as a member of an outside-the-norm category, and devalued in the process.[38] Stigmatization creates a spoiled identity, and an individual with a spoiled identity is judged as not normal. These two theoretical streams on sensemaking-identity help us wade through what does and does not make sense.

The process of stigma as a communicative process of organizing appears throughout *Supernatural*. In *Supernatural*, the "human" is discursively normative, and those that fall outside of this socially constructed boundary are stigmatized. From the common vampire to the rare djinn, shojo, and wraith, Sam and Dean regularly stigmatize these beings, referring to them as "freaks," "things," "monsters," and "sons of bitches." They are discursively framed as beyond the norm, often stigmatized as evil incarnate. Even the creatures that once used to be human are framed as having no humanity left in them. Consider the following explanation of the Windigo where sensemaking and stigmatization occur simultaneously:

> Dean: They're hundreds of years old. Each one was once a man. Sometimes an Indian, or other times a frontiersman or a miner or hunter. During some harsh winter a guy finds himself starving, cut off from supplies or help. Becomes a cannibal to survive, eating other members of his tribe or camp. Cultures all over the world believe that eating human flesh gives a person certain abilities. Speed, strength, immortality. If you eat enough of it, over years, you become this less than human thing. You're always hungry.[39]

This type of stigmatizing exposition occurs regularly in *Supernatural*.

Stigma denotes an individual as atypical. Historically, the stigmatized placated "onlookers' self-doubt by appearing as their antithesis" as a means of improving a "normal" individual's feeling of self-worth, by "establishing standards for segregating the deviant from the normal."[40] People and groups are stigmatized because they appear to transgress dominant norms or become the victims of some collective projection, as in the creation of "folk devils."[41] Sensemaking and stigmatization are both processes of organizing our environments and our identities through communicative processes.

However, the whom and what that are stigmatized in *Supernatural* changes as the series' mythology develops, and as situations become morally ambiguous, much like in *Buffy the Vampire Slayer*.[42] Lenore, for example, is a vampire that, along with her nest, no longer hunts humans. Garth is a former hunter turned werewolf, who eats only animals. Amy Pond is a katsune who once saved Sam and only kills to heal her son. The Winchesters' very human paternal grandfather turns out to be morally dubious. Crowley, a narcissistic demon, occasionally allies with the Winchesters, while angels are portrayed as unemotional bureaucrats, often unconcerned with human affairs. Or as Dean put it more than once: "Dicks."[43]

Sensemaking and stigmatization are processes of organizing shown not only in specific individual episodes, but across entire seasons, as Sam and Dean encounter demon hunting militias, bizarre religious activities and groups, and attempt to thwart the apocalypse (actually apocalypses). They are continually attempting to make sense of their surroundings, new creatures, new information, as well as their identities in relationship to all of these. How others are "organized" communicatively and discursively in popular culture is another area rich for organizational communication scholars to plumb.

CODA

This analysis of *Supernatural* is necessarily brief. However, it provides a number of different ways by which organizational communication scholars can examine popular culture artifacts. It is, of course, partial and problematic. I could have looked at *Supernatural* from a variety of other theoretical and practical views. For example, I could have examined demon hunting as "dirty work," or Sam and Dean as the embodied interrogation of downward mobility through economic discourses, or through the lens of masculine gendered work identities.[44] Or I could have examined the dives, diners, and bars (all organizations) where Sam and Dean devour massive burgers, drink beer and whiskey, and gorge on fries, through C. Wesley Buerkle's lens of "heteromasculinity."[45] Or, I could have examined how this story makes sense in the grander polymediated narrative of the series.[46] The portrayals of organizations, and the portrayals of processes of organizing are all part of the popular culture surround in which we are embedded. What can organizational communication scholars bring to popular culture? Quite a lot, actually.

To quote Dean, "We got work to do."

NOTES

1. Michaela D.E. Meyer, Linda M. Waldron, and Danielle M. Stern, "Relational Aggression on Film: An Intersectional Analysis of Mean Girls," *Popular Culture Studies Journal* 2 (2014): 5–34; Sean Brayton, "When Commodities Attack: Reading Narratives of the Great Recession and Late Capitalism in Contemporary Horror Films," *Studies in Media and Communication* 1 (2013): 150–61. redfame.com/journal/index.php/smc/article/view/234/239; Robert Andrew Dunn, "Polyreality," in *Beyond New Media: Discourse and Critique in a Polymediated Age*, ed. Art Herbig, Andrew F. Herrmann, and Adam Tyma (Lantham, MD: Lexington): 109–24; Lawrence Grossberg, "Rock, Territorialization and Power," *Cultural Studies* 5 (1991): 358–67. doi: 10.1080/09502389100490301; Andrew F. Herrmann, "Ghosts, Vampires, Zombies, and Us: The Undead as Autoethnographic Bridges," *International Review of Qualitative Research* 7 (2013): 327–41.

2. Eric M. Eisenberg, Zachary Johnson, and Willem Pieterson, "Leveraging Social Networks for Strategic Success," *International Journal of Business Communication* 52 (2015): 143–54. doi: 10.1177/2329488414560283; Andrew F. Herrmann, "Narrative as an Organizing Process: Identity and Story in a New Nonprofit," *Qualitative Research in Organizations and Management: An International Journal*, 6 (2011): 246–64. doi: 10.1108/

17465641111188411; Jane Jorgenson, "Engineering Selves: Negotiating Gender and Identity in Technical Work," *Management Communication Quarterly*, 15 (2002): 350–80. doi: 10.1177/0893318902153002; Rebecca J. Meisenbach, "Stigma Management Communication: A Theory and Agenda for Applied Research on How Individuals Manage Moments of Stigmatized Identity," *Journal of Applied Communication Research*, 38 (2010): 268–92. doi:10.1080/00909882.2010.490841.

3. Karen Lee Ashcraft and Dennis K. Mumby, *Reworking Gender: A Feminist Communicology of Organization* (Thousand Oaks, CA: Sage, 2004).

4. Joan Acker, "Gender Capitalism and Globalization," *Critical Sociology* 30 (2004): 17–40. doi: 10.1163/156916304322981668; Karen Lee Ashcraft and Lisa Flores, "'Slaves with White Collars': Persistent Performances of Masculinity in Crisis," *Text and Performance Quarterly* 23 (2003): 1–29. doi: 10.1080/10462930310001602020; Robin Boylorn, "As Seen on TV: An Autoethnographic Reflection on Race and Reality Television," *Critical Studies in Media Communication* 25(2008): 413–33. doi: 10.1080/15295030802327758; Mark P. Orbe, "Constructions of ·Reality on MTV's 'The Real Word': An Analysis of the Restrictive Coding of Black Masculinity," *Southern Communication Journal 64* (1998): 32–47. doi: 10.1080/10417949809373116.

5. Ashcraft and Mumby, 19.

6. Herrmann, "Narrative as an Organizing Process," 261.

7. Karl E. Weick, *Sensemaking in Organizations* (Thousand Oaks, CA: Sage, 1995).

8. Katherine Meizel, "Making the Dream a Reality (Show): The Celebration of Failure in American Idol," *Popular Music and Society* 32 (2009): 475–88. doi: 10.1080/03007760802217725; Keat Murray, "Surviving Survivor: Reading Mark Burnett's Field Guide and De-naturalizing Social Darwinism as Entertainment," *Journal of American & Comparative Cultures* 24 (2001): 43–54. doi: 10.1111/j.1537-4726.2001.2403_43.x.

9. Alf Rehn, "Pop (Culture) Goes the Organization: On Highbrow, Lowbrow and Hybrids in Studying Popular Culture Within Organization Studies," *Organization*, 15 (2008): 781. doi: 10.1177/1350508408093652.

10. Michael Pacanowski and Nick O'Donnell Trujillo, "Communication and Organizational Cultures," *Western Journal of Communication* 46 (1982): 115–130. doi: 10.1080/10570318209374072; Andrew F. Herrmann, "Communicating, Sensemaking, and (Dis)organizing: Theorizing the Complexity of Polymediation," in Beyond New Media: Discourse and Critique in a Polymediated Age, eds, Art Herbig, Andrew F. Herrmann, and Adam W. Tyma (Lanham, MD: Lexington Books, 2015), pp. 61–82.

11. Ashcraft and Mumby, 19.

12. Carolyn Kreber, *"The University and its Disciplines: Teaching and Learning within and beyond Disciplinary Boundaries* (New York, NY: Routledge, 2010).

13. See Art Herbig and Andrew F. Herrmann, "Polymediated Narrative: The Case of *Supernatural's* 'Fan Fiction," *International Journal of Communication* 10 (2016): 748–65. ijoc.org/index.php/ijoc/article/view/4397/1560; Alyssa Silva, "Dean Winchester: an existentialist hero?" *Sesión no numerada: revista de letras y ficción audiovisual* 2 (2012): 67–83; Joseph M. Valenzano III, and Erika Engstrom, "Homilies and Horsemen: Revelation in the CW's Supernatural," *Journal of Communication & Religion* 36 (2013): 50–72.

14. Herbig and Herrmann, "Polymediated Narrative," 749; Andrew F. Herrmann, *Re-discovering Kolchak and Twin Peaks: Elevating the Influence of the First Television Supernatural Dramas.* Paper presented at Central States Communication Association Convention, Minneapolis, MN, 2014; Andrew F. Herrmann and Art Herbig, "'All Too Human': Xander Harris and the Embodiment of the Full Human," *Popular Culture Studies Journal* 3 (2015): 84–112. mpcaaca.org/wp-content/uploads/2013/10/PCSJ-V1–N12–Herrmann-Daniel-Amos-and-Me.pdf.

15. Stacey Abbott and David Lavery, eds. *TV Goes to Hell: An Unofficial Road Map of Supernatural* (ECW Press, 2011).

16. Robert Berens, "Alex Annie Alexis Ann," *Superntnatural*, 2005.

17. Pramodita Sharma, "An Overview of the Field of Family Business Studies: Current Status and Directions for the Future," *Family Business Review* 17: (2004): 1–36. doi: 10.1111/j.1741-6248.2004.00001.x.

18. James W. Lea, "What Is a Family Business? More Than You Think," *Triangle Business Journal* 1 (1998). www.bizjournals.com/triangle/stories/1998/11/02/smallb3.

19. Sharma, p. 5.

20. Andrew F. Herrmann, "'Criteria Against Ourselves?': Embracing the Opportunities of Qualitative Inquiry," *International Review of Qualitative Research* 5 (2012): 135–52.

21. Ruth C. Smith and Eric M. Eisenberg, "Conflict at Disneyland: A Root Metaphor Analysis, *Communication Monographs* 54 (1987): 367–80. doi:10.1080/036377587093 90239.

22. Stanley Deetz and Dennis Mumby, "Metaphors, Information, and Power," *Information and Behavior* 1 (1985): 369–86; Jaime E. Bochantin,"'Morning Fog, Spider Webs, and Escaping from Alcatraz': Examining Metaphors Used by Public Safety Employees and their Families to Help Understand the Relationship between Work and Family," *Communication Monographs* (2015): 1–25. doi: 10.1080/03637751.2015.1073853.

23. Smith and Eisenberg, 1987.

24. Jun Young and Kirsten Foot, "Corporate E-cruiting: The Construction of Work in Fortune 500 Recruiting Web Sites," *Journal of Computer-Mediated Communication* 11 (2005). doi: 10.1111/j.1083-6101.2006.tb00303.x. jcmc.indiana.edu/vol11/issue1/young. html.

25. Adam Glass, "Sharp Teeth," *Supernatural*, 2014.

26. W. Gibb Dyer and Wendy Handler, "Entrepreneurship and Family Business: Exploring the Connections," *Entrepreneurship Theory and Practice* 19 (1994), 75.

27. See Katherine J. Denker. "Maintaining Gender During Work-Life Negotiations: Relational Maintenance and the Dark Side of Individual Marginalization." *Women & Language* 36 (2012): 11–34; Katherine J. Denker and Debbie Dougherty, "Corporate Colonization of Couples' Work-Life Negotiations: Rationalization, Emotion Management and Silencing Conflict." Journal of Family Communication, 13 (2013): 242–62. doi: 10.1080/15267431.2013.796946; Andrew F. Herrmann and Art Herbig, "All Too Human," 111–12; Arlie Hochschild, *The Time Bind: When Work Becomes Home and Home Becomes Work* (New York, NY, Metropolitan Books).

28. Annis G. Golden and Cheryl Geisler, "Work–life Boundary Management and the Personal Digital Assistant," *Human Relations 60, p.* 520. doi: 10.1177/ 0018726707076698.

29. Sara Dykins Callahan, "Academic Outings," *Symbolic Interaction* 31 (2008): 351–75. doi:10.1525/si.2008.31.4.351.

30. Ron Milbauer and Terri Hughes Burton, "Windego," *Supernatural*, 2005.

31. Jeffrey Hill, Maria Ferris, and Vjollca Märtinson, "Does It Matter Where You Work? A Comparison of How Three Work Venues (Traditional Office, Virtual Office, and Home Office) Influence Aspects of Work and Personal/Family Life," *Journal of Vocational Behavior* 63 (2003): 220–41. doi: 10.1016/S0001-8791(03)00042-3.

32. Nafishah Othman, Shafiz A. M. Yusof, and R. S. Osman, "A Conflict between Professional vs. Domestic Life? Understanding the Use of ICT in Teleworking for Balance in Work and Family Units," *Computer and Information Science* 2 (2009), p. 7. doi: 10.5539/cis.v2n2p3.

33. Eugenie Ross-Leming and Brad Bruckner, "Route 666," *Supernatural,* 2006.

34. Weick, 187.

35. Herrmann, "Communicating," 61–82.

36. Weick, 187.

37. Erving Goffman, *Frame Analysis: An Essay on the Organization of Experience* (London: Harper and Row, 1972), p. 10.

38. Erving Goffman, *Stigma: Notes on the Management of Spoiled Identity* (New York, NY: Prentice Hall, 1963).

39. Milbauer and Burton, "Windego."

40. Rachel Adams, *Sideshow U.S.A.: Freaks and the American Cultural Imagination* (Chicago, IL: University of Chicago Press), p 15.

41. Stanley Cohen, *Folk Devils and Moral Panics* (Oxford: MacGibbon & Key, 1972).

42. Andrew F. Herrmann, "C-can we rest now?": Foucault and the multiple discursive subjectivities of Spike. Slayage: The Journal of the Whedon Studies Association 10 (2013), p. 18. Available at: slayageonline.com/essays/slayage35/Herrmann.pdf.

43. Sera Gamble and Lou Bollo, "Are You There, God? It's Me, Dean Winchester," *Supernatural*, 2008.

44. Authors who have studied these topics and provide excellent resources for those who want to interrogate popular culture artifacts through these lenses can see: Blake E. Ashforth and Glen E. Kreiner, "'How can you do it?': Dirty work and the challenge of constructing a positive identity," *Academy of Management Review* 24 (1999): 413–34. Sarah J. Tracy and Angela Trethewey, "Fracturing the Real-Self ↔ Fake-Self Dichotomy: Moving Toward 'Crystallized' Organizational Discourses and Identities," *Communication Theory* 15 (2005): 168–95. doi: 10.1111/j.1468-2885.2005.tb00331.x; Michael Zweig, *The Working Class Majority: America's Best-Kept Secret* (Ithaca, NY: Cornell University Press, 2000); Jill Andresky Fraser, *While-Collar Sweatshop* (New York, NY: Norton, 2001); Karen Lee Ashcraft, "Resistance through Consent? Occupational Identity, Organizational Form, and the Maintenance of Masculinity among Commercial Airline Pilots," *Management Communication Quarterly* 19 (2005): 67–90; David L. Collinson, "Identities and Insecurities: Selves at Work," *Organization* 10 (2003): 527–47.

45. C. Wesley Buerkle, "Metrosexuality Can Stuff It: Beef Consumption as (Heteromasculine) Fortification." *Text and Performance Quarterly* 29 (2009): 77–93.

46. See Herbig and Herrmann, "Polymediated."

FOUR

Who's the Boss?

Leadership in the Popular Imagination

Eric M. Eisenberg

Our image of what constitutes a great leader is built over time through our experience with institutions and our exposure to media representations of leadership. But as we know, media images may differ from and significantly distort reality. This essay tracks both the reality and the media representations of leadership to show where they converge and diverge, and considers the implications of this gap for leadership practice. First, I describe the development of conceptions of leadership over the past few decades as described by researchers and practitioners. Second, I chronicle representations of leadership in popular culture over the same time period, paying special attention to representations in entertainment and in news coverage of world events. In so doing, I hope to show how popular notions of leadership are reflecting new realities in many ways but lagging in significant other respects.

WHAT IS LEADERSHIP?

Leadership is the art of influencing others to behave in ways that one favors. Leadership is an art because after more than a century of rigorous empirical study, no single formula for success has emerged; rather, there is a growing consensus that effective leaders adapt their actions to their situation and to the characteristics and inclinations of potential followers.[1] As a consequence, the nature of leadership can look very different across differing situations.

Leadership is about influencing behaviors because attitudes and beliefs are difficult to measure reliably, but actions are observable. While the rhetoric of effective leaders capturing "hearts and minds" and cultivating "shared meaning" persists in the popular imagination, what is most crucial in determining leadership effectiveness is coordinated action, whether followers behave in ways that the leader desires.[2]

Finally, leadership is about influencing behavior in ways that one favors; the purpose of leadership, regardless of context or setting, is to promote one's preferred narrative or world view in the face of a cacophony of competing alternatives. In our media-saturated, mega-bandwidth world, the competition between stories has never been more intense.

But how does leadership work? Humanity has experienced (and continues to experience) the vast number of techniques that aspiring leaders use to influence behavior and compel followership. At one extreme are force, coercion, and even extermination of the other—comply or die. Authoritarian regimes are a good example of this. At the other extreme are the subtle and pernicious workings of hegemony, wherein those with greater power not only compel certain behaviors by rigging the available behavioral options but hide their power while doing so, leaving people to believe that they are acting of their own free will. Between these poles lie a wide array of leadership styles and approaches that vary significantly in their degree of overt command and control.

But why is leadership necessary? The first challenge facing any conscious life form is how to organize either with or against other members of their species. Humans and other primates learned early on to form groups and tribes as an effective means of survival. Two archetypal forms of organizing are identifiable among early *homo sapiens*—dominator and partnership.[3] Partnership forms of organizing emphasize relationships and collaboration, while dominator forms stress hierarchy and singular leadership. Examples of both persist today, but for the most part the dominator model has prevailed. Furthermore, there are many connections between dominator models of organizing and a litany of abuses, including environmental degradation and violence against women and minorities. Moreover, in the dominator model power is consolidated and fiercely guarded by those at the top of both formal and informal hierarchies. Dominator models of organizing call out for "command and control" models of leadership, with clear lines of authority and division of labor. These models also include an implicit model of communication as one-way (orders, directives) and as focused on obedience ("do as you are told and no one gets hurt"). Much leadership today continues to be based on this model, where it is prevalent in some factories, service organizations, and multi-national corporations.

Every human being understands the dominator model, even if they do not live in an authoritarian society. With its focus on rigid hierarchy and singular leadership, this model is the default setting underlying most human organization. Up until the late twentieth century, most armies, schools, prisons, and corporations were organized in similar ways, to maximize uniformity and control of behavior. Add to this the fact that the legal systems of most societies (particularly in the Western hemisphere) are built around the idea of individual accountability and culpability, which further reinforces the need for strict hierarchy and clear rules. As I will argue below, hierarchical, command and control models of leadership have persisted long beyond their usefulness, revealing a deeply held desire on the part of many to believe that there is an omnipotent individual capable of leading us, and if not successful, who will be available to blame and to punish. Some of the earliest studies of leadership sponsored by the US military sought evidence for this "Great Man" theory, fueled by the belief that such individuals could be found. But while we now know that leadership is much more about relationships than any particular style, the desire for the charismatic leader persists. Those who long for such leaders likely also continue to believe that strict hierarchy can resolve all disputes and that someone, somewhere knows the answers and can save us from ourselves—that is, that the wizard of Oz is a real Wizard, not a deeply flawed man.

A DISRUPTION IN THE FORCE

While it remains true that hierarchical models are the default organizing tool for human organizing, a counter force has been growing for some time (and as referenced above, Riane Eisler would argue has been around since pre-history). Specifically, leaders across a wide range of industries and institutions have discovered that hierarchical solutions are ineffective in a fast-paced, turbulent and uncertain environment. The US military, for example, teaches officers how to lead in a VUCA environment (volatile, uncertain, complex and ambiguous) which requires improvisation and non-conventional tactics.[4] Margaret Wheatley made a similar point when she applied principles from the natural sciences to distinguish *order* (which could be emergent and achieved collectively) from *control* (which is pursued individually through hierarchy).[5] Meanwhile, conceptions of social power have shifted from the kind of power that one may have *over* another person—to direct or influence them to do things—to the kind of power we can achieve *with* others, the power to create and to inspire collective action. This distinction can be traced to Mary Parker Follett, who saw leadership this way in 1924:

> The skillful leader . . . does not rely on personal force; he [*sic*] controls his group not by dominating but by expressing it. He stimulates what is best in us; he unifies and concentrates what we feel only gropingly and scatteringly, but he never gets away from the current of which we and he are both an integral part. He is a leader who gives form to the

inchoate energy in every man. The person who influences me most is
not he who does great deeds but he who makes me feel I can do great
deeds. . . . Whoever has struck fire out of me, aroused me to action
which I should not otherwise have taken, he has been my leader.[6]

Most recently, a combination of increasing global competition and shifting employee values has challenged every industry and institution to
develop modes of organizing that feature less hierarchy and deeper employee engagement and participation. Traditional hierarchies are both
too slow to respond to competitive threats and not particularly satisfying
to younger employees who want their ideas to be taken seriously. In the
future, the twentieth century may be characterized as a long and challenging trek from top-down control models of organizing that have
ceased to be effective to more participative models of coordination that
feature delegation, employee empowerment and employee engagement
as engines of both productivity and desperately needed innovation.

This trend toward less hierarchical, more engaged leadership is not
limited to institutions and organizations but is also reflected in other
walks of life, from families to schools. The latest trend in higher education, for example, is to transform the classroom experience from one
where the professor plays the role of "the sage on the stage" to one where
they act as "the guide on the side." Educational researchers have consistently found better learning outcomes associated with what they call
"high-impact practices," all of which replace traditional one-way, lecture-
based interaction with more interactive and customized pedagogy.

Along with this changing notion of leadership from command to facil-
itation comes a very different expectation of what is expected of people in
leadership roles. Under the old model, the leader was expected to be
nearly superhuman, someone to obey, to possibly emulate, and to fear.
Under the new model, the leader is more of a facilitator with human
qualities and foibles. But how well do these new leadership exemplars
square with leadership imagery in the public sphere? To what extent do
leadership figures in popular culture reflect these changes, and why does
it matter? The next part of this essay explores this question in the realms
of entertainment and news.

LEADERSHIP IN ENTERTAINMENT

Popular movies and television shows are often set in institutional settings, which gives writers and others involved an opportunity to paint a
picture of leadership. Commonly portrayed organizations are police stations (*Blue Bloods*), crime labs (*CSI*), ad agencies (*Mad Men*) and law firms
(*Boston Legal*).[7] Other less common venues include churches, colleges and
schools, governments and (typically "faceless") corporations. Since portrayals of law enforcement organizations are so prevalent, I will focus

mainly on them here to illustrate how images of leadership have changed significantly over time.

While there are numerous examples one could choose, an iconic TV series that illustrated the traditional model of leadership was *Hill Street Blues* (1981–1987).[8] Much has been made in organizational theory about the death of the "social contract" between organizations and employees, wherein employee loyalty was rewarded with lifelong employment.[9] This contract was irrevocably broken at the end of the twentieth century (the debut of the comic strip *Dilbert* in 1989 provides a convenient marker for its demise) but *Hill Street Blues* was a last testament to that receding world. In that show, the Police Captain (Frank Furillo) was the pinnacle of command and control, and his lieutenants felt protective of the officers ("be careful out there" was the weekly admonition from the ranking Sergeant to those at the bottom of the pyramid). Numerous characters were at various stages of studying for the exam that would give them their next promotion along a well-defined career ladder. The world outside the precinct was portrayed as random, violent, and unpredictable, but inside its members could return to order, clear rules, and the possibility of a moral, meaningful, orderly life. Looking back on the series from today, the characters appear to be valiantly defending a receding landscape of order and control against a persistent and generally frightening onslaught of chaos, contradiction, and anomie.

The creator of *Hill Street Blues* was Steven Bochco, and six years after it ended he was inspired to create yet another police drama, *NYPD Blue* (1993–2005).[10] But the world of *NYPD Blue* could not have been more different than *Hill Street*. On *Hill Street* the Captain ruled with an iron fist, and his subordinates generally supported his position even if they disagreed with his decisions—they recognized him as having significant and valuable moral authority. In the *NYPD* incarnation the Captain (no one even remembers his name) is shunted to the side. The real police work takes place entirely through horizontal peer connections. No one is studying to move up in the organization, and the most common phrase used throughout the series has to do with the importance of "reaching out" to allies who can help you to succeed. In a brilliant move, Bochco cast the same actor (Dennis Franz) to play two contrasting roles, each reflecting the zeitgeist of the time. On *Hill Street*, Franz is Sal Bennedeto, a corrupt cop who eventually commits suicide. In *NYPD Blue*, he plays Andy Sipowicz, a deeply flawed and alcoholic officer who prevails in the end by confronting his demons and making peace with disorder and imperfection.

NYPD Blue launched in 1993, a year after the release of film director Clint Eastwood's masterpiece *Unforgiven*, which ultimately received the Academy Award for Best Picture.[11] Eastwood plays retired gunslinger William Munny who is recruited from farm life to take on one last murderous job. But without the clarity and confidence always associated with these characters, his actions become hesitant and ambiguous, blurring the lines between heroism and villainy. Looking back, Eastwood's shocking inversion of the entire Western genre (and of all the macho characters he had mostly played to that point) appears as a signal event in this shifting leadership narrative.

Jersey mob boss Tony Soprano is yet another fictional character from that time period who struggles with the collapse of clear leadership scripts. The initial airing of *The Sopranos* on HBO (1999–2007) overlapped with *NYPD Blue*, and both series convincingly created social worlds where all of the usual paradigms and anchors were coming undone and of little use to the characters.[12] Just as the social contract that held the precinct together had dissolved, the traditional Mafia code was also under fire. Throughout the series, Tony struggles to "lead" his mafia soldiers (and his family) through a world filled with anxiety and ambiguity. Decisions that would have once been straightforward are complicated by concerns about family, identity, and mental health. While some of his followers seem to want to return to a time when the boss was in complete control, others (especially the younger ones) are challenging the traditional system and pushing for change. As a result, it feels as if the traditional recipe book for leadership had been thrown out the window, leaving these protagonists on shifting ground, forcing them to improvise in order to survive.

The way leaders are portrayed in entertainment is important because it serves as a resource for audiences to use in constructing their own ideas about how to lead others across a range of situations. So how has the image of the leader changed in entertainment? It has changed in at least four ways. First, whereas in the past leaders were seen as nearly superhuman and omnipotent, now they are seen as stressed and vulnerable men and women forced to struggle daily with ordinary challenges. For example, to cope with his murderous lifestyle, Tony Soprano seeks out a therapist. Second, the path to the leader's position is no longer seen as clearly defined or logical—instead, the corporate ladder has become a loosely strung lattice that many people are not even interested in climbing. Third, it is now acknowledged that authoritarian power usually doesn't work and sometimes backfires, and that in fact horizontal relationships and connections are key to a leader's success. *NYPD Blue* officers spend all of their time working their connections on the street and at other precincts and never think of using the chain of command as a resource. Fourth, there has been a general reorientation from seeing the world as an orderly place wherein leaders can, through their actions, make steady progress and improvement, to a world where every day is just about holding back the tide, no real progress is ever made, and survival with one's sanity is the main (and possibly only laudable and achievable) goal.

While these changes were occurring in the realm of fictional leaders, the viewing public was receiving leadership lessons from the same screens but in a different context--through news stories that portrayed institutional and political leaders in particular ways. These changing representations are discussed in the next section.

LEADERSHIP IN THE NEWS

In their efforts to report on a compelling story, news organizations approach leadership in a particular way. Specifically, when a surprising (and typically traumatic) event has occurred, they begin a search for the responsible party, reflecting the public's presumed desire for a clear explanation of what happened, why it happened, and who was to blame. In this way, unlike what we saw in the discussion of entertainment, news reporters have always presumed that even the greatest and most successful of leaders is also a flawed human being, and at times even seem to enjoy revealing their foibles, especially since this predictably draws an audience.

Unfortunately, the relentless search for logical explanations and accountable persons has become less fruitful over time. Both the logic of the Cold War and the focus on state actors provided a clear formula for constructing narratives about the causes and potential impact of conflicts. But at least in the United States, the events of 9/11 signaled a very different way of thinking about these issues. In her analysis of the 9/11 transcripts, Sandra Cooper chronicled a relentless desire on the part of the investigating commission to identify accountable individuals, first on the part of the terrorists *(who did this to us?)* and later on the part of domestic institutions and agencies *(who should have been able to prevent this?)*.[13] But no single root cause could be found. In other words, a persistent attachment to a leadership narrative that emphasized singular accountability fell short in explaining what happened.

The implications of the old leadership model are also obvious in how the US government chose to respond to 9/11. In an attempt to prevent future terrorist attacks on our soil, a massive 240,000 employee bureaucratic hierarchy called the Department of Homeland Security was created, reporting to a cabinet-level secretary position. While it has been successful in a number of ways (most notably that there has not been a repeat on the scale of 9/11), challenges and priorities continue to evolve and shift as the department must focus beyond Al Queda and especially with the challenges of cybersecurity. The key question is this: Will hierarchical solutions be sufficient to adapt to these new challenges, or could there be other models worth exploring? Can we expand our leadership repertoire to include other forms of organizing?

As it turned out, the events of 9/11 revealed what many in the military had suspected for some time, that future conflicts would rarely if ever occur between organized nation-states with clear and singular command, but rather would be perpetrated by loosely connected individuals acting on behalf of semi-autonomous terror networks united by ideology. This is what the Department of Defense means when it says it is preparing for asymmetrical warfare. The enemy is not a traditional state actor, but rather a loosely distributed network of actors. As a consequence, the eventual killing of Osama Bin Laden did little to stop the actions of Al Queda, and the same may be true if we identify and destroy the "leaders" of the Islamic State (ISIS/ISIL). As the media searches for the accountable parties, the reality of distributed accountability across vast networks becomes increasingly clear.

A number of other news examples make much the same point. Post mortem analysis of the fragmented response to Hurricane Katrina and to the H1N1 virus health scare reveal many of the same issues. In both cases it was difficult to get available information to be shared across institutional silos; and in both cases traditional models of leadership and crisis response were ineffective. In the case of Katrina, confusion about FEMA's level of authority and accountability as the storm approached led to significant destruction—close analysis of the check in calls leading up to landfall show FEMA representatives ceding considerable latitude to the local Parrish leaders, many of whom had little experience with a crisis of this magnitude. Once again, we need to complicate our thinking about leadership and accountability to include the idea of shared or distributed accountability, reflecting the idea that leadership can be seen as an organizational, not an individual capability.[14]

In the case of the H1N1 threat, some similar tensions existed between the World Health Organization (WHO) and the US Centers for Disease Control (CDC). The CDC struggled from the beginning of the crisis to align their communication with the WHO while at the same time figuring out how much to share with the public. In her study of the crisis, Barbara Bennington discovered that the CDC realized early on that all of their prior models for crisis management did not apply in this case, leading them to set out in search of different models and to remain decidedly open to learning as the crisis progressed.[15]

This case leads us squarely back to the issue of how such instances are portrayed in the news media. The media represent the public's desire to know the facts—who is responsible, what happened, what should we do now? Unfortunately, definitive answers to these questions is increasingly hard to come by, whether we are talking about H1N1, global natural hazards, mysterious plane crashes, or mid-east violence. There is a widening gap between the public's desire for certainty and accountability on the one hand and the fundamental equivocality and distributed responsibility of the social world on the other. Whereas media representations tend to emphasize individual heroic action, respect for hierarchy, and the pursuit of certainty and control, the actual practice of contemporary leadership is quite nearly the opposite: Collective and systemic, networked and distributed, and vulnerable and emergent.

There is one interesting exception to this trend, and it may contain important clues for how the media can communicate with certainty about uncertain situations. Historically (before the 1990s), when anticipating a potentially catastrophic hurricane, TV meteorologists would to their best to identify the path of the storm and to warn those in the way to evacuate. In the last decade, statisticians have introduced the idea of "spaghetti" plots—originally developed to track product flow efficiency in factories—to visually communicate multiple possible tracks. Today, when a storm approaches the public has become accustomed to seeing spaghetti plots with associated probability cones that allow them to decide what to do based upon available information. The reason this is significant is because it represents a way of communicating probabilistic information in a fashion that is acceptable to and understood by the general public.

The changes of the image of the leader in news reporting differ somewhat from those in entertainment. News reports already tend to see leaders as vulnerable, and pair their public actions with their private struggles. They rarely concern themselves with the drama of how leaders rise to power and the path one must take to get there. Similar to what is seen in entertainment, however, the news does continue to focus on hierarchy and individual accountability and has difficulty with stories that cannot be traced to a single explanation or source. In the US, perhaps this is related to the fact that most news organizations are owned by large corporations that are themselves big hierarchies. But even a casual reflection over the reporting during the so-called "Arab Spring" and its aftermath show how much the media struggled with multiple causality and high levels of ambiguity.

SUMMARY

Taken together, media representations of leadership in entertainment and news share a common aesthetic, that of beleaguered individuals confronting an increasingly complex world in which the old solutions no longer work. Moreover, what they offer to viewers is nothing like optimism or hope, but rather examples of how individuals make use of the resources they have to cope with their situations. We attend to these representations because we recognize their applicability to our own lives, and see some value in observing the struggle from afar.

A recent political cartoon portrayed the headline of a newspaper that said "Everything Awful: Oh God Somebody Do Something."[16] This is the zeitgeist of our times, at least in terms of the mainstream media, who seem to have taken all the poison from postmodernism but none of the promise. Yes, the old paradigms are collapsing, the old scripts and explanations are insufficient. Yes, hierarchy and individual accountability do an incomplete job of explaining what is happening. But just as contemporary attitudes and behaviors reject grand narratives and singular authority, they at the same time open up a creative space for something different, for what might plausibly come next.

The time is ripe to re-invent our image of leadership in a way that better jibes with the complex and contradictory aspects of contemporary organizational life. Experimenting with new exemplars for leadership is the job of organizations, of governments, of schools and of the media. What we need most is a new leadership aesthetic for a new kind of world, a new leadership vocabulary even, one characterized by shared accountability and distributed intelligence, unprecedented levels of connectivity and collaboration, rapidly shifting conditions that require continuous course corrections, and a generally high degree of uncertainty. Such exemplars will both guide leader behavior and shape followers' expectations of what an effective leader can be expected to accomplish.

NOTES

1. Peter Northouse, *Leadership: Theory and Practice* (Thousand Oaks, CA: Sage, 2012).

2. Eric M. Eisenberg, "Jamming: Transcendence through Organizing," *Communication Research* 17 (1990), 139–164. doi: 10.1177/009365090017002001.

3. Riane Eisler, *The Chalice and the Blade: Our History, Our Future* (San Francisco: Harper & Row, 1988).

4. Oliver Mack, Anshuman Khare, Andreas Kramer, and Thomas Burgartz, *Managing in a VUCA World* (New York, NY: Springer, 2015).

5. Margaret Wheatley, *Leadership and the New Science* (San Francisco, CA: Berrett-Koehler, 2006).

6. Mary Parker Follett, *Creative Experience* (New York, NY: Longmans, Green & Company, 1924).

7. *Blue Bloods.* "Pilot." Directed by Michael Cuesta. Written by Robin Green & Mitchell Burgess. CBS, September 24, 2010; *CSI.* "Pilot." Directed by Danny Cannon. Written by Anthony E. Zuiker. CBS, October 6, 2000; *Mad Men.* "Smoke Gets in your Eyes." Directed by Alan Taylor. Written by Matthew Weiner. AMC, July 19, 2007; *Boston Legal.* "Head Cases." Directed by Bill D'Elia. Written by Scott Kaufer, Jeff Rake, and David E. Kelley. ABC, October 3, 2004.

8. *Hill Street Blues.* "Hill Street Station." Directed by Robert Butler. Written by Micheal Kozol and Steven Bochco. NBC, January 15, 1981.

9. Michael Keeley, *A Social Contract Theory of Organizations* (Notre Dame, IN: University of Notre Dame Press, 1988).

10. *NYPD Blue.* "Pilot." Directed by Gregory Hoblit. Written by David Milch and Steven Bochco. ABC, September 21, 1993.

11. *Unforgiven,* directed by Clint Eastwood (1992, Warner, Los Angeles), DVD.

12. *The Sopranos.* "The Sopranos." Written and directed by David Chase. HBO, January 10, 1999.

13. Sandra Cooper, "Making Sense of Complex Failure: The Case of 9–11" (PhD Diss., University of South Florida, 2007).

14. Mariaelena Bartesaghi, "Coordination: Examining Weather as a Matter of Concern," *Communication Studies* 65 (2014): 535–557. doi: 10.1080/10510974.2014.957337.

15. Barbara Bennington, "Crisis Communication: Sensemaking and Decision-making by the CDC under Conditions of Uncertainty and Ambiguity during the 2009–2010 H1N1 Pandemic" (PhD Diss., University of South Florida, 2014).

16. Matt Fraction, *Hawkeye, Vol. 1: My Life as a Weapon* (New York, NY: Marvel, 2013).

FIVE

In Space . . . Our Worst Will Make Us Scream

Reality Reflected in the Cultural Artifact Alien

Adam W. Tyma

We all have a moment—an experience—that defines what we do and what we are into. For me, it was seeing *Star Wars* in 1977 with my parents . . . in the theater.[1] I can definitely blame my dad for my overall love of the Sci-Fi genre. It is something that sticks with you.

However, I do not think that it was *Star Wars* that moved me toward my personal tastes. Oddly enough, *Star Wars* is a story of fantasy and happy endings and, though I can appreciate such stories, they seem to be the ones for me that are more out of reach or disconnected from the observable world. For me, the movie—the event—that sticks out like a bookmark in my life is *Alien*: a slimy, terror-ridden, blood-soaked bookmark. I distinctly remember watching the movie (again, with my father, but I think thanks to cable television), freaking out—and then wanting to watch it again the following day. (Thank you, Showtime.)

Yes, this is where it comes from.

Fast-forward through other movies that I have enjoyed, from *Prometheus, Event Horizon, Invasion of the Body Snatchers* (the majority of the iterations . . . except for the most recent), and *Outland* to art films like *2001:A Space Odyssey* or *Sunshine* and a pattern starts to emerge.[2] These films do not just offer a bit of escapism through the torment of the characters—they also are presenting reflections of our own lives and society at the time. Each of them offers a dystopic reality of our inevitable future. Whether we are invaded from outer space, attacked by things while in

49

outer space, or drawn to outer space and then *something happens,* the expanse of outer space is rarely presented as a utopic opportunity to become the best we can (sorry, *Star Trek*); rather, it is the opposite.[3]

If we are what we eat (at least that is what the medical community would like us to believe), then it can also be concluded that we are the media that we consume. Our exposure to moments and texts in popular culture shape who we are, both as scholars and as consumers. The purpose of this chapter is to aim this idea at the film *Alien*, working to understand the discourse that weaves throughout it and other such movies. The analysis works to both uncover the ideological positions within the film (and this critic) and perhaps discover why, when I think of the phrase "in space, no one can hear you scream," I smile.

ALIEN — A QUICK SYNOPSIS

In 1979, Ridley Scott directed *Alien*, the first of the *Alien/Prometheus* saga.[4] This initial film begins with the crew of *Nostromo*, a refining and transport vessel, being "brought to life" in deep space, off-course and following a rescue beacon signal. The vessel's computer, affectionately referred to as "Mother," has changed course toward an unknown object, specifically what is assumed to be a distress beacon in the deepest parts of space. This never bodes well for a ship's crew, whether at sea or in space.[5] The crew is woken, they land on the planet—referenced as LV 426—locate the beacon inside of a massive alien (non-Earth) spacecraft, and bring a specimen on board . . . after it attaches itself to a crew member. The rest, as they say, is history . . . a gory, messy, frightening, history that has influenced not only this author but also all of science fiction and horror films since its release.

As with most popular culture texts, the surface reading here never seems to point toward a significant collection of discourse that deserves attention. And, as with most texts, such assumptions regarding *Alien* must be reconsidered. The remainder of this chapter moves past the base plotline and examines the discourse within and underneath the text. This interrogation is accomplished by applying a theoretical lens informed by Karl Marx, Jacques Lacan, and others to the characters, plotlines, and motivations within the movie. The intent is two-fold: first, popular culture scholarship should always work to understand the deeper meanings that exist within our favorite artifacts. Second, we should never discount what a scary movie in 1979 will mean to us nearly 40 years after its release.

THE INDUSTRIAL COMPLEX . . . IN SPACE

Horror does not always have to mean that there is the dismemberment of bodies or the pooling of blood. For some, horror may equate to just that, while to others, the most horrible thing that can be conjured is the absolute loss of control to a non-descript corporate or industrial entity—for example, something simply referred to as "The Company." Within *Alien,* the commercial energy company that the crew of the *Nostromo* works for does have a name: Weyland Yutani, and we do meet the founder of the company in *Prometheus,* but the ubiquitous "company" presents both the workers and the audiences with the faceless source of their fear: their loss of control to the "machine" (in the most fundamental and Tayloristic perspective).[6] Visually, this is most striking through two images: the hauling of the refinery by the *Nostromo* and the computer interface used by both Dallas (Tom Skerritt) and Ripley (Sigourney Weaver) to communicate with "the company" and "Mother" (the UI on the ship, similar to HAL from *2001* but not nearly as advanced . . . or polite).

One key element that seems to re-appear over and over again is the panoptic nature of The Company.[7] Throughout the movie—or at least until the spaghetti dinner does not sit well with Kane (never trust the EZ meals on a boat)—the topics of "fair wage" and "contracts" come up repeatedly, and we witness sabotage-as-resistance (either performed or suggested) from those who work in the bowels of the ship toward those who signify the managers/power-holders on the ship on a few occasions. We begin to see the worker/manager binary played out through both dialogue and action. At the same time, however, there is a perpetual uneasiness in the actions and behaviors of the crew emanating from the all-seeing and conditioning gaze of The Company and its overt representation via the UI "Mother."

The Interface. It is rare that the UI for any computer system in a horror/sci-fi/suspense film is benevolent . . . except, perhaps, in the 1984 classic *Electric Dreams* (and even that one had a schizophrenic break).[8] Whether you are facing off with HAL in *2001: A Space Odyssey* or The Red Queen in the *Resident Evil* franchise, the computer system that is meant to both protect and control the human parasites living off of it is never, well, nice.[9] However, unlike those systems which become self-aware (to steal a term from *Terminator*), the UI "Mother," the liaison between the humans and the ship, does not become malevolent or "bad." It does not decide to kill them off or to control them. It operates exactly as it is meant to: it follows orders and directives. The problem, of course, is that the orders it receives are somewhat conflicting with the desires of the crew—The Company wants the specimen at all costs, while the crew just wants to survive.

When Althusser presents us with the *ideological state apparatus* (ISA) and *repressive state apparatus*, he is clear to point out that, where one acts through violence (physical, psychical, social), the other acts through unseen forces of coercion.[10] Within the reality of *Alien*, such coercion is successful through the use of "the bonus" and "the share," elements that extend directly from Marx's idea of *commodity fetishism*.[11] Crew members have lulled themselves into the hegemonic ISA and have accepted their position within it to satisfy their constructed need for more through the exchange value of these things. Moving out more broadly, consider the capital-driven dreams of 1979 and the countercultural response to the commodifying of those dreams. It is as though *Alien* was acting as a warning shot across the bow for the 1980s, the Reagan administration, and trickle-down economics. We are expendable cogs in the machine (per Frederick Taylor), so long as the machine is allowed to continue, with those at the top (management) continuing to profit.

What we see here is the computer representing the ultimate "not-caring" boss. Particularly in the early 1970s, when labor unions were possibly at their strongest and management was trying to find ways to make money for their shareholders in a unionized space, "Mother" signifies the fear that surrounds the machination of the workforce. This existential technophobic response can be seen in other films that fit within this genre, but *Alien* seems to provide a strong entry point into the conversation before the computer could be found on the top of desks across the country.[12] Consider that the first readily available personal computers did not start showing up until the early 1980s, such conversations were just starting to emerge across literary circles, echoed from mass media research coming from as far back as the Payne Studies or the birth of the Chicago School. Even so, the computer—the mechanical—begins to have sway over the person—the organic; such fears moved past the "slasher around the corner" and into "why do I even exist?"

By utilizing political economic concepts, and particularly Louis Althusser, to formally identify both the Ideological and Repressive State Apparati that are signified and enacted within *Alien*, we gain insight into how the history and context surrounding a popular culture artifact can become infused and intertwined into the various narratives. I am also able to start seeing, even then, where my own interpretive lens toward my own reality *may* have started to be formed. I was probably not considering these questions when I was six years old, but the stories at play definitely stuck with me. The next section will move the conversation from the macro-level to the critical self-reflective mirror that is constructed aboard the *Nostromo*.

BEING KILLED BY YOUR DESIRES

An element that strikes me every time I watch or think about *Alien* is this: had the greed and desires of those in power not driven them to order

Mother to wake the *Nostromo*'s crew, answer the distress call, and bring the alien (often referred to as the "face-sucker" in popular conversations) back on the ship with them—everything would be just fine. Lives would have been boring, predictable, and still moving forward. In a sense, *Alien* becomes a Lacanian cautionary tale. Lacan reminds us that, as we begin to recognize ourselves and our own identity, we also begin to see the limits of our own selves and desire that which we cannot have or become.[13] We are either driven to recognize the reflection as an idealized self that we strive (but always fail) to attain or we recognize all of the failings that we project from our own insecurities into the reflection and are forever haunted by it. That reflection of our idealized "other" overwhelms us. Hopefully, we are able to control our desires, allow logic and reason to prevail, and turn away from the mirror and look outward. Sometimes, though, the desire to look within—and get lost within that carnivalesque (a la Mikhail Bakhtin) reflection—is too strong.[14] As is so often the case, the reflection in the mirror is not reflective of our better angels but, instead, of our darker demons. Within the *Alien* universe, the xenomorph (the physiological classification for the "creature" in this movie) is not so alien to those that have faced their darker selves. Like Lacan's mirror, it presents both the fractured parts of the reflected self and the evolving self that is never complete. In fact, it could be argued that the alien signifies those things that we attempt to bury down in our psyche, away from the light of day, only to have those things erupt in the most violent and uncontrolled ways.

Each of the characters faces this fear, faces her or his darker demon through the xenomorph. For *Dallas* (the captain of the *Nostromo*, played by Tom Skerritt), the alien begins attacking him well before it ever comes on board. The moment Mother wakes him up and he receives his orders, he is instantly put back in his place. He moves from being "the captain" to "middle management," the space that Marx saw as not-quite-bourgeoisie yet no longer strictly considered a member of the proletariat—the masses. He is the only living thing that is allowed to converse with the central management. (Spoiler—even the android has more power than he does.) He is granted feigned power by The Company to manage those underneath him, yet he is bound by the same apparatus that they are. His darker demon begins to manifest in the computer interface, culminating with him climbing further and further away from his signifying stronghold (the bridge), and being consumed by his own demon in the end.

Kane (John Hurt) is the unfortunate "mother" of the demon. His reflection is only of everyone else in the crew—he shows what they are to become (food). He is the first person we see when they are all woken up—and he is the first one to fall prey to the desires of The Company. Whenever we see him, he is in the process of consuming (cigarettes, coffee, and food), expressing those basal desires that Bakhtin is so fond of showing us. It is oddly appropriate that he is to become the vessel through which the crew is to fall. He appears to be preparing himself as a host, waking from his captivity needing food only to die in his own desires (he initially falls face first into his dinner). It could be said that he signifies not so much gluttony but what the end results of that deadly sin could be.

Brett (Harry Dean Stanton) and *Parker* (Yaphet Kotto) are the perennial "workers" of this crew. Similar to *Hamlet*'s gravediggers, these two act as a mirror to the bourgeoisie while reflecting the basic wants and needs of the proletariat: the right to earn a fair wage and have their voices heard. Throughout the early part of the film, they use their socio-economic class to self-segregate from the rest of the crew. The moment they are woken early from hypersleep (that dreamless experience most sci-fi movies introduce us to, demonstrating how far away the crew really is), they begin to ask how this change from routine affects them as contracted employees. Will they be receiving proper compensation for overtime? For hazard pay? When Ripley, at this point a proper "company man," states "yeah . . . you will get what's coming to you," they are satisfied, not recognizing the ominous foreboding that statement later implies.

Though one of the characters is white and the other is black, the racial distinctions are not inherently present in the dialogue or interactions. Rather, it is identity as "performed class" that becomes the divider amongst the group. As the mechanics of the crew, they are truly "working class," living and working in the bowels of the ship. Though they eat with the officers and speak with the officers, they are corporate grunts and both act and are acted upon as such. In one scene, where Ripley confronts the workers, there is noise and industrial chaos all around them, supposedly from damage the ship has taken on. This obviously irritates Ripley, causing her to make small concessions to both workers. Once she has left the space, the workers quickly turn off the chaos, smiling the whole time. Though they did not get exactly what they were looking for, they were able to demonstrate the power they are able to exert in small ways. In this way, they are able to establish their worth (Brett attempting to trap the xenomorph; Parker aiding in defending against Ash's assault, ultimately incinerating it); however, such power is quickly overshadowed by the looming danger that faces them both. In the end, the greed of The Company overpowers their greed for "their shares."

Ash (Ian Holm) is the *Nostromo*'s science offer and is an interesting juxtaposition. Immediately, the audience is directed to not care for him all that much. More so than Ripley, Ash is definitely a company man. His willingness to countermand Ripley (the second in command under Dallas) to, it would seem, be a benevolent savior, is only countered when his interest in the parasite attached to Kane outweighs his concern for Kane himself. We also quickly begin to notice that he seems to almost "know" what Mother is thinking before Dallas does. How can this be? Once the xenomorph has moved through other members of the crew, Ash is next . . . and he survives, because he is an "it"—an android, a walking computer, the unfeeling distanced signifier for the greed of The Company personified. It could be argued that, where Mother reflects the Company's ISA (control through ideology and production) that Ash is The Company's RSA signifier, a discursive structure that reinforces The Company not through coercion but through punishment and overt oppression, an active system of control demonstrating that profit and power trump individual worth and agency. These two sides to the state apparatus are constructed through the orders (the will) that are enacted through Mother and enforced through Ash. Though latter parts of the franchise present the android as a normal part of the crew, here it is sent as a spy and sentry for The Company, reporting back and protecting The Company's interest at all cost. It is when we see Ash interfacing with Mother in "the womb"—a space we thought only Dallas could enter—that we understand the power that Ash and, thereby, The Company wield over the crew. Though we are led to see him as an extension of The Company, it is only in the reveal of his mirrored self that we see that we have been confronted with the mirror at all times. The "death" of Ash is not at the hands of the xenomorph, but by the crew. Once it is revealed that the crew is expendable (by order of The Company) through Ripley's investigation, Ash moves to eliminate the crew. This fails, and the true face of The Company is revealed. That face is not the perceived cold of Ripley, meant to defend her against what she sees as threats to her power; she would be seen as a reasonable representation of the Company. Rather, the true simulacrum of The Company with the crew is the science officer—the automaton constructed by The Company to be a pure discursive articulation of those particular company-line ideologies (the one that did not speak much, stayed in the shadows, let Kane on board after his assault, and worked to understand the growing threat).

Lambert's (Veronica Cartwright) role on the ship is as the pilot. It is her job to make sure that the *Nostromo* arrives where it is intended to be. The moment she is woken from her long sleep prematurely and forced into the pilot's chair before she is meant to be there (because that is not what the contract says), her ability to control her world around her dissipates quickly. Throughout the film, she works to understand her place on the crew. She is an officer, but appears to have no opinion about anything. She reflects the insecurities that come from wanting to be included but, it would seem, always on the periphery.

There are two women on the crew: Lambert and Ripley (Sigourney Weaver). Where Ripley presents the façade of the cold and calculating Company, Lambert wants to belong and be liked. It is this desire to be accepted that makes her complicit in bringing the infected Kane back onto the ship after he is attacked by the "facesucker." In this act of defiance against The Company (which ostracizes Ripley from the rest of the

crew, placing her as the lone person at the top of the ideological apparatus), Lambert solidifies her position amongst the crew (and, it would
appear, all of those that are marked to die throughout the movie).

Lambert's actions and behaviors are of someone who, though she
wishes to be strong and respected, her reflected self (the one she performs
when she is alone) is always someone who is afraid of the shadows—of
the things that cannot be seen. She does learn to fight in the end, but even
then her strength is overrun by her fear. As with the rest of the crew, it
seems only appropriate that, as she is confronting the creature face-to-
face, she is assaulted (and, we find out later, encased) by her fear mani-
fested. Hers is the most disturbing of the deaths—not because of the gore
of it, but the lack of it. The absolute terror she experiences as she is (what
is perceived as by the audience) raped then eviscerated by the xenomorph is horrifying because it is not seen. (It can be argued that Kane
was also violated in such a way, though his rape was presented differently to the audience, not appearing as such at first and most definitely not
experienced as such by Kane or the audience members.) Though the violation is not shown to the audience, this moment of pure terror is played
out sonically across the ship's PA system. When Ripley finds both Parker
and Lambert's bodies, her reaction fills in the blanks for the audience—
we know what happened.

WRONG PLACE + WRONG TIME = RELUCTANT HERO?

Ripley (Signourney Weaver) has been referred to as a feminist hero, an
archetype for future roles, or other such accolades.[15] While I do agree
with these arguments to an extent, here is something else to consider: she
does not become this hero to audiences—the Ripley who takes on a
Queen xenomorph not once but twice (later in the franchise), who challenges anyone who does not understand her as "right," and is willing to
sacrifice all for the greater good—until she is betrayed by the things she
holds close to her throughout the majority of the movie: The Company
and discipline. It is her forced reject of her own internal disciplining
discourse as The Company's *automaton* that creates a new space and identity for her to step into and perform.[16] It is The Company that has taken
care of her, that has given her rank, and has given her power. By embod-
ying The Company, she has taken the full form of the disciplined body,
only able to speak with the voice of The Company and responding as The
Company (in her mind, the benevolent organization that it is) would see
her respond.[17] Her mirror moment is not by facing the xenomorph
(though she does this in glorious fashion) but, rather, at the moment
where she finds out that, in classic Tayloristic fashion, she is simply another cog in the machine, easily replaceable when the desires of The
Company outweigh what she is able to provide. She is one more data

point on a profit-and-loss matrix, and it is in this moment, in the womb of "Mother," that she is confronted by her reflected self and rejects it. Like the individual leaving the mouth of the cave once the truth is known, Ripley crosses the threshold, sheds her former discursive self, and decides to "blow up the fucking ship," the thing she has been protecting throughout the whole of the movie.[18] It is this final rejection that moves her from automaton to subject within the master narrative.

Like Dallas, she attempts to utilize strategy to defeat her Lacanian reflection. With Ash, she has Parker repair him (after Ash assaults her, Parker, and Lambert) just enough to be able to ask questions. Appealing to "his" perfect sense of logic (and the arrogance that seems to come along with that across any film that has an active AI actant), she learns what she needs to learn: that the old plan (kill the creature—save the ship) no longer applies. In the final confrontation with the xenomorph, Ripley uses the equipment provided by The Company to destroy that which The Company desires more than anything. It is her logic and discipline (again, those things received conceivably and paradoxically from The Company) that aid in her destruction of the reflection and the shadows—the light (particularly as it comes from the engines and consumes the xenomorph) extinguishing the dark.

Ripley signifies not the hero in a cape, but the hero in the sense that a journey must be taken to discover the true self. The "hero" in horror is rarely better off because of the journey—he or she survives (often with substantial physical, psychological, and/or spiritual scarring) what the universe has put in front of her or him—and this is the case here. Perhaps that is why the movie is so memorable to me. It was not clean (do you ever see blood in *Star Wars*?) nor was it clear who the "good and bad" were. Throughout *Alien*, we are probably rooting for Dallas, because we have been conditioned do so.[19] It is the woman who we do not really like at all that ends up making the final turn at the end. It is the "flipping of the script" regarding the heteronormative hero that occurs—like in John Carpenter's *Halloween*—that changes the way we understand the purpose of this type of movie (horror and science fiction movies are often the closest thing we have to parables or fables in our current media spaces), creates a pedagogical space around the movie, and we begin to understand the society we live in because of the movie.[20] It is these moments of contextualization, critical interrogation, and articulation that changes us, shapes us, and gives us more as we walk away from the movie in comparison to what we walked into the movie with.[21]

WHAT DO I LEARN FROM THIS?

Popular culture was, and is, still considered by many in the Academy as mass drivel—items, songs, people, places, and visual entertainment that simply dulls the masses into a state of complacency. I would argue that, if this is the case, *Alien* is not doing a very good job of being an example of "drivel." For me, popular culture IS culture. It is the texts and discourse (and, often, they are one and the same) that weave us together and construct our collective narratives. *Alien* came out at a time where questions were seriously being asked about the corporate-industrial-military complex and what would happen if we relied too much on it for all aspects of our lives (*Aliens* presents us with a world where the military is for hire by The Company—not the best outcome). Questions had to be asked about who we are, where we are going, and should we be going there. Horror texts have always done this, from *Frankenstein* to *Cthullu* to *Thinner*. All of these are the "pop" of their day. *Alien* continues this rich, vital, and essential position. The things that scare us in the dark are not the monsters, killers, robots, aliens, or entities that are hiding around the corner or in ventilation systems. What *really* scares us are the things we see in the mirror when we close our eyes and ask those darker questions. That is why I love horror and sci-fi movies and why *Alien* speaks to me.

Or maybe I just like watching nasty creatures destroy everything in front of them with a grin . . .

NOTES

1. *Star Wars,* directed by George Lucas (1977; Los Angeles, CA: 20th Century Fox Film, 2005), Blu-Ray.
2. *Prometheus,* directed by Ridley Scott (2012; Los Angeles, CA: 20th Century Fox Film Corporation, 2012), Blu-Ray; *Event Horizon,* directed by Paul Anderson (1997; Hollywood, CA: Paramount, 2010), Blu-Ray; For *Invasion of the Body Snatchers, see:* en.wikipedia.org/wiki/Invasion_of_the_Body_Snatchers; *Outland,* directed by Peter Hyams (1981, Burbank, CA: Warner Brothers, 2012), Blu-ray; *2001:A Space Odyssey,* directed by Stanley Kubrick (1969, Beverly Hills, CA: Metro-Goldwyn-Mayer, 2008), Blu-ray; *Sunshine,* directed by Danny Boyle (2007, Los Angeles, CA: Fox Searchlight, 2007), Blu-ray.
3. See en.wikipedia.org/wiki/Star_Trek.
4. *Alien,* directed by Ridley Scott (1979, Los Angeles, CA: 20th Century Fox Film Corporation, 2004), DVD.
5. We later find out that it was actually sent there by the owners of the *Nostromo*—more on that later.
6. Frederic Taylor, *The Principles of Scientific Management* (New York, NY: Harper, 1911).
7. The concept of the panopticon is most readily accessed by way of *Discipline and Punish: The Birth of the Prison* (Michel Foucault, *Discipline and Punish: The Birth of the Prison,* trans. Alan Sheridan [New York: Vintage Books, 1995]).
8. *Electric Dreams,* directed by Steve Barron (1984, Beverly Hills, CA; Metro-Goldwyn-Mayer, 1991), VHS.
9. *Resident Evil,* directed by Paul W. S. Anderson (2002, Culver City, CA: Screen Gems, 2012), Blu-Ray.
10. Louis Althusser, *Lenin and Philosophy and Other Essays,* trans. (New York: Monthly Review Press, 2001).
11. Karl Marx and Freidrich Engels, *The Marx-Engels Reader, 2nd edition,* ed. Robert C. Tucker (New York: W.W. Norton and Company, 1978).

12. Adam W. Tyma, "The Stories They Tell—A Technophobic Narrative Analysis of America Popular Films: *Blade Runner, Terminator, The Matrix,*" *Communication & Theater Association of Minnesota Journal* 31 (2004): 51–68.

13. Jacques Lacan, "The Mirror Stage as Formative of the *I* Function as Revealed in Psychoanalytic Experience," *Ecrits: The First Complete Edition in English,* trans. Bruce Fink (New York: W.W. Norton and Company, 2006).

14. Mikhail Mikhailovich Bakhtin, *Rabelais and His World,* trans. Helene Iswolsky (Bloomington, IN: Indiana University Press, 1984).

15. Xan Brooks, "The First Action Heroine," *The Guardian*, October 12, 2009. Accessed December 10, 2015, www.theguardian.com/film/2009/oct/13/ridley-scott-alien-ripley.

16. Michel Foucault, *Discipline and Punish: The Birth of the Prison*, trans. Alan Sheridan, New York: Vintage Books, 1995

17. Althusser, *Lenin and Philosophy.*

18. This is in reference to Plato's "Allegory of the Cave," attributed to Socrates, from *The Republic.*

19. To investigate this idea of conditioned viewing of movies further, and (in particular) how it affects how the women are seen and directed for film, go to Laura Mulvey, "Visual Pleasure and Narrative Cinema," *Screen* 16 (1975): 6–18.

20. *Halloween*, directed by John Carpenter (1978; Boston, MA; Embassy Pictures, 2012), Blu-Ray.

21. Raymie E. McKerrow, "Critical Rhetoric: Theory and Praxis," *Communication Monographs* 56 (1989): 91–111. doi: 10.1080/03637758909390253; Lawrence Grossberg, "On Postmodernism and Articulation. An Interview with Stuart Hall," *Journal of Communication* 45 (1986): 45–60. doi: 10.1177/019685998601000204.

SIX

Music's Pervasive and Persuasive Role in Popular Culture

Deanna Sellnow

If a picture is worth a thousand words, what is music worth? This is a question I have been attempting to articulate intelligibly for over thirty years. In fact, I began studying music as a form of communication when I was a college forensics speech competitor. I explored the role of Richard Wagner's four opera-cycle, *Der Ring des Nibelungen,* as Nazi propaganda during Adolph Hitler's regime. The communication analysis rang true (pun intended) among judges across the country as they awarded it first place at every tournament that year, including first place honors at the National Individual Events Tournament (NIET) hosted by the American Forensic Association (AFA). I say this not to brag but instead to make an important point. Music can be an extremely powerful form of communication; a form that can be used to persuade listeners on many levels and in many ways.

Interestingly, over the course of thirty years of teaching about music as communication in my courses and examining its rhetorical potential in my research, I have never been called into question when I claim that music can and does speak to us and for us. Of course, I also realize I am not the first to make such a claim. In *The Book of Rites,* for example, Confucius is quoted as saying that "music produces a kind of pleasure which human nature cannot do without." Hans Christian Andersen is credited with saying, "Where words fail, music speaks"; and, more recently, Johnny Depp has been quoted as saying that "music touches us emotionally, where words alone can't."[1]

The question, then, is not one of whether or not music communicates but, rather, is a series of questions about what, why, and how it does so. By answering these questions, we are equipped with the tools by which to respond successfully to critics that may actually agree that music communicates, but then retort with "so what?" This chapter describes what I have learned over the years through my own examination of music as communication in popular culture, as well as what others have taught me. I have chosen to arrange it around the very questions those of us that study music as communication grapple with as we attempt to explain it to others through words alone, which in and of itself is a limitation we must overcome. I begin by offering my response to the questions people have raised regarding what music as a form of popular culture communication is and does. I follow that with a discussion about how music communicates in popular culture. Finally, I close with several reasons we ought to continue to study music as it functions in popular culture.

WHAT IS MUSIC AS COMMUNICATION IN POPULAR CULTURE?

Although nuanced definitions exist, popular culture can be understood as "comprised of the everyday objects, actions, and events that influence people to believe and behave in certain ways."[2] In other words, everything in our daily lives could be described as an aspect of popular culture. When it comes to music, we sometimes make deliberate choices to purchase and listen to a particular song or album on CD or iTunes, stream a particular radio station while working at our computer or tune one in while driving based on genre, or select a particular playlist we mixed ourselves to get motivated to exercise or to relax. Other times, musical choices are not our own, as in stores, restaurants, and other public spaces. In any case, music is a pervasive part of our daily lives and, as such, fits the definition of popular culture. In fact, with the exponential explosion of technology and new media, our access to music anytime and anyplace makes it perhaps more pervasive than it was even a decade ago.

Unlike discursive symbols (e.g., verbal/words; numerical/numbers) that tend to have fairly fixed associations (e.g., d-o-g is a four-legged furry canine; 2+2=4), music communicates via nondiscursive symbolism.[3] Nondiscursive symbols communicate using means beyond words and/or numbers. In other words, nondiscursive symbols include any nonverbal communication ranging from body language, paralanguage, and facial expression to musical sounds and visual images. Whereas discursive symbols tend to represent cognitive thoughts, nondiscursive symbols tend to represent emotions.

With regard to music specifically, music sounds the way feelings feel.[4] Important to note here, however, is that music does not *cause* emotions. Rather, it *represents* the emotions of daily living that are embodied in each of us. These emotions may be characterized as the building up of tensions and subsequent releases of them.[5] More specifically music represents human emotions by offering musical sounds and patterns that are "less pleasant to the ear [tensions]" and "more pleasant [resolutions]."[6]

As a popular culture phenomenon, music may communicate differently to us and/or for us depending on the situation: aesthetically, individually, and rhetorically. Aesthetics has to do with the creation and appreciation of art. When it comes to music as aesthetic communication, we may appreciate it (or not) based on the musical form itself.[7] For example, some people really like or really dislike certain musical genres (e.g., rock, punk, rap, hip-hop, country) regardless of composer, performer, or song. For them, the particular song that is playing isn't as important as the genre itself. The genre communicates to them in terms of their appreciation or lack of appreciation of it as a musical form.

For our purposes here, music as individual communication is conceived as unique meanings understood by an individual based on personal experiences he or she brings to the occasion. These individual interpretations are not necessarily socially grounded because they are "not widely shared by some identifiable community or group."[8] Music certainly may communicate for an individual in this way; however, others may not understand this meaning in the same way. For example, when I hear The Monkees sing "Pleasant Valley Sunday," it represents (stirs up) positive emotions in me as I enjoy the musical sound, which is pleasant to the ear and recall happy times in my childhood. Others may not interpret it this way, particularly if they are drawn to the lyrics about "rows of houses that are all the same / and no one seems to care" and "creature comfort goals, they only numb my soul."[9] Nevertheless, the individual meaning I derive is still legitimate for me personally, even if it is not what the song may be communicating in a larger sense (i.e., rhetorically).

Finally, popular culture music communicates rhetorically when it sends a unified message understood similarly to an identifiable group of people. In doing so, it proposes arguments that reinforce or challenge taken-for-granted beliefs and behaviors (i.e., social norms) regarding what is "normal/abnormal," "desirable/undesirable," "appropriate/inappropriate," and "good/bad." Examining such arguments "couched in music" and often dismissed as mere entertainment is critical because "listeners do not ordinarily anticipate persuasion and, as a result, [may not realize] its complete implications."[10]

Much of the research focused on music as rhetoric has come in the form of its role as communicating and persuading in social movements.[11] Many of these studies focus on how music crystallizes social movements that protest about social injustice and promote positive change (e.g., civil rights, temperance, women's rights, anti-war).

Other research focuses on counterculture social movements. For example, Levin and McDevitt quote the WAR (White Aryan Resistance) newsletter that claims "music is one of the greatest propaganda tools around. You can influence more people with a song than you can a speech."[12] More recently, a young boy's solo at church claiming "ain't no homos gonna make it to heaven" garnered applause by the congregation before going viral.[13] Similarly, Buju Banton's anti-gay song, "Boom Bye Bye," exists in 86 versions on YouTube and has garnered more than 17 million views.[14] In it, he encourages listeners to, for instance, shoot gay men in the head, pour acid on them, and burn them alive.

Music as rhetorical communication is not always attached to a social movement. What it does do, however, is communicate a unified message about how to believe or behave targeting particular audience(s). For example, it might come in the form of instructional communication as in children's music teaching "proper" social behavioral norms or shed light on "improper" treatment of others as in Collin Raye's "I Think About You."[15]

Music typically communicates rhetorically via the dynamic interaction between lyrical content and musical form.[16] However, sometimes music without lyrics can argue a unified message by functioning as an enthymeme. Sellnow and Sellnow conclude that "musical works can communicate as a form of enthymemes when they are associated with a previously articulated premise, when they serve to embellish that message with [congruent] emotional expression, and when they are delivered to a sympathetic audience."[17] For example, listeners of John Corigliano's "Symphony No. 1" knew it was a story of moving through the stages of grief as he lost dear friends to HIV/AIDs.[18] Thus, it communicated rhetorically for them as a socially grounded unified message.

In summary, this section answers the questions about what music as popular culture is, including what it communicates. Musical form communicates as a popular culture phenomenon by representing our emotions. Much like nonverbal cues that accompany our words when we speak (e.g., changes in volume, rate, pitch, pauses), music expresses feelings. It does so by offering patterns of tension (uncomfortable to the ear) and patterns of release (comfortable to the ear). Music as aesthetic communication focuses on the evaluation of and appreciation for (or not) the musical form. Music as individual communication focuses on unique meanings based on personal experiences with it that may not be universally shared or understood. Music as rhetorical communication focuses on socially grounded arguments conveyed in it regarding how we "ought to" or "ought not to" believe or behave.

Music as rhetoric may serve to advance positions of a social movement, reinforce cultural norms, as well as challenge cultural assumptions. It can do so through the dynamic interaction of lyrical content and musical form, as well as through musical form as enthymeme when the listeners come to the experience with a shared vision of its purpose. With these fundamental descriptions about what music as popular culture communication is in mind, we turn our attention more specifically to how such music communicates and persuades in daily life.

HOW DOES MUSIC COMMUNICATE IN POPULAR CULTURE?

As previously mentioned, music as a popular culture phenomenon communicates emotions by offering in musical form tensions and releases that represent the tensions and releases of emotions we experience in daily life. Moreover, such music might communicate aesthetically, individually, or rhetorically based on the situation. This section drills deeper into how music does so. We begin with a discussion of how music symbolizes the patterns of tension and relief from them we experience in daily life as an "illusion of life" — a symbolic representation of those feelings. Then we focus on how the various elements of musical form work together to represent these emotional patterns followed by a discussion of how lyrical content may communicate. Finally, we illustrate how musical form and lyrical content ultimately interact to communicate messages about what to believe/not believe and how to behave/not behave.

The Illusion of Life

Visual artist and aesthetic philosopher Susanne Langer came up with the notion of an illusion of life to distinguish what we experience through music (and other art forms) from actual daily life.[19] To clarify, music is a symbolic representation of the emotions we experience in life. Just as the *word* is not the *thing* itself when considering communication in the discursive verbal symbol system, so too is the *music* not the *emotions* themselves when considering communication in this nondiscursive aesthetic symbol system. Moreover, music does not cause or cure feelings. It merely sounds (represents) the way feelings (emotions we already have inside us) feel.[20]

Musical Form

We begin with a discussion of musical form because listeners are typically drawn initially to a particular song or artist based on sound. Not until after being drawn to the sound do listeners begin to focus on the lyrics. As previously mentioned, music communicates emotions through patterns of intensity and patterns of release. These patterns help us make sense of the "stresses involved in living that defy linear, discursive expression."[21] An intensity pattern in music, for example, might be communicated via a fast tempo (e.g., rate), loud dynamics (e.g., volume), short-held staccato notes, and dissonance as compared to a release pattern communicated via a slow tempo, soft dynamics, long-held and smoothly connected notes, and consonance.[22] Intensity patterns may represent any of the intensity emotions we experience in daily living (e.g., fear, shock, anger, rage, disgust, pleasure, joy, excitement, anticipation, anxiety) and release patterns any of the release emotions we experience in life (e.g., sorrow, sadness, grief, depression, resolve). Music alone (i.e., without lyrics) communicates in popular culture indexically, iconically, and symbolically.[23]

Music communicates indexically when its emotional meaning is understood because it is linked to something else by cause or association. Music communicates iconically when its emotional meaning is understood because it resembles what we expect. Music communicates symbolically when its meaning is understood by convention. Consider, for example, the theme song from the movie *Jaws*. When we hear it, we understand its emotional meaning (fear) indexically when we link it to the killer shark attack scene in the film. Iconically, its patterns of increasing intensity in the musical sound represent how the human heart rate increases when we feel fear. It also functions symbolically (i.e., by convention) when others use it to represent fear in their messages. TV commercials and late night show skits are notorious for doing so. Jack Freeman, professor of film scoring at the Berklee College of music confirms its emotional meaning staying power over the years when he said "You can't really think about the movie without the music" and "it really captures the essence of the shark."[24]

Music used alone (without lyrics) to communicate emotions in popular culture is often used for advertising and marketing. It has been used in TV commercials since the advent of TV. Consider, for example, the 1950s and 1960s happy-sounding jingles for Campbell's Soup, Oscar Meyer Weiners, Rice-a-Roni, Fritos corn chips, and Alka Seltzer. If you aren't familiar with them, a quick YouTube search will bring some up for you.

Music is still used in advertising today. For example, the happy-sounding jingle used by McDonald's has no lyrical content, but listeners immediately think "McDonald's. Mmmm, I'm lovin' it" in a positive frame. Think, too, about how the now famous 2008 Super Bowl advertisement for Budweiser beer featured Hank, the Clydesdale horse who trained himself to the musical theme from *Rocky*. The determination and persistence to succeed communicated first in *Rocky* is transposed into the commercial as viewers cheer for Hank to get picked for the team. Similarly, Chrysler's 2011 Super Bowl advertisement featuring Eminem's "Lose Yourself" communicates determination and ultimate success as a counterargument to the preconceived notions of Detroit and its automakers as losers.

Musical ascription is another tactic used to communicate via musical form.[25] In essence, musical ascription is the imitating of or borrowing from and transforming familiar musical sounds and styles. It is often used in popular culture to introduce new musical genres. Rock and roll was born as a genre by borrowing some familiar musical sounds and styles from rhythm and blues, boogie-woogie, jazz, and gospel.[26] Country music emerged from imitating some sounds and styles of country-western music, which borrowed from folk and hillbilly music.[27] And alternative rock genres such as punk and grunge capitalized on transforming sounds of mainstream rock, garage rock, and protopunk.[28]

Successful crossover music and artists also employ musical ascription. Crossover music and artists are defined as topping the charts in two or more genres with the same song(s). Examples of successful crossover artists can be documented for decades. For example, Patsy Cline topped both pop and country charts in the 1950s and 1960s. Both Elvis and Johnny Cash did so with country, gospel, and rock. Glen Campbell, Dolly Parton, Kenny Rogers, Faith Hill, Garth Brooks, Shania Twain, and the Dixie Chicks are also examples.

Today, Taylor Swift is probably one of the best-known crossover artist with hits that top both the country and pop charts. Musical ascription is the tool used by all of them to make the music popular in more than one genre. As the crossover success between country and rock continues to evolve, the use of musical ascription may actually result in the acknowledgement of a new genre: popcountry or countrypop.

Musical ascription has been used to appeal to young target audiences with potentially controversial persuasive messages. The contemporary Christian music industry has done so by borrowing musical sounds and styles from rock and pop. The Newsboys, Amy Grant, DC Talk, Michael W. Smith, and Jars of Clay not only succeeded in the Christian arena but found success in the Top 40 mainstream industry, as well. Neo-Nazi Skinhead bands have also borrowed musical sounds and styles of garage rock and punk rock to appeal to their target audience of 16- to 24-year-old white males.[29]

Today music is being produced by musicians and used by listeners in highly individualized ways thanks to the Internet. Essentially, the Internet has reduced the power of the music industry to serve as gatekeepers for what receivers ultimately get to hear. Unique musical sounds and styles may not have to borrow from existing genres to get airplay anymore. Although what lies ahead as a result is not yet clear, it is quite possible that we are in a process of transformation regarding the role of musical ascription in genre formation and the concept of crossover music and artists, as well.

Music alone has been used to communicate emotions in popular culture for decades. It has been used successfully in advertising and marketing, to introduce new musical genres, to generate crossover appeal, and to appeal to young target audiences. Certainly, music has played and will continue to play an important role in popular culture.

Lyrical Content

Communication students and scholars tend to be more comfortable examining lyrics by nature of the profession's history being grounded in words as messages. Unlike spoken or written messages, however, lyrics couched in music communicate somewhat uniquely in popular culture. This section highlights how emotional messages may be conveyed in lyrics and how these emotional messages might be understood more deeply using a variety of contemporary rhetorical perspectives.

Emotional valence communicated in lyrics can be explained as primarily comic or tragic.[30] Comic is not synonymous with humorous or funny. Rather, comic lyrics are those that "focus on the protagonist's determination to beat the odds. Failure is not an option."[31] The Perren and Fekaris song first made famous by Gloria Gaynor, "I Will Survive," is a prime example.[32] Comic lyrics can serve as an anthem of sorts, calling listeners to persevere against all odds. Bruce Springsteen's "Born To Run" is another example as he sings, "Oh, baby this town rips the bones from your back / . . . / We gotta get out while we're young / 'Cause tramps like us, baby we were born to run."[33] And "Last Resort" by Papa Roach is another: "Cut my life into pieces / This is my last resort / . . . / Don't give a f-ck if I cut my arm bleeding."[34] Thus, comic lyrics may be positive or negative; the key is that they point to perseverance at all costs and beating the odds to succeed.

Comic lyrics can also be used to rally members of a social movement in support of their mission or cause. The Live Aid anthem, "We are the World," is a classic example as an inspirational battle cry to do our part to feed the world: "There's a choice we're making / We're saving our own lives / It's true we'll make a better day just you and me."[35] Another example is "White Warriors" as a social movement battle cry of the neo-Nazi Skinhead movement: "And they'll never, never beat the warriors / White warriors, White warriors! / And they'll never, never beat the warriors."[36]

Comic lyrics can also be used as a form of instructional communication as they are in a good deal of children's music. Red Grammer's award-winning album, *Teaching Peace,* is loaded with songs teaching children to be assertive, kind, and respectful.[37] In "Say Hi," for example, Grammer instructs shy listeners to "stand up tall / . . . / take a big breath / Look 'em in the eye and say "Hi!"

Another example that comes to mind is the "Chicken Fat" song played during my elementary school gym classes in the 1960s and 1970s. The song, also known as "The Youth Fitness Song," was composed for President John F. Kennedy's Physical Fitness program and used by schools across the country to encourage children to exercise: "Go you chicken fat, go away / Go you chicken fat, go."[38] Interestingly, the song was used recently to market the *iPhone 5s.*[39] If you are not familiar with the

6:30–minute song as sung by actor Robert Preston, you can access it easily on YouTube.[40] Today, comic lyrics are also being used to instruct children about how to believe and behave in movie soundtracks. *The Lego Movie* song, "Everything is AWESOME!!!," is sung repeatedly throughout the movie. Doing so reinforces its message that "everything is great when you're part of a team" in ways that stick even after the movie is over.[41]

Tragic lyrics focus on the protagonist's attempt to hopelessly cope with fate. "I'm a loser, baby, so why don't you kill me?" as sung by Beck in "Loser" captures the essence of the tragic rhythm.[42] Other examples in popular music through the years include the Carpenter's "Goodbye to Love" where they sing that "no one ever cared if I should live or die,"[43] Eric Clapton's "Tears in Heaven,"[44] and Springsteen's academy award-winning "Streets of Philadelphia" as the protagonist infected with HIV-AIDS reflects on coping with his inevitable fate—death.[45]

Tragic lyrics have been used in popular music to reflect negative emotions people face when they feel alone, deserted, or unloved, as well as when they mourn or grieve for others. They have also been used to raise consciousness about social issues as in Springsteen's "Streets of Philadelphia" about AIDS or "Superman's Song" about power and greed by the Crash Test Dummies. In it, they sing that superman never earned a wage for saving the world from bad guys like Solomon Grundy: "And sometimes I despair / the world will never see another man like him."[46] Tragic lyrics have also been unfairly accused of causing people to commit suicide (e.g., "Don't Fear the Reaper") or to commit violent acts (e.g., Marilyn Manson's music blamed as causing the Columbine massacre). However, music does not cause or cure feelings. Rather, it represents the emotions of intensity and release we experience in our daily lives. Thus, tragic lyrics may instead be interpreted as a plea to be heard in an era when listening is becoming (if it hasn't already) a lost art.

When it comes to analysis of lyrics, a host of existing rhetorical theories can shed additional light on what and how they communicate in popular culture. For example, a dramatistic perspective can reveal motives attached to the message of the lyrics that may be offered as justification for breaking the "rules for living."[47] In "Iron Man" as sung by Ozzy Osbourne and Black Sabbath, for example, the protagonist (Iron Man) is "justified" for getting his revenge by killing "the people he once saved" because "nobody wants him / they just turn their heads."[48]

Similarly, a narrative perspective can expand the lyrical analysis to include what is offered as the "moral of the story" and "good reasons" for accepting it as valid.[49] In "Goodbye Earl," for example, the Dixie Chicks offer a number of good reasons for accepting that Earl *had to* die.[50] These reasons include physical abuse that landed Wanda in intensive care and the legal system's restraining order on Earl that didn't work.

A feminist perspective can add depth regarding roles and rules for women and men. For example, in "I Think About You," Collin Raye raises awareness about treating women with respect rather than as objects to be used and abused. He sings about seeing scantily clad models in beer advertisements that claim "drink this beer and you'll be mine" and young actresses playing "Lolita in some old man's dreams," which leads ultimately to a call for respect because all these women were once "somebody's little girl."[51] If you aren't familiar with the song, you can find a recording of it easily on YouTube.

This sampling of examples illustrates how a variety of contemporary rhetorical perspectives can enhance understanding of the lyrical message to focus not only on the emotional valence of comic or tragic rhythm, but also about the cognitive content of the stories being told in them. Perhaps what is most intriguing when studying how music communicates in popular culture, however, has to do with the interaction between lyrics and musical score in popular music.

Interaction

This section highlights how congruent and incongruent interactions between musical form and lyrical content influence the meaning conveyed, as well as the role of strategic ambiguity and ascription in such interactions. In a congruent interaction, the emotional messages in the music and lyrics reinforce each other and make the argument extremely clear and poignant. In an incongruent interaction, the emotional messages in the music contradict each other and transform the meaning in some way.

Congruent interactions may be musical release patterns combined with tragic lyrics or musical intensity patterns combined with comic lyrics. For example, the music and lyrics in Eric Clapton's "Tears in Heaven" combine tragic lyrics (coping with fate) with release patterns in the music. Together, the emotional grief and despair about losing his child is abundantly clear. We conjure up our own feelings of grief as we identify with the protagonist (in this case, Clapton himself).[52] Conversely, the music and lyrics in any number of classic rock anthems such as "Rock-n-Roll All Nite,"[53] "Born to Run,"[54] "Welcome to the Jungle,"[55] "We Will Rock You,"[56] and "I Love Rock 'n' Roll" are all examples of congruity that makes the emotionally charged argument extremely clear.[57]

Although congruent tragic release songs convey emotional meaning poignantly, doing so can be so depressing that such songs quickly lose listener appeal. Even an academy award-winning song (e.g., "Streets of Philadelphia") may be so depressing that listeners don't choose to play it very often, if at all.[58] Also, people that do choose to listen to congruent tragic release songs repeatedly may be doing so because the songs represent their feelings of sadness, loneliness, or despair and serve as a sign of their desire to be heard and valued by others (Manson, 2002). [59]

Congruent comic intensity songs, on the other hand, can function effectively as instructional communication in children's music such as in the *Teaching Peace* album and "Chicken Fat" song whose lyrics we discussed earlier. Congruent comic intensity songs can also rally people around a social movement or cause. [60] Certainly, protest songs of the 1960s serve as an excellent example. These social movement or issue rally songs may lose their ability to effectively persuade listeners to support the cause, however, when the mission "challenges the ideology of the status quo." [61] Some argue that, while the congruent comic intensity patterns in Meredith Brooks' song, "Bitch," were highly effective as an anthem for women, the song failed to appeal to many men who heard it at the time of its release (Brooks and Peiken, 1997). [62] Interestingly, however, the song does enjoy broad appeal today. Perhaps such songs that challenge the dominant ideology serve instead "as seeds for incremental persuasion over time." [63]

Incongruent interactions occur when release musical patterns are combined with comic lyrics or when intensity musical patterns are combined with tragic lyrics. Incongruent songs transform meaning from what might be gleaned from listening to either the music or the lyrics alone. To illustrate this point, let us consider two congruent comic intensity pattern songs that were remixed to be incongruent comic release pattern songs. The comic lyrics in Bruce Springsteen's original release of "Born to Run" are about the protagonist beating the odds and getting out of this "death trap" of a town. The intensity patterns in the music make the message even more poignant. Years later, he remixed the song using release patterns. Although the lyrics remained the same, the meaning was transformed to one of resolve and accepting his fate of eventually coming back home. Similarly, Toad the Wet Sprocket did a cover of KISS' "Rock n Roll All Nite" and, like Springsteen, replaced the musical intensity patterns to release patterns. The meaning changed from anticipating the fun of partying all night to reflecting on what it was like to have the energy to do so in the past.

Incongruent interactions are important in popular culture because they may result in broadening listener appeal and/or persuading listeners to accept a controversial argument as legitimate. One example of incongruent interactions that broadened listener appeal is Janet Jackson's "Together Again." The lyrics are essentially a dedication to all the friends she had lost to AIDS. By combining the tragic message with musical intensity patterns, it quickly became a song people enjoyed dancing to and, as a result, garnered broad appeal. However, the broad appeal came at the expense of misinterpretation by those unfamiliar with her purpose. They interpreted it instead as merely a catchy little dance tune. Springsteen's "Born in the USA" and "Dancing in the Dark" enjoyed similar appeal, as well as similar misinterpretation. Perhaps incongruent interactions like these need to offer lyrics at some point that make the meaning unmistakable.

Mary Chapin Carpenter's "He Thinks He'll Keep Her" and Collin Raye's "I Think About You" are two examples that did so. Each one offers incongruent interactions (intensity musical sounds combined with lyrics) and enjoyed broad appeal. However, neither suffered from misinterpretation. In both cases, the musical intensity patterns draw listeners in with what begins as fairly benign lyrics. These benign lyrics are gradually replaced with more poignant ones. This use of strategic ambiguity appears to be a way to persuade listeners incrementally to accept a potentially controversial message as legitimate.[64]

Rhetorical ascription has also been used to draw listeners in to a potentially controversial message offered via incongruent interactions and ultimately accept its argument as legitimate. "Breakfast" by the Newsboys, for example, uses both musical and lyrical ascription to couch its incongruent and potentially controversial message about accepting Christ before you die. The song is incongruent in that intensity musical patterns are combined with a tragic message about a friend that died and about people that die without knowing the Lord. They use musical ascription to sound like the other pop and rock music that appeals to their young target audience. In this rock anthem, they also employ popular culture examples that teenagers can relate to in their lyrics. For example, they speak of Captain Crunch, Cheerios, Fruit Loops, chess club, and gym class. Ultimately, the song serves as a form of evangelism. They conclude with, "When the big one finds you / may this song remind you / that they don't serve breakfast in Hell."[65] If you aren't familiar with the song, a quick Internet search can find it for you.

Congruity and incongruity among music and lyrics cannot be ignored in how they work to communicate to listeners through song. Congruent interactions make messages more poignant and can serve as an anthem for social movements, as an instructional tool with children, and to confirm feelings of sadness and grief. Incongruent interactions transform the meaning of lyrics or music alone and can broaden listener appeal and serve as incremental persuasion about potentially controversial topics. However, incongruent interactions run the risk of listener misinterpretation. Strategic ambiguity and rhetorical ascription may reduce that potential risk.

SO WHAT?

In summary, we must study music as it communicates to and for us in our daily lives. Why? We must do so because it is both pervasive and persuasive in popular culture. As explained in this chapter, music may reinforce status quo beliefs and behaviors, as well as challenge taken-for-granted roles and rules we operate by in our daily lives. As such, music can be a powerful force for change, which can be used in positive and negative ways. What is keenly important to understand is how powerfully persuasive music can be and is, particularly when people dismiss it as mere entertainment.[66]

Although music certainly may appeal to listeners for its aesthetic beauty and may communicate to listeners individually for personal reasons, over the decades music has clearly demonstrated its rhetorical role as a means of persuasion. It can argue for and against things in ways that a speech or an essay cannot. It communicates to and for us deep within our souls. Let me close with the question that opened this essay. If a picture is worth a thousand words, what is music worth? My answer now is this. Music conveys what words cannot. It communicates our inner life of feeling, of emotions, as they interact with our thoughts and beliefs about what is and what ought to be. As such, music as communication in popular culture is priceless.

NOTES

1. "Quotes About Power of Music," GoodReads.com, accessed May 21, 2016, www.goodreads.com/quotes/tag/power-of-music.

2. Deanna D. Sellnow, *The Rhetorical Power of Popular Culture: Considering Mediated Texts* (Thousand Oaks, CA: Sage, 2014): 3.

3. Suzanne K. Langer, *Feeling and Form* (New York, NY: Charles Scribner's Sons, 1953); Suzanne K. Langer, *Philosophy in a New Key*, 3rd ed. (Cambridge, MA: Harvard University Press, 1957).

4. Carroll C. Pratt, *The Meaning of Music* (New York: McGraw-Hill, 1931).

5. John Dewey, *Art as Experience* (New York, NY: Minton, Balch & Company, 1934); Langer, *Philosophy in a New Key*.

6. Terence McLaughlin, *Music and Communication* (New York: St. Martin's Press, 1970): 19.

7. Peter Kivy, *Authenticities: Philosophical Reflections of Musical Performance* (Ithaca, NY: Cornell University Press, 1995); Igor Stravinsky, *Expositions and Developments* (New York, NY: Doubleday, 1962).

8. Sellnow, *The Rhetorical Power*, 170.

9. The Monkees, vocal performance of "Pleasant Valley Sunday," by Gerry Goffin and Carole King, recorded 1967, digital file.

10. James R. Irvine and Walter G. Kirkpatrick, "The Musical Form in Rhetorical Exchange: Theoretical Considerations." *Quarterly Journal of Speech* 58 (1972): 273. doi: 10.1080/00335637209383124.

11. See John D. Bloodworth, "Communication in the Youth Counter Culture: Music as Expression." *Communication Studies* 26 (1975): 304–9. doi: 10.1080/1080/10510977509367857; R. Serge Denisoff, *Sing a Song of Social Significance*, 2nd ed. (Bowling Green, OH: Bowling Green State University Popular Press, 1983); B. Keith Murphy, "A Rhetorical and Cultural Analysis of the Protest Rock Movement, 1964–1971" (Ph.D. diss., Ohio University, 1988) ProQuest; Jerome Rodnitzky, *Minstrels of the Dawn: The Folk-protest Singer as a Cultural Hero* (Chicago, IL: Nelson-Hall, 1976); Charles J. Stewart, Craig A. Smith, and Robert E. Denton, Jr. *Persuasion and Social Movements*, 6th

ed. (Long Grove, IL: Waveland, 2012); David P. Szatsmary, *Rockin' in Time: A Social History of Rock and Roll* (Englewood Cliffs, NJ: Prentice-Hall, 1987).

12. Jack Levin and Jack McDevitt, *Hate Crimes Revisited: America's War on those Who Are Different* (Cambridge, MA: Waveland Press, 2002): 105.

13. "Child's 'Ain't No Homos Gonna Make It to Heaven' Church Performance Goes Viral," *The Huffington Post*, February 2, 2016, www.huffingtonpost.com/2012/05/30/aint-no-homos-gonna-make-it-to-heaven_n_1555735.html.

14. Spy Tekkers, "Buju Banton—Boom Bye Bye," *YouTube* video, 3:19. Posted September 19, 2007. www.youtube.com/watch?v=aIUZlzd37sI.

15. Deanna D. Sellnow, "Teaching Peace: A Rhetorical Analysis of Contemporary Children's Music," Paper presented at the annual conference of the Central States Communication Association, Cleveland, OH, April 9–12, 1992; Sellnow, *The Rhetorical Power*, 179.

16. Deanna D. Sellnow and Timothy L. Sellnow, "The 'Illusion of Life' Rhetorical Perspective: An Integrated Approach to the Study of Music as Communication," *Critical Studies in Media Communication* 18 (2001): 395–415. doi: 10.1080/07393180128090.

17. Deanna D. Sellnow and Timothy L. Sellnow, "John Corigliano's 'Symphony No. 1' as a Communicative Medium for the AIDS Crisis," *Communication Studies* 44.2 (1993): 87. doi: 10.1080/10510979309368385.

18. Sellnow and Sellnow, "John Corigliano's 'Symphony No. 1.'"

19. Langer, *Feeling and Form*; Langer, *Philosophy in a New Key*.

20. Stephen Davies, "The Expression of Emotion in Music," *Mind* 89 (1980): 67–86. doi: 10.1093/mind/LXXXIX.353.67.

21. Karen Rasmussen, "Transcendence in Leonard Bernstein's *Kaddish Symphony*," *Quarterly Journal of Speech* 80 (1994): 151. doi: 10.1080/00335639409384065.

22. Sellnow and Sellnow, "The 'Illusion of Life.'"

23. Barry Brummett, *Rhetoric in Popular Culture*, 4th ed. (Thousand Oaks, CA: Sage, 2015).

24. Matt Juul, "Why the Music of 'Jaws' is Still Terrifying," *Boston Globe*, June 15, 2015. www.boston.com/culture/entertainment/2015/06/16/why-the-music-of-jaws-is-still-terrifying.

25. Alberto Gonzalez and John J. Makay, "Rhetorical Ascription and the Gospel According to Dylan," *Quarterly Journal of Speech* 69.1 (1983): 1–14. doi: 10.1080/00335638309383630.

26. Albert Christ-Janer, Charles Hughes, and Carleton Sprague, *American Hymns Old and New* (New York, NY: Columbia University Press, 1980).

27. Piero Scaruffi, *A History of Popular Music before Rock Music: Blues, Country, Cabaret, Ragtime, Film Music, Soul, European, Latin, Jamaican, African, Arab, Indian . . .* (USA: Piero Scaruffi, 2007).

28. Adrian Boot and Chris Salewicz, *Punk: The Illustrated History of a Music Revolution* (New York, NY: Penguin, 1997); Bob Gulla, *The Greenwood Encyclopedia of Rock History: The Grunge and Post-grunge Years, 1991–2005* (Westport, CT: Greenwood Press, 2006).

29. Deanna D. Sellnow, "Music as a Unifying Social Force for Neo-Nazi Skinheads: Skrewdriver's *White Ryder* as a Case Study," (paper, annual conference of the Speech Communication Association, New Orleans, LA, November 19–22, 1994).

30. Sellnow and Sellnow, "The 'Illusion of Life.'"

31. Sellnow, *The Rhetorical Power*, 174.

32. Gloria Gaynor, vocal performance of "I Will Survive," by Freddie Perren and Dino Fekaris, released October 1978, digital file.

33. Bruce Springsteen, vocal performance of "Born to Run," by Bruce Springsteen, released August 25, 1975, digital file.

34. Papa Roach, vocal performance of "Last Resort," by Jacoby Shaddix and Tobin Esperance, released April 25, 2000, digital file.

35. USA for Africa, vocal performance of "We Are the World," by Michael Jackson and Lionel Richie, released March 7, 1985, digital file.

36. Skrewdriver, vocal performance of "White Warriors," by Ian Stuart, released 1987, stereo LP.

37. Red Grammer, *Teaching Peace*, Red Note Records, January 1, 1986, LP.

38. Robert Preston, vocal performance of "Chicken Fat," by Meredith Willson, recorded 1962, digital file.

39. Ben Yagoda, "The Strange 1960s Gym-class Anthem in Apple's New iPhone Commercial." *Slate,* June 13, 2014. www.slate.com/blogs/browbeat/2014/06/13/chicken_fat_song_apple_iphone_5s_commercial_uses_kennedy_era_exercise_anthem.html.

40. jdizzle61, "Robert Preston—Chicken Fat," *YouTube* video, 6:32. Posted [April 13, 2008]. www.youtube.com/watch?v=EFofqe26t-4.

41. Tegan and Sara featuring the Lonely Island, vocal performance of "Everything is Awesome," by Shawn Patterson, Joshua Bartholomew, Lisa Harriton, Andy Samberg, Akiva Schaffer, and Jorma Taccone, released January 27, 2014, digital file.

42. Beck, vocal performance of "Loser," by Beck and Karl Stephenson, released March 8, 1993, CD.

43. The Carpenters, vocal performance of "Goodbye to Love," by Richard Carpenter and John Bettis, released June 19, 1972, 7" single.

44. Eric Clapton, vocal performance of "Tears in Heaven," by Eric Clapton and Will Jennings, released January 7, 1992, CD.

45. Bruce Springsteen, vocal performance of "Streets of Philadelphia," by Bruce Springsteen, released February 2, 1994, CD.

46. Crash Test Dummies, vocal performance of "Superman's Song," by Brad Roberts, released March 1991, CD.

47. Kenneth Burke, *The Philosophy of Literary Form: Studies in Symbolic Action* (Berkeley, CA: University of California Press, 1974): 293–304.

48. Ozzy Osbourne, vocal performance of "Iron Man," by Tony Iommi, Ozzy Osbourne, Geezer Butler, and Bill Ward, released October 1971, 45 RPM.

49. Walter R. Fisher, "Narration as a human communication paradigm: The case of public moral argument," *Communication Monographs* 51 (1984): 7–9. doi: 10.1080/03637758409390180.

50. Dixie Chicks, vocal performance of "Goodbye Earl," by Dennis Linde, released February 29, 2000, CD.

51. Collin Raye, vocal performance of "I Think about You," by Don Schlitz and Steve Seskin, released February 26, 1996, CD.

52. Clapton, "Tears in Heaven."

53. KISS, vocal performance of "Rock and Roll All Nite," by Paul Stanley and Gene Simmons, released April 2, 1975, 7" Single.

54. Springsteen, "Born to Run."

55. Guns N' Roses, vocal performance of "Welcome to the Jungle," by Axl Rose, Michael McKagan, Izzy Stradlin, Saul Hudson, and Steven Adler, released September 28, 1987, CD.

56. Queen, vocal performance of "We Will Rock You," by Brian May, released October 7, 1977, 7" Single.

57. Joan Jett, vocal performance of "I Love Rock 'N' Roll," by Alan Merrill and Jake Hooker, released 1975, 7" Single.

58. Timothy L. Sellnow, and Deanna D. Sellnow, "The Appeal of the Tragic Rhythm: Bruce Springsteen as a Case Study," *Speaker and Gavel* 27 (1990): 38–49.

59. Michael Manson, "Interview." In Micheal Moore (Director). *Bowling for Columbine* (Los Angeles, CA: United Artists, 2002).

60. Stewart, Smith, and Denton, Jr., *Persuasion and Social Movements*.

61. Sellnow, *The Rhetorical Power*, 177.

62. Meredith Brooks, vocal performance of "Bitch," by Meredith Brooks and Shelly Peiken, released May 20, 1997, CD.

63. Sellnow, *The Rhetorical Power*, 178.

64. Deanna D. Sellnow, "Music as Persuasion: Refuting Hegemonic Masculinity in 'He Thinks He'll Keep Her,'" *Women's Studies in Communication* 22 (1999): 66–81.

65. Newsboys, vocal performance of "Breakfast," by Steve Taylor and Peter Furler, released February 20, 1996, CD.

66. James R. Irvine and Walter G. Kirkpatrick, W., "The Musical Form in Rhetorical Exchange: Theoretical Considerations," *Quarterly Journal of Speech 58* (1972): 272–84. doi: 10.1080/00335637209383124.

SEVEN

Reflection and Deflection

An Approach to Popular Culture and Politics

Trevor Parry-Giles, Will P. Howell, and Devin Scott

From ancient Greek theater to contemporary streaming video, from William Shakespeare's plays to Oliver Stone's films, humans bring politics into their artistic creations, and vice versa. Governing institutions and processes offer scenes of drama and suspense, characters that are larger than life and poignantly venal, and plots with high stakes and behind-the-scenes banality. Politics, in short, is the stuff of which both tragedy and comedy are made. Politics translates well to these dramatic forms because it is fundamentally erratic and unpredictable.

The volatility of political affairs makes great entertainment, but that quality also complicates how we study political cultural artifacts. These may capture the instability of political affairs, but they cannot definitively depict political "reality." Faced with this conundrum, scholars sometimes gravitate to arguments about how accurately popular art—usually television shows, music, or movies—captures or affects the realm of governance. Such arguments reveal little more than the obvious truism that art imitates (political) life incompletely and/or inaccurately. At the very best, these arguments are rooted to specific circumstances and difficult to translate across situations.

Therefore, we encourage scholars of popular culture and politics to start from the notion that art cannot accurately or fully capture political reality. Certainly, art constructs a sense of the world, but Theodore Adorno rightly argues that consumers know "the difference between art and empirical reality in [their] spiritual make-up."[1] Even if consumers lost that knowledge, the broad and complex nature of campaigning, governing, decision-making, and other political processes would still defy mimesis. Recognizing how closely art and politics intertwine, we are comfortable with framing studies that quantitatively gauge how art *contributes* to political opinions.[2] Problems arise, though, when such scholarship ventures claims approaching objectivity. For instance, communication scholars R. Lance Holbert, David Tschida, Maria Dixon, Kristin Cherry, Keli Steuber and David Airne praise NBC's drama *The West Wing* for providing an "insider's view of what it is like to be president on a daily basis."[3] Historian Richard Shenkman builds a critical case upon some undefined objectivity when he bemoans "Hollywood's failure to depict adequately the presidents of the United States."[4] Left unsaid in these conclusions is what would constitute "adequately" depicting the presidents. HBO's *Veep* and ABC's *Scandal*, for instance, feature fictional female Vice Presidents of the United States for a country that has never elected a female vice president.[5] Are these shows inadequate? Of course not. Do they influence and entertain, shaping viewers' sense of politics and political culture in the United States? Absolutely.

Realities—political or otherwise—are fluid, fragmented, and constructed. Ideally, analytic approaches must accept that discursive fragments "do not stand still long enough to analyze," as Michael Calvin McGee suggested.[6] It follows, therefore, that the culture—of which such fragments are composed—cannot hope to reach a truly static, and therefore objective, state. When reaching political judgments, Ronald Beiner argues that citizens treat appearances as reality; scholars, then, would be wise to do the same. Politics is thus not a definite field, but rather "a space of appearances," where people can compare their experiences to decide on the best courses of action.[7] This comparison happens largely through cultural exchange and gives works of art significant "responsibility towards the public realm."[8] Therefore, scholars of popular culture and politics should aim to study these cultural exchanges.

We also encourage scholars to eschew searches for popular culture's instrumental political effect. Scholarship about political satire sometimes highlights this issue. Some scholars who see citizens increasing knowledge or changing beliefs, correlate that change with exposure to political humor, and then proceed to claim humor caused the change.[9] Lindsay Hoffman and Dannagal Young, for example, argue that "consuming satire or parody and traditional TV news affect political participation."[10] More humanistically inclined scholars, like Roderick Hart and Johanna Hartelius, occasionally venture claims such as "Jon Stewart & Co . . . force us into one and only one way of imagining the world."[11] Diana Mutz and Lilach Nir move these claims beyond humor to say that "fictional content can affect respondents' political attitudes and policy positions."[12] We understand the strong desire to assess the influence of these popular entertainment pieces, but deterministic claims diminish the complexity of political influence. Such claims encourage readers to isolate variables that cannot and should not be isolated.

Nonetheless, we agree that popular art affects politics to some degree—and that it was necessary to argue for such influence in the not-so-distant past. Since cultural studies came to academic prominence in the 1970s, some scholars have resisted the idea that popular culture is powerful.[13] These scholars believed that rationality governs political deliberation, and thus privileged traditional political communicators—news outlets, politicians, and advocates, for example. Earlier scholars had to confront the presumed-superior credibility of traditional political sources and argue that art and culture carried weight as well—often more so than traditional sources.[14] We believe this battle has been won.

In the aftermath, we attempt to model a critical approach for isolating artistic representations of political themes such as institutions, executive leadership, and ideology. Looking at the graphic novel/film *Watchmen*, we ask how these texts *reflect* and *deflect* political *realities*. By "reflect," we mean how does *Watchmen* mirror aspects or dimensions of its contemporary political affairs? Somewhat uniquely in popular culture, politically based texts or texts with political subject matter face an additional burden of verisimilitude. Such texts are more or less true to the commonly understood "reality" of political life and political culture; the critical task is not assessing the degree or quality of the imitation, but in finding the relevance of the verisimilitude to the meanings put forth by the text. By "deflect," we mean: how does *Watchmen* align, but clash, with aspects of its contemporary political affairs? In this sense, our suggested approach embraces Anne Norton's vision of "the political as an aspect of culture, and culture as the field in which politics is conceived and enacted."[15] Ideally, this approach will help scholars push beyond the narrower realms of "politics" or "popular culture" toward arguments about culture broadly—how values, processes, and norms track across a group of people via the complex interactions and entanglements of our politics with our popular culture. Of course, this is not entirely novel, but it strives to confront the persistent mimetic problem faced by political popular culture critics.

With a critical framework based on reflection and deflection, the critic of political popular culture is able to explicate and make meaning from the differences and similarities between artifact and subject, illustrating, thusly, patterns of cultural exchange. Works of art—whether paintings or symphonies, films or graphic novels—"construct and periodically reconstruct perceptions and beliefs [underlying] political actions," notes Murray Edelman. "It is art," Edelman believes, "that evokes idealizations, threats, and beliefs about the proper place of masses, leaders, obedience, heroism, evil, and virtue."[16] The critic of political art and art about political matters recognizes, with Edelman, that "art helps create a public more aware of its own interests than it was before and more sensitive as well to the stultifying effects on thought and political action of a great deal of political language."[17] As scholars, we must recognize the plurality and changeability inherent in popular culture about politics.

Several scholars are using the approach we encourage. They often operate from a rhetorical sensibility, attend to both aesthetic and political meanings, and resist positivistic claims about effect. Crucially, their powerful claims implicate the broader culture within which popular culture and politics operate. Kristina Horn Sheeler and Karrin Vasby Anderson, for instance, trace how fictional female presidents are constructed within "the contours of presidentiality." In "the performances of primary characters, the storylines of selected episodes, and the journalistic and academic framing of each text," Sheeler and Anderson find cultural beliefs about executive leadership and gender.[18] Similarly, when Don Waisenan and Amy Becker examine comedic personae, they consider "the many roles created [for or by vice presidents] . . . across media spaces."[19] Then, rather than claiming that a particular rhetoric—say, "Sarah Palin's tortured syntax"—affects how Vice President Joe Biden presents himself, Waisenan and Becker argue that Biden's choices engage the many "circulating personae" within the vice presidency.[20] Trevor Parry-Giles and Shawn Parry-Giles assess the symbolic capacities of the first four seasons of *The West Wing* as the program articulates a vision of US nationalism rooted in long-standing dynamics of gender, race, and militarism.[21] Through an interrogation of these popular, political culture artifacts, these works offer critical perspectives on contemporary culture.

While these critics examine overtly political texts, popular culture need not be overtly political for it to be worthy and valuable of critical attention. There are certainly cultural artifacts using characters, settings, and plots to overtly engage the political system. Examples of this category might include the television show *House of Cards* (2013–), the film *Lincoln* (2012), the musical *Hamilton* (2015), or the novel (and later film) *Thank You for Smoking* (1994 and 2005, respectively). Other cultural artifacts may take up non-political settings, with non-political characters enacting non-political plots, even as they manifest political themes—say, leadership, decision making, and power. Recent examples of this second category could include AMC's television show *The Walking Dead* (2010–) or Kendrick Lamar's album *To Pimp A Butterfly* (2015). In examples like these, scholars can develop insights about society's values, processes, and norms by looking for *reflections* and *deflections* between politics and popular culture.

REFLECTIONS AND DEFLECTIONS:
WATCHMEN IN ITS POLITICAL CONTEXTS

To illustrate how attending to textual reflections and deflections enable critical insights, we turn to the 1986–1987 graphic novel *Watchmen* and its 2009 film adaptation. DC Comics syndicated the *Watchmen* comic series and then collected those comics as a graphic novel. The graphic novel won a Hugo Award, is ranked as one of *Time's* top one hundred English-language novels, and has been reprinted at least twenty-three times.[22] The film adaptation, released in March 2009, earned over $184 million worldwide at the box-office and over $98 million in domestic video sales.[23] *Entertainment Weekly* critic Ken Tucker called the film "the most 'political' movie" of 2009 because it "captur[ed] what [was] in the air at the moment" of its release.[24] Inspired by Tucker's comments, we briefly consider how the reflections and deflections between *Watchmen* and its nonfictional political contexts open up space for non-instrumental arguments.

For would-be scholars seeking entry points, we suggest an artifact's settings, characters, and themes. In *Watchmen*, for example, the setting is a related, but deflected, historical trajectory that reflects elements of Cold War America—namely, the expansion of executive power and the prevalence of fear. The setting's reflections and deflections suggest an array of arguments about how significant political events leave their mark upon a culture. If scholars want to make arguments about leadership, they might consider reflections and deflections between characters and politicians. Presidents Ronald Reagan and George W. Bush are reflected in three *Watchmen* characters who exercise executive power. One of those characters is, indeed, the president—Richard Nixon—but the other two are superheroes. Through these three characters, *Watchmen* disturbs the idea that excellent leaders deserve, or can effectively wield, broad executive power. Thematic reflections and deflections can support arguments about ideology. By simultaneously reflecting a concern for American exceptionalism, and deflecting the gravity of that concern, *Watchmen* offers concerned readers/viewers a counterpoint as they (re)evaluate the ideology. We will consider each area in turn—setting, character, and theme—before offering some final thoughts about using this approach to study popular culture and politics.

While *Watchmen* unfolds in a distinct historical context, it deflects the history that readers would know. It is set in 1985 with Richard Nixon in his fifth term as the US president—an office that, in reality, can only be held by an individual for two terms, and which was held by Ronald Reagan in 1985. With the help of a nuclear-powered super-being named Dr. Manhattan, Nixon won the Vietnam War in 1971. Despite this victory, *Watchmen's* America, like the nonfictional America of 1986–1987, remains threatened by the possibility of nuclear war with the Soviet Union. By deflecting readers' historical context, *Watchmen*'s setting clears space to reflect two elements from readers' political contexts: expanded executive power and potential nuclear annihilation.

Both the novel and film reflect political contexts in which executive power expanded to meet public safety concerns. Both Ronald Reagan and George W. Bush requested additional powers during the Cold War and post-September-11th years, respectively, to keep America safe.[25] They did not have *absolute* power, and the legislative and judicial branches usually kept the presidents' power in check. Nonetheless, many citizens questioned the power shift. In *Watchmen*, the president's power expanded for similar reasons but was not similarly checked; indeed, *Watchmen*'s Congress only does Nixon's bidding. *Watchmen*'s America holds elections, but citizens choose between "Nixon or the commies." Nixon abolished the two-term limit for presidents, and is now omnipresent as demonstrated by the "Nixon: Four More Years" posters in both the comic and film backgrounds. Neither Reagan nor Bush were so audacious; but to the extent that *Watchmen* reflects real-world growth of executive power, it raises the specter of possibility. The deflection between popular culture and politics curbs the threat's immediacy, and invites readers/viewers to reconsider Reagan and Bush's new powers.

The fictional story also reflects "real" Americans grappling with the looming fear of war. One of the masked crime fighters in *Watchmen* laments that he "can just feel this anxiety, this terror bearing down." Another masked crime fighter calls it "an era of stress and anxiety, when the present seems unstable and the future unlikely," leading people to "retreat and withdraw from reality." A journalist senses "war paranoia," in which people are "empty and disillusioned" as they await World War III. These descriptions could have come from 1980s or 2000s news reports; and by reflecting what readers/viewers are seeing in the news, *Watchmen* builds a bridge between lived experiences and fictional possibilities. One such possibility is the total collapse of social order. In the first two terms of Nixon's presidency, masked crime fighters helped keep the peace—but in 1977, Nixon outlawed "costumed adventuring." By 1985, *Watchmen*'s America teems with rioting, mob violence, prostitution, and similar desperate acts. What then, for the "real" Americas of the 1980s and 2000s, without masked crime fighters to offer the possibility of external protection? The novel/film's dark deflections, and uncomfortable reflections, call attention to Americans' fear of social upheaval and the collapse of order.

But *Watchmen* does more than simply comment on setting; it also explores executive leadership through three characters. Would-be scholars might look for reflections between these three characters and the American presidency, and advance arguments about the power vested in that office. In the most reflective sense, for example, *Watchmen*'s President Richard Nixon exercises the extent of political possibilities, while the masked crime fighter Ozymandias exhibits super-human—yet still human—leadership outside the political system. Finally, the super-being Dr. Manhattan demonstrates possibilities beyond the realm of human frailty. These powerful leaders do a great deal, but their shortcomings suggest that even the most gifted or powerful leaders cannot lead perfectly.

Watchmen's Richard Nixon, for example, is hamstrung by both his humanity and his political system. *Watchmen's* Nixon reflects the "real" Nixon's covetous relationship to power. To protect his authority, *Watchmen's* Nixon constructs himself to be the guarantor of all safety and security. He marginalizes the once-popular masked crime fighters and compels them (by a change in law) to "look the other way." "Real" Cold War presidents were capable of launching nuclear war with the push of a button, but *Watchmen's* Nixon expresses this idea with a rawness unlike anything in the political world: "I say when doomsday is approaching." And *Watchmen's* Nixon did what the "real" Nixon could not: he brought about an American victory in the Vietnam War. Yet, *he*—a human, limited by the political realities of the situation—did not end the war; rather, he asked the radioactive Dr. Manhattan to intervene, and this request was "something that his predecessors would not ask," Dr. Manhattan notes. This total deflection of American history and temporality raises crucial questions about the American presidency: if a president can act decisively, should he or she? How is the willingness to act decisively a valuable quality in a president, and how is it harmful? These questions, and many more, are available to scholars who look for the reflections and deflections between *Watchmen's* Nixon and an abstract, unnamed, "real" American president.

If *Watchmen's* Nixon is constrained by his humanity and his political system, Adrian Veidt (who goes by the moniker "Ozymandias") is unbounded by systemic limits. Ozymandias is super-human—fast enough to dodge a bullet and "the smartest man on earth"—but still human. Nixon may claim to determine doomsday, but Ozymandias actually has that power—the power to either cause or prevent nuclear destruction. His power is external to any representative body or process, simply by virtue of his intelligence and abilities. This independence leads him to perceive that "a world united in peace [requires] sacrifice," and empowers him to dispassionately sacrifice a segment of the population to achieve peace. Without electoral or political repercussions, Ozymandias can "[step] beyond conventional solutions" and act outside the political system to "frighten governments into co-operation."[26] People will die from his plan, but Ozymandias believes he is "killing . . . millions, in order to save billions." This statement may reflect, say, President Truman and the justification for using the atomic bomb, but Ozymandias deflects most American presidents. So, when his destructive, extra-governmental scheme ends the Cold War and produces world harmony, readers/viewers confront several thought-provoking questions: what decisions should leaders make in the absence of electoral repercussions? To whom should we extend the power to make unilateral decisions? In considering these questions, citizens and scholars alike must acknowledge that Ozymandias is still Adrian Veidt—he still reflects humanity, and the limitations inherent to all humans.

Dr. Manhattan, on the other hand, deflects both humanity and political limitations. Dr. Manhattan was *once* human, but after he was exposed to a nuclear energy field he became telekinetic and clairvoyant, capable of subatomically manipulating the physical world. Some people call him a "superman" or "god," but he stresses that he is "just a puppet who can see the strings." Still, over and over again, he deflects humanity—both emotionally and physically. In a particularly illustrative quip, Dr. Manhattan observes that "a live body and a dead body contain the same number of particles. Structurally, there's no discernible difference." But despite Dr. Manhattan's progressively tenuous grip on humanity, characters repeatedly claim that "as long as people think [he's] still watching us, we'll be all right." *Watchmen*, then, reflects our hope for leaders: that they will make us feel safe. Yet our presidents deflect Dr. Manhattan: they lack both his ability to control the physical world, and his disengagement with humanity. As with Veidt and Nixon, scholars can explore what Dr. Manhattan's reflections and deflections say about American political leaders: should they be empathic? Should they be able to manipulate the physical world at will? Should they be made of the same fiber as us, or something greater?

In sum, all three characters reflect and deflect the American presidency in ways that open up potentially useful arguments. Nixon's democratically extended power was tenuous, and he overcame that tenuousness through repressive means. Furthermore, extending this power to a human brought a host of known limitations; Nixon himself entrusts "humanity" to "a higher authority than mine." A truly exceptional human like Ozymandias, whose power came from his exceptionalness, could make painful decisions he felt were necessary for the greater good even as he too was limited by his temporality and, as Dr. Manhattan reminded readers of the novel, "Nothing ever ends" except human life. Finally, Manhattan's "god" power—the power to "end all worlds"—brought absolute safety and security to citizens, but lacked the empathy to do anything more than defend them. Collectively, these characters demonstrate the limitations of autocratic power, regardless of who the individual leader is.

But scholars may also want to consider how characters reflect and deflect the communication practices of contemporary individual leaders—in *Watchmen*'s case, Ronald Reagan (novel) or George W. Bush (film).[27] For instance, the exhortations of *Watchmen*'s Nixon (e.g., "We can't let these fuckers think we're weak") occasionally reflect those of

George W. Bush (e.g., "terrorist attacks . . . are invited by the perception of weakness.")[28] Bush's America deflects key settings of Nixon's America in *Watchmen*—the widespread vigilantism, say, or the diffuse desperation. Does this mean Bush's rhetoric was overwrought, given his situation? Our contention is that critics might probe deflections of setting for meaning, and then read that meaning back on the reflection between characters. This approach navigates a frequent challenge with popular cultural scholarship: comparing "something "real" with something "imagined."

Yet insights might be gained from studying how "imagined" characters reflect and deflect other "imagined" characters. For instance, *Watchmen*'s Dr. Manhattan reflects Superman's heroic leadership and extrahuman capabilities. Whereas Superman lives a relatively human life, Dr. Manhattan's detachment from humanity is stressed over and over. This deflection raises several key questions about leadership in American culture: do Americans want leaders—heroic or otherwise—who maintain connections to "the common man"? How do such connections influence how a leader exercises his/her skills? By asking these questions about, and looking for reflection and deflections between, "imagined" characters, scholars and citizens alike are unbound from what is temporally possible.

This line between "real" and "imagined" tends to be clearer with characters and settings than with themes. American exceptionalism, for example, means relatively the same in *Watchmen* as it does in contemporary American politics. That is, since 1630, when John Winthrop charged the new American colony to be "a city upon a hill," American political discourse has reverberated with the idea that everything about America is better than everything elsewhere. In his farewell address, Reagan reiterated that America was "still a beacon, still a magnet for all who must have freedom"; and Bush called America "the greatest nation on earth."[29] *Watchmen* reflects this ideology, but it manifests differently in its fictional setting. One of the masked adventurers, for example, laments that citizens do not love America anymore: "like coke in green glass bottles . . . they don't make [American love] anymore." At the end of the Vietnam War, another masked adventurer damningly muses that "if we'd lost here in Vietnam, it might have driven us crazy as a country." This quip deflects the historic loss of the Vietnam War, while paying homage to the anxieties and fears concerning American superiority in the years after the war. By deflecting the outcome of the Vietnam War, while calling attention to the effects of that humiliating defeat, *Watchmen* reflects and highlights the incredible resilience of our collective sense of American exceptionalism. Is this a marker of resilient ideology? Misplaced ideology? Transcendent ideology? Potential scholars can propose answers to these questions when they search for thematic reflections.

CONCLUSION

Our somewhat cursory reading of *Watchmen* is not intended to argue for or against particular interpretations of the graphic novel and film. Rather, we offer this abbreviated discussion of *Watchmen* to illustrate our over-arching critical argument: the search for reflections and deflections be-tween a popular culture artifact and a political context can open up a text for scholars of popular culture and politics. Settings, characters, and themes provide particularly useful entry points to a text, and mediate between "reality" and entertainment. Most importantly, our approach gives scholars a productive alternative to deterministic claims that popu-lar culture accurately captures or deterministically affects politics, or vice versa. Recognizing this fact is of paramount importance. Art's fiction will never match up with an objective "reality"—and such "attempts to claim objectivity," John Street rightly argues, are primarily about "the exercise of power and the attempt to legitimate that power."[30]

And when power is in question—as it always is in political discus-sions—it is incredibly important to understand how people make sense of their situations. Kenneth Burke saw people doing this through litera-ture and dubbed such literature "equipment for living"; it strikes us that his observation applies to other forms of culture, too.[31] Popular culture artifacts are crucibles in which the political gets forged, broken down, and repurposed for new projects. Such a process is mercurial even to the super-being Dr. Manhattan, who ponders, "A world grows up around me. Am I shaping it, or do its predetermined contours guide my hand? . . . Who makes the world?" These questions are not easily an-swered, but we encourage scholars of popular culture and politics to keep on asking them.

NOTES

    1. Theodor W. Adorno, "Culture Industry Reconsidered," translated by Anson G. Rabinbach, *New German Critique* (1975): 18.
    2. Maria Elizabeth Grabe and Erik Page Bucy, *Image Bite Politics: News and the Visual Framing of Elections*, 1st edition (New York, NY: Oxford University Press, USA, 2009); Penina Wiesman, "We Frame to Please: A Preliminary Examination of *The Daily Show*'s Use of Frames," in *The Daily Show and Rhetoric: Arguments, Issues, and Strategies*, ed. Trischa Goodnow (Lanham, MD: Lexington Books, 2011).
    3. R. Lance Holbert et al., "*The West Wing* and Depictions of the American Presi-dency: Expanding the Domains of Framing in Political Communication," *Communica-tion Quarterly* 53 (2005): 506, doi:10.1080/01463370500102228.
    4. Peter Rollins, *Hollywood's White House* (Lexington, KY: University Press of Ken-tucky, 2005), x.
    5. Eventually, the vice-president in *Veep* becomes president, an even further break from the American political "reality."
    6. Michael C McGee, "Text, Context, and the Fragmentation of Contemporary Cul-ture," *Western Journal of Speech Communication* 54 (1990): 287.

7. Ronald Beiner, *Political Judgement*, 1st edition (New York, NY: Routledge, 2009), 12.

8. Ibid, 23.

9. Josh Compton, "More than Laughing? Survey of Political Humor Effects Research," in *Laughing Matters: Humor and American Politics in the Media Age.*, ed. J. C. Baumgartner and J. S. Morris (New York, NY: Routledge, 2008), 39–63.

10. Lindsay H. Hoffman and Dannagal G. Young, "Satire, Punch Lines and the Nightly News: Untangling Media Effects on Political Participation," *Communication Research Reports* 28 (2011): 164, doi: 10.1080/08824096.2011.565278; See also: Robin L. Nabi, Emily Moyer-Gusé, and Sahara Byrne, "All Joking aside: A Serious Investigation into the Persuasive Effect of Funny Social Issue Messages," *Communication Monographs* 74 (2007): 29–54, doi: 10.1080/03637750701196896; Amber Day, "Shifting the Conversation: Colbert's Super PAC and the Measurement of Satirical Efficacy," *International Journal of Communication* 7 (2013): 414–29; Lauren Feldman, "Cloudy with a Chance of Heat Balls: The Portrayal of Global Warming on *The Daily Show* and *The Colbert Report*," *International Journal of Communication* 7 (2013): 430–51; Amy Xenos, Michael, Waisanen, Don Becker, "Sizing Up *The Daily Show*: Audience Perceptions of Political Comedy Programming," *Atlantic Journal of Communication* 18 (2010): 144–57; Kenton Bird et al., "'It's Better than Being Informed': College-Aged Viewers of The Daily Show," in *Laughing Matters: Humor and American Politics in the Media Age.*, ed. J. C. Baumgartner and J. S. Morris (New York, NY: Routledge, 2008).

11. Roderick P. Hart and E. Johanna Hartelius, "The Political Sins of Jon Stewart," *Critical Studies in Media Communication* 24 (2007): 269. doi: 10.1080/07393180701520991.

12. Diana C. Mutz and Lilach Nir, "Not Necessarily the News: Does Fictional Television Influence Real-World Policy Preferences?" *Mass Communication and Society* 13 (2010): 210. doi:10.1080/15205430902813856.

13. For an excellent and thorough assessment of this tendency, see Stuart Hall, "Cultural Studies and Its Theoretical Legacies," in *Stuart Hall: Critical Dialogues in Cultural Studies*, ed. Kuan-Hsing Chen and David Morley (New York, NY: Routledge, 1996).

14. For an excellent review of this transition, see R. Lance Holbert, "A Typology for the Study of Entertainment Television and Politics," *American Behavioral Scientist* 49 (2005): 436–53. doi:10.1177/0002764205279419.

15. Anne Norton, *95 Theses on Politics, Culture, and Method* (New Haven, CT: Yale University Press, 2004), 12.

16. Murray J. Edelman, *From Art to Politics: How Artistic Creations Shape Political Conceptions* (Chicago, IL: University of Chicago Press, 1995), 9.

17. Ibid, 144.

18. Kristina Horn Sheeler and Karrin Vasby Anderson, *Woman President: Confronting Postfeminist Political Culture*, 1st ed. (College Station, TX: Texas A&M University Press, 2013), 43.

19. Don J. Waisanen and Amy B. Becker, "The Problem with Being Joe Biden: Political Comedy and Circulating Personae," *Critical Studies in Media Communication* 32 (2015), 257.

20. Ibid, 258.

21. Trevor Parry-Giles and Shawn J. Parry-Giles, *The Prime-Time Presidency: The West Wing and US Nationalism* (Urbana: University of Illinois Press, 2006).

22. 1988 Hugo Awards," *The Hugo Awards*, accessed October 31, 2015, www.thehugoawards.org/hugo-history/1988-hugo-awards/; Richard Lacayo, "All-TIME 100 Novels," *Time*, January 6, 2010, entertainment.time.com/2005/10/16/all-time-100-novels/; "Watchmen [First Printing]," *Grand Comics Database*, accessed October 31, 2015, www.comics.org/issue/43793/.

23. "Watchmen (2009)—Financial Information," *The Numbers*, accessed October 31, 2015,www.the-numbers.com/movie/Watchmen.

24. Ken Tucker, "'Watchmen': Why Rush Limbaugh Isn't Gonna Like It," *Entertainment Weekly*, March 8, 2008,www.ew.com/article/2009/03/08/watchmen-rush-l.

25. The film was released in March 2009, two months into Barack Obama's presidency, but the film planning and production took place during George W. Bush's tenure as president. Thus, we will draw the parallel with Bush's presidency rather than Obama's.

26. There are minor variations in Ozymandias' plot between the graphic novel and the film. In the film, Ozymandias sets off nuclear explosions in many major cities, including New York, London, and Moscow. In the graphic novel, Ozymandias instead teleports an "alien" to New York, which explodes with telepathic force to massacre the population. Despite these differences, both "sacrifices" reflect cold war anxieties while serving similar purposes.

27. Again, we discuss George W. Bush because the film was planned and produced during Bush's presidency, even though it was released during Barack Obama's presidency.

28. George W. Bush, "War on Terror," *US Department of State Archive*, September 7, 2003,2001-2009.state.gov/p/nea/rls/rm/23897.htm.

29. Ronald Reagan, "Farewell Speech," *WGBH—American Experience*, 1988,www.pbs.org/wgbh/americanexperience/features/primary-resources/reagan-farewell/.

30. John Street, *Politics and Popular Culture* (Philadelphia, PA: Temple University Press, 1997), 176.

31. Kenneth Burke, *The Philosophy of Literary Form: Studies in Symbolic Action* (Berkeley, CA: University of California Press, 1974), 293.

EIGHT

Public Relations Representations in Popular Culture

A "Scandal" on Primetime Television

Cheryl Ann Lambert, Jessalynn Strauss, and Natalie T. J. Tindall

In the past two decades, new technology has extended the reach of popular culture to an ever-expanding audience. Thanks to digital streaming and video services, viewers can now watch entire seasons of television programs. The participatory nature of social media has fostered online, real-time communities that allow individual viewers to watch television programs while engaged in shared digitized discussions. Multiple touch points enable media to create narratives that inevitably shape public discourse. Likewise, multiple meanings of American culture are constructed by viewers and program creators. Whether engaging in popular culture alone or within groups in live or mediated contexts, audiences share a social experience in which they co-create cultural meanings. In this chapter, we turn our sights to discourse in mediated context with a focus on televised representations of fictional public relations (PR) characters in the United States (US). The authors employ a cultural studies framework to analyze the professional representations of PR on two televised shows, *Scandal* and *Ray Donovan*.

Scandal (2012) and *Ray Donovan* (2013) both began at a time of profound social, political, and cultural change in the United States. Barack Obama was re-elected the first Black president of the United States in 2012, which revealed racial divisions soon conveyed in public discourse. Cultural ideologies were deepened, too, when twin bombs at the 2013

89

Boston Marathon were set off by men who practiced extremist Islam. Political wrangling over gun laws—mostly around entrenched positions yielding no change in access—quickly devolved into public sentiments against government leadership. Mistrust of the government increased with revelations that a US government agency had been collecting private information from American citizens through their cell phones. Although Olivia Pope of *Scandal* and Ray Donovan exist in represented realities, their worlds are never fully divorced from the lived realities of viewers.

PUBLIC RELATIONS SCHOLARSHIP IN POPULAR CULTURE

For several decades, public relations representations have shaped viewer assumptions about professional identity, social status, and personal relationships. According to Carol Ames, "Since 1995, the American public has had weekly exposure to long-running television series related to PR."[1] Yet there is a dearth of popular culture-related public relations scholarship. Thus far, media representations have been the most productive stream of literature. Scholars have conducted analyses of public relations representations in television, in film, and in a combination of media.[2] Karen S. Miller's historical analysis of fictional portrayals of public relations practitioners found that the representations of public relations were "woefully inadequate in terms of explaining who practitioners are and what they do."[3] The characterizations of public relations professionals fell into multiple categories: ditzy (shallow but loveable), obsequious, cynical and sarcastic; manipulative and predatory; money-minded; isolated; accomplished; and unfulfilled. Kate Fitch, who analyzed a fictional public relations campaign in HBO's series *True Blood* from the post-feminist tradition, called for critical-cultural alternatives to public relations representations.[4] With this call in mind, the authors employed the circuit of culture to interrogate media representations of public relations in popular culture.[5]

THE CIRCUIT OF CULTURE FRAMEWORK

The circuit of culture model is a cultural studies framework to understand how the media function as cultural products.[6] The model encompasses five continuously intersecting moments during which meaning is produced: regulation, production, representation, consumption, and identity. *Regulation* comprises the guidelines by which program developers operate to regulate cultural practices.[7] Media producers are bound by community norms for social practice. For example, programs deemed outside the social and political mainstream air on designated networks. Program creators comment on society's ideological problems by embedding assumptions into media during *production*.[8] Producers are engaged in a complex, multifaceted approach to create cultural products encoded with meanings.[9] Production involves the use of narrative, dialogue, and character behaviors to assign meanings to social behaviors. *Representation* involves using images, signs, and language to represent the world to people according to renowned cultural studies scholar Stuart Hall. Media representations function as a window to the world and "an essential part of the process by which meaning is produced and exchanged between members of a culture."[10] During *consumption*, viewers actively construct their realities by interpreting media.[11] They share these constructions with others as indicators of who they are and are not by ascribing specific meanings to the media stories they see and hear. When viewers identify with media presentations, they are experiencing the moment of *identity*.

US television producers have constructed a representation of public relations through consistent narrative features, leading viewers to consume specific images of the industry, informing the identity of the field. In order to examine the cultural meaning of public relations, we explore how production, representation, consumption, and identity intersect within *Scandal* and *Ray Donovan* and inform regulation.

OLIVIA POPE AND RAY DONOVAN AS PUBLIC RELATIONS PROFESSIONALS

Scandal is an ABC drama centered on the life of Olivia Pope, an attorney and crisis management expert who owns and manages her own Washington, DC–based public relations agency, Olivia Pope & Associates (OPA).[12] The self-proclaimed fixer for DC's elite is a former White House communications director for the Fitzgerald (Fitz) Grant administration.[13] The titular scandal involves her personal life: She is a single African American woman who for much of the series is having an affair with the married, White, Republican President of the United States, Fitz Grant. The other scandal refers broadly to her high-profile clients in crisis.

The Showtime program *Ray Donovan* features a slick problem solver employed by a high-end Los Angeles law firm whose dysfunctional family relationships often cause as many problems as his clients. Ray has a laser-like focus on client protection at the expense of ethical principles. Ray's father, Mickey Donovan, is a career criminal whose illegal actions often make Ray's look reasonable in comparison. Ray's efforts to protect his family, especially his wife and two children, belie a softer side to the ruthless actions he undertakes on behalf of his clients. The ongoing irony of *Ray Donovan*'s title character is that he can fix the problems of his clients — often by hiding murders and blackmailing potential assailants — but he cannot maintain a good relationship with his family.

Olivia Pope and Ray Donovan conform to a persistent myth about public relations practitioners as highly efficient, highly unethical, and highly effective. Their upper-class residences convey the idea that unethical behaviors leads to financial stability.

Several plots featuring dishonest politicians who finally get caught for their misdeeds must resonate with viewers who mistrust the US government. Other narratives hew more closely to current events. A storyline in the fictional Grant administration wherein rigged Ohio election ballots guarantee his election seems inspired by state-wide voting irregularities during the 2004 US presidential election.[14] The ideals of democracy inform the narrative as Olivia attributes the consequences of the rigged election to forgoing the will of the people. Citizens' rights are also front and center in a *Scandal* episode when a hacker threatens to reveal that the American government has been secretly spying on American citizens. The plot hearkens back to the NSA story of accessing private phones. By creating compromised characters, circulating the common anti-hero trope in American television, producers have effectively normalized their range of behaviors.[15]

THE FIXER

In sharp contrast to the majority of practicing public relations professionals, Olivia Pope and Ray Donovan are both *fixers*. The two are exceptionally gifted at brokering deals with law enforcement officials, media professionals, religious leaders, and political party front-runners—all to protect their clients. The means they use for client protection reveals the contested nature of a fixer, however. According to *Ray Donovan* producers, a fixer is "a person who arranges for bribes or payoffs of corrupt police or government officials, or other criminals, to enable a criminal to avoid punishment." Audiences are presented with the image of Ray as ultimate protector of both his family and his clients and they incorporate this archetype into their conception of the public relations professional as a "fixer." For Olivia, a self-identified fixer, her role is to "solve problems, manage crises, and save reputations." Nevertheless, Olivia Pope & Associates (OPA) employees have traded sexual favors with the medical examiner to obtain critical case information, coerced cooperation from police officers and business executives through threats of revealing private sexual information, and bribed hotel witnesses in order to ensure their silence about an OPA client. It could be argued that Ray is a criminal engaged in public relations while Olivia is a public relations practitioner facilitating crime; after all, Olivia conducts background research, preps clients for interviews through media training, and develops long-term plans for image restoration. Ray Donovan and Olivia Pope hold a like-minded commitment to advocating for their high-profile clients and companies. Advocacy connects these characters' representations of public relations to their real-life counterparts.

THE PUBLIC RELATIONS STEREOTYPE

Manipulation and coercion reflect a common cultural understanding of the public relations industry despite the fact that such representations are incompatible with our professional identity. The US-based Public Relations Society of America has created a shared meaning of professionalism in the public relations community by regulating how members should behave. The professional association's code of ethics constitutes six professional values and six provisions and guidelines.[16] The only aspects of the code that Olivia and Ray adhere to consistently are advocacy, expertise, and loyalty. Program producers present these characters as exceptionally skilled problem solvers during their debut episodes. When viewers first meet Olivia Pope, she is negotiating with Russian kidnappers of an American Ambassador's son—with less than the agreed-upon funding to secure the child's release. Olivia quickly defuses the situation by threatening to put the kidnappers' names on the terrorism watch-list, thereby restricting their travel access and potential future interactions with the US government. The kidnappers accept the money, Olivia departs, and she calls her client to say, "It's handled." The pilot episode of *Ray Donovan* shows its title character simultaneously solving two clients' problems—one, a male action star, has been caught in a tryst with a transgender woman; the other, a popular music artist, has woken up in bed with a woman who has died of a drug overdose. By creating compromised characters, circulating the common anti-hero trope in American television, producers have effectively normalized their range of behaviors by tapping into viewer preconceptions about glamorized criminals.

MORALLY AMBIGUOUS CHARACTERS

Viewers can, and do, ascribe their own meaning to represented realities during the moment of consumption. As viewers become invested in Ray Donovan and Olivia Pope—and ratings suggest they are, they will likely expect those characters to be motivated by good will, only acting with justification.[17] Program creators have developed the quintessential *morally ambiguous characters*, those who exhibit behaviors that appear to be at odds with the traits they typically display.[18] Although public relations scholars have not explored moral ambiguity, many have identified character traits consistent with the construct.[19] *Ray Donovan* establishes identity through difference, as its title character takes actions so blatantly unethical and illegal that viewers no doubt feel secure in their own moral status, regardless of what small-scale errors they may have committed.

Even the most sinister of their actions appear to have selfless motivations.[20]

Through their vulnerabilities, these characters are reconstructed as fallible individuals. *Ray Donovan* producers have created a proscribed extralegal world in which Ray's actions are guided only by the need to solve his clients' many problems. With little respect to laws or ethics, Ray operates primarily under two guiding principles: He must succeed at his job by fixing the problems his clients bring to him, and he must protect his family, primarily his teenage children. His identity as an unconventional warrior-antihero is designated by his frequent physical injuries, many of which are to his face, visually demonstrating his status to the viewer. In representing a father-protector, Ray is unable to show emotional vulnerability or acknowledge any complexity or conflict in his decision making.

THE FAMILY BUSINESS

The cultural understanding of family informs narratives on *Ray Donovan* and *Scandal*. Olivia Pope and Ray Donovan are shaped by patriarchal norms because their professional status exists as a result of their relationship to powerful fathers. As an Irish-American originally from working-class South Boston ("Southie") who represents high-profile West Coast clients, Ray embodies a particular segment of the American dream. He has geographically separated his family (including his wife, two children, and two brothers) from the criminal elements of his family's past by relocating to a wealthy suburb of Los Angeles (LA) County. The upper-class identity he has created collapses when his father, an active member of the Boston criminal underworld, is released from prison and travels to California to join his sons. The social status of both characters is often at risk due to potential exposure of extra-legal activities. Ray pays prisoners for some jobs; Olivia Pope & Associates (OPA) employees are all ex-convicts. Ray bribes individuals to complete certain tasks; OPA employees commit bribery, blackmail, and violent interrogations on Olivia's orders. Nevertheless, the program employs verbal and visual appeals to invite viewers to co-create a moral high ground for Olivia. Her frequent assertions that she "wears the white hat," a trope signifying the protagonist, along with her white attire and accessories function to convey her innocence.[21] Her purported innocence highlights the contrast between her statements and her lived reality. Like Ray, she remains irrevocably linked to her estranged father despite his many transgressions.

TRADITIONAL GENDER ROLES

Olivia Pope is constantly renegotiating her professional and personal identity in response to patriarchal ideology embedded in her relationships. Her father Eli Pope is "Command" of B6-13, a CIA-like security organization operating outside the purview of the government. Because B6-13 is not an official agency, Eli employs any number of illegal information-gathering techniques without fear of reprisal. He uses brute force to demand compliance from his employees as well as total respect from his daughter. Despite the considerable talents Olivia has demonstrated, she maintains only intermittent success against Eli. His vast network of soldiers ready to do his bidding reinforce his patriarchy, echoed in his verbal assuredness: "You can't take Command." Gender also constrains her romantic relationship with the president. She struggles to express her own agency through much of the series, alternately resisting and embracing her pursuit of love. Viewers learn in the debut episode that Olivia initiated the end of their affair; they learn soon after the consequences of her decision: A staged reconciliation and pregnancy with his wife in order to convey the illusion of a happy marriage to the media. Three seasons later when Olivia publicly reveals her relationship with President Grant, her professional identity is overshadowed by her presumed new role as First Lady. We witness her transform from a formidable businesswoman to a reluctant greeter/hostess/advisor as the president moves her into the White House without consulting her first. Viewers who struggle for autonomy in their own lives might identify with Olivia's plight.

RACE ON THE MARGINS

As the first network television drama with an African American woman in the lead role since *Get Christie Love* in 1965, *Scandal* debuted at a time when networks were increasingly coming under fire for their lack of programs with people of color.[22] Yet race exists on the periphery of the production and representation. Before *Scandal*, producer Shonda Rhimes had proven the viability of programs featuring diverse casts with the long-running drama *Grey's Anatomy* and its successful spin-off, *Private Practice*. Since then, her production team developed the second network television drama with an African American woman in the lead role since 1965—*How to Get Away with Murder*. Still, Shonda maintains her color-blind casting is a rational response to societal changes that reflect her post-Civil Rights sensibilities.

Media representations in television often develop characters through specific cultural identity markers, highlighting the stories of some while downplaying those of others.[23] In the post-racial world of *Scandal*, however, the narrative, character interactions, and verbal markers rarely signify any point of difference.[24] It is unfortunate that the issue of race and culture so prevalent in viewers' lives is not fully reflected in the program. A compelling storyline around the subject of race occurs when Olivia creates a crisis management plan to manage the dissolution of the president's marriage and eventual remarriage to Olivia. According to the plan, Olivia and Fitz's relationship would spark a dialogue about race in America and their relationship would provide a refreshing change for the Republican Party. Fitz's eventual marriage to Olivia would be seen as "monumental in the redemption of America." Unfortunately for viewers, the plan never comes to fruition.

Arguably the most overt reference to racial identity occurs during an episode in which Olivia represents an African American man whose unarmed son was killed by the police. The episode marks the only time viewers see Olivia inhabit a traditionally Black social space. This positioning of racial identity is all the more curious because the role is inspired by African American attorney and communication expert Judy Smith who served in the Republican administration of President George H. W. Bush and currently works as a consulting producer on *Scandal*. Paradoxically, lead actress Kerry Washington was a staunch supporter of the Obama administration.

A SCANDAL-OUS CONCLUSION? UNDERSTANDING PROFESSIONAL IDENTITY THROUGH TELEVISION

Robin Redmon Wright and Jennifer A. Sandlin wrote, "Television viewing, in particular, is an increasingly ubiquitous space of cultural consumption, as television audiences consume, decode, and make meaning of the cultural texts presented through this medium."[25] Interrogating these programs through the lens of the circuit of culture reveals important aspects of the constructed public relations professional. We view these programs as cultural products encoded with meaning that audiences use to formulate their identities. Media texts can and do influence identity by reinforcing social status.[26]

We can offer preliminary insights about the moment of regulation by situating these programs within the popular media landscape. Production in the US entertainment media environment is beholden to its economic and social realities. A business driven by ratings and return on investment relies on financial backing from advertisers to maintain studio support.[27] Thus, production of *Scandal* and *Ray Donovan* can only continue if they maintain profitable business models. Program producers function as gatekeepers for fictional narratives, helping to shape viewers' understanding of the real world. Given their broad appeal, it is unfortunate that *Scandal* and *Ray Donovan* promote a lifestyle of money, power, intrigue, and lasciviousness that is unattainable for the majority of viewers and that cannot be reconciled with the realities of current professional life.

INSIGHTS FOR EDUCATORS

Media portrayals inform the meaning people ascribe to the public relations profession. According to Melvin L. DeFleur and Sandra Ball-Rokeach: "It may be possible to mediate the conduct of individuals as they derive definitions of appropriate behavior and belief from suggested interpretations communicated to them."[28] These images and representations can form as a socialization mechanism of what students and future professionals believe is the correct way of doing public relations and being a practitioner.

What does this mean for educators who are teaching strategic communication and public relations students who aspire to have careers similar to Olivia Pope and Ray Donovan? Public relations educators are uniquely qualified to utilize media representations of public relations as a powerful teaching tool. Inaccurate representations can negatively affect public relations by influencing how society views the profession, thus perpetuating erroneous assumptions.[29] Shannon A. Bowen argued that student expectations related to public relations as a career are influenced by interpersonal interactions (e.g., meeting and emulating influential student leaders) or mass media.[30] Robina Xavier, Amisha Mehta, and Ingrid Larkin confirmed that mass media influenced Australian students' understanding about the public relations profession, which could have had deleterious effects on the number of students enrolling in the area of study: "Despite the often negative portrayal of public relations in the mass media, students were still selecting the courses; however, many other students are probably being deterred from taking up this profession."[31] These authors confirmed Bowen's findings that students were more interested in publicity and event coordination/management "as both these areas have tangible outcomes and are often represented in media portrayals of public relations."

A strategy that professors can use to critically dissect these mediated portrayals could be connecting the past to the present. At least one industry trade publication has called for the media to present our profession in a positive light.[32] Nowadays, misrepresentations of public relations have become popular topics for industry blog posts. Although recent representations of public relations professionals as "fixers" would appear to be new portrayals, these images date back to the beginnings of the public relations origin story. In the history of public relations, two names inevitably rise to the top: Ivy Lee and Edward Bernays. A former newspaper man, Lee gained notoriety as he helped fix the problems of companies like Standard Oil and the Pennsylvania Railroad; Bernays attempted to fix the declining sales of cigarette makers by popularizing their product's use by women in his "Torches of Freedom" march. As these forefathers of public relations sought to improve client reputations by changing public opinion, it should come as no surprise that today's popular fictional stories contain a kernel of truth from our past.[33]

NOTES

1. Carol Ames, "PR Goes to the Movies: The Image of Public Relations Improves from 1996 to 2008," *Public Relations Review* 36 (2010): 164–70. doi: 10.1016/j.pubrev.2009.08.016.
2. Ames, "PR Goes to Movies," Kate Fitch, "Promoting the Vampire Rights Amendment: Public Relations, Postfeminism and True Blood," *Public Relations Review* 41 (2014): 607–14. doi:10.1016/j.pubrev.2014.02.029. Jane Johnston, "Girls on Screen: How Film and Television Depict Women in Public Relations," *PRism* 7 (2010): www.prismjournal.org; Emily Kinsky and Coy Callison, "PR in the News: How a Sample of Network Newscasts Framed Public Relations," *Public Relations Journal* 3 (2009): 1–17; Lambert, Cheryl A. and White, Candace, "Feminization of the Film? Occupational Roles of Public Relations Characters in Movies," *Public Relations Journal* 6 (2012); Mordecai Lee, "The Image of the Government Flack: Movie Depictions of Public Relations in Public Administration," *Public Relations Review* 27 (2001): 297–315. doi: 10.1016/S0363-8111(01)00088-1; Mordecai Lee, "Flicks of Government Flacks: The Sequel," *Public Relations Review* 35 (2009): 159–61. doi:10.1016/j.pubrev.2008.09.017; Karen S. Miller, "Public Relations in Film and Fiction: 1930–1995," *Journal of Public Relations Research* 11 (1999): 3–28. doi: 10.1207/s1532754xjprr1101_0; Joe Saltzman, "The Image of the Public Relations Practitioner in Movies and Television, 1901–2011," *The IJPC Journal* 3 (2012): 1–50; Youngmin Yoon and Heather Black, "Learning about Public Relations from Television: How is the Profession Portrayed?" *Communication Science* 28 (2011): 85–106.
3. Miller, "Public Relations Film Fiction," 23.
4. Fitch, "Promoting the Vampire Rights," 608.
5. Paul du Gay, et al., *Doing Cultural Studies: The Story of the Sony Walkman* (London: Sage, 2013), xix; Stuart Hall, Jessica Evans, and Sean Nixon, eds., *Representation* (London: Sage, 2013), xviii.
6. Björn Bollhöfer, "'Screenscapes': Placing TV Series in their Contexts of Production, Meaning and Consumption," *Tijdschrift Voor Economische en Sociale Geografie* 98 (2007): 165–75. doi: 10.1111/j.1467-9663.2007.00389.x.
7. Horace Newcomb and Paul M. Hirsch, "Television as a Cultural Forum," *Quarterly Review of Film Studies*, Summer (1983): 561–573. doi: 10.1080/10509208309361170.
8. Barry Dornfeld, *Producing Public Television, Producing Public Culture* (Princeton, NJ: Princeton University Press, 1998), 16.
9. Hall, Evans, and Nixon, "Representation," xxi.
10. Stuart Hall, *Media and Cultural Regulation,*(London: Sage, 1997) 208.
11. Tanzina Vega, "A Show Makes Friends and History: 'Scandal' on ABC Is Breaking Barriers," *The New York Times*, January 6, 2013, www.nytimes.com/2013/01/17/arts/television/scandal-on-abc-is-breaking-barriers.html?_r=0.
12. Vega, "A Show Makes Friends."
13. Dornfeld, *Producing Public Television*, 16.
14. Lambert and White "Feminization of the film."
15. Hall, Evans, and Nixon, "Representation," 1.
16. Christopher Hitchens, "Ohio's Odd Numbers," *Vanity Fair*, March, 2005, www.vanityfair.com/news/2005/03/hitchens200503.
17. "Public Relations Society of America (PRSA) Member Code of Ethics," *Public Relations Society of America*, accessed February 6, 2016, www.prsa.org/AboutPRSA/Ethics/CodeEnglish/index.html#.VrZ-OfldUuc.

18. Anna Everett, "Scandalicious: *Scandal,* Social Media, and Shonda Rhimes' Auteurist Juggernaut," *The Black Scholar* 45 (2015): 34–43. doi: 10.1080/00064246.2014.997602. Willa Paskin, "Network TV is Broken. So How Does Shonda Rhimes Keep Making hits?" *The New York Times Magazine,* May 9, 2013, www.nytimes.com/2013/05/12/magazine/shonda-rhimes.html?ref=magazine&_r=0&pagewanted=all.

19. K. Maja Krakowiak and Mina Tsay-Vogel, "What Makes Characters' Bad Behavior Acceptable? The Effects of Character Motivation and Outcome on Perception, Character Liking, and Moral Disengagement," *Mass Communication and Society* 16 (2013): 179–99. doi: 10.1080/15205436.2012.690926.

20. Arthur A. Raney, "Expanding Disposition Theory: Reconsidering Character Liking, Moral Evaluations, and Enjoyment," *Communication Theory* 14 (2004): 348–69. doi: 10.1111/j.1468-2885.2004.tb00319.x.

21. Ames, "PR Goes to the Movies," 169, Lee, "Flicks of Government Flacks," 161, Miller, "Public Relations Film Fiction," 14–15, and Saltzman, "The Image of the Public Relations Practitioner," 15 and 35.

22. Beth Braun, "The X-Files and Buffy the Vampire Slayer: The Ambiguity of Evil in Supernatural Representations," *Journal of Popular Film and Television* 28 (2000): 88–94. doi: 10.1080/01956050009602827.

23. Ruud Kaulingsfreks, Geoff Lightfoot, and Hugo Letiche, "The Man in the Black Hat," *Culture and Organization* 15 (2009): 151–65.

24. Allison Samuels, "Black Women Seize Center Stage at Last," *The Daily Beast,* July 17, 2013, www.thedailybeast.com/articles/2013/07/17/black-women-seize-center-stage-at-last.html.

25. Michael Pickering, *Research Methods for Cultural Studies* (Edinburgh, UK: Edinburgh University Press, 2008), 22. Amanda N. Edgar, "R&B Rhetoric and Victim-Blaming Discourses: Exploring the Popular Press's Revision of Rihanna's Contextual Agency," *Women's Studies in Communication* 37 (2014): 138–58 offers a compelling example of US television employing cultural identity to re-construct a social narrative.

26. Bollhöfer, "'Screenscapes,'" 167.

27. Robin Redmon Wright and Jennifer A. Sandlin, "You are What You Eat!?: Television Cooking Shows, Consumption, and Lifestyle Practices as Adult Learning," (May 28, 2009). *Adult Education Research Conference.* Paper 70, newprairiepress.org/aerc/2009/papers/70. Wright and Sandlin.

28. Willa Paskin, "Network TV is Broken," *The New York Times Magazine,* May 9, 2013, www.nytimes.com/2013/05/12/magazine/shonda-rhimes.html?ref=magazine&_r=0&pagewanted=all; William M. Kunz, "Prime-Time Television Program Ownership in a Post-Fin/Syn World," *Journal of Broadcasting & Electronic Media* 53 (2009): 636–51. doi: 10.1080/08838150903327181.

29. Melvin L. DeFleur and Sandra Ball-Rokeach, *Theories of Mass Communication* (New York, NY: Pearson, 1989.)

30. Lambert and White, "Feminization of the Film."

31. Shannon A. Bowen, "'I Thought It Would Be More Glamorous': Preconceptions and Misconceptions among Students in the Public Relations Principles Course," *Public Relations Review* 29 (2003): 199–214. doi:10.1016/S0363-8111(03)00012-2.

32. Shannon A. Bowen, "All Glamour, no Substance? How Public Relations Majors and Potential Majors in an Exemplar Program View the Industry and Function," *Public Relations Review* 35 (2009): 402–10. doi:10.1016/j.pubrev.2009.05.018.

33. Robina Xavier, Amisha Mehta, and Ingrid Larkin, "Destination Public Relations: Understanding the Sources that Influence Course Selection for and Career Preferences of Postgraduate Students," *PRism* 5, nos.1and 2 (2007/8): praxis.massey.ac.nz/prism_on-line_journ.html.

NINE

Critical Rhetoric and Popular Culture

Examining Rhetoric's Relationship to the Popular

Art Herbig

Aboard, about, above . . . I remember them all too well. They are words of context. Merriam-Webster tells us that a preposition is "a word or group of words that is used with a noun, pronoun, or noun phrase to show direction, location, or time, or to introduce an object."[1] Prepositional phrases often offer specificity, such as the rhetoric of Abraham Lincoln or rhetoric in the Lyceum Movement. These phrasings suggest a voice or a context for rhetoric that implores further exploration and critical attention. So, it is not inconsequential when we find "Rhetoric of Popular Culture" courses in university catalogues throughout the nation (including mine).[2] It is worth considering the implications of the most prominent textbook about rhetoric and popular culture in our field being titled *Rhetoric in Popular Culture.*[3] The words "of" and "in" in these instances suggest a relationship between rhetoric and popular culture. However, for critical rhetoric, the examination must begin with, Why a preposition at all? Answering that question is my objective in this chapter.

When we discuss the "Rhetoric of Popular Culture" or "Rhetoric in Popular Culture," we suggest popular culture has a voice or is a context for rhetoric. "Rhetoric of Popular Culture" treats popular culture as if it speaks and creates. It has its own rhetoric, as it were. Rhetoric in Popular Culture seems to insinuate that rhetoric is a dimension of popular culture as if there are dimensions of popular culture that exist without rhetorical implications. Building on the works of Michel Foucault,[4] Raymie E. McKerrow,[5] and Michael Calvin McGee,[6] I would like to suggest a new formulation for the relationship of popular culture and the study of rhetoric: Popular Culture is Rhetoric.

To understand my position, I must begin with my understanding of contemporary research in rhetoric. While describing "Research in Rhetoric," McKerrow makes a salient point:

> In one sense, nothing is "rhetorical" until it is given meaning. It is not the case that death, in and of itself, is rhetorical. It is not the case that what we call a painting is, in and of itself, rhetorical. Death is death; a painting is composed of watercolors or oils with varying texture or strokes culminating in an image. What is rhetorical is how we respond to death, or a painting—the use we make of it in giving it meaning or significance.[7]

Not all of culture is rhetoric, but popular culture is culture's discursive form. Understanding popular culture this way distinguishes popular culture from culture based on the idea that the word "popular" suggests that people are attempting to create and manage meanings of the many different forms culture can take. For example, Kim Kardashian can exist in the world without being popular culture, while a discursive *Kim Kardashian* becomes a centerpiece for discussions about gender, wealth, and reality.

In recent years, scholars have taken a variety of approaches to defining popular culture. According to Alexander Buhmann, Lea Hellmueller, and Louis Bosshart, "defining and systematically putting a finger on the somewhat opaque phenomenon of popular culture may cause some difficulty."[8] John Fiske defined popular culture in opposition to the dominant.[9] Lawrence Grossberg depicts it as "a sphere in which people struggle over reality and their place in it."[10] According to Bob Batchelor, it is "the connections that form between individuals and objects."[11] Henry Jenkins sees, in the emergence of new media, a return to a grassroots version of the popular.[12] While attempting to "rethink popular culture," Chandra Mukerji and Michael Schudson suggest that the term "refers to the beliefs and practices, and the objects through which they are organized, that are widely shared among a population."[13] The tensions of mass versus public or high versus low can still be seen in some of these definitions, but what crosses all of them is the belief that the popular is a means for expression and sensemaking. So, for rhetoric scholars, why not treat popular culture as an ever evolving and changing discourse formation spanning endless other formations in the tradition of Michel Foucault? A rock is just a rock until it is a pet rock. It is through its rhetorical expression that it enters the popular.

According to Lisa Silvestri, rhetoric scholars have already been moving toward the study of discourse in line with Foucault.[14] Building on the work of Michael Calvin McGee in combination with Foucault, Silvestri argues that discourse "represents ways of constituting knowledge, together with the social practices, forms of subjectivity, and power relations that inhere in such knowledge(s) and the relations between them."[15] Silvestri goes on to point out that this shift toward McGee and Foucault coincides with the expansion of media into just about every dimension of our lives. Similarly, Mary Stuckey recently began to theorize the idea of rhetorical "circulation" based on the work of McGee.[16] The work in that special edition of *Rhetoric & Public Affairs* focused on how everything from sound bites to images can evolve and change through discourse.[17] As polymediation has become part of our communicative landscape,[18] we have begun to realize that we need better tools to manage the multitude of messages that enter our lives. Critical rhetoric is uniquely placed at the crux of this problem. Studying meaning is the unique skillset for which a rhetorician is trained. The ways in which people can and are making meaning using popular culture is a natural fit.

In this chapter, I would like to reconsider the notion that, for critical rhetoric, popular culture can be approached as something that has a voice (rhetoric of popular culture) or a location where rhetoric can be found (rhetoric in popular culture) and embrace the fundamentally rhetorical nature of popular culture. In order to do so, I would like to begin with a discussion of the relationship between critical rhetoric and popular culture. Then I will move to how the impulses of the critical rhetorician can be applied in popular contexts. Ultimately, we have reached a period of time where critics should not simply attempt to study rhetoric "in" or "of" popular culture. The tools for the dissemination of rhetoric have made it possible for critics to operate inside popular culture as well.

CRITICAL RHETORIC AS DISCOURSE INSIDE POPULAR CULTURE

To be frank, much of what I am arguing for is not entirely new. In 2004, David Zarefsky wrote an article based on the work of the Alliance of Rhetoric Societies where he argues for a need for a "Public Face of Rhetoric."[19] As part of that goal, he noted that rhetoricians should "respond to public issues and promote productive exchanges of ideas and participation in public discourse" as well as advocate for a website that would "profile rhetorical scholars who are actively engaged in the public interest." I concur with the group's appraisal that rhetorical scholars need to do more to reach out and promote their scholarship; however, what I am advocating for is not just about finding alternative places for traditional scholarship. What I would like rhetorical scholars to discover is the power in the rhetorical form of popular culture and create scholarship in those forms. Critical rhetoric's potential rests on the impulse to exist *inside* the discourses it seeks to critique. That type of scholarship needs to move beyond questions of what to when, why, and how.

In his foundational discussion of "Critical Rhetoric: Theory and Praxis," Raymie McKerrow argues that in the tradition of Foucault's notion of permanent criticism one of the goals of critical rhetoric is "to unmask or demystify the discourse of power."[20] As I discussed above, if we are to believe scholars such as Fiske, Grossberg, and Jenkins, then popular culture is a space for intersecting discourses about power. It would seem that the two were made for each other. However, the complicating factor in much of the scholarship of critical rhetoricians exists outside of what most would consider popular forms of dissemination. Therefore, the forms it takes and its outlets for dissemination diminish the power of critical rhetoric's perspectives on power. This disconnect alienates critical rhetoric from the audiences that would benefit from its insights.

With this in mind, of eight principles outlined by McKerrow in his article defining critical rhetoric, for me the eighth is probably the most important and the most revolutionary: "Criticism is a performance."[21] In connection with this perspective, Michael Calvin McGee wrote:

> Critical rhetoric does not begin with a finished text in need of interpretation; rather texts are understood to be larger than the apparently finished discourse that presents itself as transparent. The apparently finished discourse is in fact a dense reconstruction of all the bits of other discourses from which it is made.[22]

Whether they are discussed as moments, fragments, events, or texts, what is fundamental to this type of approach is that objects of analysis are never fixed in meaning. In fact, by making them an object of analysis, they are changed. Take, for instance, a once kitschy, low-rated vampire television program named *Buffy the Vampire Slayer*. One cannot avoid how the lasting impact of that program has been shaped, in part, by the scholarly attention it has received.[23] The intersecting discourses in which *Buffy the Vampire Slayer* has become intertwined make the discursive existence of that program every bit as compelling as its individual episodes. So, why has so much of the research on *Buffy* been confined to academic books and scholarly journal articles?

If popular culture is rhetoric and critical rhetoric aims to participate in the discourses that it seeks to critique, then it is time for critics to expand what it means to critique popular culture. According to McKerrow, "the reversal of 'public address' to 'discourse which addresses publics' places the critic in the role of 'inventor.'"[24] That level of invention is more than what can be accomplished in just a journal article or in a book chapter. We need to be training critics in a variety of rhetorical tools and forms of dissemination. We need to be creating spaces where we engage one another outside conference room walls. Modern media have created spaces where discourse is possible and it is time to use those spaces as something more than just a text in need of distanced critique. In the case of *Buffy the Vampire Slayer*, where are the critical commentary tracks recorded like directors' commentaries? Where are the online critical roundtables like podcasts?

We need to learn from popular culture as well as learn about popular culture. According to Jason Mittell,[25] the storytelling in the serial narratives of contemporary television is enthralling audiences. Audio podcasts such as *Serial* merge journalism with narrative to capture imaginations. Documentaries with critical positions and high production values such as *Happy Valley* take on issues close to academics while also inspiring critical thought and action. Now, I realize the irony of advocating this position inside of an academic book. It almost seems disingenuous. So, let me address that point for a moment. I am not advocating for an end to academic publishing in books or journal articles. In fact, I think a move toward more public acts of criticism and dissemination can help to resolve one of the major tensions in research on rhetoric. In recent years, I have been around many a rhetorical scholar who has bemoaned the amount of publications that address methodological issues and the lack of actual criticism. The fact is, turning to our colleagues in order to discuss method or theory is exactly the right audience for those conversations. Those are academic conversations that allow us to reflect on the critical enterprise and hone our critical lenses. The audiences for conversations about method and theory read journals such as *The Quarterly Journal of Speech*. Since we have cultivated that audience, we need to find venues for criticism where we can reach other audiences and use tools other than the word processor. For instance, Dean Scheibel encourages students to create their own "comic reflections" on communication research with the goal of allowing students to "experience new insights and make a deeper connection with the course material".[26] This student assignment might allow for those types of connections, but what is to prevent a scholar from creating comics as a means for distributing certain kinds of research findings like those that are sometimes found in medicine?[27] In order to do so we must first think about the issues that need to be addressed in order for us to do this type of work.

Maybe the most complex dimension of popular culture research is time. There was a period of time in which a two-year peer-review period for an academic journal article might have been appropriate for publishing thoughts and insights about a film or cultural issue, but we now live in a time where we accept that cultural events, discourses, and texts have almost instantaneously shifting meanings. Even before the Internet was fully embraced as a home for mass information dissemination and social networking, McGee wrote that

> scholars are analysts at heart, but nothing in our new environment is complete enough, finished enough, to analyze—and the fragments that present themselves to us do not stand long enough to analyze. They fly by so quickly that by the time you grasp the problem at stake, you seem to be dealing with yesterday's news, a puzzle that solved itself by disappearing.[28]

It would be easy to agree with McGee and hope that the world will open back up to academic time, but what McGee is not around to witness is the ways in which the very media that caused his concern have opened up new opportunities for scholarship and new platforms for criticism.

Academics now find themselves in a world of competing times. The first is academic time. Academic time is purposefully slow and reflective. It asks that authors, reviewers, editors, and scholars negotiate both time and process in order to produce cultural commentary and scholarship that fully acknowledge the scope and implications of the arguments it makes. Then, there is the kind of time that we operate in every day. Breaking news, zeitgeist cultural moments, and instant response to events are part of this kind of time. The key to our relationship with time is that we recognize both and adapt when necessary.

One of the masters of this kind of scholarship is Henry Jenkins. On top of being one of the leading thinkers about media of his time,[29] Jenkins engages audiences with his *Confessions of an Aca-Fan* blog.[30] One important dimension of *Confessions of an Aca-Fan* is that it is not just an archive of the musings of a scholar. Jenkins takes on timely issues as well as academic concerns. He challenges his audiences to challenge him. He blends academic insight with fan appreciation. Jenkins is able to manage the complexities of theory and method in books such as *Convergence Culture* and *Spreadable Media*, while also confronting topical issues and bringing important critical insights to his blog. However, while it is not unlike him to include a trailer or clip to help serve his point, Jenkins is still operating in the world of written language.

Central to the practice of critical rhetoric in the study of popular culture is to introduce material consistent with the discourses in popular culture. For instance, CarrieLynn D. Reinhard and Christopher Olson have attempted to manage multiple spaces. Reinhard and Olson coedited *Making Sense of Cinema: Empirical Studies into Film Spectators and Spectatorship*.[31] On top of that form of traditional publication, they also co-host a podcast—*The Pop Culture Lens*—that "look[s] back at the media of yesterday through the lens of today in order to determine if it has any relevance to the contemporary experience. We structure the podcast so that the format loosely resembles an academic paper, but one that everyone can understand."[32] Their podcast is unique in that it follows the mode of distribution being used by other culture commentators such as *The Nerdist* and National Public Radio's *Pop Culture Happy Hour*.[33] The Podcast is a unique format that blends radio with episodic storytelling in ways that harken back to the original days of radio as well as providing an accessible form of commentary that anyone can download straight to their phone.

Nonfiction media are not the only way in which scholars can reach out to new audiences. Patricia Leavy has written fiction books, such as *Low-Fat Love* and *Blue*,[34] that address issues related to popular culture. In an interview for *Blue*, Leavy described her rationale for the project: "I wanted to show how we use pop culture and art to help us understand and get through our own lives. I think we can understand our lives, things we can't yet even name, through art."[35] Leavy's recognition of how scholars can participate in popular culture with work that reflects their critical positions and storytelling touches on important critical and methodological issues. Fundamentally, it beckons a question that has been confronted by performance and autoethnographic scholars for a long time: what constitutes scholarship? Leavy's work shows that participation comes in many forms and the space for that type of work must be seen as an integral branch of public scholarship moving forward.

We can learn from the study of popular culture and that learning can be put to use in creating scholarship for those outside of academia. If we are to believe myself and Andrew F. Herrmann,[36] then we are arriving to this conversation at a very important time in history. Joseph Campbell has documented how storytelling and mythologizing has remained remarkably consistent throughout the span of human history;[37] but, as Walter J. Ong theorized, our interactions with media have the power to fundamentally alter our understandings of the world.[38] The rise of transmedia contexts has brought about the polymediated narrative. These are narratives driven by world-building and discourse, not necessarily characters. If critical rhetoric is to respond, it will need to examine the relationship between distribution, discourse, and narrative.

For me, this conversation is not an idle musing. On top of my work on projects such as this book, I have been engaged in trying to incorporate film and online media into the practice of critical rhetoric. Under the guise of what myself and Aaron Hess discussed as convergent critical rhetoric,[39] I also directed a film entitled *Never Forget: Public Memory & 9/11*.[40] Alongside Alix Watson and Aaron Hess, we built from our research interests in public memory to try to connect the issues raised by those who study memory with audiences outside of academe. We also built a production Facebook page that became an outlet for discourse and updates about the project.[41] With the film, we found a way to take those ideas to film festivals in Seattle, Louisville, and Paris while also interacting with audiences in subsequent question-and-answer sessions. As part of the experience, I conducted interviews with academics for what I have lovingly called my "visual literature review." In those interviews, I pushed the scholars to explain their ideas to people who knew nothing about memory as well as those who had clear ideas about history. This film was for someone who had not read Marita Sturken,[42] James E. Young,[43] or Barbie Zelizer.[44] With the Facebook page, we gave audiences a glimpse into the crafting of scholarship complete with pictures and videos. It is designed as scholarship in the grammar of popular culture.

Given that I have only directed two film projects as part of my academic work, I cannot claim to have extensive experience in the area.

However, in reflecting on the work I have done so far, there have been some important lessons I have been able to glean from that work. First and foremost, what I have learned is that doing this kind of work is not an either/or proposition; instead it is a both/and. The beginnings of doing this type of work have been building for years. Scholars in visual rhetoric have been teaching us about the powerful language of the camera.[45] We have learned the power of sound, music, and auditory stimulation.[46] We have studied the integration of text with images and audio. We see rhetoric out in the world and study it in the field. We know the capacity of light and shadow to shape character and create complexity. What we had not been acknowledging was that we were learning all of these things in order to incorporate them into our own works.

Also, what might be the biggest obstacle to this type of scholarship is what I consider to be one of its biggest strengths: it requires collaboration. As the credits role on your favorite film, you will notice that more than one name appears. Projects like the ones I am proposing are often not the product of a single author toiling away in front of a computer screen; but instead they are a product of several people putting skills to work in order to complete something greater than its individual parts. For instance, Dr. Lynn Harter teamed up with filmmaker Evan Shaw to create films that have explored the role of art in a variety of contexts.[47] Beyond just film and scholarship, in the coming years I hope to expand upon these ideas and explore new polymediated contexts. I hope others will join me.

GRAB A CAMERA, A MICROPHONE, ANIMATE, FIND A NEW WAY

Ultimately, critical rhetoric embraces the notion that what is produced by the rhetorician should be critiqued, commented on, and considered alongside of the materials upon which he or she comments. This is not to say that we no longer need the next David Zarefsky to study Lincoln or a budding Karlyn Kohrs Campbell to bring us insight into the rhetoric of women's suffrage—we do! What we also need to do is train critics who can take the work of Zarefsky and Campbell and bring it to life in a new medium and for different audiences. Open access journals such as *The Journal of Contemporary Rhetoric* and new formats such as *In Media Res* have given scholars new timelines and venues for their writing. However, these new spaces are still places of "media literacy." The problem is that media literacy treats people as "audiences," "consumers," or "readers" of the content produced by others. If we are going to break that mentality, we will also need to break it for ourselves.

As part of a reflection on the contiguous relationship between rhetoric and performance, Phillip Wander outlined the fundamental paradox critics face:

Now it is true that academic work sometimes thingifies, objectifies, and even silences its subjects. Moreover, professional notions of purpose sometimes devolve into scrambles for job security and obsessions with academic hierarchies and opportunities for moving up. But, and this is the point, academic work can also roll the rock back from the front of the cave to reveal something vital, liminal, and hopeful—even in dark times. Consider the words "critic," "performer," and "theorist." I ask myself who I am and who I am not, what this text is saying and what it is not, who is part of my audience and who is not, and how I perform my text in relation to different audiences. When what lurks in the shadows of a text is made visible and/or audible, when we get a feel for what is being said, it adds new and sometimes surprising dimensions to who we are and what we ought to be doing.[48]

Like Wander, McKerrow argued that criticism is practice. It is fundamentally performative. Pointing back to Foucault, McKerrow points to an important distinction in this process: "Foucault believes it is more important to raise questions than to locate and privilege final answers."[49] Critical rhetoric does not occupy a privileged position where the critics possess answers to culture's critical questions; instead we come from educated positions in order to bring complexity and depth to issues that seemingly avoid the complications that they imply. According to Foucault, "as soon as one questions that unity, it loses its self-evidence; it indicates itself, constructs itself, only on the basis of a complex field of discourse."[50] We need to be involved in the creation, critique, re-creation, and re-critique process if we are to fully understand modern discourse in all of its forms.

Be it camera angles, Foley audio, or the positioning of the racks in a department store, rhetoric is all around us. Therefore, the study of rhetoric must continue to explore ways to study film that does not reduce an interaction between characters into a few lines from a script and continue to expand the study of a Macy's in ways that incorporate field observations. For many familiar with critical approaches to popular culture, these ideas are not new. In fact, there are great examples of scholars who have incorporated field methods into their work or have layered their textual analyses with deep descriptions of the many facets of mediated texts.[51] These areas are growing, but there is more to do to reach beyond the academic audience.

The next step in this evolution is to change the medium. This is not a change that transplants old techniques into new formats such as a MOOC or a Blog. My recommendation is about taking our focus away from the twenty-five-page essay from time to time in order to produce a series of three-minute short films that can be posted, reposted, liked, favorited, commented on, and responded to. Reaching out to audiences in the polymediated age is about more than just action, it is interaction.

Let us also avoid the idea that speaking to popular audiences represents a "dumbing down" or "dilution of the rigor" of research. Those of us who study rhetoric are aware that crafting content differently does not belie the rigor that went into its execution. In fact, finding a give and take where audiences could be introduced to academic conceptions of words such as "hegemony," "polyvalence," and "gender" could benefit public conceptions of communication research as well as those with which we interact. In a time where education, and especially liberal arts, are under attack,[52] it would be to our benefit to bridge the divide between these audiences.

Rhetoric is not "in" popular culture like a vegetable in a grocery store ready to be plucked out and examined. Rhetoric is not "of" popular culture as if popular culture was an actor with a unified voice. Popular culture is rhetoric, in all of its forms and through all of its media. This volume embraces the idea that popular culture can act as a binding force that brings people together through their ability to share and reflect on communication as well as a divisive force that alienates and obscures. Given that importance of popular culture, there has never been a time where rhetoric and criticism have been more relevant. Studying and critiquing the content of communication in popular contexts and through popular distribution is important. Teaching others to do the same is equally as important. Speaking *with* audiences instead of *at* or *around* popular audiences will be the next prepositional challenge we have to face.

NOTES

1. "Preposition," *Merriam-Webster*, accessed December 8, 2015, www.merriam-webster.com/dictionary/preposition.

2. There are actually two Rhetoric of Popular Culture courses at my institution: one in Communication and one in English. "Com 44001: Rhetoric of Popular Culture," Indiana University—Purdue University, Fort Wayne, accessed December 5, 2015, bulletin.ipfw.edu/preview_course_nopop.php?catoid=33&coid=91536. "English & Linguistics @ IPFW," Indiana University—Purdue University, Fort Wayne, accessed December 5, 2015, www.ipfw.edu/dotAsset/271152.pdf.

3. Barry Brummett, *Rhetoric in Popular Culture*, 4th ed. (Los Angeles: Sage Publications, 2015).

4. Michel Foucault, *The Archaeology of Knowledge & the Discourse on Language*, trans. A. M. Sheridan Smith (New York: Pantheon Books, 1972).

5. Raymie E. McKerrow, "Critical Rhetoric: Theory & Praxis," *Communication Monographs* 56, no. 2 (1989): 91–111. doi: 10.1080/03637758909390253; Raymie E. McKerrow, "Critical Rhetoric in a Postmodern World," *Quarterly Journal of Speech* 77, no. 1 (1991): 75–8. doi: 10.1080/00335639109383945; Raymie E. McKerrow, "Critical Rhetoric and the Possibility of the Subject," in *The Critical Turn: Rhetoric and Philosophy in Postmodern Discourse*, eds. Ian Angus and Lenore Langsdorf (Carbondale, IL: Southern Illinois University Press, 1993): 51–67; Raymie E. McKerrow and Jeffrey St. John, "Critical Rhetoric and Continual Critique," in *Rhetorical Criticism: Perspectives in Action*, ed. Jim A. Kuypers (Lanham, MD: Lexington Books, 2009); Raymie E. McKerrow, "Research in Rhetoric: A Glance at our Recent Past, Present, and Potential Future," *The*

Review of Communication 10, no. 3 (2010): 197–210. doi: 10.1080/15358590903536478; Raymie E. McKerrow, "Foucault's Relationship to Rhetoric," *The Review of Communication* 11, no. 4 (2011): 253–271. doi: 10.1080/15358593.2011.602103; Raymie E. McKerrow, "Criticism is as Criticism Does," *Western Journal of Communication* 77, no. 5 (2013): 546–549. doi: 10.1080/10570314.2013.799284; Raymie E. McKerrow, "'Research in Rhetoric' Revisited," *Quarterly Journal of Speech* 101, no. 1 (2015): 155. doi: 10.1080/15358590903536478.

6. Michael Calvin McGee, "Text, Context, and the Fragmentation of Contemporary Culture," *Western Journal of Speech Communication* 54, no. 3 (1990). doi: 10.1080/10570319009374343.

7. McKerrow, "'Research in Rhetoric,'" 155.

8. Alexander Buhmann, Lea Hellmueller, and Louis Bosshart, "Popular Culture and Communication Practice," *Communication Research Trends* 34, no. 3 (2015): 6.

9. John Fiske, *Understanding Popular Culture*, 2nd ed. (London: Routledge, 2010): 35–39.

10. Lawrence Grossberg, *Dancing in Spite of Myself: Essays on Popular Culture* (Durham, NC: Duke University Press, 1997): 2.

11. Bob Batchelor, "Editorial: What Is Pop Culture?," *Popular Culture Studies Journal* 1, no. 1 (2013): 1.

12. Henry Jenkins, *Convergence Culture: Where Old and New Media Collide* (New York: New York University Press, 2006): 135–137.

13. Chandra Mukerji and Michael Schudson, "Introduction: Rethinking Popular Culture," in *Rethinking Popular Culture: Contemporary Perspectives in Cultural Studies*, ed. Chandra Mukerji and Michael Schudson (Berkeley: University of California Press, 1991): 3.

14. Lisa Silvestri, "A Rhetorical Forecast," *The Review of Communication* 13, no. 2 (2013). doi: 10.1080/15358593.2013.789121.

15. Silvestri, "A Rhetorical Forecast," 130.

16. Mary Stuckey, "On Rhetorical Circulation," *Rhetoric & Public Affairs* 15, no. 4 (2012).

17. Megyn Foley, "Sound Bites: Rethinking the Circulation of Speech from Fragment to Fetish," *Rhetoric & Public Affairs* 15, no. 4 (2012); Sean Patrick O'Rourke, "Circulation and Noncirculation of Photographic Texts in the Civil Rights Movement: A Case Study of the Rhetoric of Control," *Rhetoric & Public Affairs* 15, no. 4 (2012).

18. Adam W. Tyma, Andrew F. Herrmann, & Art Herbig, "Introduction: The Beginnings: #WeNeedaWord," in *Beyond New Media: Discourse and Critique in a Polymediated Age*, eds. Art Herbig, Andrew F. Herrmann, and Adam W. Tyma (Lanham, MD: Lexington, 2015): xix-xx.

19. David Zarefsky, "Institutional and Social Goals for Rhetoric," *Rhetoric Society Quarterly* 34, no. 3 (2004), 36–37.

20. McKerrow, "Critical Rhetoric: Theory and Praxis," 91.

21. McKerrow, "Critical Rhetoric: Theory and Praxis," 108.

22. McGee, "Text, Context, and the Fragmentation," 279.

23. For instance, one only has to access the online journal *Slayage: The Journal of Whedon Studies* (www.whedonstudies.tv/slayage-the-journal-of-whedon-studies.html) to access a treasure trove of *Buffy*-related scholarship.

24. McKerrow, "Critical Rhetoric: Theory and Praxis," 101.

25. Jason Mittell, *Complex TV: The Poetics of Contemporary Television Storytelling* (New York, NY: New York University Press, 2015).

26. Jennifer Masunaga, "Comic Reflections on Academic Work," *LMU/LA Library News*, November 5, 2014, lmulibrary.typepad.com/lmu-library-news/2014/11/comic-reflections-on-academic-work.html.

27. See *Graphic Medicine*, accessed June 10, 2016, www.graphicmedicine.org/.

28. McGee, "Text, Context, and the Fragmentation," 286–287.

29. Jenkins has a lengthy C.V. and has published across a number of contexts including fandom, technology, and content analysis. Two of his most prominent works

are: Jenkins, *Convergence Culture*; Henry Jenkins, Sam Ford, and Joshua Green, *Spreadable Media: Creating Value and Meaning in a Networked Culture* (New York: New York University Press, 2013).

30. Beyond his academic publications, Jenkins writes extensively in his own blog: Henry Jenkins, *Confessions of an Aca-Fan: The Official Weblog of Henry Jenkins* (blog), December 22, 2015, henryjenkins.org/.

31. CarrieLynn D. Reinhard and Christopher J. Olson, eds., *Making Sense of Cinema: Empirical Studies into Film Spectators and Spectatorship* (New York: Bloomsbury Academic, 2016).

32. Christopher J. Olson and CarrieLynn D. Reinhard, "About the Podcast," *The Pop Culture Lens* (podcast), January 5, 2016, thepopculturelens.podbean.com/p/about-the-podcast/.

33. Chris Hardwick and a Many Headed Beast, *The Nerdist* (blog), January 5, 2016, nerdist.com; Linda Holmes, ed., "Pop Culture Happy Hour (podcast)," *Monkey See: Pop-Culture News and Analysis from NPR* (blog), *NPR*, January 5, 2016, www.npr.org/sections/monkeysee/129472378/pop-culture-happy-hour/.

34. Patricia Leavy, *Low-Fat Love* (Netherlands: Sense Publishers, 2011); Particia Leavy, *Blue* (Netherlands: Sense Publishers, 2015).

35. "An Intimate Interview with Author Patricia Leavy about her New Novel Blue," by Robyn Hussa Farrell, *WeAretheRealDeal.com*, November 2, 2015, wearetherealdeal.com/2015/11/02/an-intimate-interview-with-author-patricia-leavy-about-her-new-novel-blue/, para. 12.

36. Art Herbig and Andrew F. Herrmann, "Polymediated Narrative: The Case of the Supernatural Episode 'Fan Fiction,'" *International Journal of Communication* (2016),

37. Joseph Campbell, *The Hero with a Thousand Faces*, commemorative ed. (1949; Princeton, NJ: Princeton University Press, 2004).

38. Walter J. Ong, *Orality and Literacy: The Technologizing of the Word* (1982; London: Routledge, 2001).

39. Art Herbig and Aaron Hess, "Convergent Critical Rhetoric at the 'Rally to Restore Sanity': Exploring the Intersection of Rhetoric, Ethnography, and Documentary Production," *Communication Studies* 63, no. 3 (2012): 269–289, doi:10.1080/10510974.2012.674617.

40. Art Herbig, Alix Watson, and Aaron Hess, *Never Forget: Public Memory & 9/11*, Film, directed by Art Herbig (2015; Fort Wayne, IN: Living Text Productions).

41. LivingText Productions' Facebook Page, accessed June 10, 2016, www.facebook.com/LivingText/.

42. Marita Sturken, *Tangled Memories: The Vietnam War, The AIDS Epidemic, and the Politics of Remembering* (Berkeley, CA: University of California Press, 1997); Marita Sturken, *Tourists of History: Memory, Kitsch, and Consumerism from Oklahoma City to Ground Zero* (Durham, NC: Duke University Press, 2007).

43. James E. Young, *The Texture of Memory: Holocaust Memorials and Meaning* (New Haven, CT: Yale University Press, 1993); James E. Young, *At Memory's Edge: After-Images of the Holocaust in Contemporary Art and Architecture* (New Haven, CT: Yale University Press, 2000).

44. Barbie Zelizer, *Remembering to Forget: Holocaust Memory through the Camera's Eye* (Chicago, IL: University of Chicago Press, 2000); Barbie Zelizer, "Reading the Past Against the Grain: The Shape of Memory Studies," *Critical Studies in Mass Communication* 12, no. 2 (1995), doi:10.1080/15295039509366932.

45. For example, Robert Hariman and John Louis Lucaites, *No Caption Needed: Iconic Photographs, Public Culture, and Liberal Democracy* (Chicago, IL: University of Chicago Press, 2007); Cara A. Finnegan, *Picturing Poverty: Print Culture and FSA Photographs* (Washington, DC: Smithsonian Books, 2003).

46. For example, Greg Goodale, *Sonic Persuasion: Reading Sound in the Recorded Age* (Urbana, IL: University of Illinois Press, 2011).

47. Tom Hodson, "Documentary Filmmakers Discuss the Making of 'Creative Abundance'" *WOUB*, September 8, 2015, woub.org/2015/09/08/documentary-filmmakers-discuss-making-creative-abundance/.

48. Phillip Wander, "Contiguous Fields of Study," *Text and Performance Quarterly* 34, no. 1 (2014), doi: 10.1080/10462937.2013.848465.

49. Raymie McKerrow, "Foucault's Relationship," 262.

50. Foucault, *The Archaeology of Knowledge*, 23.

51. For examples of rhetorical fieldwork, consult Michael Middleton, Aaron Hess, Danielle Endres, and Samantha Senda-Cook, *Participatory Critical Rhetoric: Theoretical and Methodological Foundations for Studying Rhetoric in Situ* (Lanham, MD: Lexington Books, 2015); Sara L. McKinnon, Robert Asen, Karma R. Chávez, and Robert Glenn Howard, *Text + Field: Innovations in Rhetorical Method* (University Park, PN: Penn State University Press, 2016). For examples of alternative layers of criticism, consult Steven C. Combs, *The Dao of Rhetoric* (New York: SUNY Press, 2005).

52. See Fareed Zakaria, *In Defense of a Liberal Education* (New York, NY: W. W. Norton, 2015); Kirstin R. Wilcox, "How to Advocate for the Liberal Arts: The State-University Edition," *The Chronicle of Higher Education*, June 8, 2015, chronicle.com/article/How-to-Advocate-for-the/230743/; Beckie Supiano, "How Liberal-Arts Majors Fare Over the Long Haul," *The Chronicle of Higher Education*, January 22, 2014, chronicle.com/article/How-Liberal-Arts-Majors-Fare/144133/.

TEN

"Prison is Bullshit"

An Intersectional Analysis of
Popular Culture Representations of
the Prison Industrial Complex
in Orange is the New Black

Michelle Kelsey Kearl

At the time of this writing, *Orange is the New Black (OITNB)* has been signed for three more seasons as a Netflix original series.[1] The show's premise is likely familiar to readers: white, middle-upper class, hetero-normative, young, and attractive Piper Chapman is charged with felony money laundering and drug trafficking after delivering a suitcase full of drug money 10 years previous to her conviction. The trajectory of the first season follows Piper's unlikely prison stay as she encounters and becomes accustomed to the daily routine of prison. As season two and three developed, Piper's role becomes increasingly peripheral in the show. Indeed, this was the subversive goal of the show's creator Jenji Kohan when she pitched the series to television executives; Piper was to be a Trojan horse wherein the stories and representations of women of color could materialize in the consciousness of the show's predominately white audience.[2]

Set in a prison and about relationships negotiated in prison, prison itself is a significant structural/institutional force in the show. Like Piper, the Prison Industrial Complex (PIC) is not simply a fictitious character confined to the show's script. Instead, the unique complexity of the show is its "based in real life" ethos. All told, *OITNB* takes a version of reality,

Piper Kerman's memoirs and the prison system, and builds around it a fictionalized world.[3] And while audiences may well understand the show is a mix of fiction and reality, we might rightfully be more critical of the presentation of those stories, characters, and structures that help fuel the material reality of the PIC. The materiality of the PIC is undeniable and its existence is persistently buttressed with cultural narratives that manifest our collective authorization of the project itself; it is quintessentially hegemonic.[4] How, then, does the show represent the prison industrial complex? And, in what ways are these representations empowering or disempowering for people of color? This chapter proceeds with an explanation of the PIC, then charts an intersectional analysis of *OITNB*, and finishes with conclusions and implications.

THE PRISON INDUSTRIAL COMPLEX AND POPULAR CULTURE

The rapid, exponential growth of the prison industrial complex cannot be understated. In 1972, 200,000 people were imprisoned in the United States today, upward of 2.2 million people are imprisoned with an additional 4.7 million people on parole or under surveillance.[5] Of course, nothing about the PIC is inevitable; instead, legal, economic, and cultural forces fuel its power.[6]

Legally, the PIC was set into motion through the combination of public interests and private industry, a relationship that dates back to 1973 with the introduction of the Rockefeller drug laws creating mandatory minimums for drug crimes in New York.[7] Richard Nixon's declaration of a war on drugs, perpetuated by most presidents since, encouraged national adjustments on mandatory minimums, three strikes laws, and other sentencing practices that had the direct effective of incarcerating more people for longer sentences.[8] In the 1980s alone the Comprehensive Crime Control Act, the Anti-Drug Abuse Act, the Omnibus Drug Bill, and the Immigration Reform and Control Act were all passed with the additional mandatory minimums for nonviolent offenses.[9]

With state prisons already over-populated and underfunded and a public uninterested in financing new prisons, the private prison industry emerged to pick up the slack. They also reassured the public that a putative model of punishment would continue to depress crime and increase incarceration rates.[10] This meant that, to sustain itself, the PIC must necessarily fail at reducing crime in order to fuel its own demand for prisoners. The PIC works because of the cycle of crime that it helps institutionalize that keeps people incarcerated longer, moves them far from the kinship and social networks that might reduce recidivism, and releases them after long prison stays with no meaningful way of reentering society.[11] The PIC, then, through this cycle of incarceration, teaches people *to become* prisoners.

The mass incarceration of black men has traditionally consumed public discourse around the PIC. Black women, too, have shouldered the burden of the PIC. The imprisonment of women jumped by over 800 percent since 1997, two thirds of whom are women of color.[12] African American women in particular are incarcerated at three times the rates of white women.[13] The conditions that precipitate the disproportionate incarceration of women of color are the same social and economic conditions that keep some people of color cycling through the PIC. Racism, generations of poverty, the school to prison pipeline, over policing in black neighborhoods, racial profiling, and police violence perpetuate social conditions of black alienation.[14] The mass incarceration of people of color is not inevitable; indeed, the direct, purposeful result of the war on drugs was the isolation of black populations.

While the fear of criminality remains a part of the cultural imaginary, social interest in the material conditions of prisons and prisoners is marginal at best. The act of imprisonment itself encourages public disinterest in prisons—we put people "away" and hope that they will return "better." Political and cultural narratives encourage contradictory understandings of the prison context. On the one hand, prisoners can find rehabilitation in prison, learn from their mistakes, and reenter society after their time is served; while, on the other hand, the conditions in prison are often idealized as too good. Prisoners have access to privileges many free people do not, making their time in prison comforting, not rehabilitative.[15] Private prisons are purposefully constructed out of sight and out of mind of the public where they can take advantage of depressed economic conditions in rural locations while also trimming the perceived luxuries and privileges of state facilities.[16] Although private prisons appear to be an economic boon, they effectively marginalize perceptions of prison contexts, and treatment of prisoners specifically.

Culturally, representations of the PIC have largely depicted "individual stories of crime, victimization, and punishment, and the stories are typically told from the point of view of law enforcement," effectively suggesting that the legal system works because guilty people are convicted and imprisoned.[17] Indeed, the resolution of heightened fears and anxieties of crime must be realized through the proper capturing and punishment of wrongdoers.[18] These representations also guarantee "that issues of class bias and institutional racism in the criminal justice system are never raised, much less addressed. Prisons *are* because they exist."[19] Serial crime dramas thus perpetuate a sense of continued incarceration. At each episode's conclusion, there is always the promise of a new crime, with a new criminal who warrants incarceration. In this way, television representations of crime function as a microcosm of the troubling realities of a PIC that disproportionately intrudes on the material experiences of people of color.

INTERSECTIONALITY

Kimberlé Crenshaw's development of intersectionality as a black feminist
theory that centers the lived experiences of women of color provides an
apt basis for understanding the PIC as it is represented in *OITNB*.[20] Crenshaw found constraining systems of power in the enactment of affirma-
tive action policies that specifically excluded black women in hiring practices. To lodge a legal complaint, black women were forced to file as
women or as African American; but could not file as African American
women, ensuring that regardless of how they articulated themselves to
the court, they would lose. Crenshaw also recognized the radical potential of intersectionality to explain legal and social situations, as well as
how women of color were, and continue to be, constrained by both racism and sexism demonstrated in popular culture representations.[21]
Building on Crenshaw's work, Bonnie Thornton Dill and Ruth E. Zambrana take an intersectional approach to popular culture because "representations of groups and individuals in [popular] cultural forms create
and sustain ideologies of group and individual inferiority/superiority
and support the use of these factors to explain both individual and group
behavior."[22] Intersectionality offers nuanced critiques of popular culture
representations as they organize the material experiences of women of
color.

Intersectional studies can take up representations of difference as they
materialize in a single character or a type of character, how difference is
taken up in several different characters, or interpret the context of difference in an entire show.[23] According to Michaela de Meyer, "intersectional representation" is how a show treats difference across characters and
plot lines.[24] Regardless of how a critic discusses popular culture, Patricia
Hill Collins calls for four interventions in the methodological application
of intersectionality. First, scholars must place the lived experience of marginalized people at the starting point of study. Second, interrogating
complexities of identity cannot edge into essentialism. Third, scholars
must make explicit the relations of power structuring oppression. Fourth,
and finally, we must always engage in a critical praxis—linking research
and activism to close gaps between the academy and social change.[25]
Working from an understanding of discourses of power as both constraining and productive, the analysis proceeds through the assumption
that the representations in *OITNB* exercise power in ways we might both
and simultaneously celebrate and criticize.[26]

I argue that an intersectional approach provides a nuanced way to
study how *OITNB* encourages audiences to be critical of the private prison industry, while failing to condemn the foundations upon which the
PIC operates. Thus, although audiences can support the critical perspective of the show's condemnation of the PIC's economic exploitation, they
are allowed to remain unmoved by the systemic racism, biased and vio-

lent policing, and differential sentencing practices that feed the demand of the industry. Through this intersectional critique, I can examine how representations on *OITNB* challenge viewers' passive acquiescence to the PIC's structural and economic force while it simultaneously defers critical challenges to social narratives of criminality, and may, in effect, reinforce audiences' normative assumptions about the justness of the justice system more broadly.

ANALYSIS

In its third season, the writers of *OITNB* developed a clear critique of the PIC by introducing Management & Correction Corporation (MCC) as a savior from the imminent closing of Litchfield prison. The storyline of the conversion from a state institution to a private prison is rightfully negative—MCC is exclusively profit driven, with a concealed, but no less clear, top-down hierarchy of decision making that is removed from the prison context, and is free of any long-term commitment to or interests in the well-being of prisoners. Indeed, within two episodes of MCC's takeover, Danny, MCC's "man-on-the-ground," is reminded by his Senior Vice President father that their investors "will not be around long enough" to be responsible for the violation of inmates' rights.[27]

MCC comes complete with neoliberal benefits that encourage its approval. MCC contracts with an expensive lingerie company, Whispers, to provide higher wages for the inmates' labor. Despite the wage increases, Whispers stands to benefit most from the agreement. In the cafeteria, Piper narrates the benefits of prison labor in describing her new job to her girlfriend Alex. Understanding the disparity between the retail price of the underwear and the women's wages, Piper suggests "it's basically slave labor."[28] To which another inmate, Cindy, adds, "technically, it's more like indentured servitude."[29] Underlining the exploitative nature of Whispers is much needed and helps demonstrate the exploitation of prison labor broadly.

The exploitation of labor is also illustrated among the prison's correctional officers (COs). Under MCC, all COs must be rehired. The company then cuts their hours, while also hiring inexperienced COs at lower wages and without benefits. As the veteran guards develop an awareness of the trajectory of this economic relationship, they work toward unionization, and in the final episode go on strike. Danny, to save time and money, after just fifteen minutes of deescalation and self-defense training, assigns each new guard to a veteran and calls it an apprenticeship.[30] Unsurprisingly, the new COs are quick to escalate conflict instead of curb it, abuse their power over the women through sexual violence and rape, negligently refuse to protect particularly vulnerable inmates, and generally misunderstand the prison process.[31] There is shockingly little oversight of the new COs who are given weapons, power, and the authorization, but no training, to exercise force over the women of Litchfield.

Other unethical cost-saving strategies of MCC include new contracts with food vendors. The prison ships in mass quantities of low quality bagged foods.[32] Requests for new books in the library, particularly legal texts to help inmates work on their cases, and job training are plainly rejected.[33] The final episode of season three rounds out a reality of private prisons. Litchfield becomes home to two busloads of new inmates. As the audience sees the women file into the prison, the camera cuts to newly constructed bunks that double their sleep capacity.[34] The criticism of the economics of the PIC is clear, striking, welcomed, and appropriately pitched but, as I will illustrate, neglects the social and political forces that structure and perpetuate the PIC. This show participates in neoliberal fantasies and discourses that conceal the raced, classed, and gendered oppressions of the PIC betraying the intersectional potential Kohan promises.

Consistent with neoliberal discourses of the PIC, particularly in popular culture, the women in *OITNB* are presumably justifiably incarcerated.[35] There is, to date, no discussion of wrongful convictions, biased or violent policing, or differential sentencing leading to a character finding herself in prison. *OITNB* uses dramatized flashbacks to give the immediate context to each character's crime, confirming in each case the character to be guilty of a punishable crime—justifying her prison stay. For some characters, the flashbacks reveal an entirely different context for their crimes than the character lets on; yet still, they confirm guilt. The flashbacks approach intersectional experiences of poverty, racism, domestic abuse, unemployment, addiction, lack of educational opportunity, and/or mental illness; however, these issues are not cast as systemic intersectional inequalities constraining freedom that the PIC exploits to populate prisons. Instead, audiences witness the uniqueness of each woman's situation and the individual choice each made to land in prison. When systemic inequalities are articulated, they do not fuel a critique of the racist foundations of the PIC.

The scripting of YaVonne (Vee) Parker and Tasha (Taystee) Jefferson's relationship demonstrates the undermining of the political and cultural operation of the PIC. Taystee grows up in foster care and by the age of 16 is in a juvenile prison; she has "been in institutions [her] whole life."[36] While Taystee is desperate for a family, she attempts to survive in a group home while working at a fast food restaurant, but eventually, and for unexplained reasons, approaches Vee for a job.[37] When Taystee suggests that this is not her "forever career," Vee retorts, "Girl, you're from this hood, you don't get a career, you get a job. This is the best paying job around."[38] This flashback pits Taystee's math skills and social, cultural knowledge against the temptation of Vee's family structure. In this way, the systemic problems associated with fleeting educational opportunities, poverty, abusive or violent group homes, experiences in the foster system, and over-policing in black neighborhoods is emptied of its systemic operation and individualized through the highlighting of a series of choices made by both Vee and Taystee.

Efforts are made to construct "the system" as interfering in the lives of the black women; however, these are often deferred to individual choice as well. Most pointedly, when RJ, Vee's adopted son dies at the hands of a cop, she comforts Taystee who is clearly upset about her brother's death. Taystee complains that nothing will be done because RJ's murderer was a cop. Vee responds, "They claimed he was armed, I don't know, baby, maybe he was. I told him to not carry a piece. A black man walking around the city at night." [39] This appears, on its face, to edge toward a critical understanding of racist policing. It is not until ten episodes later that viewers learn that Vee orchestrated the murder. She teams with a corrupt cop who finds RJ walking to a store at night, tosses him a gun, and then shoots him. There are two troubling implications here. First, Vee's response to Taystee suggests that RJ would have been somehow *more* guilty if he were carrying a weapon. Second, the combined discourse of Vee's explanation to Taystee and the realization that Vee is responsible for the murder takes the material conditions under which many black men and women are murdered, and refuses to critique racist policing and casts suspicion on the lived experience of profiling and uses of deadly force.

Taystee's release and subsequent return to Litchfield demonstrates to some extent the reality of the PIC in the lives of black women serving time. Upon her return Taystee details the parole expectations on "the outside" including strict curfews, relentless job searching and interviews, concluding "at least in prison you get dinner." [40] Poussey challenges Taystee's choice to return to prison but Taystee persists:

> Minimum wage is some kind of joke. I got a part time working at Pizza Hut and I still owe the prison $900 in fees I gotta pay back. I ain't got no place to stay. . . . Everyone I know is poor, in jail, or gone . . . and I got fucked up in the head ya know. I know how to play it here, where to be and what rules to follow. [41]

This exchange is heartfelt and difficult to watch in its palpable desperation. Systems of poverty and disconnectedness are charted here in compelling ways. The exchange makes clear that prisons cannot sufficiently address the social and cultural conditions that alienate people as they reenter society. With a felony record and no marketable skills, as well as Taystee's lack of access to a social support system, the show represents, in part, the reality of some released women, particularly of those imprisoned by private facilities far from their families. [42] While Taystee is not geographically dislocated, she nonetheless finds no support outside of prison. This view of the transition back into society helps to explain, at least in part, high rates of recidivism among felons.[43] Taystee's reentry suggests the PIC has taught her how *to be* a prisoner.

While "the system" figures as the formative institution in Taystee's childhood despite (or perhaps motivating) her strong desire for a family structure, *OITNB* drains the racist forces of foster care, lack of educational opportunity, and cycles of poverty by emphasizing individual choice related to Taystee joining Vee's "family" and Vee's relationship with corrupt police. Audiences, then, could just as easily read the corrupt police officer as an apparition to be cast out of the narrative of good police keeping communities safe and Taystee as so desperate for a family that she chooses a life with Vee over the hard work of getting out of "the system." In either case, the audience is focused on the individual instead of the institutional forces that influence and limit the available options for individual freedom.

In addition to lacking a precise interrogation of systemic racism and biased and violent policing, *OITNB* is largely evasive on differential sentencing and rehabilitation practices.[44] The audience is privy to the sentencing of Piper.[45] Beyond Piper, there are few instances where audiences might gain an understanding of the sentencing structure of the prison. Audiences know, for example, that Chapman is serving fifteen months. Morello tells Piper she has thirty-four months.[46] Poussey is two years into a six-year sentence.[47] Gloria has been in prison for two and a half years, with no indication of how long she has left.[48] With over twenty different characters, the silence around sentencing prevents the disparities related to mandatory minimums for drug offenses as well as racial disparities that structure the lived experiences of the women in prison to emerge.

In reality, sentencing is a measure by which the PIC can be exposed for its institutional racism. African American women, on average, spend over four months longer in sentences than white women for the same crimes and for violent crimes their sentences can be up to 33 percent longer.[49] Any number of systemic failures in the criminal justice system impact the means by which people of color are charged with more serious crimes, given longer sentences, and generally assigned to more violent prisons including "law enforcement arrest decisions, prosecutorial charging practices, indigent defense representation, presentence investigation procedures" among other practices including the disproportionate benefits whites receive for providing information or making a plea deal.[50]

While the evasion of unjust sentencing practices is a missed opportunity to engage a more enduring critique of the PIC, I argue that the representation of Piper as realizing prison as a space for self-actualization further distances the audience from a racialized understanding of the PIC. Neoliberal discourses of the space of prison encourage audiences to see it as an opportunity for self-reflection, growth, reform, and a temporary time. One of the implicit comforts of the show, particularly for white audiences, is Piper's short, only fifteen-month sentence, the temporality of which is consistently emphasized.[51] While Piper is indeed guilty of a punishable crime, the ways in which she reflects on her time in prison is distinct from other prisoners. Piper expresses self-reflection, growth, and rehabilitation. In the first season, Piper has an often studied moment with her mother Carol.[52] Some argue that this scene is meant as a comedic relief to Piper's mother's scapegoating of Alex for Piper's crime. Carol is engaged in a clear attempt to distance herself, primarily, and her daughter, secondarily, from the prison context. Piper resists these attempts: "I am in here because I am no different from anyone else in here. I made bad choices. I committed a crime. And being here is no one's fault, but my own."[53] Carol, clearly unwilling to hear Piper, quips, "Sweetheart, you're nothing like any of these women. . . . Darling, you're a debutant."[54] Reading this scene as enabling audiences to see how privilege crosses class and race lines in the PIC is plausible in the context of season one.[55] However, given the development of the three seasons, I argue here for a different reading. If the audience is to take Piper seriously, there are at least two troubling implications. First, the crimes for which all of the women have been convicted are free of biased policing and arrest practices in communities of color, a set of circumstances that fly in the face of material reality.[56] Second, this positionality defers an understanding of how race and class coalesce to create the conditions under which "bad choices" are made. To see Piper as "no different from anyone else" in the prison is to refuse the raced, gendered, and classed foundations of the PIC.

For women of color in particular accessing the narrative of rehabilitation is near impossible. Cycles of poverty, drug and alcohol addiction, mental illness, unaddressed trauma from sexual violence, and much more overwhelmingly drive the incarceration of African American women; these conditions are virtually ignored in deference to "a prevailing attitude . . . : [that] it serves them right" to be incarcerated, re-centering the marginal status of prisoners and bolstering discourses of individual choice.[57] Because of these social and economic conditions, combined with targeted policing of black communities, as well as the violence and victimization incarcerated black women are more likely to experience, it is no accident that the narratives of rehabilitation do not imagine a black subject.

Ultimately, Piper's perspective is inaccessible to Taystee whose relationship to the PIC necessarily prevents a story of rehabilitation precisely because of the intersectional power lines that crisscross her lived experience. To imagine rehabilitation already rejects the social and cultural conditions that propagate cycles of incarceration to begin with. Taystee, in contradistinction to Piper, ultimately finds prison a predictable, reliable home, while Piper's race and class privilege allow her to imagine prison as a temporal space in which she has found herself. Taystee's experience of prison is constrained by the presence of the PIC throughout her life, however unarticulated by the show. This does not suggest the inevitability of crime or criminality, but demands a more nuanced understanding of the material inequalities that delimit the lives the women in the story can experience.

The logics of the PIC are cemented in *OITNB* at the expense of intersectional understanding of how people of color have become the demand side of the private prison industry, a demand met by systemic racism, biased policing, differential sentencing, and narratives of rehabilitation. *OITNB* laudably humanizes the lives of its women characters, bringing their stories into the homes of millions of Americans and many more people abroad, and features perhaps more people of color in an assembled cast than most other television shows. The show also facilitates much needed criticism of the economic structures of the PIC palatable to contemporary cultural criticism of unrestrained, amoral accumulation of wealth at the expense of treating people humanely; particularly since the 2008 recession, cultural conversations about the trouble of unrestrained free-market capitalism have found wider, more accepting audiences. This critique is perhaps enough to encourage audiences to be reflexive about the economy of the PIC—but the critique does not go far enough to speak to the social and legal foundations that filled the demand for private prisons. Perhaps more dangerously, the show's participation in neoliberal discourses of individual choice, rehabilitation, and the justness of the characters' incarceration justify the perception of the justness of incarceration as a social practice.

Jenji Kohan has, to some extent, made good on her promise to bring to life the stories of women of color that audiences might not otherwise welcome. Given the centrality of the PIC to *OITNB*, it is important to insist that Piper's character acts as the Trojan horse she was meant to be. Critiques of the PIC do not simply stop at the economic problematics. This limited critique offered by *OITNB* does not challenge the show's white viewers to approach or internalize the racial disparities in surveillance, arrests, and sentencing and rehabilitation of people of color. Clear from the analysis above, Piper's whiteness and class privilege frequently mark a unique experience with the criminal justice system that is simply not afforded to characters of color. Intersectionality reveals how women of color populate the fictional landscape of Litchfield with their imprisonment always already justified. At the expense of a truly radically challenging critique of the PIC, *OITNB* settles for a more palatable economic criticism of private prisons, the wealthy that profit from them, and the political wrangling that manages them with disinterest in the material realities and lived experiences that produced them.

OITNB remains an important popular culture location for intersectional analyses. Future intersectional analyses could take a different tack and focus more specifically on the experiences of several characters as they intersect a host of identities. For example, Suzanne, Bennett, and Tiffany are characters whose mental or physical disability intersects with their race, class, or gender to produce complex discourses about and around each that should be of interest to scholars of communication and popular culture alike. With the promise of three new seasons, surely by publication of this chapter more potential areas of intersectional criticism will emerge.

Following the guidelines charted by Patricia Hill Collins, the intersectional analysis here demonstrates the complex matrix of power and identity as they work through the PIC. Paying close attention to the lived experiences of people of color in relationship to the PIC helps reveal the economic focus of *OITNB*'s criticism. The departure from the ideologies that structure the PIC, and to a significant degree the relationship between some African American communities and the state, refuses the realities of racial profiling, over policing, and disproportionate arrests and sentencing practices that construct an essentialized view of black criminality and violence. While this criticism may seem strident, the memoirs and characters upon which *OITNB* is built are real people: Piper Kerman articulates herself as a prison reform activist, and Kohan herself underscores the importance of the show in connecting audiences to diverse representations. If Michelle Alexander is right that the PIC is the new Jim Crow, the mechanisms by which the PIC can exercise power, accumulate wealth, and perpetuate itself deserves a nuanced, intersectional representation.[58] Popular culture is not dislocated from the praxis; indeed, despite the fictional nature of television and other forms of popular culture, they "carry in disguise certain thoughts, attitudes, or political and social convictions" that we must use to make decisions "with serious outcomes for ourselves and others."[59]

NOTES

1. Kwame Opam, "Orange is the New Black is Getting Three More Seasons," *The Verge*, last accessed February 8, www.theverge.com/2016/2/5/10922190/orange-is-the-new-black-netflix-three-season-renewal.

2. "'Orange' Creator Jenji Kohan: 'Piper Was My Trojan Horse'" *Fresh Air,* First broadcast on August 13, 2013 by National Pubic Radio, directed by Terry Gross.

3. Piper Kerman, *Orange is the New Black: My Year in a Women's Prison* (New York: Spiegel & Grau, 2011).

4. Antonio Gramsci, Selections from *The Prison Notebooks of Antonio Gramsci* (New York: International Publishers, 1995, copyright 1971), 337.

5. Nicole D. Porter, "The State of Sentencing 2015: Developments in Policy and Practice," *The Sentencing Project*, last accessed January 16, 2016, sentencingproject.org/doc/publications/State-of-Sentencing-2015.pdf.

6. David Ladipo, "The Rise of America's Prison Industrial Complex" *New Left Review*, 7 (2001), 110.

7. Vanessa Barker, *The Politics of Imprisonment: How the Democratic Process Shapes the Way America Punishes Offenders* (New York: Oxford University Press, 2009), 151. Eric Schlosser, "The Prison-Industrial Complex" *The Atlantic,* December 1998, last accessed February 16, 2016: www.theatlantic.com/magazine/archive/1998/12/the-prison-industrial-complex/304669/.

8. Ibid.

9. Ladipo, "The Rise of America's Prison Industrial Complex," 115.

10. Ibid., 112.

11. Marc Mauer, *Race to Incarcerate* (New York: The New Press, 1999), 11; Silja J. A. Talvi, "On the Inside with the American Correctional Association," in *Prison Profiteers: Who Makes Money from Mass Incarceration,* ed. Tara Herival and Paul Wright (New York: The New Press, 2007).

12. Lenora Lapidus, Namita Luthra, Anjuli Verma, Deborah Small, Patricia Allard, and Kirsten Levingston, "Caught in the Net: The Impact of Drug Policies on Women and Families," American Civil Liberties Union, 2005, last accessed March 27, 2016, www.aclu.org/files/images/asset_upload_file431_23513.pdf.

13. Ibid.

14. Ibid.

15. Paul Wright, "The Cultural Commodification of Prisons" *Social Justice, 27,* no. 3 (2000), 15–21.

16. Ibid.

17. Michelle Alexander, *The New Jim Crow: Mass Incarceration in the Age of Colorblindness* (New York: The New Press, 2012), 59.

18. Ibid.

19. Wright, "The Cultural Commodification of Prisons," 20; Aurora Wallace, "Better Here Than There: Prison Narratives in Reality" In Charles J. Ogletree, Jr. and Austin Sarat, *Punishment in Popular Culture* (New York: New York University Press, 2015).

20. Kimberlé Crenshaw, "Mapping the Margins: Intersectionality, Identity Politics, and Violence Against Women of Color," *Stanford Law Review 43,* no. 6 (1991): 1241–1299.

21. Kimberlé Crenshaw, "Demarginalizing the intersection of race and sex: A black feminist critique of antidiscrimination doctrine, feminist theory and antiracist politics." University of Chicago Legal Forum (1989), 139.

22. Bonnie Thornton Dill and Ruth Enid Zambrana, *Emerging Intersections: Race, Class, and Gender in Theory* (New Brunswick, New Jersey: Rutgers University Press, 2009).

23. Michaela D. E. Meyer, "'I'm Just Trying to Find My Way Like Most Kids': Bisexuality, Adolescence and the Drama of *One Tree Hill,*" *Sexuality and Culture,* 13 (2009); Becca Cragin, "Beyond the feminine: Intersectionality and hybridity in talk shows," *Women's Studies in Communication,* 33, no. 2 (2010); Michaela D. E. Meyer, "The 'Other' Woman in Contemporary Television Drama: Analyzing Intersectional Representation on *Bones,*" *Sexuality & Culture,* 19, no. 4 (2015); Danielle M. Stern, "It Takes a Classless, Heteronormative Utopian Village: Gilmore Girls and the Problem of Postfeminism," *The Communication Review* 15 (2012).

24. Michaela D. E. Meyer, "The 'Other' Woman in Contemporary Television Drama: Analyzing Intersectional Represenation on *Bones*" *Sexuality & Culture,* 19, no. 4 (2015)

25. Patricia Hill Collins, *Black Feminist Thought: Knowledge, Consciousness, and the Politics of Empowerment* (New York: Routledge, 2000).

26. Raymie E. McKerrow, "Critical Rhetoric: Theory and Praxis," *Communication Monographs* 56 (1989): 91–111.

27. "Fear and Other Smells," *Orange is the New Black,* first broadcast June 11, 2015, by Netflix, directed by Mark Burly and written by Nick Jones.

28. "Ching Chang Chong," *Orange is the New Black,* first broadcast June 11, 2015, by Netflix, directed by Anthony Hemingway, and written by Sara Hess.

29. Ibid.

30. "Tongue Tied," *Orange is the New Black*, first broadcast June 11, 2015, by Netflix, directed by Julie Anne Robinson, and written by Sian Heder.

31. "A Tittin' and a Harin'," *Orange is the New Black*, first broadcast June 11, 2015, by Netflix, directed by Jesse Peretz, and written by Lauren Morelli; "Don't Make Me Come Back There," *Orange is the New Black*, first broadcast June 11, 2015, by Netflix, directed by Uta Briesewitz, and written by Sara Hess; "We Can Be Heroes," *Orange is the New Black*, first broadcast June 11, 2015, by Netflix, directed by Phil Abraham and written by Sian Heder.

32. "Tongue Tied."

33. "Fear and Other Smells."

34. "Trust No Bitch," *Orange is the New Black*, first broadcast June 11, 2015, by Netflix, directed by Phil Abraham and written by Jim Danger Gray.

35. Rose M. Brewer and Nancy A. Heitzeg, "The Racialization of Crime and Punishment: Criminal Justice, Color-Blind Racism, and the Political Economy of the Prison Industrial Complex," *American Behavioral Scientist* 51, no. 5 (2008), 625–644.

36. "Fucksgiving," *Orange is the New Black*, first broadcast July 11, 2013, by Netflix, directed by Michael Trim and written by Sian Heder.

37. "Looks Blue, Tastes Red," *Orange is the New Black*, first broadcast June 6, 2014, by Netflix, directed by Michael Trim and written by Jenji Kohan.

38. Ibid.

39. Ibid.

40. "Fool Me Once," *Orange is the New Black*, first broadcast June 6, 2014, by Netflix, directed by Andrew McCarthy and written by Sara Hess.

41. Ibid.

42. Michelle Alexander, *The New Jim Crow*, 230.

43. Brewer and Heitzeg, "The Racialization of Crime," 637.

44. Johanna Christian and Shenique S. Thomas, "Examining the intersections of race, gender, and mass imprisonment, *Journal of Ethnicity in Criminal Justice,* 7 (2009), 72–73.

45. Piper explains to Healy in "I Wasn't Ready" that she pleads to a lesser charge to avoid the mandatory minimums during trial. Healy makes a gesture toward unjust sentencing standards: "I got a crack dealer who is doing 9 months and then I have a lady who accidentally backed into a mailman who is doing four years. I just don't get it." The crack dealer has no subjectivity outside of her trade, which is coded as black and deserves a tougher sentence than the, presumably white, "lady" who was simply mistaken. Healy at once indexes a problem in the criminal justice system, affirms traditional sentencing practices of the PIC, and through his inflection solidifies racial stereotypes.

46. "I Wasn't Ready."

47. "Fool Me Once."

48. "Mother's Day," *Orange is the New Black*, first broadcast June 11, 2015, by Netflix, directed by Andrew McCarthy and written by Jenji Kohan.

49. The Sentencing Project, "Women in the Justice System: Briefing Sheet," 2007, last accessed March 29, 2016, www.sentencingproject.org/doc/publications/womenincj_total.pdf.

50. Tushar Kansal, "Racial Disparity in Sentencing: A Review of the Literature," The sentencing Project, 2005, last accessed March 29, 2016 www.sentencingproject.org/doc/publications/rd_sentencing_review.pdf.

51. While the series' first episode uses temporality as a comfort to Piper's character, and, I argue, the audience, there are a host of notations of Piper's short sentence throughout the series. See episodes: "I wasn't ready," "Lesbian Request Denied," "Mother's Day," "Fucksgiving," "Tongue Tied."

52. Suzanne M. Enck and Megan E. Morrissey, "If *Orange is the New Black*, I Must Be Color Blind: Comic Framing of Post-Racism in the Prison-Industrial Complex," *Critical Studies in Media Communication*, 32, no. 5 (2015).

53. "WAC Pack," *Orange is the New Black*, first broadcast July 11, 2013, by Netflix, directed by Micheal Trim and written by Lauren Morelli.

54. Ibid.

55. Enck and Morrissey, "If *Orange is the New Black*," 5–7.

56. Michelle Alexander, *The New Jim Crow*.

57. Alicia R. Isaac, Lettie L. Lockhart, and Larry Williams, "Violence Against African American Women in Prisons and Jails," *Journal of Human Behavior in the Social Environment*, 4, no. 1–3, 150.

58. Michelle Alexander, *The New Jim Crow*.

59. Barry Brummett, *Uncovering Hidden Rhetorics: Social Issues in Disguise* (Thousand Oaks, CA: Sage Publishing, 2008), 1.

ELEVEN

Polymediating the Post

Reclaiming Feminism in Popular Culture

Danielle M. Stern and Krista J. Catalfamo

Mirca Madianou and Daniel Miller define polymedia as "an emerging environment of communicative opportunities that functions as an 'integrated structure' within which each individual medium is defined in relational terms in the context of other media."[1] Adam Tyma, Andrew F. Herrmann and Art Herbig expand this definition to signify the various forms media take in the current era, as well as the many types of interactions that occupy those forms.[2] According to Michelle Calka, polymediation is a product and process of identity performance that is ubiquitous, shape-shifting in its authorship, simultaneously fragmented and merged, and both divisive and communal.[3] Danielle Stern and Chelsea Henderson applied this idea to feminist activism via the polymediated platforms of the Representation Project, which they found allowed for both formal and informal organizing around feminist gathering spaces online and offline.[4] Their interviews with young women who practiced feminism on the various Representation Project polymediated platforms demonstrated a convergence of ideas, conversations, and commitments to a unified cause. However, how might conventions articulated by young women actively identifying as feminists operate in similar spaces but also resist a totalizing movement identity?

In a polymediated environment that fostered the emergence of collective feminist action via #NotBuyingIt, #MissRep, and #YesAllWomen, a backlash was bound to follow. Enter Women Against Feminism (WAF), a Tumblr blog that began July 3, 2013, with a photo of a young, conventionally attractive, white woman holding a handwritten note that read, "This is what an anti-feminist looks like."[5] The note closed with a smiley face and has generated thousands of posts on the WAF Tumblr. The majority of posts provide more of the same as that initial image: selfies of young women from their computers or in front of mirrors with handwritten notes explaining why they do not need feminism, how feminism has hurt men, or how the feminist movement clings to victimhood and therefore makes women's lives worse. The Tumblr account assures protection of the anonymity of sources who submit a photo, a screenshot of an online conversation, or a snarky statement superimposed over celebrity images. According to a BBC report, the content curator also maintains her own anonymity online for fear of online bullying by feminists.[6]

A Facebook account associated with the WAF Tumblr account—but providing no individual identity markers—was created January 3, 2014, with a note titled, "Why I Am Against Feminism" and a photo of a white woman with red hair, red lips, and lined eyelids holding a note that read, "As a woman in the Western world, I am not oppressed, and neither are you." The Facebook account garnered more than 31,000 likes as of July 2015. But not until *The Guardian* published a widely read article about the anti-feminist movement (that did not specifically mention WAF) by feminist activist and journalist Jessica Valenti on July 7, 2014, did the WAF backlash pick up social media steam.[7] On July 8, the #WomenAgainst-Feminism hashtag appeared on Twitter with a link to Valenti's story from @GinaMMM, a UK artist and writer. According to topsy.com, more than 76,000 tweets with #WomenAgainstFeminism were generated in July 2014, with approximately 40 percent of those tweets emerging in the last 10 days of July when mainstream media, including *USA Today*, the BBC, *The Today Show*, and *Time* began covering the dialogue.[8] As Twitter often does, it accelerated the already existing conversation, igniting anger from feminists and encouraging anti-feminist discourse and images like those on the original Tumblr blog.

This chapter interrogates the anti-feminist discourse of Women Against Feminism, whose anti-movement/non-movement relies on post-feminist ideals of individual choice within polymediated, fragmented media practices.[9] As women increasingly claim agentic spaces online,[10] it is more important than ever to interrogate the uses of that agency. According to Stern and Henderson, the "symbiotic relationship between social action and mediated identity is the foundation of citizenry and activism in the polymediated era."[11] Studies of polymediated (anti) activism about gender politics, which occupies a primary popular culture practice today, enhances our understanding of how young women frame their identity with and through popular culture. We contextualize our critique of the WAF within postfeminism because, as Andrea Press has argued, scholars must interrogate the "everyday concepts that ordinary speakers/citizens/media consumers use to describe the phenomena that we study,"[12] in this case young women's understandings of feminist identities. Identity expression in the Women Against Feminism polymediated environments operates within neo-liberal sensibilities of individualism and American ethnocentrism, that when coupled with anti-feminist discourse, risks dehistoricizing feminism in popular culture.

FEMINISM AND POPULAR CULTURE

Feminism, in all its various forms and waves, has made its presence known via institutional forms of popular culture. There is no single, correct way to be a feminist, as Walker has declared.[13] The multiple strands and movements of feminism can be distinguished from each other by their aims and actions. The most prevalent method has been to categorize feminist movements according to waves, contrasting the work of first wave women's suffragists—beginning with the Seneca Falls Conference of 1848 and ending with the passage of women's suffrage in 1920—with that of second wave feminists who fought for women's liberation beginning in the 1970s. But the use of wave terminology becomes problematic because this demarcation often does not allow for the contextual space between and within waves, especially concerning the 1990s emergence of third wave feminists concerned with struggles of culture, sexuality, class, race, and ethnicity.[14] This fragmented nature of third wave feminism has led to another descriptive term for the movement—postfeminism— though many academics would argue against the congruous relationship.[15]

Heywood and Drake defined the difference between postfeminism and third wave feminism in this way: "Postfeminist characterizes a group of young, conservative feminists who explicitly define themselves against and criticize feminists of the second wave."[16] The young, conservative feminists the authors implicated included Naomi Wolf and Christina Hoff Sommers, among others, whose work they argued is essentially a backlash against feminism that asserts the movement's ideals have been achieved. Along with the assumed end of the women's movement, postfeminists also have called for "individual women to make personal choices that simply reinforce these fundamental societal changes,"[17] a call to action that contradicts the third wave movement's inclusiveness and collective action.

As Lotz argued, a majority of individuals learn about feminism based on coverage in and construction by media texts.[18] Popular media, however, may be the culprit for a misrepresented, botched feminism presented to consumers. "Clearly, the mainstream media—not the women's movement—heralded these mass-market, pop-culture prima donnas as postfeminist poster girls."[19] John Fiske found that the criticism and publicity of the popular press, a secondary text which in the polymediated era includes blogs and Twitter as part of the press, promotes particular meanings of primary texts.[20] This intertextuality helps popular culture consumers make sense of the revolving door of feminist texts and movement. According to Stuart Hall, the media naturalize certain values and practices of the dominant ideology,[21] including those of movements such as feminism. Consumers and citizens may become accustomed to one-note representations of feminist politics and movements.

THE APOLITICAL, ETHNOCENTRIC ENVIRONMENT OF WOMEN AGAINST FEMINISM

Angela McRobbie identified an "undoing of feminism,"[22] where feminist tenets at the individual level have been substituted in place of organized feminist movement in political and institutional life. "These new and seemingly 'modern' ideas about women and especially young women are then disseminated more aggressively, so as to ensure that a new women's movement will not re-emerge."[23] Individualization has become a primary component of postfeminism, which privileges self-improvement over structural change. Rebecca Munford and Melanie Waters identify popular culture as the site for postfeminist gains: "Postfeminist popular culture, itself a commodified, politically empty feminism, gives the consumer all the feminism she requires."[24] To this, we add that the fragmented, social (polymediated) spaces that permeate popular culture today might help contribute to the relationship between consumerism and feminist movement. While we still embrace polymediated technologies and practices for their potential to unite people seeking gender parity and social justice, these spaces equally allow for anti-feminists to come together to resist feminist gains.

Sarah Banet-Weiser expands on the postfeminist values articulated by other critics to include cynicism toward consumer culture and political movement,[25] meaning that the current generation of young women see themselves operating outside both the limits and opportunities of these primary markers of social life. Moreover, polymediated practices increase the likelihood of this cynical, third-person effect to gather steam. The mission statement of Women Against Feminism demonstrates this skewed understanding of political movement:

> This page is not sponsored by any organization and does not promote any organizations whatsoever. By submitting your photo you are not automatically consenting to join any organization (that's your own decision). This page has no official spokesperson because each of these women is her own spokesperson! Other people can speak their own mind and don't need permission from this page (free speech, right?). . . . The focus of this page is just to post women's responses to

feminism and those photos *should* speak for themselves. If that starts a "movement" then great! Thank you.

While we want to avoid generalizing about markers of privilege based on photos on Tumblr, the selfies and perspectives shared on WAF and its Twitter and Facebook accounts make it hard to ignore the participants' whiteness and limited range of understanding of intersectional oppression and the role of political organizing. The race and class privilege of WAF contributors is representative of feminist scholars' critique of the privileged space occupied by women who resist the feminist movement. As Elana Levine has argued, postfeminist traits of empowerment and choice, while limited to a "narrow range of privileged women," are "naturalized as universal."[26] This naturalization process complicates resistance to hegemonic popular culture practices and texts and likely affords the space to self-proclaimed anti-feminists to project their messages successfully.

WAF contributors shared the belief that they do not need feminists to be their representatives in society. They do not want a social movement to tell them how to think: "I don't need feminism because I can form my own opinions without the influence of other women, politicians, and liberal college professors." The women who contribute to WAF do not like feminists being the spokespeople of women: "I don't need feminism because I am capable of critical thinking and I do not need other women representing me." The belief that feminists speak for women as a whole has led some women to feel silenced: "I don't need feminism because I never asked to be represented by a collective of people who think they have the right to speak on my behalf just because I have a vagina. Your vaginas can't silence my voice." Anti-feminists want to be their own representatives and not have feminists speak on their behalf.

The irony is that feminist movements have been founded upon hearing marginalized voices. This is not to assert that conventionally attractive, likely straight, white women occupy a marginalized space in popular culture. However, similar to the way that the Christian Right has proclaimed a war on Christians via conservative-leaning news outlets, anti-feminists have been able to individually share their voices across polymediated spaces under the united name of Women Against Feminism to rise up against their so-called oppression. As such, WAF has worked within a popular culture that successfully inverts understandings of privilege and marginality to convince a generation of young women that feminism is not necessary. Some WAF posts do step outside the bubble of American understandings of feminism, but when they do they risk ethnocentric, patronizing expressions of feminism. For example, "I need feminism because I am a white, middle class, American woman. Oh, wait, that's right I don't need feminism, I am really not oppressed"; "Being a woman is not a disadvantage"; and:

> I don't need feminism because men and women are created for differ-
> ent purposes to help each other. They each have different things they
> are good at and praising one gender more than another isn't equality.
> Women in different countries who are abused every day for wanting
> their rights need feminism. They need the right to be equal and get to
> have the change to work as a team with a man.

This post builds upon Susan Douglas' arguments about "the turn within"
resulting from technological expansion and corporate conglomeration
that allowed for a collapsing of economic and political worldviews.[27]
Decreased news coverage of international issues by American media corporations, with the exception of sensationalized stories of global terrorism and gender atrocities such as rape and mutilation in "other" coun-
tries, shifts us from what Marshall McLuhan envisioned as a global village toward ethnocentric isolation.[28] This inward focus coincides with
neoliberal government and corporate policies that privilege individual
responsibility and nationalism. For all of its abilities to connect, polymediation can equally aid in dividing us. To be clear, we are not veering
toward technological determinism. Tumblr, Facebook, and Twitter do
not create this division (nor unity in the case of organizing around a
common cause). Rather, these polymediated spaces make it easier for
people with an already limited viewpoint to perpetuate that ideology.

VICTIMS OF HETERONORMATIVE, PRIVILEGED BODIES

Popular culture that embraces a lens of postfeminist individualism reinforces contradictory (as well as heteronormative) notions of femininity,
such as independence and vulnerability, but not at the risk of scaring
away potential (male) partners. Many bloggers have expressed on the
WAF Tumblr that they want to be able to choose whatever they want to
be, whether a mother or a CEO. A young woman posted: "I don't need
feminism because it defiles my dream to become a loyal, loving stay at
home wife." These anti-feminists believe that feminists look down on
women who choose a more traditional heteronormative lifestyle. "I believe women should be supportive of one another regardless of where
they choose to work"; "I don't need feminism because my husband and I
respect each other and I'm the breadwinner." These posts, especially the
statement from the "breadwinner" also indicate a misled belief that feminism puts down women who do not fit into traditional gender roles.
These juxtaposed readings of feminism point to the continued antagonistic space that feminist movements occupy in popular culture: feminists
put down women who have claimed more power in their personal and
professional relationships while also demonizing women who have the
privilege of seeking a domestic, "wife" role.

Anti-feminists of WAF also leave no space for non-heteronormative relating. References to relationships also overwhelmingly reinforce heteronormative performances of bodies. Some WAF identify as such because they do not want to be told how they are supposed to dress or look. For example, "I don't need feminism because I enjoy being feminine," perpetuating the stereotype of gendered dress styles that feminist women are assumed to defy. "I don't need feminism because I like men looking at me when I look good. That's why I do this." The belief that feminists do not condone women showing their beauty or sexuality has led some women to not support feminism. One WAF post includes a picture of a woman's cleavage holding a sign that reads, "Women have agency!!! If I dress like this, I want you to look." Women are against feminism because they want the right to dress and look in whatever way they choose and to not be judged for their choices. WAF contributors revisit this conflation of heteronormative bodily performance and post-feminist choice frequently.

Several posts on the Women Against Feminism Tumblr show young women's fondness of and appreciation toward men. "I don't need feminism because my boyfriend treats me right" implies that women who are feminists have been in negative relationships with men. Another post takes this idea one step further, "I don't need feminism because I was raised to be an independent woman, not a victim of anything and because I love my man." This post could be interpreted as women who are feminists have had negative interactions with men and have assumed the role of victim. This is further evidence that many of the contributors to WAF dislike feminism because of the skewed belief that feminists hate men.

Instead of putting down men, women who are against feminism want equality between the sexes. Clearly, the irony of that feminist goal is lost on WAF supporters. WAF posts share a view of feminism as a movement for women to try to become superior to men, whereas they seek equality because they "respect men and women." "I don't need feminism because I believe in equality, not entitlements and supremacy." Anti-feminists' dislike of the feminist movement stems from the stereotype of feminism aiming to move women to a higher social position than men. The rise of WAF along with men's rights activism is no coincidence, although the WAF Facebook page declares that WAF does not affiliate with men's rights organizations—or any organizations. In turn, Women Against Feminism do not want to be given anything they do not deserve: "I don't need feminists to give me an undeserved pay increase for working less than a man. I want equality, not special privileges." Anti-feminists want to work for everything that they have and not be given anything just because they are female, which WAF contributors label "entitlements." Nowhere on WAF did we find posts that embrace non-heteronormative ideologies of intimacy or workplace issues. This privileged intersectional position points to the opportunities cultivated by feminist movements to which many anti-feminists are impervious.

In her focus group discussions with young women about feminism and media, Andrea Press found that media outlets paradoxically reinforce the goals of feminist movements and repudiate feminist gains:

> My data indicate that the partial social revolution accomplished by feminist-inspired efforts has thrust women into a kind of "double jeopardy," in which they are exposed to what they perceive as the demands of the feminist world—to achieve in the public realm—even as more traditional demands on women—to shoulder the bulk of work in the family, to present themselves as desirable sex objects—remain in place. These dual pressures may account both for the ambivalence that sociological studies of women's attitudes tell us many women hold toward feminism as an identity and for the radical disjuncture between scholarly and popular viewpoints about feminism.[29]

The postfeminist landscape Press described is prevalent in all popular culture forms, from television and film to music and Internet culture.[30] The passions expressed by the young women who post on the WAF page are no exception to this "double jeopardy," evidenced in part by how contributors to WAF share that they did not always identify as anti-feminist.

In fact, some identified as feminists earlier in their lives: "I used to think I was a feminist [because] I thought feminism was about equality but honestly most feminists today are all about blaming men for everything. . . . So when someone asks me if I'm a feminist I don't know what to say anymore [because] I don't want them to think that I'm *that* kind of feminist." Just as postfeminist popular culture privileges individual action, it also contributes to a misunderstanding of "blame" for gender equality. WAF contributors point to man-blaming or man-hating rather than understanding that feminism seeks systemic social change to achieve equality. The stereotype that feminists hate men has changed how some former feminists see men. One WAF contributor shared: "When I first got into feminism I was all like 'feminists don't hate men!! Men can be feminists too, that's really cool!!' and two years later I am starting to hate men." With not wanting to be seen as a man-hater, former feminists are changing their label: "I'm not a feminist anymore, I am now a humanist . . . there's too many feminists that hate men or want females to be dominate/a higher class." The above comments identify the feminist movement as encouraging hatred toward men, resulting in a victim mentality that women are oppressed by men in general rather than institutional sexism.

Anti-feminists on WAF do not want to be considered oppressed, nor do they want to be considered victims. Some of these bloggers see feminists having a victim complex, blaming everyone else for what is wrong in their lives except for themselves. These women who submit to the Tumblr WAF feel like they "don't need feminism because victim mentality is a personality disorder." One young woman wrote, "I don't need feminism because my self-worth is not directly tied to the size of my victim complex," suggesting that she owns up to her own faults and does not blame others and thereby continue the myth of individualism in a neoliberal, postfeminist popular culture landscape. Sexual assault survivors on WAF also embrace anti-feminism related to a rejection of the victim complex. "Feminists are just trying to have a reason to hate all men. Just because a man looks at you or compliments you, doesn't mean he's raping you!!" The woman who submitted that post also stated that she had been raped and abused, yet still believes women falsely call "rape" too often. These anti-feminist bloggers want other women to admit their mistakes: "I don't need feminism because getting drunk at a party and having sex with a stranger is just irresponsibility, not rape!" And, "I don't need feminism because I am a rape survivor but I am not afraid of men!" Equating "fear" with "feminist identity" ties into the fear-baiting of a 24/7 news cycle in a polymediated, postfeminist culture that scholars and feminists alike need to counter with inclusive narratives and polymediated practices.

CONCLUSION

According to Elana Levine, popular culture depends on the "sort of individual tailoring that threatens to make the very notion of a collective social experience moot."[31] This struggle makes popular culture practices of Women Against Feminism a crucial counterpoint to feminist movement. Perusing the written statements and screenshots of messages of WAF supporters indicates a mixed understanding of feminism. Some WAF users advocate for "humanism" while others indicate a postfeminist stance, particularly that they and their peers have achieved equality, so feminists need to cease their whining. In an ironic twist, the very act of establishing their agency against feminist movement positions the Women Against Feminism within feminist ideals of voice and agency.[32] Upon reviewing thousands of WAF posts and contextualizing them within historic and current understandings of feminism, we are not ready to identify these self-proclaimed anti-feminists as vengeful about feminist gains. Rather, they are perpetuating popular culture myths that communicate feminism and feminist identity in limited ways that build upon conflict and fear from protected, privileged spaces. These myths also affirm a continued postfeminist popular culture landscape that applauds competitive ways of knowing rather than communal ways of knowing. Individualistic, masculinist culture pushes back at feminist organizing that focuses on the collective.[33] Anti-feminists are successfully using polymediated popular culture to communicate their individual successes as reasons why they do not need the organized feminist movement.

Even though it is difficult to speculate on identity markers of class, race, and sexuality without completing ethnographic research, the women who use these polymediated platforms to voice their concerns about feminism—at least based on appearance—occupy a privileged space of whiteness, a problem the anti-feminists have in common with mainstream feminist movements. The fact that WAF contributors employ smart phones and computer technology to generate photos and memes, as well as comfortably assert agency in a public forum, likely signifies a certain level of socioeconomic or educated status. Evidenced by the growing number of young women blogging, microblogging, and posting images and short videos to express their social and political (non-) affiliations, there clearly exists a desire to connect with young women today.[34] Moreover, this connection is not centrally located, but rather dispersed across multiple social networks and expanded on in traditional popular culture spaces and practices.

The "modern" feminism that so many WAF members advocate against must rally to be more inclusive, offline as well as online, to act as an intervention against sexism and feminist backlash. Perusing the sea of white faces on the WAF polymedia pages should make feminists just as aware of the limited space visibly occupied by non-white, non-straight, less socioeconomically privileged feminists in popular culture. Yes, we must still interrogate rape culture and the gender wage gap. But we must also critique heteronormativity in social institutions, transphobia, racism, class oppression, and global inequality. How can polymediation aid in this process? How can we polymediate an inclusive feminism that helps us turn outward, away from individualism and toward global concerns to eradicate intersectional gender oppression? As scholars of feminism and popular culture we need to examine the dispersed, symbiotic, and polymediated curation of and reaction to misogyny, of which the anti-feminism practiced by WAF surely is. We have an opportunity to remind our colleagues, students, families, and community members why feminism across technological and geographical borders is more necessary than ever.

NOTES

1. Mirca Madianou and Daniel Miller, "Polymedia: Towards a New Theory of Digital Media in Interpersonal Communication," *International Journal of Cultural Studies* 16 (2012): 170, doi: 10.1177/1367877912452486.

2. Adam W. Tyma, Andrew F. Herrmann, and Art Herbig, "Introduction. The Beginnings: #WeNeedaWord," In *Beyond New Media: Discourse and Critique in a Polymediated Age*, ed. Art Herbig, Andrew F. Herrmann, and Adam W. Tyma (Lanham, MD: Lexington, 2015), xx.

3. Michelle Calka, "Polymediation: The Relationship between Self and Media," In *Beyond New Media: Discourse and Critique in a Polymediated Age*, ed. Art Herbig, Andrew F. Herrmann, and Adam W. Tyma (Lanham, MD: Lexington, 2015), 15.

4. The Representation Project began as a documentary and K-12 curriculum titled, Miss Representation. It includes online tools and multiple social media platforms. Danielle Stern and Chelsea Henderson, "Hashtagging Feminism: Tetradic Polymediated Activism," In *Beyond New Media: Discourse and Critique in a Polymediated Age*, ed. Art Herbig, Andrew F. Herrmann, and Adam W. Tyma (Lanham, MD: Lexington, 2015), 127.

5. All quoted references from the WAF blog can be accessed at www.womenagainstfeminsm.tumblr.com.

6. "#BBCtrending: Meet the 'Women Against Feminism'," *BBC*, July 24, 2014, www.bbc.com/news/magazine-28446617.

7. Jessica Valenti, "Punching Gloria Steinem: Inside the Bizarre World of Anti-feminist Women," *The Guardian* July 7, 2014, www.theguardian.com/commentisfree/2014/jul/07/anti-feminist-women-hobby-lobby-decision-great.

8. 27,139 uses of #WomenAgainstFeminism were tweeted on July 21 alone.

9. The curators of the WAF Facebook account, which has the most information of the various WAF social media platforms, identify that WAF is not associated with any organizations and that individual women represent their own voices. See www.facebook.com/WomenAgainstFeminism/info?tab=page_info; Calka, "Polymediation," 15.

10. Mary Madden and Kathryn Zickuhr, "65% of Online Adults use Social Networking Sites," *Pew Research Internet Project*, August 26, 2011, www.pewinternet.org/2011/08/26/65–of-onlin-adults-use-social-networking-sites/.

11. Stern and Henderson, "Hashtagging Feminism," 139.

12. Andrea Press, "Feminism and Feminist Media in the Post-feminist Era: What to Make of the 'Feminist' in Feminist Media Studies," *Feminist Media Studies* 11 (2011): 111, doi: 10.1080/14680777.2011.537039.

13. Rebecca Walker, *To Be Real: Telling the Truth and Changing the Face of Feminism* (New York: Anchor, 1995).

14. Cathryn Bailey, "Making Waves and Drawing Lines: The Politics of Defining the Vicissitudes of Feminism," *Hypatia* 12 (1997): 20, doi: 10.1111/j.1527-2001.1997.tb00003.x.

15. Ellen Riordan, "Commodified Agents and Empowered Girls: Consuming and Producing Feminism," *Journal of Communication Inquiry* 25 (2001): 279–297, doi: 10.1177/0196859901025003006.

16. Leslie Heywood and Jennifer Drake, *Third Wave Agenda: Being Feminist, Doing Feminism* (Minneapolis, University of Minnesota Press, 1997), 1.

17. Catherine Orr, "Charting the Currents of the Third Wave," *Hypatia* 12 (1997): 34), doi: 10.1111/j.1527-2001.1997.tb00004.x.

18. Amanda Lotz, "Communicating Third-Wave Feminism and New Social Movements: Challenges for the Next Century of Feminist Endeavor," *Women and Language* 26 (2003): 2–9.

19. Jennifer Pozner, "The 'Big Lie': False Feminist Death Syndrome, Profit, and the Media. In *Catching a Wave: Reclaiming Feminism for the 21st Century*, ed. Rory Dicker and Alison Piepmeier (Boston: Northeastern University Press, 2003), 34.

20. John Fiske, *Television Culture* (London: Methuen,1987).

21. Stuart Hall, "Encoding/Decoding," In *Culture, Media, Language: Working Papers in Cultural Studies, 1972–9*, ed. Stuart Hall (London: Routledge, 1980), 128–138.

22. Angela McRobbie, *The Aftermath of Feminism: Gender, Culture, and Social Change* (London: Sage, 2009), 4.

23. McRobbie, *Aftermath*, 1.

24. Rebecca Munford and Melanie Waters, *Feminism & Popular Culture: Investigating the Postfeminist Mystique* (London: IB Tauris, 2014), xi.

25. Sarah Banet-Weiser," What's Your Flava: Race and Postfeminism in Media Culture," In *The Media Studies Reader*, ed. Laurie Ouellette (New York: Routledge, 2013), 384.

26. Elana Levine, *Cupcakes, Pinterest, and Ladyporn: Feminized Popular Culture in the Early Twenty-First Century* (Urbana: University of Illinois Press, 2015), loc 159 para 1, Kindle book.

27. Susan Douglas, "The Turn Within: The Irony of Technology in a Globalized World," In *The Media Studies Reader*, ed. Laurie Ouellette (New York: Routledge, 2013), 94.

28. Marshall McLuhan, *Understanding Media: The Extensions of Man* (New York: McGraw-Hill, 1964).

29. Press, "Feminism,"110.

30. For critiques of postfeminist narratives on television, see Danielle Stern, "It Takes a Classless, Heteronormative, Utopian Village: Gilmore Girls and the Problem of Postfeminism," *The Communication Review* 15 (2012): 167–186, doi: 10.1080/10714421.2012.702005; Jane Arthurs, "Sex and the City and Consumer Culture: Remediating Postfeminist Drama," *Feminist Media Studies* 3 (2003), 83–98, doi: 10.1080/1468077032000080149; Banet-Weiser, "What's Your Flava"; for film critiques, see McRobbie, *The Aftermath*; Hilary Radner, *Neo-Feminist Cinema: Girly Films, Chick Flicks, and Consumer Culture* (London: Routledge, 2010). For postfeminist analysis of popular music, see Munford and Waters, *Feminism & Popular Culture*; of Internet culture, see Anita Harris, "Young Women, Late Modern Politics, and the Participatory Possibilities of Online Cultures," *Journal of Youth Studies*, 11 (2008): 481–495. doi: 10.1080/13676260802282950; Jessica Ringrose, "Are You Sexy, Flirty, Or A Slut? Exploring 'Sexualisation' and How Teen Girls Perform/Negotiate Digital Sexual Identity on Social Networking Sites," In *New Femininities Postfeminism, Neoliberalism and Subjectivity*, ed. Rosalind Gill and Christina Scharff (London: Palgrave MacMillan, 2011), 99–116.

31. Levine, *Cupcakes*, loc 178 para 1.

32. Susan K. Foss and Cindy L. Griffin, "A Feminist Perspective on Rhetorical Theory: Toward a Clarification of Boundaries," *Western Journal of Communication*, 56 (1992): 330–349.

33. For a summary of how popular culture frames masculine and feminine spheres, see Andrew F. Herrmann and Art Herbig, "All Too Human: Xander Harris and the Embodiment of the Fully Human, "In *The Popular Culture Studies Journal*, 3 (2015): 85–112 .

34. Harris, "Young Women,": Jessalyn Marie Keller, "Virtual Feminisms," *Information, Communication & Society*, 15 (2012), 429–447, doi: 10.1080/1369118X.2011.64289.

TWELVE

Thinking Conjuncturally about Countercultures

Lawrence Grossberg

Politics in the United States—I leave open questions of other places, and also the broader questions of global politics—have been strange for well over fifty years and they are getting stranger every year, and almost every week.[1] Intermittently, during this half-century, they have become increasingly scary, although I have to continue reminding myself that I thought the previous moment (Reagan, Bush, etc.) was about as bad as I could imagine. Yet, I continue to think—again—that it cannot get any stranger or scarier than *this* moment. I have been trying for some time to think about the uncanny nature of contemporary politics, and why it increasingly seems to shade into the threatening, and how it is so powerfully articulated through and to the popular.

Any history of the present has to have multiple starting points, but regardless of what story one is trying to tell, one of the starting points has to be the 1960s, and it is not coincidental that, over the past years, comparisons of the present have increased dramatically: Obama and JFK, Iraq-Afghanistan and Vietnam, the Cold War and the War on Terrorism, and most controversially, the counterculture and the Tea Parties.

In fact, I might hypothesize that the forms and configurations of contemporary politics are the result of two fundamentally interrelated strategic vectors that "originated" in the 1960s: on the one hand, Nixon's invention and deployment (after his defeat by JFK) of a strategy built upon a politics of *ressentiment*, setting "ordinary" folks against the socio-cultural elite (although it was the very ability to affectively distribute the population into these categories that was the heart of this strategy).[2] This became, and has remained, a dominant political practice of many key fractions of the "new right," by which I mean the changing and variegated articulations of forms of conservatism (anti-government, religious, nationalist, and anti-socialist as well as emergent practices of racism, sexism, etc.) to equally variegated forms of pro-capitalism.[3]

And on the other hand, from the left as it were, the politics of the past fifty years have been shaped by the vectors defined, set loose and precluded by the so-called counterculture of the 1960s. In fact, the new right emerges in part as a reaction against the counterculture and its consequences, but it also has adopted, over the decades, a variety of countercultural strategies. In fact, the question I want to explore is whether one might (or even should) describe these developments on either or both the right and on the left as contemporary countercultures. Or to put it differently, I wonder if the concept of a counterculture may not be useful in understanding key moments of US politics over the past half-century, including the present moment.

But if that is the case, we have to think about what is at stake in the notion of a counterculture. The term was, after all, invented in the 1960s, ostensibly to describe what its inventor, Theodore Roszak, thought to be a new phenomenon.[4] Yet, as insightful and popular as his original work may have been, I want to suggest that Roszak confused empirical description with conceptual invention. In Roszak's terms—and apparently, according to many of its current defenders who vehemently object to the term being applied to any right-wing movements such as the Tea Parties, any counterculture would have to closely resemble that of the 1960s; but this seems to me to preclude any effort to use the concept to understand the specificity of the political assemblage in ways that might prove useful beyond the specific actualization in the 1960s. That is, I want to think of countercultures both conceptually and conjuncturally. I do not want to define them by the 1960s, but rather, to define the 1960s as one conjunctural actualization of a counterculture.

Let me then try to define the specific discursive formation or machinic assemblage that constitutes the existence of a countercultural politics. For the moment, I do not assume that they are all necessary but I do assume that, taken together, they are sufficient for the existence of a counterculture. I would propose six characteristics:

1. A counterculture exists without a singular identity; it has no single unifying value, politics, ideology, and so on. It is rather a space of variation, hybridity and experimentation, the practices, movements, formations and struggles of which are dispersed throughout the spaces of social institutions and everyday life. That heterogeneity can be described in any number of different dimensions or cartographies including: (a) political (e.g., using Williams' distinctions between oppositional, alternative and independent on the one hand, and dominant, residual and emergent on the other); (b) normative—as a map of values and themes (the map of

the 1960s counterculture included central notions of love, experience, creativity, the present, authentic individuality, and so on, as well as any number of contradictions, such as individual/community), but there are no guarantees what those values are or how they are differently configured; (c) pragmatic—as a map of the variety of practices, including political, spiritual, communal-lifestyle, and cultural; and finally, (d) a subcultural map, describing the dispersed space that, in the 1960s, would have included the political radicals, the new communalists (and spiritualists) and the more aesthetico-political groups such as the Yippies, with much of the space filled in by various—in fact the majority population—hybrid formations, groups and individuals.

2. If a counterculture is a space of diversity and multiplicity, it also occupies a unique temporality, which I will call a temporal ambivalence. This ambivalence gives rise to a specific ambiguity about its own sense of agency and its place in time or, to put it differently, about the inevitability of change and hence, about its role or responsibility to that change. This was, in the 1960s, embodied in the very idea of the Age of Aquarius, which was coming whether we accepted it or not, although at the same time, the members of the counterculture assumed that they had a responsibility to usher in that new era, if not to bring it about. Perhaps more John the Baptist than Jesus, the very act of heralding change brings about the very change it announces. This is perhaps the root of the idea of a prefigurative politics.

3. A counterculture is lived by its population as a vital (and sometimes overwhelming) reality; it transforms the affective experience of everyday life, defining an integral and highly charged intensive part or dimension of shared life. While it is not necessarily lived as a visible subcultural identity (although it is for some, at least at certain times), it does provide a self-defining sense of one's place within the larger social spaces.

4. Despite number (1) above, a counterculture does have a sense of unity, which is best characterized as an affective unity, and lived as cartographies of orientations and mobilities. That sense of unity may be ideological represented partly by a shared sense of opposition (see number 5) or, again, as in the 1960s, by an assumed, shared, sociological identity (e.g., generational). More often than not, that unity is representationally created from the outside (by the media) and depends on the central role of culture in countercultures (see no. 6).

5. A counterculture stands against the "mainstream/dominant" culture; its judgment is totalizing, rejecting the ground of fundamental structures, the ways of being, established and protected by the existing formations and practices of power. At least in the 1960s, taken as a unity, the counterculture had no design on or desire to take over the institutions of power, or at least, it was a revolution against the state itself as both a historically and geographically specific site of power. Seen from another angle, the counterculture can be understood to have stood against power

itself, even though it seemed at times to want to change specific relations and institutions of power.

6. All of this both demands and is made possible by the centrality of culture in a counterculture. Culture is its pervasive environment. Countercultures work on, in, with and through cultural formations and practices; they are bound together through the popular—drugs, style, and music—so that we can say that the counterculture produced the very culture that in turn constituted its very unity and gave expression to its totalizing judgment of the status quo. It is/was the culture that defines a field—a set of apparatuses—of belonging for its population. Culture defines not a shared identity (there are many identities, including some subcultural identities, possible within a counterculture) but a space and logic of identifications. And consequently, it simultaneously defines a system of vectors of attraction and movement into the counterculture (or what in more traditional terms might be described as mechanisms of recruitment).

The centrality of culture may help to explain the crucial importance of education (and the university) in the 1960s. But the result of the structuring dominance of the popular as a set of affective regimes and formations to the counterculture's sense of itself and its position against the dominant culture was that it left the "enemy" largely undefined (the system, the man, Catch-22) and under-analyzed, so that many different groups understood it differently. In an odd sense, the fact that the core of the counterculture is located in the popular means that it is always more likely that its attention will be focused on forms of difference from (and even resistant—broadly defined—to) the mainstream, rather than on researching and theorizing that mainstream.

Understanding the emergence of such a cultural-political "machine" requires locating it within its conjuncture, in this case at least, post WWII United States, characterized by, on the one hand, the hegemony of a particular set of institutional structures and compromises, combining specific forms of capitalism, democracy, difference and exclusion, social mobility, cold war politics (nuclear and containment militarisms), and more; and on the other hand, a particular complex and contradictory structure of feeling constituted by, at the very least, a demand for conformity and consensus based on a sense of accomplishment, relief, comfort (economic boom) and superiority, a powerful experience of anxiety (the bomb, communism), the celebration of expertise on the one hand and youth on the other. Articulated together, these shaped the fragile establishment, the apparent victory, of a certain way of being modern, a certain understanding of "America," although it had been in the making for at least fifty to seventy years, comprising what I have called "liberal modernity."[5]

But this is an insufficient conjunctural story, for just as this formation was becoming hegemonic (or at least appeared to be), it was also being resisted, attacked and sometimes just ignored as a way of living and as a way of being modern. What is really interesting is that such struggles against the mainstream came from all directions, from all sides and aspects of the political, social and cultural life of the nation. It is in this context that I understand the emergence of the particular configuration of youth and popular music/culture that I have called the "rock formation."[6] Refusing for the most part (except at very specific moments, often as much by the mainstream as by those in the formation itself) to be articulated to either ideological or institutional politics, it offered an affective politics aimed against the dominant structure of feeling and its lived expression in everyday life.[7] It defined a different kind of politics (I am not claiming that it was historically new or unconditioned), refusing the reification of the political and its demand for unities.[8] The counterculture emerged out of this quotidian and affective formation, as the result of a series of events and articulations.

After thirty years of attacks from the right and the left, from various identity formations and even various capitalist formations, the liberal modern mainstream has become little more than a veneer. In fact, it has been supplanted by a series of less stable, less confident scenarios, constituted by continuously morphing struggles, as a variety of temporary settlements among various fractions and alliances, seeking to establish a new dominant and within it, perhaps less necessarily, perhaps less obviously, a new mainstream, which taken together would again define a new American modernity, a new way of being modern and American. This new affective topography (comprised of various structures of feeling), however difficult to pin down, is characterized by an increasing sense of anxiety and insecurity (brought on partly through government deregulation, allowing risk to be moved down the economic scale, and new technologies), a sacralization of markets as defining both freedom and morality, a sense of national decline with an almost paranoid sense of superiority and/or inferiority, and a growing partisanship and refusal not only to compromise but to grant any respect to the other side (cutting across politics, culture and knowledge) and characterizing a growing array of social, cultural and political positions. I might suggest that if the liberal modernity of the post-war formation established everyday life as the primary plane on which people define their lives (and power struggles appear to be waged), the contemporary conjuncture has at the very least made everyday life increasingly precarious, and might even be in the process of dismantling everyday life itself.

That means that, increasingly but beginning after the Second World War, politics is being played out on the plane of affective, quotidian politics, the plane on which, first, the rock formation, and then the counterculture were established. Raising the question of counterculture today is then not a matter of nostalgia (although there may be positive moments of nostalgia involved) nor a question of judging when and if some authentic counterculture has been "co-opted,"[9] either by the right or the left. In the contemporary context, the question of countercultures raises—in no uncertain terms—the problem of the popular and the cultural side of the problematics of capitalism on the one hand and democracy on the other (against all vanguardisms).[10] It makes visible—almost unavoidable—questions about how one mobilizes people's affective alienations—dissatisfactions, anger, uncertainties, collapsed dreams—and expectations, hopes, and dreams, with the state of society, into new forms of political practice and agency. It returns us, albeit read differently, to Gramsci's understanding of hegemony as working on and through the popular and to a reformed problematic of political agency: how one mobilizes people affectively into or away from political projects.

If I am right to suggest that the conditions of hegemonic struggle, as well as the structures of feeling, have changed so much, then the terms of analysis with which one might have understood the "rock formation" are unlikely to work today, although I do not mean to suggest that the rock formation does not continue to have an affective presence and force at least at some social sites. But it no longer describes the most powerful logics and articulations of the popular. This is not to say that popular culture—or popular music—does not matter to its fans, but that it does not matter in the same way, for very complex reasons, including the changing affective place of "youth," the increasing importance of both technology and economics as sites of popular insecurity and investment, the transformations of generational relations, and the proliferation of media/cultural forms available for and even addressed to "youth."

The real question is whether it is useful (analytically, politically) to talk about the present conjuncture (marked by the generally increasing power, albeit differentially, across various domains, sites and machines of power, since the late 1970s, of various "new right" alliances) of the continuing presence, emergence, and articulation of countercultures. One has to, following on what I have said here, ask what formations, what struggles, what spaces emerging and existing today can or even should be described as countercultures or whether they are, despite superficial similarities, something else conceptually. Here I can only begin to speculate and offer some observations about the right and the left (recognizing that these terms do not work as effortlessly and seamlessly as they were thought to in the past, and that many people would refuse such binary designations).

I want to suggest that the contemporary left is in fact characterized by just the sort of space of differences and creativity that is the beginning of a countercultural formation. This includes the anti- and alter-globalization movements; new and long-standing communalist groups, sometimes referred to as the "social and consciousness movement,"[11] some versions of social entrepreneurialism; new spiritualisms; techno-utopians; various progressive political struggles; certain popular music formations (e.g., techno-nomads, continuations of politicized punk); and various groups committed to a variety of cultural, performative and aesthetic practices of politics. In fact, this explosion of diversity and creativity far exceeds anything in the 1960s, so that it can sometimes seem like there are just too many groups, too many issues, and so on. This is partly explainable because of the increasing global awareness and operation of such groups juxtaposed to their often increasing localism, the increasing tendency to organize in terms of single-issue struggles (even if they do understand that everything is connected) and the increasing sense of the possibilities for struggle (and hence for more pragmatic strategies) within "the mainstream" itself.

Many of these groups and formations overlap. All of them believe in alternative futures, alternative worlds, alternative economies, although they may mean different things by such terms. For many of the participants in these many groups and practices, these struggles are vital and constitutive elements of their lives without constituting a simple or single identity. And yet, while all of this suggests the existence of something we might want to call a counterculture, at least two interesting and significant elements seem to argue against it. First, even while some of these groups do see themselves as part of a "movement of movement," more often than not, that space of unity is limited to their own formation. Many of these groups and formations simply do not know that the others exist or, just as problematically, they do not acknowledge a commonality with each other. For example, too often, the splits that emerged in the 1960s between hippies, Yippies and politicos (an artificial distinction since most countercultural participants existed in the hybrid spaces between these formations) have become even more reified as different political strategies (independent, alternative and oppositional—but now one would have to add yet another category for resistance within the mainstream) become increasingly grounded in and justified by forms of moral absolutism and ontological certainty.

Second, and perhaps even more importantly, the enormous diversity of what one might initially see as a counterculture, not only in terms of values, definitions of "the enemy," strategies and practices, and groups, has resulted in or gone along with enormous social diversity as well. This is no longer a generationally centered counterculture,[12] but one dispersed across all the possible social categories, including generations, nationalities and ethnicities, classes, sexualities, and more. It is not surprising, therefore, that there is no common culture—admittedly, this is also partly the result of the explosion of media and forms of popular culture—but I think, the current potentiality of a counterculture (or of a multiplicity of countercultures) is constrained by the apparent absence of any cultural forms or practices capable of constituting an affective space of belonging together, a space of identification and, as I have already argued, a space by which people can follow vectors into the counterculture. This largely explains the paradox: if the potential counterculture is as large and active as I have suggested, why is it so invisible? The question is: Is it possible to have a counterculture without a popular discourse, "without a song"?

The situation on the right is even more difficult, especially since the landscape is continuously and rapidly changing. I have argued before that the success of the New Right (with and following the rise of Ronald Reagan, etc.) depends in part on its ability to appropriate and rearticulate a variety of countercultural strategies from the rock formation and the 1960s counterculture.[13] Yet, the left continues to tell the same stories and dismiss such popular movements as based in false consciousness, or ignorance, or even bigotry. Such decisions to ignore "where people are" and to refuse to engage with the popular hopes, fears, languages and logics of calculation—as well as with the strategies of other political positions engaged in the same struggle over the imagination of the coming modernity is one of the very reasons that the various articulations of a new conservatism continue to reassert themselves in sometimes very successful and influential ways. After all, bad stories make bad politics! If nothing else, the left, it seems to me, has failed to see or take seriously just how polarized the political culture of the United States has become, and how various left fractions have themselves contributed to many of the dimensions of this polarization, with its own enactments of certainty and absolutism.

The new right has in my opinion to be understood as the evolution through three overlapping formations. It started in the 1950s and 1960s as a broad social movement which, in its first instantiations, was open to diversity across many dimensions, although it had its own rigid and uncompromising elements. Yet it was a movement aimed primarily at state politics (attempting to "win" the Republican Party, beginning with the nomination of Barry Goldwater in 1964). The response to Goldwater's catastrophic defeat was two-fold: first, a strategy to literally control the party through involvement at the precinct level, and second, the recognition of the need to engage in a more popular politics, to operate on the terrain of the popular and common sense. The result was the impressive victory of Ronald Reagan, a victory that many of the left saw as both impossible and incomprehensible, the beginning of the end of liberal modernity.

The "Tea Party movement"—yet another moment of apocalyptic catastrophe in the minds of the left—was called into existence at the intersection of George W. Bush's failed presidency (failed because, retrospectively—and only retrospectively—it failed to meet the expectations and hopes of certain conservative fractions largely outside of government) and the election of Barack Obama (that apparently expressed the resurgence of liberalism). The Tea Party movement is more ambiguously placed in relation to traditional party politics—both inside and outside. Defining themselves somewhere between the political (against big government and taxes) and the cultural (nationalism, constitutionalism, often religion), between the local and the national, the Tea Parties are, without any doubt, a populist movement, without any obvious leaders — although they do have a variegated and even contradictory set of expressive spokespersons taken from various public domains, each speaking to some sub-set of groups and issues. The movement started out, I believe, as a space of diversity—and yes, even creativity and experimentation— with some groups leaning toward party and electoral politics and others more ambiguously expressing dissatisfaction with the political and social direction of the country and engaging in often more cultural forms of protest. It has always been difficult to define its membership (or the criteria of membership) despite the stereotyping and reductionism that often characterize left descriptions. Instead, in terms of values, practices or politics, the Tea Party movement was a formation without a center.

However, even more recently, the formation has transformed itself yet again, resulting in yet another apocalyptic and apparently even more frightening, political contestation. In the past few years, elements of the movement have become increasingly more extreme, less open to compromise (even if it is a necessary condition of governance) and more devoted to seeing itself as the presence of a disruptive social movement within the state itself. In this, the Tea Parties have become less determining and dominant, simply one player in a more diverse, but paradoxically less open, field of political struggle, often linking single-issue movements with broader agendas in an increasingly internally hostile field in which compromise becomes the mark of treachery. While the social movement/ party politics that characterized Reaganism was built upon a sense of unity in difference—the eleventh commandment was, "thou shalt not attack other Republicans"—the contemporary articulation of the new right is built on an apocalyptic rhetoric of purification, battling as much against incumbents who were once seen as part of the common movement as against the liberal enemies. While the new right has always include a certain threat of violence (even to the point of explicitly forming alliances with the militia movement), the increasing use of rhetorics of violence and absolution, of humiliation and victimage, and of intolerance and exclusion has resulted in a unique (albeit perhaps not entirely new) version of "American fanaticism."

That the movement in each of these incarnations is largely affective is rather obvious, because their "ideological position" is so visibly contradictory. It is an anti-democratic war waged in the name of democracy. It is willing to defend the Constitution at all costs, including violating the most fundamental principles and articles of the Constitution. In the name of the people, it attacks the popular. And in the name of the popular, it attacks the people who would dare assert their values over that of the market or the movement. But if we try to understand it ideologically, we will fail—because what drives it is less a coherent political position, or a set of values and principles, but a loosely configured chaos of responses to a profoundly troubled and deeply felt affective dissatisfaction or alienation; it is the expression of widely felt fears—in a context of norms and hopes that are no longer possible to actualize. And consequently, these movements enact their politics largely in and through cultural forms rather than the more traditional and obvious political tactics. But unlike the left, they speak to a sense of immediacy and frustration that is both deeply personal and deeply historical. It comes not from a position of ethical judgment (or an economy of abstract political sympathy) but from a sense of the lived impossibility of the current conjuncture. And because it speaks of and through the popular, in cultural terms that are widely accessible, it has the potential to have a profound impact. At the very least, we need to take seriously the possibility that it is, in significant ways, enacting a historical struggle over the strategic value of a counter-cultural movement of movements.

NOTES

1. An earlier version of this was published as Grossberg, 2014. The arguments here have been elaborated in Grossberg, 2005 and 2015.
2. Obviously, it is not a matter of Nixon's authorship, but rather his ability to make such a practice viable over a span of decades. I am well aware that Nixon is often accused of having formulated a contemporary politics of race, and while this is also true, the uniqueness of his appeals to racism was precisely their articulation into this more general politics.
3. In my opinion, the use of "neoliberalism" to describe this formation simply hides its historically changing and even contradictory and competing commitments and practices.
4. There is some controversy about the origin of the term, but the most common story supports Roszak's claim.
5. Lawrence Grossberg, *Caught in the Crossfire: Kids, Politics, and America's Future* (Herndon: Paradigm Publishers, 2005).
6. Lawrence Grossberg, *We Gotta Get Out of This Place: Popular Conservatism and Postmodern Culture* (New York: Routledge, 1992).
7. I use everyday life here not as equivalent with daily life but as a specific historical possibility, following Lefebvre and my own writings on the subject.
8. This is not the same as an alliance politics, which is based on a series of compromises between various unities.
9. After all, the 1960s in the US was a moment in which largely commercial popular culture (origins do not after all determine one's place in an economic system) was, in a variety of ways, articulated to the political. This was the source of at least some of both its weaknesses and its strengths.
10. In that sense, the US counterculture of the 1960s is more useful at this moment than the intellectually and politically more interesting European versions, whether in France or Italy, in the 1960s.
11. Paul Hawken, *Blessed Unrest* (New York: Viking Press, 2007); David Korten, *The Great Turning* (San Francisco: Kumarian Press, 2007).
12. Actually, I think the generational identity of the counterculture was an over-played ideological construction—imposed to a large extent by mainstream media and the rock formation, and rendered invisible by the enormous social diversity of the actual movement of movements.

13. Grossberg, *We Gotta Get Out*.

THIRTEEN

Rethinking Studies of Relationships and Popular Culture

Notes on Approach, Method, and (Meta)Theory

Jimmie Manning

Although popular culture has an impact on relationships,[1] just as relationships also impact popular culture, too often popular culture research evades examining close relationships or interpersonal communication in depth. As I have noted in earlier essays, the overwhelming majority of research about popular culture is either effects-based (i.e., examining what effects media have on someone's perceptions or behaviors),[2] or are identity-oriented textual criticism studies about who people are encouraged to relate with and how.[3] Other studies examine what kinds of relationships are represented through visual media, especially television.[4] Although these approaches to examining popular representations of relationships have value and have started important discussions, their potential—in terms of generating robust, sophisticated, and multilayered theoretical understandings—are limited. As Craig and numerous other scholars have noted,[5] theoretical knowledge, and the practical implications it offers, tends to thrive when a number of paradigmatic and methodological approaches are taken to a given topic. Additionally, reviewing past research about relationships and popular culture indicates that the relational aspects of such studies are limited. Most tend to explore a particular relational identity, especially how that identity is accepted, rejected, marginalized, or celebrated within a particular culture. Actual studies exploring relational interaction, whether as it is represented or produced in popular culture or as it results from popular culture consumption, are limited and difficult to find.

My goal in writing this chapter, then, is to offer new approaches, methods, and theories for studying popular culture. In many cases, these ideas or tools have been used in other contexts and would appear to make a good fit for exploring relationships and popular culture. When applicable, additional sources for exploration are offered—especially for methodological and theoretical approaches. I also point to scholars who have been using novel approaches to studying popular culture and relationships. My overall goal for the chapter is to provide relationship researchers inspiration for how they might engage studies of relationships and popular culture in new and productive ways.

METAPHORS FOR UNDERSTANDING POPULAR CULTURE IN RELATIONSHIP STUDIES

To begin, I urge for close relationship scholars—especially those who study interpersonal communication—to consider the metaphors that guide their research. Returning to the three dominant types of research about relationships and popular culture, it would appear three metaphors are often used. For effects studies, the metaphors of *popular culture as relational motivators* (i.e., popular culture motivates people to feel sexual or violent toward others) and *popular culture as relational assumption-maker* (i.e., some close relationships seem more normal than others) frequently come into play. That latter metaphor also works for many content analysis studies, although content analysis studies also deal with representation. For the humanist studies that critique relationships—or, more often, relational identity—a third metaphor is also apt: *popular culture as relational informant*. That is, for better or worse, representations of relationships in popular culture can deeply impact how individuals, cultures, and societies respond to the relationships and the people who are in them.

Here I offer five additional metaphors that could guide valuable research. In addition to explaining each, I provide some examples of research that could serve as a beginning guide for more extensive inquiry.

Popular Culture as Significant Relational Moment

First, and perhaps most obvious, popular culture is a part of—and often actually constitutes—the significant moments people share in their relationships. I spend less space explaining this metaphor because it is almost completely self-evident: a couple fondly remembers the first movie they saw together in a theater, a family gleefully looks forward to their trip to Disney World, a father takes his son to a baseball game for the first time, a mother shares her favorite album with her daughter. Popular culture can mark relationships, helping people to remember specific connections in a given place and time. Popular culture can set the mood for relationships, setting atmosphere or mood or even cruelly juxtaposing what is happening in a conversation. As Patricia Leavy recently explained,[6] popular culture is a soundtrack and collection of visual hallmarks marking our life experiences. It can create, enhance, sustain, or even constitute a given relational moment. Yet, little research about the role of popular culture in relationships is to be found. This metaphor is revisited later in this chapter, specifically the notion of popular culture being constitutive of relationships.

Popular Culture as Connector

As the first metaphor implies, popular culture is significant to relationships because it allows for connection. These relational connections can be pre-existing and made deeper through a new shared popular culture interest; yet it might be some aspect of popular culture itself that draws people together. This has been noted by many scholars, although not often in the context of close relationships. For example, in her germinal work exploring online fan communities, interpersonal communication scholar Nancy Baym examined the close relationships that formed between soap opera viewers as they joined together in a Usenet group to discuss their favorite characters and stories.[7] In addition to being mutual fans of the series, many members of the online forum became close friends. Such studies explore how people come together in offline spaces as well. For instance, a common reoccurring theme in Ben Bolling and Matthew J. Smith's collection of ethnographic essays about Comic-Con International is the politics of relationships and relating for those who attend.[8]

As these studies indicate, shared popular culture interests create and sustain relationships. As Thomas Verschelde argues, it would be worthwhile to consider how such shared interests might serve as a tipping point, of sorts, that encourages someone to take a chance on someone else.[9] In his work, he shares an anecdote of seeing a woman at a party and not being able to catch her attention until she realized that he liked the television show *Arrested Development*. After that, they talked about the show together and eventually entered into a long-term romantic relationship. It is important to consider how popular culture serves as a relational connector beyond meeting, too. Given that most every relationship has its ups and downs, it might be that popular culture allows as the common connection that allows that relationship to continue. A married couple who has hit a lull might be in a rut with little to say, but the shared ritual of watching a weekly television show might pull them through until better times approach. The only time two friends might get together is when their favorite band returns to perform, and perhaps that is enough to sustain their relationship.

It is also likely that popular culture can help people to connect about a certain idea or topic. Two women might already be well-connected with many common interests, but after seeing a film with a storyline about rape they might open up and share their own experiences with the top-ic—perhaps allowing a deeper connection and a new dimension to their friendship. A student in my advanced interpersonal communication class once shared that he and his family had stopped talking after the death of his big brother until watching a television movie about parents grieving a dead son. After the movie, the family cried together and started to talk about their hurt. Popular culture has long been acknowledged for its potential to invoke conversations about politics and social issues, as well as its portrayals of difficult life situations. These topics, and the conversa-tions and feelings that accompany them, surely have an impact on rela-tionships.

Popular Culture as Indicator

Popular culture—or, rather, popular culture preferences—also sug-gest *who* we are relating with and *how* we might go about doing it. As parents notice the popular culture their children gravitate to, they likely gain a better sense of how to go about relating with them. Of course, that assumes that parents are okay with their children's popular culture choices. In fact, as a child performs particular popular culture apprecia-tion, it might be a source of conflict. As one example, a father who sees that his son is playing with Barbie dolls might encourage him to switch to a toy perceived as more masculine. As another, a father might tell his rap-loving son that he needs to turn off his "black people ghetto music" and take down that son's Chief Keef posters while he is away at school. Both of those scenarios are likely to be explored in terms of identity, gender/ sexuality, and/or race in scholarly studies, but few studies would look at these popular culture preferences in terms of how they indicate where relational discord is likely to happen.[10]

It would be interesting to study the potential for other relationships based on people's popular culture interests and what they indicate to others. Would women be more or less likely to date a man who identified as a Bronie? More interestingly, why? What are the assumptions made about such a person, and how do they tie into relational wants and de-sires? Relationship research using the metaphor of *popular culture as indi-cator* could also test more mundane, taken-for-granted assumptions made about popular culture preferences. One possible line of questioning: Do single women who enjoy romantic comedies really long for a stable, com-mitted, long-term relationship more than other women? What about women who read bridal magazines? Cultural rhetorics suggest these women might be looking hard and fast for a husband, [11] but empirical research would likely produce results that would temper those assumptions. Taking such questions to a broader level could create just as interesting questions with just as illuminating findings. Do our popular culture preferences indicate who we are as a relational partner? [12] How about what we want in a relationship? Research answering these questions could paint a fuller picture of how relationship realities defy relationship myths or expectations.

Popular Culture as Relational Artifact

Whereas popular culture is often viewed—or, more likely in research is treated—as text, it would also be beneficial to consider it as artifact. For starters, conceptualizing popular culture as artifact in relationship studies would allow scholars to look at the meaning of objects in relationships. Such objects could include gifts to mark special occasions, family heirlooms passed from one generation to the next, or a collection of action figures two brothers accumulate together as they grow up. These objects might become more infused with meaning as a relationship continues (e.g., a movie ticket stub from a first date continues to grow in emotional value with each wedding anniversary), could immediately become infused with meaning based on a past experience (e.g., a DVD of the same movie, given on an anniversary, immediately has worth because of what movie it is even though the object is new to the relationship), or could transform in meaning over time (e.g., after a bitter divorce, a wife wants to be rid of the stub and DVD because it reminds her of the failed relationship) and in relation to a specific person in the relationship (e.g., but the husband smiles as he looks at both objects, reminded of the beauty that once was).

Unlike many of the previous metaphors explored in this essay, there is actually ample research about relational objects, especially gifts. Some of this research comes from disciplines where relationships are typically studied, such as communication studies or psychology, [13] but a large body of this research comes from disciplines ranging from philosophy to consumer studies. [14] The focus of such studies is often on the complexity of gifts, especially as they serve as a symbolic gesture that is read/interpreted by many. To that end, on a cultural level gifts can indicate social class, rhetorical savvy, an understanding of social mores, and a sense of ceremony. On a relational level, gifts can indicate affection, gratitude, closeness, and level of intimacy. Continuing to consider how these rhetorical or symbolic dimensions of gifts or other objects tie into current popular fads as well as current relational expectations could allow for a more holistic understanding of relationships as well as popular culture.

Popular Culture as Relational Building Block

In many ways, objects become extensions of relationships, and in many cases it is likely that some objects are a more central part of a relationship's constitution. That is, once a couple who is enamored with *The Simpsons* purchases a Bart Simpson statue together, that relational object is part of the make-up of their relationship. It might not be a particular salient or highly meaningful ingredient, but as it sits there in *their* living room as *their* joint purchase representing *their* shared interest, it continues to reinforce the *their*-ness of them. In that sense, the statue becomes one of many building blocks of their relationship. These building blocks need not be tangible objects. They can be ways of performing, the use of certain words or phrases when interacting, or ways of touching each other. They also can be, and probably frequently are, popular-culture oriented. This idea that the objects, behaviors, thoughts, and discourses that constitute a relationship are popular-culture oriented is more complex than it might seem at first glance.

For example, many of the discourses that inform a relationship and that are invoked within it likely originate, in part, from popular culture. To use a more obvious example, a husband, wanting to initiate foreplay with his wife, hides her towel and clothes while she is showering. As she sneaks out of the bathroom to try and find them, he picks her up and yells, "Bazinga!" He then tosses her on the bed where she laughs and he begins to kiss her. Because they watch *The Big Bang Theory* together, she gets that "Bazinga!" is the saying emoted by the character Sheldon Cooper when he pulls a prank on someone. Although the couple probably did not give much thought to the use of the word "bazinga," it invoked a sense of playfulness that comes from a comedy program they both enjoy. Along those lines, because the husband used humor to initiate sex, if he were rejected by his wife he might not feel as much shame or embarrassment, if any, if she turned down his advances. In this scenario, the popular culture source being incorporated into the relationship allows a sense of comfort and lightheartedness.

The intertextual nature of popular culture and relationships can be obvious when a discourse, action, or object more directly mimics something from popular culture.[15] It may also be that the intertextual aspects of popular culture are subtle, with one or more relational partners not understanding the origin of a behavior or discourse. The same husband and wife from the previous example—who clearly enjoy spontaneous sexual activity on some level—might find themselves with opposing attitudes in another situation. For example, the wife might be surprised when her husband rejects sexual advances on an empty, moonlit beach. Despite her pleas and reassurances that no one is watching, he continues to say no. To him, it seems dirty and messy.

"How can you say that?" she asks in disbelief. "I thought it was everyone's fantasy. It's hot!" Even though the wife suggests it is everyone's fantasy—and, more than that, truly believes that most people would want to have sex on the beach—clearly her husband does not have the same idea. In this hypothetical example, no one has ever shared their desire to have sex on a beach with the wife, whether a friend, lover, or otherwise; and unlike other fantasies, it was not something she thought up on her own, either. Rather, she remembers seeing a beach makeout scene in *From Here to Eternity* as a young girl and thinking it was hot. She also remembers a hot sex scene featuring Tom Cruise in *The Firm* that she watched as a teenager. As both of those beach images resonated with her, she began to build a fantasy—and when she saw opportunity, she tried to make it happen. In a subtle way, she was pulling those popular images into her relationship.

So why might it be important to consider the intertextual nature of relationships and popular culture? First, given that good communication is often pointed to as one of the most important, if not the most important, aspects of a relationship, it is beneficial to know what distal discourses (i.e., outside sources) are informing the proximal discourses shared between relational partners.[16] It might be that if the husband were able to know more about how the fantasy developed, he might be more open to it—especially if he looked at some of the source material for that fantasy. Moreover, as people become more cognizant of how the discourses within a relationship are shaped by outside discourses, they might also let go of the idea that relational partners are monadic individual actors who make independent choices of their own free will. Rather, relational social control often imposes will on relational partners who feel they must do or make the "correct" or "right" choice in a relationship. Developing a literacy of how popular culture discourses and representations impact relationships allows people the opportunity to separate the oughts from the wants, or can allow relational partners a sense of agency about *what is right for them* rather than what popular culture sources invoke as being the way to do relationships.[17]

EXPANDING USE OF METHODS FOR STUDYING RELATIONSHIPS AND POPULAR CULTURE

Although certainly not exhaustive, the metaphors offered to this point open up dialogue about what can be learned from studying relationships and popular culture as well as point to new directions for such studies. Many of the approaches discussed in the last section could be explored using the experimental, content analysis, and textual-critical methods that are often used with effects-oriented, content analytic, and humanistic studies, respectively. To truly expand knowledge about popular culture and relationships, new methodological terrain will need to be explored. Here I briefly review four methods that could be or have been fruitful.

Dyadic and Multiadic Interview Approaches

Many of the metaphors listed here, and the research questions they likely involve, could be answered through open-ended qualitative interviews. Whereas some research questions will only require interviews with one member of a relational entity, researchers should strongly consider whether it would be of benefit to interview all members. After all, if a relationship is being researched, then it makes sense to look at as many members of a relationship as possible. For many studies, it can be especially beneficial for each member of the relational entity to be interviewed separately with the same protocol. In addition to allowing a sense of each relational member's experience, it also allows the opportunity to compare and contrast across interviews to get a stronger sense of meaning.[18] As Eiskiovits and Koren also note, a stronger sense of narrative validity can also be gained by looking across separate interviews.[19]

As another approach, it can also be beneficial to interview participants separately before bringing them back together using the same interview protocol. This multiadic approach to interviewing accounts for how relational partners often behave differently when they are together than when they are separate.[20] In other words, multiadic approaches allow researchers to better understand both individual and relational perspectives. Multiadic approaches can especially allow a strong sense of what voices might be marginalized or stifled in a relationship.[21] For a complete overview of using dyadic and multiadic qualitative approaches, see the essay Adrianne Kunkel and I wrote for *Journal of Family Communication*.[22]

Diary Methods

Although interview methods provide a good sense of how people respond and think in the moment, they also rely heavily on memory of events that may be far in the past and, because of the expectation of an immediate response, might not allow for the deepest reflection. Interviews also happen at one point in time, meaning that change or growth cannot easily be measured. That means that methods that allow more time for careful reflection, such as a survey, could be beneficial. Another alternative, participant diaries, is a longitudinal approach that can allow for perspectives to be viewed as they change over time. Similar to dyadic or multiadic approaches, diaries can also be collected from multiple partners in one particular relationship. I encourage researchers to consider using diaries for two reasons. First, as mentioned earlier in this essay, people might not fully realize how they carry a popular culture discourse with them in a relationship. That is, they might not be cognizant of how they are invoking something they learned from popular culture over time. Diaries would allow a better opportunity for those fleeting moments to be captured by the researcher, especially as they might come into play with future entries or follow-up interviews.

Second, depending on the questions offered to those completing diaries, the open-ended nature of the responses participants will make could allow for insights about what questions might be asked about relationships and popular culture next. That is, the possibility for inductive understandings of the connections between relationships and popular culture could be robust. Those advantages noted, it is important to consider that many participants flake on diary studies—especially if no compensation is offered for participating. It is also common that some participants provide little or cursory information. Those interested in conducting diary studies are strongly encouraged to consult Jean-Philippe Laurenceau and Niall Bolger's excellent primer as well as to seek out journal articles where other researchers have carried out diary studies.

Autoethnography

As an alternate or in addition to asking others to share their narratives through interviews, surveys, and diaries, researchers should also consider how they can share their own stories regarding relationships and popular culture. Specifically, autoethnography can serve as an excellent method for developing theoretical insights from lived experience. As a method, autoethnography foregrounds personal experience (*auto*) as it relates to cultural identities and contexts (*ethno*) and articulated via writing, performance, art, or other creative approaches (*graphy*).[23] It is essential that all three elements be part of an autoethnography. A personal story alone does not constitute research—it must be reflexively embedded in culture and, through writing that is often evocative, develop deeper understandings both for the author and for the potential audiences.[24]

Tony Adams and I point to five strengths that autoethnography allows popular culture research.[25] We argue that autoethnography allows people to place their experiences alongside a popular culture text or event to examine how personal experiences are informed by or resemble popular culture; allows response to popular culture texts that do not match their personal experiences, especially those that might be harmful; describe their personal interaction with popular culture phenomena; examine their personal experiences with creating or producing popular culture; and/or create scholarship about popular culture that can be read and understood by multiple audiences, including those without academic research training. In that same essay, we offer suggestions for those who are interested in doing autoethnographic research about popular culture; and in another,[26] we explore how family relationships can be explored through autoethnography. Those looking to do this work can start there and should supplement those readings with a more thorough guide such as Carolyn Ellis' *The Ethnographic "I"*.

Research-Informed Criticism

In addition to the methods listed above, research about relationships and popular culture has recently been expanded via work that ostensibly involves humanistic criticism but that draws from empirical research and empirically generated theories in order to do so. In other words, those who are enacting rhetorical, media, literary, or cultural criticism are using empirically generated theories or findings to critique popular culture content as well as extract deeper meaning. For a particularly clever example of this approach, see Michaela D.E. Meyer's essay where she uses relational dialectics theory, an interpretive-empirical theory, to analyze a narrative arc about a gay teen's coming out on the television program *Dawson's Creek*.[27] By applying the theory in her criticism, she is able to consider both the nuances of how multiple relationships are portrayed as part of the show, but also reflexively uses her findings to contribute to the development of the theory.

A FINAL THOUGHT:
DIVERSIFYING (META)THEORETICAL TERRAIN

Given the novelty of the metaphors offered here as well as the largely interpretive, inductive-oriented methods, it is likely that, if engaged, new theories about how relationships and popular culture interact will be developed. These theories have the potential both to inform how popular culture is created and sustained, and also how relationships are made intelligible and navigated via popular culture. As mentioned at the beginning of this essay, the more diverse this theoretical terrain, the more likely competing perspectives can be compared and contrasted across theoretical paradigms to develop strong practical insights for interpersonal relationships.[28] To that end, dominant theoretical approaches to relational popular culture studies such as cultivation theory or queer theory should continue to be considered,[29] but so should those that are still developing or that have received scant attention from those who study relationships and popular culture to this point.

For example, two studies reviewed in this essay have explored relationships and popular culture through a lens of relational dialectics theory,[30] and both in different ways.[31] Given its focus on distal and proximal discourses, and the ease with which those can be aligned with popular and personal discourses, respectively, RDT would be a good candidate for immediate further exploration.[32] Given that popular culture also appears to be a building block of relationships in varied and dynamic ways, it also becomes important to consider the communicative elements of the thoughts, behaviors, discourses, and objects related to popular culture. To that end, further exploration—and perhaps a clearer articulation—of the communication as constitutive of relationships (CCR) perspective should be explored.[33]

It would also be beneficial to consider how people see their relationships both in and deflected by popular culture, perhaps through a theory such as symbolic placement that directly examines how people do identity work by placing themselves in symbols.[34] Feelings and emotions are also likely to be theoretically relevant to such studies, and so the ongoing theoretical work being labeled as affect theory will also likely offer insights.[35] Regardless of the combination of perspectives, theories, and methods one chooses to use in their pursuit of better understanding connections between relationships and popular culture, given the lack of attention to the research area, any well-considered, methodologically sound, and theoretically informed approach would be welcome. As Anne Harris notes, popular culture has the power to both "reflect our experiences" as well as "co-create them."[36] It is time to better understand how this power is being used, both by the creators of popular culture as well as ourselves.

NOTES

1. Steve Duck, *Rethinking Relationships* (Thousand Oaks, CA: Sage, 2010): 32.

2. Jimmie Manning, "Exploring Family Discourses about Purity Pledges: Connecting Relationships and Popular Culture." *Qualitative Research Reports in Communication* 15 (2014): 92–93. doi:10.1080/17459435.2014.955597.

3. Jimmie Manning, "Because the Personal *Is* the Political: Politics and the Unpacking the Rhetoric of (Queer) Relationships," in *Queer Identities/Political Realities*, ed. Kathleen German and Bruce Dreshel (Newcastle, UK: Cambridge Scholars, 2009): 7.

4. See, for example, Dana E. Mastro and Susannah R. Stern, "Representations of Race in Television Commercials: A Content Analysis of Prime-Time Advertising," *Journal of Broadcasting and Electronic Media* 47 (2003): 638–47. doi:10.1207/s15506878jobem4704_9.

5. Robert T. Craig, "Communication Theory as a Field," *Communication Theory* 9 (1999): 120. doi: 10.1111/j.1468-2885.1999.tb00355.x. See, for example, François Cooren, "Pragmatism as Ventriloquism: Creating a Dialogue Among Seven Traditions in the Study of Communication," *Language Under Discussion* 2 (2014): 1–26; or, for a more relationship-centered exploration, Jimmie Manning, "A Constitutive Approach to Interpersonal Communication Studies," *Communication Studies* 65 (2014): 432–40. doi:10.1080/10510974.2014.927294.

6. Patricia Leavy, *Blue* (Rotterdam, Netherlands: Sense Publishers, 2016): xv.

7. Nancy Baym, *Tune In/Log On: Soaps, Fandom, and Online Community* (Thousand Oaks, CA: Sage, 2000): 199.

8. Ben Bolling and Matthew J. Smith. *It Happens at Comic-Con: Ethnographic Essays on a Pop Culture Phenomenon* (Jefferson, NC: McFarland, 2014).

9. Tom Verschelde, "New Approaches to Theory in Interpersonal Communication: Incorporating Media Perspectives" (paper, Central States Communication Association Annual Convention, Kansas City, MO, April 6, 2013): 2.

10. One noteable example is Manning, "Exploring Family Discourses," where family members who participate in the study both individually and as a collective group explain that generational differences in musical preferences are to be expected; and that parents will always be critical of their children's musical choices. Rather than seeing this as something that threatened their parent-child relationships, they saw it as reinforcement of what that relationship is supposed to be. In other words, they claimed they were doing what parents and children are supposed to do: fight over musical preferences.

11. To be fair, many women are stereotyped as liking romantic comedies, not only single women; but, nonetheless, single men are warned about signs of women who are too eager to get married, including an obsession with romantic comedies and flipping through bridal magazines. See, for example, Will Lloyd, "Five Mistakes Single Women Make in Trying to Date a Man," *Singles Scene by It's Just Lunch* (blog), October 4, 2015, www.itsjustlunchblog.com/2015/10/the-3-biggest-dating-mistakes-women-make-with-tips-for-how-to-avoid-them.html.

12. Andrew Ledbetter has started doing work in this area, although it is in early stages. See Andrew Ledbetter, "'Why Don't We See What's on TV?:' Shared TV Viewing, Relational Maintenance Behavior, and Romanticism as Predictors of Romantic Relationship Quality" (paper, Central States Communication Association Annual Convention, Grand Rapids, MI, April 16, 2016).

13. See, for example, Hairong Feng, Hui-Ching Chang, and Richard Holt, "Examining Chinese Gift-Giving Behavior from the Politeness Theory Perspective," *Asian Journal of Communication* 21 (2011): 301–17. doi:10.1080/01292986.2011.559257.

14. In philosophy, Mark Osteen, for instance, has edited an impressive collection of essays that examines the philosophies of gift giving across different times and civilizations. See Mark Osteen, *The Question of the Gift: Essays across Disciplines* (New York, NY: Routledge, 2013). Although it makes sense, there are an impressive number of gift-oriented studies that come from Consumer Studies scholars. As one example, see Morgan K. Ward and Susan M. Broniarczyk, "It's Not Me, It's You: How Gift Giving Creates Giver Identity Threat as a Function of Social Closeness," *Journal of Consumer Research* 38 (2011): 164–81. doi: 10.1086/658166.

15. Several scholars talk about the intertextual aspects of relationships, most notably Leslie A. Baxter, *Voicing Relationships: A Dialogic Perspective* (Thousand Oaks, CA: Sage Publications, 2011) and Duck, *Rethinking Relationships*.

16. For a more robust discussion of distal and proximal discourses, see Baxter, *Voicing Relationships*, 121–51. For an example of analysis involving distal popular culture discourses in interplay with proximal relational discourses, see Manning, "Exploring Family Discourses."

17. To be clear, I am not suggesting that all relational social control is a bad thing. On the contrary, much of it can be good, especially discourses discouraging behaviors such as physical abuse, sexual coercion, and the like. I am more taking aim at non-harmful, non-normative relational compositions, identities, behaviors, and beliefs. As one example, if a husband and wife decide to defy gender norms with the husband staying home and the wife working, then that really hurts no one. The couple might thrive under that arrangement, and yet it is likely they would still receive teasing and even shaming because of expectations about how relationships are supposed to be done.

18. Jimmie Manning and Adrianne Kunkel, "Qualitative Approaches to Dyadic Data Analyses in Family Communication Research: An Invited Essay," *Journal of Family Communication* 15 (2015) 186. doi:10.1080/15267431.2015.1043434.

19. Zvi Eisikovits, and Chaya Koren, "Approaches to and Outcomes of Dyadic Interview Analysis," *Qualitative Health Research* 20 (2010): 1643. doi:10.1177/1049732310376520.

20. For examples of this method in action, see Manning, "Exploring Family Discourses" or Jimmie Manning, "Paradoxes of (Im)purity: Affirming Heteronormativity

and Queering Heterosexuality in Family Discourses of Purity Pledges," *Women's Studies in Communication* 38.1 (2015): 99–117. doi: 10.1080/07491409.2014.954687.

21. Manning and Kunkel, "Qualitative Approaches," 186.

22. Manning and Kunkel, "Qualitative Approaches."

23. Arthur P. Bochner and Carolyn S. Ellis, "Autoethnography," in *Communication As . . . : Perspectives on Theory*, ed. Gregory Shepherd, Jeffrey St. John, and Ted Striphas (Thousand Oaks, CA: Sage Publciations, 2006): 110.

24. Tony Adams, Stacy Holman Jones, and Carolyn Ellis, *Autoethnography* (New York, NY: Oxford University Press, 2014): 3.

25. Jimmie Manning and Tony E. Adams, "Popular Culture Studies and Autoethnography: An Essay on Method," *The Popular Culture Studies Journal* 3 (2015): 199–200. mpcaaca.org/the-popular-culture-studies-journal/volume-3.

26. Tony Adams and Jimmie Manning, "Autoethnography and Family Research," *Journal of Family Theory & Review* 7 (2015): 350–66. doi: 10.1111/jftr.12116.

27. Michaela D. E. Meyer, "'It's Me. I'm It.': Defining Adolescent Sexual Identity through Relational Dialectics in *Dawson's Creek*," *Communication Quarterly* 51 (2003): 262–276. doi: 10.1080/01463370309370156.

28. Manning, "A Constitutive Approach," 438.

29. Grounded theory helps to explain how being exposed to television programming influences beliefs and perceptions of the world. See James Shanahan and Michael Morgan, *Television and Its Viewers: Cultivation Theory and Research* (Cambridge, UK: Cambridge University Press, 1999) for a contemporary perspective. For an excellent overview of Queer Theory, see Gust A. Yep, "The Violence of Heteronormativity in Communication Studies: Notes on Injury, Healing, and Queer World-Making," *Journal of Homosexuality* 45 (2003): 11–59. doi: 10.1300/J082v45n02_02.

30. Meyer, "It's Me," 262–276.

31. Meyer, "It's Me" taking a humanistic approach akin to rhetorical criticism and Manning, "Exploring Family Discourses" taking a more traditionally empirical approach. See also Jimmie Manning, ""Ipsedixitism, Ipseity, and Ipsilateral Identity: The Fear of Finding Ourselves in the Fissures between Phishing and *Catfish*," in *Beyond New Media: Discourse and Critique in a Polymediated Age*, ed. Art Herbig, Andrew F. Herrmann, and Adam Tyma (Lanham, MD: Lexington Books, 2015): 83–107 for yet another approach, this one involving autoethnography.

32. Relational dialectics theory is often simply referred to as RDT, or now also RDT 2.0 based on Baxter's new iteration that relies more on the discursive nature of the theory.

33. See Leslie A. Baxter, "Relationships as Dialogues," *Personal Relationships* 11 (2004): 1–22. doi: 10.1111/j.1475-6811.2004.00068.x for a general overview or Jimmie Manning and Katherine J. Denker, "Doing Feminist Interpersonal Communication Studies: A Call for Action, Two Methodological Approaches, and Theoretical Potentials," *Women & Language* 38 (2015): 133–42.for notes in a more applied context.

34. See Jimmie Manning, "Finding Yourself in *Mad Men*," in *Lucky Strikes and a Three-Martini Lunch: Thinking about Television's Mad Men*, ed. Danielle S. Stern, Jimmie Manning, and Jennifer C. Dunn (Newcastle, UK: Cambridge Scholars, 2012): 89–96.

35. Affect theory is a field of theory that specifically examines the various intensities that pass from one body to another. For an introduction, see Melissa Gregg and Gregory J. Seigworth. *The Affect Theory Reader* (Durham, NC: Duke University Press, 2010).

36. As quoted in Leavy, "Blue," xiii.

FOURTEEN

Public Opponents Cooperating

Possibilities for Dialogue
in Popular Culture Controversies

Rob Anderson and Kenneth N. Cissna

The language *wars*? A *war* on women? Culture *wars*? Contemporary media daily encourage the assumption that polarizing tactics work well for leaders in deep value conflicts, when good-versus-evil's winners and losers collide.[1] Popular journalism, once thought to moderate social tensions, increasingly thrives on polarized conflict and the drama it builds.

Strong leaders, in this view, do not change their minds; that would be "flip-flopping" or "going soft" on the other side. Strong leaders follow polls, clicks, and tweets, seeking rewards for neutralizing and humiliating opponents. Nowhere are examples of this more dangerous than in the political arena as it increasingly adopts the ethos of entertainment culture. A publicity-sensitive business executive and host of a popular reality television series is currently being taken seriously as a presidential candidate; he claims that opponents are not simply wrong but are "stupid" and "losers." Other leaders dig in further for their accusations. To them an opposing candidate is secretly a new Hitler who is "not one of us," a deranged, unhinged threat who has plotted against ordinary citizens all along. Self-appointed saviors must defeat evil and deceitful threats by escalating the rhetorical stakes. Polarizing techniques are not new, but they have become omnipresent, business as usual in a contemporary mediated culture where listening carefully to opposing arguments is equated with capitulation.

Enter proponents of dialogue, at times accused of naïvete when they teach specific skills of listening, collaboration, spontaneity, multiple perspectives, and openness to new solutions as common elements of dialogic communication.[2] Dialogue studies could do a better job of conceptualizing and accounting for unequal power relations.[3] Nevertheless, culturally rich dialogue can recast opponents as collaborators across sharp disagreements and often deliver unexpectedly productive results, as we have argued elsewhere.[4]

One knotty assumption about dialogue, though, can be understood both as invitation and barrier: the notion that successful dialogue, even between opponents, is essentially open-ended and unrehearsed. Some practitioners believe that because dialogue is emergent and cannot be scripted ahead of time, attempts to manage or present it are doomed to failure or irrelevance. It is a necessarily messy process, full of surprise.

Yet are all of dialogue's surprises helpful, especially for public audiences? Nearly buried in intellectual history are traces of a personal relationship, between famed psychologists B. F. Skinner and Carl Rogers, that clarify this question and illuminate larger dilemmas of polarization in public dialogue. We wish to excavate it as a small exploratory case study. First, we describe the context of media celebrity surrounding the participants in controversy; second, we note the moves made by them to minimize the dangers of polarized public argument; finally, we offer implications of their informal model for public dialogue.

SKINNER, ROGERS, AND DIALOGUE

For decades in the mid-twentieth century, American behaviorist and humanistic psychologists clashed over how to define human experience. Today it is hard to imagine how fully this controversy animated such a wide range of opinions in the popular media. Two of the most famous intellectuals of their era emerged as "key influencers" through their several public exchanges: psychologist B. F. Skinner of Harvard, the foremost proponent of behaviorism and its associated technologies of conditioning and education; and psychotherapist Carl R. Rogers, the most famous representative of humanism in psychology.[5] Skinner argued that social planners should embrace new techniques of control in order to produce better citizens. Rogers countered that the entire enterprise of social control dehumanized persons, who were capable of healthy self-direction and freedom of choice in social relations. Their seemingly divergent worldviews left little room for agreement about basic philosophy. If one was right, the other must be basically wrong in a form of "paradigm debate" involving "irreconcilable differences."[6] Academics and the public chose sides. In an argument that "dichotomizes into bipolar, antagonistic points," humanists characterized behaviorists as "manipulative,

depersonalizing, and controlling slaves to scientism, concerned with forcing men into submission, conformity, and docility," while humanists
were accused of being "softheaded, nonscientific, vague, sentimental,
and hopelessly caught up in nonoperational, meaningless values."[7]

Popular media portrayed Skinner and Rogers as antagonists. However, we discovered in their private correspondence a respect that developed into friendship. It transcended their philosophical differences and
inflected their appearances in the public sphere. This private relationship
was based on practical ideas for subtly structuring dialogue, minimizing
polarization, and maximizing opportunities for listeners to understand
controversial claims for themselves.

Public intellectuals rarely received rock-star levels of publicity before
the Skinner-Rogers sparring. Skinner's claim that science can control human behavior for socially desirable results, however, found an "astound-
ing reception in wide circles of education, medicine, business, and science," partly because he "managed to capitalize on a growth industry—
behavioral technology—to become the spokesperson for it in many na-
tions."[8] He achieved a "remarkable cultural dissemination" of his ideas
from the 1940s through the 1970s.[9] He was featured on the cover of *Time*
magazine for September 20, 1971, during a period in which he was "at
times obsessed with his own image."[10] He was the focus of numerous
network television programs, news reports, and journalistic interviews,
as befits someone "who had acquired the celebrity of a movie or TV
star."[11] Skinner became a cultural phenomenon symbolizing the behaviorist project of well-chosen technologies of control leading to social harmony and individual happiness. He stimulated a "widespread discourse" for which he was his own "master marketer."[12] His books, particularly the novel *Walden Two* and *Beyond Freedom and Dignity*, became
best-sellers in part because the marketer in Skinner knew when and how
to merge scientific research with popular culture, appealing to popular
media outlets through speculation, application, and controversy.[13] *Walden Two* sold nearly 2 ½ million copies before Skinner died, and *Beyond
Freedom and Dignity* "incited an enormous backlash from critical audiences and the lay public" and "ignited the press like wildfire."[14]

At roughly the same intellectual moment, Carl Rogers also had captured the public imagination, although perhaps with less avid self-mar-
keting and for a seemingly antithetical project. His pioneering work in
nondirective and client-centered therapy had earned him a strong professional reputation and burgeoning fame as a public cultural commentator
on the potential of persons to direct their own destinies. Professionally,
Rogers had been elected as president of the American Psychological Association (APA), as well as the American Academy of Psychotherapists
and the American Association of Applied Psychology. The APA also
honored Rogers with its Distinguished Scientific Contribution Award
and the Distinguished Professional Contribution Award. His public im-

age was equally impressive as he became one of the best-known psychologists worldwide. *On Becoming a Person* became a crossover bestseller.[15] A documentary film about one of Rogers' growth groups received an Academy Award, and he also was the subject of a *Time* magazine profile and numerous media interviews. Later in his career, he would expand his status as a public celebrity, authoring trade books on marriage, education, encounter groups, and personal power. Rogers died in 1987 before he learned of his nomination for a Nobel Peace Prize honoring his international workshops promoting intercultural trust.

BACKSTAGING THE DIALOGUE

We do not know when or how Rogers and Skinner first met.[16] The earliest correspondence between them that we found was a 1952 letter from Rogers to Skinner granting Skinner permission to quote from an article he'd recently published.[17] In his letter, Rogers also expresses interest in Skinner's forthcoming book because, he says, "this problem of the place of science in relation to human behavior . . . has concerned me even more since I wrote the paper to which you refer."[18] Skinner probably was clearing permissions for his book, *Science and Human Behavior*, which appeared the next year.[19]

Three years later, Rogers writes to request a copy of a Skinner paper mentioned in what Rogers called a "tantalizing little clipping from my daily paper."[20] In his second paragraph, Rogers writes:

> I don't know any American psychologist today with whom I feel a deeper philosophical disagreement, but I have a hearty and general respect for you because you are forthright and honest in stating your views. I wish that some time we might have a chance to talk together and explore what I believe are our differences.[21]

Rogers is straightforward, almost blunt, in expressing both his profound disagreement with Skinner and his simultaneous respect grounded in Skinner's own forthrightness. Rogers also mentions his interest in talking with Skinner face to face about their differences, which, of course, is the basis for deeper dialogue. This provided the first seed for their exchanges over the next decade.

Skinner's response accepts Rogers' invitation, saying "I, too, wish that we might have a chance to talk together and explore our differences."[22] Skinner invites Rogers to visit him at his summer place in Maine if he has occasion to come east during the next month or two. He also suggests that they might meet at the next APA convention. Although he says it "might be a more profitable session if we kept the public out of it," he then raises the possibility of proposing a program on the control of human behavior for the next APA convention, and asks Rogers, "What do you think?" In reply, Rogers thanks Skinner for a reprint he'd sent, says he won't be able to come to Maine, but expresses interest in the meeting at the APA convention.[23]

Five months later, Skinner sends an article in *American Scholar* that he had told Rogers he was writing. Although he says he expects Rogers to be in strong disagreement with it, he reiterates his suggestion of "airing our points of view" at an APA meeting.[24] In a series of letters exchanged during January and February, Rogers and Skinner explore the specifics of the proposal: Would it be a round table discussion or a more structured event? A debate with rebuttals? Involving one or more third parties? Would they invite responses from the floor? Who would be moderator? What would the exact topic and title be? Who would initiate the submission?[25] Rogers puts Skinner in charge—saying in a hand-written letter that he is willing to participate if Skinner will take the initiative in arranging it, and that he accepts Skinner's list of possible chairs for the program.[26]

On March 2, 1956, Skinner writes to Richard Solomon to propose the program.[27] Rogers later questions only the brief title Skinner gave the session ("The Control of Human Behavior"), and suggests several more expanded versions, all of which contain the phrase that Skinner proposed.[28] Skinner accepts one of Rogers' suggestions, "Some Issues Regarding the Control of Human Behavior."[29]

Rogers' two-page reply in May assumes the proposal will be accepted and he begins to explore the specifics of the arrangements. He suggests that Skinner speak first, as he is "a little bit more of a proponent of a new point of view than I am in this connection." He asks Skinner if he could have his paper done well ahead of time (two months later), because "the more closely our papers are related to each other the more the meeting will have a significant flow of thought and the less we will be battling straw men or heading off toward unrelated goals." Finally, he suggests that, in the style of a debate, which he says "is only a partially true description of the meeting," Skinner should have the last comment.[30] A week later, Skinner responds that he would be happy to give his paper first, and says he should have it, or a detailed outline, available by the date Rogers suggested. He preferred the earlier deadline even though, originally, he was thinking of a later date that would allow him to work on it during his vacation at his summer place in Maine—adding "in fact [I] ought to do so if I am to protect my vacation."[31]

Later in May, Rogers describes this session's purpose as not to debate one another, but to "think through myself and think through with you the important questions" that are involved. He notes that although they may be "different in ideas," they "have no difficulty working together."[32] They also agree on a division and sequencing of the time: 30 minutes for Skinner, 40 minutes for Rogers, and 10 minutes for Skinner's response.[33]

On July 16, Skinner sends a draft of his paper.[34] Two weeks later, Rogers sends his own draft, as well as asking for Skinner's "reaction to some developments which have occurred since we last corresponded."[35] Edward P. Morgan, an influential commentator for the American Broadcasting Company (now ABC News) had approached Rogers after reading one of his papers, surely sensing an opportunity to report on an unusual event.[36] Rogers writes that he favors creating some publicity around their discussion of these issues of behavioral control, because "it would be good to get the public thinking, and I believe it would be good for our profession in that it presents psychologists as a definitely significant group."[37] Someone from *Time* magazine had approached him about the controversy as well. Rogers is willing to share whatever spotlight this media attention might provide, and he also wants to make sure that Skinner is okay with this publicity. On August 20, Skinner sends a handwritten postcard to Rogers saying he is revising the draft of his opening paper, and will have the rebuttal done within a week. He asks for the addresses of the two journalists so he can send them copies as well. In parentheses, he adds, "I think I am beginning to see light—a real area of agreement between us. So far—a very creative experience for me."[38]

Their session at the convention occurs on Tuesday evening, September 4. Rogers and Skinner resume their correspondence within a week with Skinner suggesting another publication option and joking that their exchange "was all very reinforcing!" and Rogers responding two weeks later, telling of a contact from *Scientific American* that could present a publication possibility and joking back that he is "delighted that we *chose*" to participate in the session.[39] He also offers, quite seriously, that he suspects that "both of us found that we do not have all the answers."[40] The humor, of course, referred to two contested concepts—reinforcement and choice—on which they differed. Their exchange was published in *Science*, the prestigious journal published by the American Association for the Advancement of Science, and was used by Morgan as the basis for an ABC broadcast.[41]

They continue to correspond occasionally, sharing publication plans, papers, reprints, proofs, and upcoming travel plans.[42] In mid-December 1956, Rogers writes again: "I believe that we have been unusually successful in doing exactly what we started out to do, namely to call the attention of the wide group to the issues which are involved. I take off my hat to you for your initiative in getting this whole venture underway. It has been a very satisfying experience all around."[43] Skinner replies that he, too, "feel[s] that the whole thing was very worthwhile and that we have started something which may have a long and healthful history."[44]

The significance of their correspondence and of their relationship can be found in one additional anecdote from one of those letters. Rogers writes to Skinner asking for some reprints or references related to applying Skinner's ideas to the field of education. Then he writes: "I think that *if learning could be arranged for in the ways I believe you are trying to do, then from my point of view that would leave room for education to take place on top of it.* I suspect you might not agree with this latter idea, but at any rate, I would like very much to get all the information I can in this area" (emphasis added).[45] Skinner responds quickly, sending Rogers a copy of his first paper in what he calls this "rapidly expanding" and "very exciting" field. He then adds that "I am glad to leave room for whatever you mean by 'education.' Indeed one object of the machines is to free the student for more effective discussion and the kind of personal interchange between teacher and student which has almost disappeared from American education."[46] Each becomes a bit more open to the other's ideas. Over twenty years later, after Skinner's retirement and while he is writing his autobiography, he asks for Rogers' permission to quote the italicized portion of Rogers' letter above, saying "I think this is a good statement of your position then and, I suppose, now, and would like to use it in the text."[47]

After a face-to-face meeting at a small conference organized by the American Academy of Arts and Sciences in December 1960, Rogers and Skinner met again publicly in the summer of 1962. They were invited jointly to the University of Minnesota, Duluth, to participate in a two-day "dialogue," which became their first unscripted encounter.[48] The topic became "Education and the Control of Human Behavior: A Dialogue."[49] As the event approaches, Skinner writes that the schedule will encourage a "genuine exchange" between them and that he appreciates this opportunity to "clear up [their] differences."[50] The program shows two opportunities for "informal exchange" between Skinner and Rogers along with opening and closing statements, small group sessions, and a question and answer period with audience members.[51] In April of the following year, after the conference, Skinner writes that he and Rogers met recently and "discussed the question of editing a two-hour portion of the conference." Skinner says he has a person who is willing to do the editing from a fuller transcript.[52]

In 1965, Rogers writes Skinner seeking permission for a local radio station to air part of the dialogue. He is glad to have met Skinner's wife and daughter when they visited the Rogers' home in La Jolla, California, and says how happy he and his wife are with their decision to move there (and to leave traditional university life). However, he realizes that this "is not a place where your wife would be happy."[53] Perhaps the Skinners had been considering a move to southern California, as Skinner replies that "he is sorry that I have missed this chance to see you oftener." He also grants Rogers permission to make any use he likes of any version of their dialogue in Duluth.[54] Although later they had perhaps their strongest personal disagreement, concerning whether tape recordings of their Minnesota meeting should be made available, four hours of tapes were eventually made available commercially on cassettes, and a transcript was published.[55]

The final correspondence we have seen comes from 1982. A 75th birthday celebration has been arranged for Rogers at the APA convention that fall, and Skinner expresses his regret at not being able to attend: "Sorry I can't be with you on October 9. We could exchange views on intellectual self-management in old age. You obviously have your own system, and it would be fun to see how we differ. I always thought we went on playing the same old tunes after our exchanges, but we did tune the fiddles a little more accurately." Skinner signs the letter "All best wishes."[56] Rogers responds: "Thanks for your cordial and witty note on the occasion of the celebration of October 9. I appreciated it very much. I hope you are well. I continue to be active and expect you do the same. Our differences do not prevent me from signing this Affectionately."[57]

With both of them in their mid-seventies, their relationship at least thirty years old, and on the occasion of a celebration to honor one of them, they both used quite intimate forms for closing their letters. Rogers died February 4, 1987 at age 85; Skinner died August 18, 1990, at age 86.

IMPLICATIONS FOR PUBLIC DIALOGUE

Revisiting the Skinner-Rogers letters helps to foreground fresh implications for public dialogue. Society can mitigate the popular obsession with polarized leadership if appropriate dialogic backstaging from leaders became recognized as an essential element in preparing a space for public talk. This insight raises important questions. Does it mean that public opponents need to like or fully appreciate each other? Are effective and successful instances of public dialogue fully spontaneous? Carefully planned and controlled? Fully honest in exchanges of accusation and defense? What is the relationship between spontaneous and honest expression of disagreement or anger, on the one hand, and careful preplanning of the presentations, on the other? Could productive opposition depend in part on certain kinds of cooperation with those you oppose? Are alternative forms of empathy necessary for public dialogue? Does the dynamic of the Skinner-Rogers relationship suggest different ways to reconceptualize social expectations of polarization and accusation? Precise answers to such questions are surely not possible in a brief exploratory essay, but our study can at least offer clues. We discovered, for example, several implications that rhetors and critics could use as touchstones.

Recognizing the Fragile Interdependence of Spontaneity and Planning

In some public presentational forms, the temptation is to sequence slick packages of scripted ideas. In others, it is clear that the participants are simply winging it. But if public dialogue is truly desired, the choices involved are far more nuanced. Spontaneity does not preclude preparation or even coordination, if participants are trying to clarify and sharpen their audience's understanding of basic issues. Preparation can facilitate the forms of spontaneity that matter most to audiences—staying on point, sensing moment by moment what is most relevant in participants' rhetoric for listeners, providing effective internal summaries, inviting full explanations in fair and nonsarcastic ways, pointing out the most persuasive points the other makes, and taking ideas seriously without taking oneself overly seriously. In other words, dialogic spontaneity and planning for it can be seen as interdependent. Through a dynamic interplay of these tensions, dialogue can offer audiences oppositions and distinctions, and also offer opportunities for synthesis and reconciliation. Dialogue takes listeners and participants alike beyond their static initial positions to the fluid potential for change. As Rogers wrote to Skinner prior to their APA convention joint appearance, "I feel it would be profitable if the meeting contains some newness for us as well as the audience."[58]

Considering an Alternative Sense of Empathy

Empathy in public argument has often been described as a soft skill, a wouldn't-it-be-nice attitude on the part of one participant to another (roughly, "I can sense your different reality, and imagine what that must be like," although Rogers' scholarly definitions were more precise). Without denigrating the value of such cognitive acts and their expression, the notion of *backstaging* dialogue illustrated in the Skinner-Rogers relation suggests a different type of empathic concern for communicators in public conflict—one we might call *mutualized clarification* while working with the other side(s). In addition to empathic attempts focused on the opponent's ideas, the Skinner and Rogers correspondence shows how each also prioritized empathizing with their audiences, imaginatively taking the role of listeners who were attempting to listen coherently to a breadth of new terms, research findings, and conflicting philosophical positions. Their correspondence demonstrates how the two psychologists wanted to provide minimal, but crucial, structure for their meetings in order to clarify issues, not just present arguments. If we trust the motives expressed in their letters, Skinner's and Rogers' concern for facilitating listeners' understanding was a primary collaborative goal, in some ways eclipsing any individual desire to score points or defeat the other's argument.

Of course, we must be realistic. Each still wanted to present his own ideas persuasively, and each thought the other to be seriously misguided about human nature. Yet it is possible to discipline the temptation to demonize the opponent, and to polarize the different groups of followers. Skinner and Rogers hit upon one such way: think first about the difficulties of listeners new to the controversy, and collaboratively create a dialogue-enhancing strategy of issue clarification. This does not mean that taking sides will not occur; it means that needless polarization can be minimized by leaders' simple but practical shared empathy with the difficulties of a public listening to complicated rhetoric.

Ratifying the Importance of Greeting

The political theorist Iris Marion Young observes that dialogue in conflict situations "cannot begin without preliminaries in which the parties establish trust or respect."[59] This is a "logical and motivational condition of dialogue," a "moment of communication" in which participants "recognize one another in their particularity."[60] She labels this phenomenon *greeting*, emphasizing the relatively content-free speech acts associated with acknowledging the other—such as "how are you doing?," "let's talk," "take care," and so forth. The concept of *greeting* also includes "mild forms of flattery, stroking of egos, and deference."[61] These practices, along with a sensitivity to such tonal issues as invitation, civil leave-taking, and the absence of personal insult or dismissal, can be powerful reminders for leaders in conflict. We see many vivid examples of *greeting* in the Skinner-Rogers correspondence, of course. Young argues that theorists of deliberative democracy tend to disregard this concept, and how it can counteract anger and fear during public dialogue. Strikingly, Skinner and Rogers usually maintained such a relationship without the pettiness often displayed by self-involved adversaries. They modeled openness to the other while arguing.

CONCLUSION

Critics of popular media culture worry about excessive polarization of positions and people in the public sphere. This polarization is a countertrend to, and perhaps a justification for, renewed interest in public dialogue. We have offered here a preliminary exploration of a nearly forgotten but significant moment over fifty years ago in which two cultural icons with conflicting visions for democracy nevertheless work hard in private to ensure more dialogic and less polarized public encounters. Perhaps their attitudes and choices have in some small way helped contemporary psychologists to recognize that behaviorism and humanism are not mutually exclusive goals. Krasner envisioned this when he wrote in 1978 that the future (which we are now experiencing) involves "behaviorist-humanists" with the two camps collaborating to craft a "positive mutual goal" of "assisting people to design their own environments for a humane, humanistic world of 'reasonably satisfied' people."[62]

NOTES

1. See Michael McCluskey and Young Mie Kim, "Moderatism or Polarization? Representation of Advocacy Groups' Ideology in Newspapers," *Journalism and Mass Communication Quarterly* 89, no. 4 (2012): 565–84; and John J. Pauly, "Is Journalism Interested in Resolution, or Only in Conflict? *Marquette Law Review* 93, no. 1 (2009): 7–23.

2. See David Mathews, *Politics and People: Finding a Responsible Public Voice*, 2nd ed. (Urbana: University of Illinois Press, 1999).

3. Scott C. Hammond, Rob Anderson, and Kenneth N. Cissna, "Problematics of Dialogue and Power," in *Communication Yearbook 27*, ed. Pamela J. Kalbfleisch (Mahweh, NJ: Erlbaum, 2003), 125–57.

4. Rob Anderson and Kenneth N. Cissna, *The Martin Buber-Carl Rogers Dialogue: A New Transcript with Commentary* (Albany: State University of New York Press, 1997); Kenneth N. Cissna and Rob Anderson, *Moments of Meeting: Buber, Rogers, and the Potential for Public Dialogue* (Albany: State University of New York Press, 2002).

5. Leonard Krasner, "The Future and the Past in the Behaviorism-Humanism Dialogue," *American Psychologist* 33, no. 9 (1978): 800.

6. Patrick K. Dooley, "Kuhn and Psychology: The Rogers-Skinner, Day-Giorgi Debates," *Journal for the Theory of Social Behaviour* 12, no. 3 (1982): 277–83; Krasner, "The Future and the Past," 801.

7. Carl E. Pitts, "Twelve Years Later: A Reply to Carl Rogers," *Journal of Humanistic Psychology* 13, no. 1 (1973): 75.

8. William R. Woodward, "Introduction: Skinner and Behaviorism as Cultural Icons: From Local Knowledge to Reader Reception," in *B. F. Skinner and Behaviorism in American Culture*, ed. Laurence D. Smith and William R. Woodward (Bethlehem PA: Lehigh University Press, 1996): 8.

9. Ibid.

10. Daniel W. Bjork, *B. F. Skinner: A Life* (New York: Basic Books, 1993), 192.

11. Elizabeth Hall, "Will Success Spoil B. F. Skinner?" *Psychology Today*, November, 1972, 68.

12. Woodward, "Introduction," 22, 18.

13. B. F. Skinner, *Walden Two* (New York: Macmillan, 1948); B. F. Skinner, *Beyond Freedom and Dignity* (New York: Knopf, 1971).

14. Bjork, *B. F. Skinner*, 162; William O'Donohue and Kyle E. Ferguson, *The Psychology of B. F. Skinner* (Thousand Oaks, CA: Sage, 2001), 202.

15. Carl R. Rogers, *On Becoming a Person* (Boston: Houghton Mifflin, 1961).

16. Our studies of the Martin Buber–Carl Rogers dialogue (e.g., Anderson and Cissna, 1997; Cissna and Anderson, 2002) led us to the Carl R. Rogers Collection in the Manuscript Division of the Library of Congress, among other archives. While searching for relevant letters and other materials, we were surprised to find correspondence between Rogers and B. F. Skinner that revealed a collegial and friendly personal relationship that developed amidst their contentious public encounters. We copied these and set them aside for too long. In 2004, Art Herbig visited the Harvard University Archives as a co-researcher and searched the Skinner collection. He found many additional letters and documents that are relevant to this project, and we are deeply indebted to Art for his assistance and generous spirit. Quotations from materials in the HUA courtesy of the Harvard University Archive.

17. Rogers to Skinner, September 23, 1952, B. F. Skinner Collection, HUGFP 60.10 (Box 2, Misc. Correspondence 1950–54 Folder), Harvard University Archives.

18. Ibid.

19. B. F. Skinner, *Science and Human Behavior* (New York: Macmillan, 1953).

20. Rogers to Skinner, July 14, 1955, B. F. Skinner Collection, HUGFP 60.15 (Box 3, 1955 Letters and Documents Folder), Harvard University Archives.

21. Rogers to Skinner, July 14, 1955, B. F. Skinner Collection, HUGFP 60.15 (Box 3, 1955 Letters and Documents Folder), Harvard University Archives.

22. Skinner to Rogers, July 20, 1955, B. F. Skinner Collection, HUGFP 60.15 (Box 4, 1956 Letters and Documents Folder), Harvard University Archives.

23. Rogers to Skinner, July 26, 1955, B. F. Skinner Collection, HUGFP 60.15 (Box 4, 1956 Letters and Documents Folder), Harvard University Archives.

24. Skinner to Rogers, December 27, 1955, B. F. Skinner Collection, HUGFP 60.15 (Box 4, 1956 Letters and Documents Folder), Harvard University Archives and Carl R. Rogers Collection, Box 80, Folder 7, Manuscript Division, Library of Congress.

25. Rogers to Skinner, January 18, 1956, B. F. Skinner Collection, HUGFP 60.15 (Box 4, 1956 Letters and Documents Folder), Harvard University Archives; Skinner to Rogers, January 30, 1956, B. F. Skinner Collection, HUGFP 60.15 (Box 4, 1956 Letters and Documents Folder), Harvard University Archives; Rogers to Skinner, February 12, 1956, B. F. Skinner Collection, HUGFP 60.15 (Box 4, 1956 Letters and Documents Folder), Harvard University Archives.

26. Rogers to Skinner, January 18, 1956, B. F. Skinner Collection, HUGFP 60.15 (Box 4, 1956 Letters and Documents Folder), Harvard University Archives.

27. Skinner to Richard Solomon, March 2, 1956, Carl R. Rogers Collection, Box 80, Folder 7, Manuscript Division, Library of Congress.

28. Rogers to Skinner, March 20, 1956, Carl R. Rogers Collection, Box 80, Folder 7, Manuscript Division, Library of Congress and B. F. Skinner Collection, HUGFP 60.15 (Box 4, 1956 Letters and Documents Folder), Harvard University Archives.

29. Skinner to Rogers, March 27, 1956, B. F. Skinner Collection, HUGFP 60.15 (Box 4, 1956 Letters and Documents Folder), Harvard University Archives.

30. Rogers to Skinner, May 14, 1956, Carl R. Rogers Collection, Box 80, Folder 7, Manuscript Division, Library of Congress and B. F. Skinner Collection, HUGFP 60.15 (Box 4, 1956 Letters and Documents Folder), Harvard University Archives.

31. Skinner to Rogers, May 21, 1956, Carl R. Rogers Collection, Box 80, Folder 7, Manuscript Division, Library of Congress and B. F. Skinner Collection, HUGFP 60.15 (Box 4, 1956 Letters and Documents Folder), Harvard University Archives.

32. Rogers to Skinner, May 24, 1956, Carl R. Rogers Collection, Box 80, Folder 7, Manuscript Division, Library of Congress and B. F. Skinner Collection, HUGFP 60.15 (Box 4, 1956 Letters and Documents Folder), Harvard University Archives.

33. Ibid.; Skinner to Rogers, May 29, 1956, B. F. Skinner Collection, HUGFP 60.15 (Box 4, 1956 Letters and Documents Folder), Harvard University Archives.

34. Skinner to Rogers, July 16, 1956, B. F. Skinner Collection, HUGFP 60.15 (Box 4, 1956 Letters and Documents Folder), Harvard University Archives.

35. Rogers to Skinner, July 30, 1956, Carl R. Rogers Collection, Box 80, Folder 7, Manuscript Division, Library of Congress and B. F. Skinner Collection, HUGFP 60.15 (Box 4, 1956 Letters and Documents Folder), Harvard University Archives.

36. Edward Morgan to Rogers, May 8, 1956, Carl R. Rogers Collection, Box 80, Folder 7, Manuscript Division, Library of Congress.

37. Rogers to Skinner, July 30, 1956, Carl R. Rogers Collection, Box 80, Folder 7, Manuscript Division, Library of Congress and B. F. Skinner Collection, HUGFP 60.15 (Box 4, 1956 Letters and Documents Folder), Harvard University Archives.

38. Skinner to Rogers, August 20, 1956, Carl R. Rogers Collection, Box 80, Folder 7, Manuscript Division, Library of Congress.

39. Skinner to Rogers, September 10, 1956, B. F. Skinner Collection, HUGFP 60.15 (Box 4, 1956 Letters and Documents Folder), Harvard University Archives; Rogers to Skinner, September 24, 1956, B. F. Skinner Collection, HUGFP 60.15 (Box 4, 1956 Letters and Documents Folder), Harvard University Archives.

40. Rogers to Skinner, September 24, 1956, B. F. Skinner Collection, HUGFP 60.15 (Box 4, 1956 Letters and Documents Folder), Harvard University Archives.

41. Carl Rogers and B. F. Skinner, "Some Issues Concerning the Control of Human Behavior: A Symposium," *Science* 124 (1956): 1057–66. Johanne Current (Secretary to Morgan) to Rogers, September 13, 1956, Carl R. Rogers Collection, Box 80, Folder 7, Manuscript Division, Library of Congress.

42. Rogers to Skinner, September 24, 1956, B. F. Skinner Collection, HUGFP 60.15 (Box 4, 1956 Letters and Documents Folder), Harvard University Archives; Skinner to Rogers, September 27, 1956, B. F. Skinner Collection, HUGFP 60.15 (Box 4, 1956 Letters and Documents Folder), Harvard University Archives; Skinner to Rogers, October 2, 1956, B. F. Skinner Collection, HUGFP 60.15 (Box 4, 1956 Letters and Documents Folder), Harvard University Archives; Skinner to Rogers, October 22, 1956, B. F. Skinner Collection, HUGFP 60.15 (Box 4, 1956 Letters and Documents Folder), Harvard University Archives; Skinner to Rogers, November 1, 1956, B. F. Skinner Collection, HUGFP 60.15 (Box 4, 1956 Letters and Documents Folder), Harvard University Archives and Carl R. Rogers Collection, Box 80, Folder 7, Manuscript Division, Library of Congress; Rogers to Skinner, November 5, 1956, B. F. Skinner Collection, HUGFP 60.15 (Box 4, 1956 Letters and Documents Folder), Harvard University Archives; Skinner to Rogers, November 11, 1956, Carl R. Rogers Collection, Box 80, Folder 7, Manuscript Division, Library of Congress; Skinner to Rogers, no date, Carl R. Rogers Collection, Box 80, Folder 7, Manuscript Division, Library of Congress.

43. Rogers to Skinner, December 14, 1956, B. F. Skinner Collection, HUGFP 60.15 (Box 4, 1956 Letters and Documents Folder), Harvard University Archives.

44. Skinner to Rogers, December 21, 1956, B. F. Skinner Collection, HUGFP 60.15 (Box 4, 1956 Letters and Documents Folder), Harvard University Archives.

45. Rogers to Skinner, December 11, 1957, B. F. Skinner Collection, HUGFP 60.10 (Box 2, Transfer File 1956–57 Folder), Harvard University Archives.

46. Skinner to Rogers, December 16, 1957, B. F. Skinner Collection, HUGFP 60.10 (Box 2, Transfer File 1956–57 Folder), Harvard University Archives.

47. Skinner to Rogers, November 15, 1979, B. F. Skinner Collection, HUGFP 60.10 (Box 33, R (L-Z) Misc. Correspondence 1974–79 Folder), Harvard University Archives.

48. Gerald Gladstein to Skinner, January 11, 1962, B. F. Skinner Collection, HUGFP 60.10 (Box 6, Misc. Correspondence 1962 Folder), Harvard University Archives.

49. Program: Education and the Control of Human Behavior: A Dialogue, no date, B. F. Skinner Collection, HUGFP 60.15 (Box 5, 1962 Letters and Documents Folder), Harvard University Archives.

50. Skinner to Gladstein, May 2, 1962, B. F. Skinner Collection, HUGFP 60.10 (Box 6, Misc. Correspondence 1962 Folder), Harvard University Archives.

51. Program: Education and the Control of Human Behavior: A Dialogue, no date, B. F. Skinner Collection, HUGFP 60.15 (Box 5, 1962 Letters and Documents Folder), Harvard University Archives.

52. Skinner to A. W. Tamminen, April 9, 1963, B. F. Skinner Collection, HUGFP 60.15 (Box 6, 1963 Letters and Documents Folder), Harvard University Archives; Skinner to A. W. Tamminen, August 5, 1963, B. F. Skinner Collection, HUGFP 60.15 (Box 6, 1963 Letters and Documents Folder), Harvard University Archives.

53. Rogers to Skinner, May 18, 1965, B. F. Skinner Collection, HUGFP 60.10 (Box 7, Misc. Correspondence 1964–65 Folder), Harvard University Archives.

54. Skinner to Rogers, May 24, 1965, B. F. Skinner Collection, HUGFP 60.10 (Box 7, Misc. Correspondence 1964–65 Folder), Harvard University Archives.

55. See Carl R. Rogers, "In Retrospect: Forty-six Years," *American Psychologist* 29 (1974, February): 115–23; and B. F. Skinner, "Comment on Rogers," *American Psychologist* 29 (1974, August): 640; Carl R. Rogers and B. F. Skinner, *Rogers/Skinner Dialogue: A Dialogue on Education and the Control of Human Behavior*, ed. by Gerald A. Gladstein (New York: Psychology Today Library Cassettes, 1975); and Howard Kirschenbaum and Valerie Land Henderson, eds., *Carl Rogers: Dialogues* (Boston: Houghton Mifflin, 1989), 79–152.

56. Skinner to Rogers, September 8, 1982, B. F. Skinner Collection, Harvard University Archives arc #11529.

57. Rogers to Skinner, November 5, 1982, B. F. Skinner Collection, Harvard University Archives arc #11529.

58. Rogers to Skinner, May 14, 1956, Carl R. Rogers Collection, Box 80, Folder 7, Manuscript Division, Library of Congress and B. F. Skinner Collection, HUGFP 60.15 (Box 4, 1956 Letters and Documents Folder), Harvard University Archives.

59. Iris Marion Young, "Communication and the Other: Beyond Deliberative Democracy," in *Democracy and Difference: Contesting the Boundaries of the Political*, ed. Seyla Benhabib (Princeton, NJ: Princeton University Press, 1996), 129.

60. Ibid.

61. Ibid.

62. Krasner, "The Future and the Past," 803.

FIFTEEN

"You Don't Know Me"

Portrayals of Black Fatherhood and Husbandhood
in T.I. and Tiny: The Family Hustle

Siobhan E. Smith, Ryessia Jones, and Johnny Jones

In December 2011, the Harris family, which consists of Tip "T.I." Harris, his wife "Tiny" (Tameka), and their five children, emerged on the reality television show *T.I. and Tiny: The Family Hustle*. The program features rapper "T.I." and his family dynamics in the hyper-mediated world of commercial hip-hop. The show debuted on VH1 just four months after T.I.'s release from a federal prison in Arkansas, and it features T.I. returning to his work as a rapper, actor, and businessman while also introducing his and Tiny's blended family of six children to the business. The family includes Tiny's daughter from a previous relationship, Zonnique "Niq Niq" Pullins; T.I.'s two sons and daughter from previous relationships, Messiah, Domani and Deyjah, respectively; and Tiny and T.I.'s sons King and Major. The Harrises recently welcomed a seventh child, daughter Heiress Harris, to their family, in March 2016.

In the years since its debut, *The Family Hustle* has evolved into a platform that draws attention to the tensions surrounding portrayals of Black masculinity, specifically fatherhood and husbandhood. Throughout the program's narrative existence, T.I. attempts to revamp his gangster rapper image into one that is more family friendly. In addition, with their blended family on display on *T.I. and Tiny: The Family Hustle*, T.I. and Tiny are determined to construct their own account of the twenty-first-century Black family.

According to Mark P. Orbe, academic research that focuses on Blacks in the media "has called attention to the ways that images of Blacks in the media historically have remained largely invisible, marginalized to the point of insignificance, or been limited to specific stereotypes."[1] These limited images of Blacks in the media often result in individuals constructing their perceptions of Blacks; these viewpoints are often woefully incomplete.[2] In essence, an examination of *The Family Hustle* suggests that the show presents the Black family, while expanding the perception of Black fatherhood and husbandhood. Shows like *The Family Hustle* also create a space where viewers can confront the issues concerning the creation and maintenance of Black male persona in today's hyper-mediated world.

Almost thirty years earlier, in 1984, the "Father Laureate,"[3] Heathcliff Huxtable, made his debut on NBC's *The Cosby Show*. This narrative program, though fictional, maintained authentic touches from Bill Cosby's life, such as his experience as an educated man who enjoys upper-middle-class success with his family. *The Family Hustle* is just one of the recent television offerings that attempt to share varied dimensions of Black life. The shows often take the form of situation comedies (e.g., *The Cosby Show, My Wife and Kids, All of Us, The Hughleys, The Bernie Mac Show*) and reality television shows (e.g., *The Family Hustle, Run's House, Snoop Dogg's Father Hood, Marrying the Game*). Granted, though sitcoms tend to present variations of the American nuclear family, and reality TV regularly features gangster rappers as fathers, both situate the middle-class Black family as headed by a patriarch. With these issues at the forefront of discussion, this chapter reviews past presentations of fathers before exploring T.I.'s presentation of Black fatherhood and husbandhood on *The Family Hustle*. By exploring these past presentations, this analysis illustrates how T.I. challenges the current representations of Black males in their familial roles. In focusing on T.I. as a Black father and husband, this chapter reveals how T.I. discredits Tiny's parenting and business entrepreneurship skills in order to be portrayed as an adequate parent and provider despite his troubled past. Two themes emerged from the text: Black fatherhood and husbandhood. The first theme, Black fatherhood, focuses on what T.I. views to be his fatherly duties, which is to keep his daughters out of strip clubs, keep his sons out of prison, and help each child develop their own "hustle." The second theme, husbandhood, focuses on T.I. making the transition to head of household after his prison sentence.

PORTRAYALS OF FATHERS AND FAMILIES IN TELEVISION

Research has explored the portrayals of fatherhood and families in popular culture. In the televisual context, Timothy Pehlke, Charles Hennon,

Elise Radina, and Katherine Kuvalanka's study of 12 non-animated sitcoms derived three themes: father-child interactions, negative messages about fatherhood, and racial/ethnic and socio-economic issues in fathering.[4] Concerning the latter, the analysis of three shows featuring minority characters (e.g., Black families on *My Wife and Kids* and *All of Us*, a Latino family on *The George Lopez Show*) found these fathers to be particularly emotionally supportive of their children. These fathers were also members of the middle-class, and unlike blue-collar fathers, did not display buffoonish behaviors. This particular discovery echoes past findings of television families.[5]

Focusing on the portrayals of Black families on television, a brief exploration of the 1985–1986 season focused on just three shows, *The Cosby Show*, *227*, and *Charlie & Company*.[6] Despite the few programs that featured African Americans, the researchers found positive portrayals of Black families. Family members were well-dressed, competent, and were headed by employed parents. Further, the majority of interactions were between wives and husbands, suggesting that the latter were very much a part of their families. Ultimately, this study provided evidence of a more positive image of Black families, in contrast to previous research.[7]

Research regarding the Black family has also studied how these families have been portrayed in reality television via hip-hop celebrities. For example, Ryessia Jones, Johnny Jones, and Siobhan Smith focused on Black motherhood,[8] finding that *T.I. and Tiny: The Family Hustle* portrays Tiny as a mother caught between her own desires ("the devoted finance and compromised stage mother")[9] and her devotion to her husband and family ("the deferential hip-hop wife").[10] Studies have also focused on Black fathers/rappers. Debra Smith argues that *Run's House* features a family more reminiscent of *The Cosby Show*,[11] with its emphasis on celebrity friends, "loving and fun" fathering,[12] and the parents' encouraging their children to be successful. While Snoop Dogg is not always presented in a positive manner in *Father Hood*, both shows emphasize positive dynamics of the Black family, Black fathers who are present in their children's lives, and Black males who are active partners with their wives. Although *The Cosby Show* was critiqued because it tended to ignore tensions surrounding Black socio-political issues, *Father Hood* regularly refers to Snoop's impoverished background and his desire to provide his children with a better life. Ultimately, while research reveals a history of progression in the portrayals of Black families and Black fathers in popular culture, our analysis considers T.I.'s contribution to this progression but also critiques how his performance of fatherhood and husbandhood digresses due to the patriarchal standards of *The Family Hustle* that are inherent in popular culture television.

T.I. and Tiny: The Family Hustle was originally one of the celeb-reality offerings from Cris Abrego and Mark Cronin's 51 Minds Entertainment (e.g., *Strange Love*, *My Fair Brady*), premiering on December 5, 2011. *The*

Family Hustle takes an angle that is different from the couple's previous two reality TV shows, *Road to Redemption* and *Tiny & Toya*, by seemingly blending the subject matter of both. The show uses familiar reality TV visual cues (e.g., confessionals via *The Real World*) and focuses closely on the dynamics of the family in a situation comedy (e.g., *The Osbournes* and *Run's House*).[13] However, what makes *The Family Hustle* unique is that it privileges the perspective of a Black man, T.I., as he attempts to manage his marriage to Tiny and meet the various needs of his children. Throughout the show, T.I. regularly embodies a Cliff Huxtable persona. The character is influenced by his own image and identity as he wears sweaters and discusses his life as a Black father and husband who is a successful business-educated man in the hip-hop industry who also enjoys upper-middle-class success with his family.

FROM TIP TO T.I.

Born Clifford Joseph Harris, Jr., but often known as T.I.P. or King of the South, T.I. debuted in 2001 with his album *I'm Serious*. He released the critically acclaimed *Trap Muzik* (2003) and *Urban Legend* (2004) before releasing his most popular work at that time, *King* (2006). This album featured several hits, and paved the way for his fifth studio album, *T.I. vs. T.I.P.* (2007). He also began forays into acting with *ATL* and *American Gangster*. His 2014 album, *Paperwork*, peaked at No. 2 on Billboard's 200. Along with his most recent film *Sleepless Night* (2016), T.I. continued his music industry enterprises when he signed a distribution deal with Jay Z's Roc Nation for his latest album, *Dime Trap* (2016), and also became one of several major hip-hop/pop artists to become a minority artist-owner of Jay Z's Tidal online music streaming service.

While achieving his musical and acting successes, T.I. has also had his fair share of legal battles. He has been arrested many times, including for violating his probation (2003), for possession of firearms (2007), and for possession of marijuana (2010). He has also served prison time. During this time period, Tiny appeared on the reality television show *Tiny & Toya*, which aired from 2009–2010 on Black Entertainment Television (BET); the show aired for two seasons. The show spotlighted T.I.'s lack of a presence, offering audiences only glimpses of the rapper. In fact, the audience has to rely on family phone conversations and Tiny's narratives to get a sense of T.I. Meanwhile, another reality show, *T.I.'s Road to Redemption* (2009), focused on his efforts to complete 1,000 hours of community service to reduce his sentence for weapons charges. As the cameras follow T.I., the audience is able to see him perform community service by speaking to schools and community groups about the importance of staying out of trouble. It is also in this reality television show that T.I. first welcomes the audience into his personal life. For instance, the audience is able to see the birth of his and Tiny's son, Major, the release of his *Paper Trail* (2008) album, and his understanding the consequences of his actions. Despite T.I. being more open about his personal life, the audience sees little interaction between T.I. and his family. It was *The Family Hustle* that actually broke this ground. Our exploration of *The Family Hustle* revealed that T.I.'s image on the show coalesced around two themes: Black fatherhood and husbandhood. Ultimately, these themes reveal that even though T.I. prioritizes "God, family, and then, hustle" on the first episode, the show truly presents hustle and family—the Harrises are not particularly portrayed as religious. Even more striking is that "family" really refers to T.I.'s relationships with his children, not the one with his wife.

T.I. AS BLACK FATHER AND HUSBAND

Black Fatherhood

To illustrate how T.I. performs Black fatherhood, it is necessary to examine what T.I. considers to be his fatherly duties. As mentioned previously, the Harris Family is a blended family. Despite not being the biological father of Zonnique ("Niq Niq"), T.I. still refers to her as his daughter. Furthermore, the audience sees T.I. taking an active parenting role in Domani, Messiah, and Deyjah's lives, despite having joint custody of them. For this reason, the relationships T.I. has with his children illustrate how he performs Black fatherhood. We discovered two mini-themes regarding T.I. as a father: (a) fatherly goals and (b) family hustle.

In *T.I. and Tiny: The Family Hustle*, T.I. mentions he has two major goals as a father: (1) to keep his daughters out of strip clubs and (2) to keep his sons out of prison. Though T.I. knows he is not a model citizen, he hopes that his children will respect him, despite having been absent from their lives. Furthermore, T.I. realizes that his function as a father is to have his children learn from his mistakes, thus allowing him to be a more positive role model for them.[14]

When T.I. returns from serving his sentence in Arkansas, he is shocked to see King misbehave. In "King of the House," the audience sees King refuse to do homework and go to bed. Furthermore, King seems to ignore all of the house rules. Because of King's behavior, T.I. decides to take a more active parenting role. In doing so, T.I. discredits Tiny's ability to discipline her children, but also her ability to be a mother. What is particularly interesting in T.I.'s critique of Tiny's disciplinary techniques is that Tiny maintained the household for almost three years while T.I. was absent due to his legal troubles. T.I decides to take King and his other sons to his old neighborhood to "show them some struggle." By taking the boys to the old neighborhood, although T.I. does not mention it, he teaches his sons about being privileged and draws attention to their current socioeconomic status. If T.I. were not a successful entrepreneur, the old neighborhood would be the Harris family's living situation.

Further, to ensure that T.I. keeps his daughters out of trouble, T.I. focuses on teaching them to respect themselves. In the episode "Bad and Sneaky," T.I. learns that Deyjah has a boyfriend. When discussing boys with her, T.I. tells his daughter that boys will tell her anything to get her "sugar." In their conversation, Dejyah thinks her father is referring to kisses. However, the audience understands that T.I. is referring to sex. T.I. instructs Deyjah to never give away all her "sugar" because she "only has one cup of sugar to give." T.I. encourages his daughter to not engage in any sexual activities until she is old enough and unless she finds the right person. In essence, to ensure that his daughters "stay out of the strip club," during conversations about sex, T.I. attempts to instill a sense of respectability to them. T.I. encourages his daughter to not engage in any sexual activities unless she finds the right person. Patricia Hill Collins notes politics of respectability is "characterized by cleanliness of person and property, temperance, thrift, polite manners, and sexuality."[15] By having his daughters embrace a politics of respectability, they challenge the dominant stereotype of Black women's sexual immorality while helping T.I. fulfill his fatherly duties of making sure his daughters "stay out of the strip club."

T.I. also stresses the importance of receiving an education. Throughout the season, the audience sees T.I. disciplining Deyjah and Domani because of their low grades. Deyjah's poor grades cause her to lose the privilege of her electronics. It is worth mentioning that Deyjah's mother provides the terms for her punishment and T.I. agrees. Furthermore, T.I. warns Deyjah that her Christmas gifts will be affected if she does not improve her grades. In another instance, T.I. makes an offer to Domani to encourage him to improve his grades. If Domani improves and completes additional schoolwork, he will have the opportunity to shoot his first music video. T.I.'s approach works, and Domani's grades do indeed improve. On one hand, the show's display of T.I.'s concerns for his children's education is a simple plot point in the program's narrative. On another hand, it illustrates the gendered aspects of his fathering and privileges his parenting. In fairness, T.I. does take time to speak privately with both children about their academic performance. But what's interesting is how he treats them differently. Though both children are the same age, Deyjah is punished, while Domani is ultimately rewarded. In fact, the viewers never learn what happens to Deyjah's grades; Domani's grade successes, in addition to the fact that the show suggests that T.I.'s parenting attempts always work, imply that Deyjah improved her grades. But the viewers never see this, because the situation is never mentioned again. By contrast, the show spends time showing Domani record his music video with T.I.'s help. In this instance, T.I.'s sons appear to trump his daughters. In addition, the show argues that T.I.'s discipline is more effective than Tiny's—this is discussed in more detail below.

In addition to fathering his children, T.I. explicitly states that one of his goals for his children is to help them find their own "hustle," or a financially lucrative career path. Throughout season one, the audience sees each child develop their own hustle. The audience is privy to Zonnique's developing music career with the OMG Girlz as she participates in her first national tour. Also, the audience learns that Messiah is a children's book author. As stated above, T.I. provides Domani with an opportunity to perform an original rap and to shoot his first music video. To help King and Major start their acting careers, Tiny and T.I. take the boys to Los Angeles to meet with an agency for child actors and develop skills as child models/actors. In addition, all of the children have the opportunity to reenact Messiah's book as a play and participate in a fashion show for T.I.'s Akoo clothing line. In encouraging his children to find their own hustles, T.I. is acting as a supportive father who is integrating his children's lives into the commercial hip-hop industry. His interactions with his children are used to validate his brand as the ultimate hustler, which is considered a key component in succeeding in the industry. This portrayal is certainly different from Snoop Dogg's portrayal as a less-than-ideal role model. T.I. not only uses the hustle as a mode toward respectability, but it also places him closer to Cliff Huxtable's persona as a father who often encouraged the value of work and education on his children alongside Claire Huxtable, who functioned as the family values disciplinarian. With *The Family Hustle*, T.I.'s fatherhood is privileged as he operates from the position of a hip-hop businessman capable of giving his children access to business opportunities and teaching them values, discipline, and work ethic simultaneously. Ultimately, his fatherhood becomes an embodiment of the progressive values of mothers and fathers in the portrayals of the Black family in popular culture television. The problematic of this fatherhood and masculinity is that it overlooks the mother's role in the process.

The Husbandhood Hustle

In addition to T.I.'s focus on developing his relationships with his children and assisting them in their hustles, the show also features his relationship with Tiny. Their relational dynamic is presented as T.I. often overruling Tiny's previous guidelines for the children, T.I. not respecting Tiny as a business woman, and not concerning himself with her personal development, which also feeds into the presentation of T.I.'s hustle as the brains and breadwinner of the family. While this portrayal aligns with sitcoms and reality TV shows that both situate the middle-class Black family as headed by a patriarch, it further establishes T.I.'s agency as a patriarch. He stifles Tiny's evolution as a wife and mother, thus portraying a relationship that supports T.I.'s husbandhood hustle as productive and Tiny's supportive role as nonproductive.[16]

Both *Tiny & Toya* and the first portion of the first episode of *The Family Hustle* explain that during T.I.'s incarceration, Tiny had to maintain the family. However, on his return, he is not happy with a range of issues, from the cleanliness of their home to Tiny's management of the children as they grow up. As mentioned above, in "Bad and Sneaky," T.I. is horrified to learn that Deyjah has a boyfriend. He is even more distraught when he learns that Tiny knew about the relationship—she just hadn't told *him* about it. In "Baby Girl," T.I. makes it his business to patrol the video shoot for the OMG Girls. He is upset to discover that Zonnique and the other young ladies in the group are wearing heels and lipstick. He declares in a confessional to the audience that girls who performed these behaviors were considered loose and he did not want Zonnique to be perceived that way. In both instances, Tiny attempts to point out that T.I. is overreacting. Concerning Deyjah's boyfriend, she states that there exists a double standard; though he doesn't want Deyjah dating, he encourages his sons to do so (viewers are privy to these conversations throughout the season). Further, she insists that the wardrobe for the video shoot is cute and appropriate for the girls' age. T.I.'s view of Tiny's lax parenting is privileged by the show, as he is given the final word. After making changes to the OMG Girls' clothes, he declares, "My work here is done." His statement suggests that Tiny had not done any work to maintain the girls' youthful image, so he had to get involved. Furthermore, this portrayal presents a "father knows best" mentality and the assumption that Tiny does not do her job as a mother. Showing T.I. appearing on set for the girls' video shoot and overriding many of his wife's choices demean her as a partner in their marriage as well as in their family businesses. Considering Tiny's presence during T.I.'s absence due to his incarceration, the reality televisual portrayal reveals contradictions in T.I.'s husbandhood in that he has not been alone in instilling values in his children. According to the show, he does not work in conjunction with his wife in making family decisions and teaching their children, a patriarchal and inherently sexist image that dismisses the possibility for the portrayal of an egalitarian marriage produced by the show.

The show also presents T.I. as the more business-oriented and financially responsible parent. In "Sixty Forty," Tiny is often showed arguing with her business partner and stylist Shekinah about their hair dryer prototype. By contrast, viewers see T.I. calmly and quickly recording tracks in the studio with R&B superstar Usher. In another instance, in "I Will Put My Foot on Your Back Pocket," scenes of Tiny getting a consultation from a plastic surgeon are shown back to back with clips of T.I.'s going to Los Angeles to promote his book, *Power & Beauty*, at a signing. From there, he appears at a radio station for an interview. As the narrative goes back and forth between them, it is apparent that the show presents T.I. as *still* working, thus hustling. Tiny has done little, if any work at all. The message is clear: T.I. works, Tiny plays. In "Sixty Forty," T.I. uses the children to mock Tiny's business ventures: even youngest son Major replies "no" when T.I. asks him, "Should Mommy and Auntie Shekinah work together?" Instead of asking Tiny should she and Shekinah work together, T.I. chooses to ask their three-year old child. By asking Major this question, T.I. insinuates that a toddler has more common sense than Tiny. But more importantly, T.I. is unwilling to support Tiny's aspirations and hustles, despite supporting their children's hustles.

In addition to mocking Tiny as a businesswoman, T.I. rarely seems concerned about Tiny's personal development or deepening the bonds of their marriage. As mentioned above, T.I.'s main concern appears to be making sure that his children are productive and that they are developing their own hustles. Unfortunately, this leaves little time for T.I. and Tiny's relationship. Only in the "Booty Tag" episode does T.I. finally show his appreciation for Tiny and the sacrifices she has made. Despite planning a childfree candlelight dinner for Tiny to express his gratitude, the majority of the episodes suggest T.I. treats Tiny as one of the children. When he convenes family meetings, he does not consult Tiny before these gatherings, but tells *her* and the children what is expected of them. This exemplifies *The Family Hustle's* presentation of the Black family as one dominated by patriarchal Black fatherhood and husbandhood hustle, thus presenting a space where viewers can question the issues concerning the creation and maintenance of Black male persona in the hyper-mediated world of hip-hop, television, and Black popular culture. While the portrayal of T.I. can be viewed positively on some levels, each positive depiction is met with a problematic portrayal to the detriment of Tiny and therefore the Black family as a whole. Our analysis is not an attempt to debate over the sympathy that should be offered to either Tiny or T.I., but it reveals how the reality television show presents a positive Black family that is respectable in spite of its blended construction and T.I.'s past, but also how the dynamics of T.I. and Tiny's marriage roles are troubled by patriarchy in the husband and a lack of agency for the wife. This discovery is inherent in popular culture television sitcoms and reality shows.

SUMMARY

Our analysis of T.I.'s portrayal on *The Family Hustle* produced two major themes, Black fatherhood and husbandhood. Therefore, this analysis brings attention to and offers visibility concerning the historical portrayals of Blacks in media. Although we reveal how T.I. challenges stereotypes of black fatherhood, we also recognize how his performance of husbandhood marginalizes portrayals of his wife, Tiny. Special emphasis is put on raising children and helping them find their interests and careers, to the detriment of marriage. Limited media images of the Black family such as these often result in individuals constructing their perceptions of Blacks; these viewpoints are often extremely incomplete and inconsistent with research that has revealed commercial television's ability "to be a rhizomatic construct, which encompasses myriad social, political, and ideological issues."[17] Although T.I. presents some progressive perspectives of Black male identity via reality television, our analysis still provides evidence for the need to present more televisual narratives consistent with blackness, including identity construction and collectivity in the Black family and community that responds to more parochial images of Blacks.

Because *The Family Hustle* is a reality television show, the audience is left to ask, "what happens when the cameras are off?" For instance, when examining T.I.'s 2012 album, *Trouble Man: Heavy Is the Head*, one cannot help but notice the gun that T.I. holds on his illustrated album cover. Although the gun is not real, one is left to ask if T.I. has actually learned from his past mistakes. Furthermore, this portrayal also questions how T.I. is challenged to mediate his reality television and his hip-hop hyper-masculine identities. According to Mark Anthony Neal, "hip-hop has been a primary site for the articulation of distinct forms of black masculinity."[18] These forms are filled with contradictory narratives and iconic images from many of its most popular artists that not only reveal more three-dimensional (albeit problematic) individuals, but it shows how reality TV and other popular culture media can limit those identities. Although T.I.'s performance of Black fatherhood on *The Family Hustle* coincides with the values and consciousness that rappers articulate about their children in hip-hop music—T.I.'s primary medium—the possibilities to present a more progressive performance of Black husbandhood is limited on *The Family Hustle*. For instance, T.I. has recorded multiple songs ("Got Your Back" [2010] and "Stay" [2014]) that articulate his dedication to his wife. This appreciation is overlooked on *The Family Hustle* for the sake of upholding the hustle, but also the patriarchal standards of reality television and society. Ultimately, T.I. reproduces a patriarchy on the reality television show to the detriment of a three-dimensional identity formation of hip-hop hyper-masculinity.[19]

Throughout the show, T.I.'s interactions with his children and wife harken back to Cosby's portrayal of fatherhood and husbandhood as Cliff Huxtable. Of course, both Bill Cosby and Tip Harris have had unsavory elements of their private lives threaten to upstage their more palatable personality aspects (e.g., accusations of infidelity, issues surrounding children from extra-marital relationships, run-ins with law enforcement). This presents a challenge to Black men of Harris' and Cosby's statuses of having to both work to control their mediated image, while also simultaneously presenting a particular view of the Black family amid problematic performances and markings of Black male identities and masculinities.

In essence, this chapter highlights how *T.I. and Tiny: The Family Hustle* allows polarized images of Black males to emerge in reality television. In the episode titled, "America's Sweetheart," T.I. performs with Taylor Swift. In the interview confession, T.I. reveals to viewers that he has not performed for a large audience since his eighteen-month prison sentence, which he refers to as his "hiatus." When preparing for the performance, T.I. jokes about trying not to curse in front of Taylor Swift's young fan-base because he does not "need that look." Also in the episode, T.I. jokes with his wife and rappers Young Jeezy and Nelly about the differences between a hip-hop concert and a Taylor Swift concert. In discussing pro-fanity and the concert backstage differences, viewers are made aware of the dichotomy between T.I's gangster persona (e.g., explicit song lyrics and prison sentence) and his family-friendly persona (e.g., performing in front of a predominantly young, white audience with "America's Sweet-heart," Taylor Swift). While *T.I. and Tiny: The Family Hustle* helps T.I. achieve this G-rated image, thus causing the show to challenge the nega-tive stereotypes of Black males in the media, this show also becomes a space for patriarchy. Throughout the program, T.I. often undermines Tiny's authority and achievements. In discrediting Tiny, the show por-trays her as an inadequate mother and failed businesswoman. These are false notions; viewers and fans are aware of Tiny's ability to raise a blended family while T.I. was incarcerated and her successful music ca-reer as an artist and songwriter. Popular culture is the space in which we will learn just how far T.I.—and reality TV—is willing to go to challenge the negative notions of Black males in the media.

While our analysis of *The Family Hustle* discovers the inherent patriar-chy that lies in a somewhat progressive portrayal of Black masculinity in T.I., this also gives implications to the multi-faceted nature of Black mas-culinity through the performance of fatherhood and husband. In this examination of celeb-reality television, we recognize how a hip-hop superstar uses his privilege to give his family a presence in popular cul-ture, to promote life values toward a reformed and progressive Black manhood, and present a blended family with loving parents. Despite his past, T.I. performs this identity in an entertaining manner that makes it presentable to popular culture audiences that might not sense the inher-ent patriarchy beyond the charm and humor of the show. Our analysis reveals that while the Black family can provide a progressive and even lucrative place in television, more portrayals that challenge patriarchy in family television shows can benefit blackness as it is portrayed in the media. While T.I. contributes to the progression of this image with *The Family Hustle*, it further proves that Black masculinity can push for more advanced portrayals that confront the construction of masculinity and patriarchy in the hyper-mediated world as a whole.

NOTES

1. Mark P. Orbe. "Constructions of Reality on MTV's "The Real World": An Analysis of the Restrictive Coding of Black Masculinity," *Southern Journal of Communication* 64, no. 1 (1998): 33.

2. Douglas Kellner, *Media Culture: Cultural Studies, Identity Politics Between the Modern and the Post-Modern* (London: Routledge, 1995).

3. Anne Chan, "Bill Cosby: America's Father," in *Black Fathers: An Invisible Presence in America*, ed. Michael E. Connor and Joseph White (London: Routledge, 2006), 125.

4. Timothy Allen Pehlke II, Charles B. Hennon, M. Elise Radina, and Katherine A. Kuvalanka, "Does Father Still Know Best? An Inductive Thematic Analysis of Popular TV Sitcoms," *Fathering* 7, no. 2 (2009).

5. Richard Butsch, "Class and Gender in Four Decades of Television Situation Comedy: Plus Ca Change . . . " *Critical Studies in Media Communication* 9, no. 4 (1992).

6. Bishetta Merritt and Carolyn A. Stroman, "Black Family Imagery and Interactions on Television," *Journal of Black Studies* 23, no. 4 (1993).

7. Gordon L. Berry, "Television and Afro-Americans: Past Legacy and Present Portrayals," in *Television and Social Behavior: Beyond Violence and Children*, ed. Stephen. B. Withey and Ronald P. Abeles (London: Routledge, 1980); Bradley S. Greenberg and Kimberly Neuendorf, "Black Family Interactions on Television," in *Life on Television: Content Analyses of U.S. TV Drama*, ed. Bradley S. Greenberg (Ablex: Norwood, New Jersey, 1980).

8. Ryessia Jones, Johnny Jones, and Siobhan E. Smith, "From 90s Girl to Hiphop Wife: An Analysis of the Portrayal of Tiny as Black Mother in Reality Television," in *Black Women Are Loud! A Critical Analysis of Black Women's Portrayals on Reality Television*, ed. Donnetrice Allison (Lanham, Maryland: Lexington Books, 2016).

9. Ibid., 45.

10. Ibid., 48,

11. Debra C. Smith, "Critiquing Reality-Based Televisual Black Fatherhood: A Critical Analysis of Run's House and Snoop Dogg's Father Hood," *Critical Studies in Media Communication* 25, no. 4 (2008).

12. Ibid., 402.

13. Richard M. Huff, *Reality Television* (New York: Praeger, 2006), 25.

14. L. Malone-Colon and Alex Roberts, *Marriage and the Well-Being of African American Boys*, Institute for American Values: Center for Marriage and Families, 2006, no. 2.

15. Patricia Hill Collins, *Black sexual politics: African Americans, gender, and the new racism*, 2nd ed. (New York: Routledge, 2005), 71.

16. Jones, Jones, Smith 2016.

17. Bambi Haggins, "Afterword: Television in the Age of Digital: New Frontier and Brave New World," *Emergences: Journal for the Study of Media and Composite Cultures* 11, no. 1 (2001): 129.

18. Mark A. Neal, *New Black Man* (New York: Routledge, 2006), 129.

19. Derek Iwamoto, "Tupac Shakur: Understanding the Identity Formation of Hyper-Masculinity of a Popular Hip-Hop Artist," *The Black Scholar* 33, no. 2 (2003).

SIXTEEN

Video Gaming

Aggressively Social

Robert Andrew Dunn

Research about the negative aspects of video gaming abounds, particularly the effects of violent content on aggression.[1] However, the validity and strength of these effects have been questioned.[2] Moreover, research publications have shown evidence of bias in favor of such negative effects studies, and scholars have paid less attention to the so-called prosocial aspects of gaming: particularly that of cooperation, social connectivity and cohesion, and community building. Early researchers promoted the potential of virtual and cyberspace communities.[3] And some even pointed to early online gaming, particularly Multi-User Dimensions (MUDs), text-based Internet games, and their potential to promote collaboration and instill cohesion.[4] But what of today's worlds? *Worlds of Warcraft* and *Minecraft*?[5] Worlds of *Borderlands* and *Rock Bands*?[6] Worlds of aliens and zombies? What do the games of today provide or engender in terms of collaboration between partners, social cohesion within hunting parties, and community building amongst the online hoards? To answer such questions, one must delve into the video game industry and understand its nature.

The video game industry has evolved into a complex, massive, and lucrative industry, earning $15.4 billion in 2014.[7] Social gaming accounts for a large portion of that industry, as 39 percent of frequent gamers said they play social games.[8] In addition, frequent gamers said they play social games more than any other games, and, at 56 percent, more than half said they played games with other people including friends (42 percent), family (21 percent), parents (16 percent), and spouses/partners (15 percent).[9] This seems to challenge the antisocial narrative that has been painted by negative effects research over the years. This is true even among school-aged children, who are thought to be particularly vulnerable.[10]

> The gaming industry is producing a steady stream of games that continue to expand in their nature and impact—they can be artistic, social, and collaborative, with many allowing massive numbers of people from all over the world to participate simultaneously.[11]

COOPERATION

Michael Argyle has argued that cooperation is an essential stepping-stone to social behavior.[12] He defined cooperation as our capacity "to engage in joint behaviour with others."[13] He said it is more than just working toward a common goal. He wrote: "More crucial than this, I suggest, is following a shared programme, which generates coordinated behaviour, which in some cases is an end in itself, as in games, music, and dance."[14] Given that games among more than one person require cooperation, it makes sense that engaging in gameplay with others is a prosocial behavior in itself. There are abundant research findings on violent video games and aggression.[15] However, other research has found that cooperative video game play can actually reduce aggressiveness, even when the video game is a violent one.[16]

Researchers who have studied both violent content and prosocial behavior in gaming found that playing prosocial games correlated with prosocial traits such as helping behavior, empathy, emotional awareness, cooperation, and sharing. And though the researchers found that playing violent games overall seemed either to be negatively related to or less positively related to prosocial traits overall, playing violent video games was indeed found to be positively related to cooperation and sharing and emotional awareness. Thus, both prosocial and violent video games are linked to cooperation.[17] Research has also shown that when video gamers are placed in either competitive situations or cooperative situations, those in the cooperative situations are more likely than those in competitive situations to engage in tit-for-tat behavior, mirroring the behaviors others have shown them, including cooperative ones.[18]

A group of Canadian researchers explicitly studied video games with a cooperative function. The scholars identified four positive cooperative performance metrics, which included simultaneous expressions of laughter and excitement by the players, deliberations on strategy among players during the game, mutual extensions of helpful advice among players during the game, and adherence to a global strategy among all players.[19] The researchers also identified some struggles with cooperative game play, that of players sometimes getting in the way of one another in the game and waiting for other gamers, often less skilled, to catch up.[20] Research that is more recent found that cooperative play led to more effort than competitive play in video games. Also, when playing a video game cooperatively, friends were more committed to the game's goals than strangers were.[21] Such findings do not seem to speak to a cold world of aggressive, anti-social gamers that other scholars have painted of video games. Other research has shown that playing video games cooperatively, as opposed to playing solo, engendered unity and trust and fostered collaboration.[22]

SOCIAL CONNECTIVITY AND COHESION

The online video game can be seen as a social conduit, a place where people connect with one another.[23] Nick Yee, in his studies of Massively Multiplayer Online (MMO) games, found that people are motivated to play such games by the promise of achievement, the lure of immersion, and the desire to connect socially with others.[24] That social connection included a desire for casual chat, helping others, making friends, building personal relationship, self-disclosing to others, finding and giving support, collaborating as a team, working with others in groups, and achieving goals with groups.[25] In his other research, he identified three types of social groupings one finds within MMOs: "combat groups (temporary collaboration between a few users), guilds (persistent user-created membership organizations), and ideological alliances (agreements between guilds or "racial" groups)."[26] Thus, the MMO accounts for a particularly social kind of game, one in which the player often depends on making friends, joining groups, and even building communities in order to truly advance in the game.[27] Ferguson argues that as a result, gamers often feel a strong link to their in-game social network.[28] Yee cited relationship building as a prime motivation for why people play MMOs.[29] This relationship motivation is built on the idea that gamers are looking to make significant connections with others, who will reciprocate support.[30]

Romantic and Familial Connections

Sherry Turkle discovered both in her original discussions twenty years ago and in her most recent research that people have found and continue to find love via online gaming.[31] She wrote about a text-based video game, a MUD, set in the world of *Star Trek*.[32]

> Through typed descriptions and typed commands, they create characters who have casual and romantic sexual encounters, hold jobs and collect paychecks, attend rituals and celebrations, fall in love and get

married. To the participants, such goings-on can be gripping; "This is more real than my real life," says a character who turns out to be a man playing a woman who is pretending to be a man.[33]

Many years later, Turkle would judge this mediated approach to romance with a bit more of a critical eye. She introduced the world to Pete, a man who is married with kids to a woman in real life and is married to another person (assumedly a woman named Jade) in the online video game Second Life, which Turkle describes as more of a virtual environment than a true game with winners, losers, or objectives. Pete and Jade communicate via type and text, have virtual sex via computer animation, and discuss topics he feels uncomfortable discussing with his real-life wife. Pete considers this second love life a vital part of his offline existence.[34]

> Second Life gives me a better relationship than I have in real life. This is where I feel most myself. Jade accepts who I am. My relationship with Jade makes it possible for me to stay in my marriage with my family.[35]

Though Turkle goes on to suggest this is an irony, and looked askance at the relationship overall, one must wonder if this is our place to do?[36] Yes, the relationship is an extramarital affair, even polygamous in a sense. But that is not what troubles Turkle. It is the cold, impersonal, online, and ever-present nature of it. Pete is not just having an affair; he is living another life, a Second Life.[37] Is not that what he is supposed to do? Is not that what the game is there for? We change; we adapt. We live multiple lives, as Turkle points out. Reality becomes polyreality.[38]

Yee found within Massively Multiplayer Online Role-Playing Games that romantic couples who play together were quite common.[39]

> Thus, not only do MMORPGs have wide and strong appeal, but the likelihood of co-usage with individuals who are emotionally close to the user is also quite high. The stereotypical video gamer is characterized as socially withdrawn and playing alone, but the co-usage findings together with the fact that the MMORPG user is in an environment with hundreds of other users show that MMORPG users clearly do not fit this stereotypical profile. The substantial portion of MMORPG users who have a romantic partner or family member who also participates in the same MMORPG opens up the potential to explore how their virtual interactions differ or impact their real-life interactions.[40]

More recent research backs up these assertions. A survey of 2,865 *World of Warcraft* gamers revealed that 30 percent played the game with a romantic partner.[41] Kim-Phong Huynh, Si-Wei Lim and Marko M. Skoric found three distinct types of romantic relationships among online gamers: "splitters," those who kept their online relationships separate from their real life; "migrators," those who dabbled in mixing online and real life; and "blenders," those who established no differences between online and real life.[42]

Friendship

As mentioned above, the Entertainment Software Association's most recent research on frequent gamers showed that 42 percent play with friends and 54 percent said video games help to stay connected with friends.[43] Turkle interviewed many Second Life gamers who look to the game as a means of spicing up their social life, describing it as a source for new friendships.[44] Is this a surprising finding? In an age when many have lamented that we no longer know our neighbors, is it surprising that many might turn to online sources to diversify themselves socially? Where do people turn in a time when volunteerism, membership in social organizations, and entertaining others socially has steadily been on the wane?[45] For one, Second Life. The game that is not a game has a number of uses for people seeking deeper connections, even help. Recent research into support groups in Second Life showed that participants found them to be particularly satisfying and rewarding.[46]

> Cancer Caregiver group members comment on the love, deep understanding, and close friendships they develop in the group. Alcoholics Anonymous members describe their group as family, best friends, loving community, admired others, and dedicated people. Participants see themselves as connected to each other in close relationships.[47]

Yee, in his studies of MMOs, found that gamers had shared intimate secrets with their online friends that they had not told their real-life counterparts. He also found that 53.3 percent of women and 39.4 percent of men found their friendships online to be the same or better than their real-life friends.[48] In their research on *Halo: Reach*, a multiplayer first-person shooter video game, Winter Mason and Aaron Clauset found that more than half of the players involved in the study had played the game with another player in the study.[49] Gamer respondents were also more likely to say another respondent was an online or offline friend than in other forms of social media.[50] The researchers also found that playing with friends improved the gamers' own performance, improved their team's performances, and yielded more overall prosocial behavior.[51]

COMMUNITY BUILDING

Early on, online gaming communities fell into two categories, those text-based MUDs driven by adventure gaming and those text-based MUDs driven by socialization.[52] These MUDs featured role-playing participants, which were stratified into social hierarchies of deified super users with special privileges and average users with no privileges.[53] Later Burger-Helmchen and Cohendet identified three user communities associated with video games.[54] The first are the testers, those who beta test games and are in direct communication with the company to help it improve its games.[55] The second are the players, those who are enthusiastic about the game. They may be modders, those that modify the games into new versions, or they may be organizers, those who run online guilds or in some way assist other gamers and new gamers acclimate to the game and assist them in immersing in the game experience.[56] The final user group is developers, those with a sophisticated set of skills who actually may be called upon to assist in the creation of a game or a portion of a game.[57] These categories still speak to hierarchies established on knowledge. However, they do not speak to the relationships that develop within those communities. Hierarchy does not necessarily connote dysfunction or absence of community.

Turkle introduced a man, Joel, who would span a few of these community categories.[58] Joel beta-tested Second Life, but did not enjoy it.[59] As a software designer and artist by trade, he later returned to the game when he found a "community" (a word Turkle uses here but later offers that she uses incorrectly) of like-minded creative types who relished the sandbox aspect of the game.[60] He became a popular, well-connected figure in the game. His magnetism drew in at least one gamer, who sought his counsel on her real-life problems and struggles with suicidal thoughts. Given his social capital and technical skill/knowledge, Joel is in the upper echelon of the Second Life hierarchy. But he takes the time to attend in-game weddings, create in-game gifts for people, and he even offers what counsel he can to a fellow gamer which much less capital.[61] Is that not indicative of a caring community?

Matthieu Guitton studied a *Star Wars*–inspired realm in *Second Life*, populated by a role-playing community.[62] When interviewed, members of the community offered a variety of reasons for why they are committed to the community or why the community maintains its cohesion. Members mentioned a variety of reasons, including their friendships and connections with others, their feeling a sense of home, and their activities in role-playing, helping others, and working for the community at large.[63]

CHALLENGES TO VIDEO GAME SOCIALIZATION

The impermanence of relationships in online gaming is a hindrance to their quality and, perhaps, their meaningfulness and usefulness. Turkle, while discussing the enthusiasm Second Life gamers had for making new friends or even finding new loves, pointed out that many times these connections were short-lived.[64] The relationships lack a certain maturity, and, as the newness wears off or the emotional drama increases, the relationship ends as immature relationships often end—abruptly.[65] Turkle alludes to this being an artifact of feeling, saying, and doing things online we might not otherwise do in real life, a finding supported by research into the Proteus Effect.[66] So were they truly friends to begin with? Truly loves? It would seem that Turkle would suggest no. But even she admits that to many, they are real and meaningful.[67] Even if one has been catfished, that is hoodwinked in a fake online relationship, does it mean that the relationship never existed and was devoid of meaning? Or does it mean it just ended badly, as many real-life relationships do? Still, Turkle makes a fair criticism here. The quality, to some extent, does suffer. Thus, there is a challenge in the lack of maturity of online gaming relationships.

Research into MMO guilds finds that these communities suffer from bloat and can become unwieldy with high membership turnover. A magic number of sorts appears to be 35 members or fewer, which makes the guild manageable.[68] These guilds are particularly effective when they match the kind of team-based groups one sees in the business world.[69] Also, despite thousands, even millions of gamers online, and despite a wealth of groups and guilds to join, most MMO gamers play much of the game alone. However, they do not seem to notice or mind this lack of socialization.[70] As Turkle pointed out, this seems to be indicative of modern society.[71] And as Rheingold pointed out more than 20 years ago, this may not be our place to judge it negatively.[72]

Because the gaming community is both a product and reflection of the real world, it is similarly challenged. Thus, the same societal ills one sees in the real world, one sees in the gaming community. For instance, the recent #GamerGate controversy showed how discourses of gender continue to erupt in online spaces as conservative critics, anti-feminist gamers, and conspiracy theorists attacked female gamers, female game creators, and, ultimately, feminist scholars.[73] The controversy began over accusations that a female video game developer had slept with a video game journalist in return for a favorable game review, which evolved into an overall criticism of the role of feminism in gaming, of journalism ethics, and of academic research.[74] Equality among the sexes within gaming continues to be a struggle. Video game development is still a male-dominated industry at 78 percent male.[75] However, this is not to say that gaming in general is male-dominated. In fact, the Pew Research Center found in 2015 that 42 percent of women owned a game console versus 37 percent of men.[76]

Another challenge that mirrors society in gaming is that of racism. Though odd to consider race as being an issue in video games, given one can choose to be any race they want or even be a race that does not exist while playing, there are still disappointing examples of racism that persist even in electronic worlds. Tanner Higgin discussed how Sony Online Entertainment had created a black race, the Erudites, for its EverQuest MMORPG.[77] However, the race was separated from the other races and proved to be less popular.[78] When SOE created the sequel, EverQuest II, the Erudites were no longer black.[79] Gamers of color, including celebrities and professional gamers, have experienced racism from other gamers.[80] Racial epithets along with sexist and homophobic language are commonplace in the gaming world.[81] However, these are less indicative of a problem with gaming than a problem with society in general. Thus, in this respect, the virtual world and the real world are essentially the same, and challenges to community and cohesion abound on both sides of the screen.

GAMING: A SHARED CULTURE

Given the collectivism and commercialism that gaming has developed over the years, it is doubtful that one can find people who have not been in some way swept up into its ambit. Perhaps no game really captures this zeitgeist of shared popular culture than *Minecraft*, a sandbox game with far-reaching social implications.[82] "*Minecraft* is a game about breaking and placing blocks. At first, people built structures to protect against nocturnal monsters, but as the game grew players worked together to create wonderful, imaginative things."[83] The game has successfully taught players about construction, problem solving, science, math, and artificial intelligence.[84]

> *Minecraft* has succeeded by mining the rich gap in our media between games and tools. It offers players something considerably more than a conventional 3-D sketching program, but something considerably more creative than what most games offer. [*Minecraft* Creator Markus] Persson, inadvertently or not, struck gold by calling on the *Minecraft*'s players to collaborate, deeply, in the process of creation (including the creation of the game itself). Millions of amateur creators responded eagerly to this challenge by embracing a game that let them be more than an audience and a little more than players too.[85]

And indeed, almost 22.6 million people have downloaded the computer version of the game to learn, to share, to build, to create, to commune.[86] *Minecraft* is also available on all major gaming consoles and mobile apps.[87] Beyond the game itself, a culture has developed. Minecraft offers its own social network, *Minebook*.[88] There is an online museum dedicated to the game.[89] And the game has moved from the screen into the world of toys and collectibles like other pop culture machines.[90]

This ability of video games to transcend the boundaries of "just a video game" is what makes them a growing and aggressively social part of our collected, shared culture. This transcendence is what the detractors who focus solely on the connections between gaming and aggression overlook. Video games have spawned other forms of media, including books, comic books, movies, and TV shows. Conversely, nearly all forms of media have been converted into video game forms. With this media fluidity comes social cohesion via fan culture. Video game fans purchase games, buy collectibles, wear branded gear, and participate in convention cosplay. Social identity is also derived from video game play. A study of LAN party gamers (those who network their computers together to play video games collectively) found that the main reason participants attended such a party was a social motivation, to be with other gaming enthusiasts like themselves.[91] And now, perhaps as an example of the zenith of pop culture for video games, developer Nintendo has announced it plans to open a theme park based on its beloved video game characters and worlds.[92] So indeed, video games are popular culture. However, given the demographics of gamers and money earned in the industry cited above, there is a strong case to be made that gaming is inseparable from modern culture.[93] Mainstream media, while still relying on tired pejoratives for gamers, have even legitimized video games as big business and sound investments.[94]

CONCLUSION

Despite some challenges or perceived drawbacks, online gaming does seem to be fertile ground for cooperation, social connectivity/ cohesion, and community building. Moreover, gaming in general is a vital part of our shared culture today. The constant drum beat to demonize video games as nothing more than antisocial dreck overlooks the obvious positive and meaningful impact that video games play in people's lives. Ferguson has spent many years and much copy discussing what he sees as unnecessary fears over violent video games.[95] He has suggested that there are parallels between the moral panic he sees over video games and the moral panics of the past over comic books, *Dungeons & Dragons* tabletop games and the *Harry Potter* book series. His concerns are noteworthy as one can also find socialization and culture among all of these previously feared forms of media. Comic book conventions are found all over the world, bringing out thousands of fans to commune with one another. Tabletop gaming tournaments continue to bring devotees to the table, even at a time when such games can be reasonably, if not perfectly, simulated in a video game setting. And Harry Potter fans can experience their own bewitching adventures at Hogwarts thanks to Universal Studios' Orlando, Florida, theme parks. Essentially, Ferguson's critiques of video games ring true. Moreover, criticism and fear of a facet of society does not negate its existence. Fear of how one socializes does not make it any less social nor does it negate the importance of that culture.

NOTES

1. See Craig A. Anderson and Brad J. Bushman, "Effects of Violent Video Games on Aggressive Behavior, Aggressive Cognition, Aggressive Affect, Physiological

Arousal, and Prosocial Behavior: A Meta-analytic Review of the Scientific Literature," *Psychological Science* 12, no. 5 (2001): 353–59; John L. Sherry, "The Effects of Violent Video Games on Aggression," *Human Communication Research* 27, no. 3 (2001): 409–31.

2. See Christopher John Ferguson, "The Good, the Bad and the Ugly: A Meta-analytic Review of Positive and Negative Effects of Violent Video Games," *Psychiatric Quarterly* 78, no. 4 (2007): 309–16; Christopher J. Ferguson, "Blazing Angels or Resident Evil? Can Violent Video Games Be a Force for Good?," *Review of General Psychology* 14, no. 2 (2010): 68–81; Christopher J. Ferguson, "Video Games and Youth Violence: A Prospective Analysis in Adolescents," *Journal of Youth and Adolescence* 40, no. 4 (2011): 377–91; Christopher J. Ferguson et al., "Violent Video Games and Aggression: Causal Relationship or Byproduct of Family Violence and Intrinsic Violence Motivation?," *Criminal Justice and Behavior* 35, no. 3 (2008): 311–32.

3. See Christopher J. Ferguson, "Evidence for Publication Bias in Video Game Violence Effects Literature: A Meta-analytic Review," *Aggression and Violent Behavior* 12, no. 4 (2007): 470–82; Douglas A. Gentile et al., "The Effects of Prosocial Video Games on Prosocial Behaviors: International Evidence from Correlational, Longitudinal, and Experimental Studies," *Personality and Social Psychology Bulletin* 25, 2009, doi: 10.1177/0146167209333045; Isabela Granic, Adam Lobel, and C. M. E, "The Benefits of Playing Video Games," *American Psychologist* 69, no. 1 (2014): 66–78, doi: 10.1037/a0034857; Howard Rheingold, *The Virtual Community: Homesteading on the Virtual Frontier* (Addison-Wesley Longman Publishing Co., Inc., 1993); Marc A. Smith and Peter Kollock, *Communities in Cyberspace* (London: Routledge, 1999).

4. Sherry Turkle, *Life on the Screen: Identity in the Age of the Age of Internet* (New York: Simon and Schuster, 1995).

5. See Blizzard Entertainment, *World of Warcraft*, 2004; Mojang. *Minecraft*, 2011.

6. See Gearbox Software, *Borderlands*, 2009; Harmonix. *Rock Band*, 2007.

7. Entertainment Software Association, "Essential Facts About Games and Violence" (Entertainment Software Association, 2015), www.theesa.com/wp-content/uploads/2015/04/ESA-Essential-Facts-2015.pdf.

8. Ibid.

9. Ibid.

10. See Craig A. Anderson, Douglas A. Gentile, and Katherine E. Buckley, *Violent Video Game Effects on Children and Adolescents* (New York: Oxford University Press, 2007), www.researchgate.net/profile/Douglas_Gentile/publication/222094716_Violent_video_game_effects_on_children_and_adolescents_Theory_research_and_public_policy/links/0fcfd50ed8fcc2ab96000000.pdf; Douglas A. Gentile and William Stone, "Violent Video Game Effects on Children and Adolescents: A Review of the Literature.," *Minerva Pediatrica* 57, no. 6 (2005): 337–58; Douglas A. Gentile et al., "The Effects of Prosocial Video Games on Prosocial Behaviors: International Evidence from Correlational, Longitudinal, and Experimental Studies," *Personality and Social Psychology Bulletin*, March 25, 2009, doi: 10.1177/0146167209333045.

11. "NMC Horizon Report > 2014 K-12 Edition," accessed October 30, 2015, www.nmc.org/publication/nmc-horizon-report-2014-k-12-edition/, 38.

12. Michael Argyle, *Cooperation (Psychology Revivals): The Basis of Sociability* (Routledge, 2013), xi.

13. Ibid.

14. Ibid.

15. See Craig A. Anderson and Brad J. Bushman, "Effects of Violent Video Games on Aggressive Behavior, Aggressive Cognition, Aggressive Affect, Physiological Arousal, and Prosocial Behavior: A Meta-analytic Review of the Scientific Literature," *Psychological Science* 12, no. 5 (2001): 353–59; John L. Sherry, "The Effects of Violent Video Games on Aggression.," *Human Communication Research* 27, no. 3 (2001): 409–31.

16. Jessica M. Jerabeck and Christopher J. Ferguson, "The Influence of Solitary and Cooperative Violent Video Game Play on Aggressive and Prosocial Behavior," *Computers in Human Behavior* 29, no. 6 (2013): 2573–78.

17. Douglas A. Gentile et al., "The Effects of Prosocial Video Games on Prosocial Behaviors: International Evidence from Correlational, Longitudinal, and Experimental Studies," *Personality and Social Psychology Bulletin*, March 25, 2009, doi: 10.1177/0146167209333045.

18. David R. Ewoldsen et al., "Effect of Playing Violent Video Games Cooperatively or Competitively on Subsequent Cooperative Behavior," *Cyberpsychology, Behavior, and Social Networking* 15, no. 5 (2012): 277–80.

19. Magy Seif El-Nasr, Bardia Aghabeigi, David Milam, Mona Erfani, Beth Lameman, Hamid Maygoli, Sang Mah, "Understanding and Evaluating Cooperative Games," in *Proceedings of the SIGCHI Conference on Human Factors in Computing Systems* (ACM, 2010), 253–62, dl.acm.org/citation.cfm?id=1753363.

20. Ibid.

21. Wei Peng and Gary Hsieh, "The Influence of Competition, Cooperation, and Player Relationship in a Motor Performance-Centered Computer Game," *Computers in Human Behavior* 28, no. 6 (2012): 2100–2106.

22. Tobias Greitemeyer and Christopher Cox, "There's No 'I' in Team: Effects of Cooperative Video Games on Cooperative Behavior," *European Journal of Social Psychology* 43, no. 3 (2013): 224–28.

23. Constance A. Steinkuehler and Dmitri Williams, "Where Everybody Knows Your (Screen) Name: Online Games as 'Third Places'," *Journal of Computer-Mediated Communication* 11, no. 4 (July 1, 2006): 885–909, doi: 10.1111/j.1083-6101.2006.00300.x.

24. Nick Yee, "Motivations for Play in Online Games," *CyberPsychology & Behavior* 9, no. 6 (2006): 772–75, doi: 10.1089/cpb.2006.9.772.

25. Ibid.

26. Nick Yee, "The Psychology of Massively Multi-user Online Role-playing Games: Motivations, Emotional Investment, Relationships and Problematic Usage," in *Avatars at Work and Play* (Springer, 2006), 187–207, link.springer.com/content/pdf/10.1007/1–4020–3898–4_9.pdf, 5.

27. Jane Barnett and Mark Coulson, "Virtually Real: A Psychological Perspective on Massively Multiplayer Online Games.," *Review of General Psychology* 14, no. 2 (2010): 167–79.

28. Christopher J. Ferguson, "Blazing Angels or Resident Evil? Can Violent Video Games Be a Force for Good?," *Review of General Psychology* 14, no. 2 (2010): 68–81.

29. Nick Yee, "The Psychology of Massively Multi-user Online Role-playing Games: Motivations, Emotional Investment, Relationships and Problematic Usage," in *Avatars at Work and Play* (Springer, 2006), 187–207, link.springer.com/content/pdf/10.1007/1–4020–3898–4_9.pdf.

30. Ibid.

31. Sherry Turkle, *Life on the Screen: Identity in the Age of the Internet* (New York: Simon and Schuster, 1995); Sherry Turkle, Alone Together: Why We Expect More from Technology and Less from Each Other (New York: Basic Books, 2012).

32. Sherry Turkle, *Life on the Screen: Identity in the Age of the Internet* (New York: Simon and Schuster, 1995).

33. Ibid, 10.

34. Sherry Turkle, *Alone Together: Why We Expect More from Technology and Less from Each Other* (Basic books, 2012).

35. Ibid, 159.

36. Ibid.

37. Ibid.

38. Robert Andrew Dunn, "Polyreality," in *Beyond New Media: Discourse and Critique in a Polymediated Age*, ed. Art Herbig, Andrew F. Herrmann, and Adam W. Tyma (Lanham, MD: Lexington Books, 2014), 109–24.

39. Nick Yee, "The Demographics, Motivations, and Derived Experiences of Users of Massively Multi-user Online Graphical Environments," *Presence* 15, no. 3 (2006): 309–29.

40. Ibid, 19.

41. See Blizzard Entertainment, *World of Warcraft* (2004); Diane J. Schiano et al., "The 'lonely Gamer' Revisited," *Entertainment Computing 5*, no. 1 (January 2014): 65–70, doi: 10.1016/j.entcom.2013.08.002.

42. Kim-Phong Huynh, Si-Wei Lim, and Marko M. Skoric, "Stepping Out of the Magic Circle: Regulation of Play/Life Boundary in MMO-Mediated Romantic Relationship," *Journal of Computer-Mediated Communication 18*, no. 3 (April 1, 2013): 251–64, doi: 10.1111/jcc4.12011.

43. Entertainment Software Association, "Essential Facts About Games and Violence" (Entertainment Software Association, 2015), www.theesa.com/wp-content/uploads/2015/04/ESA-Essential-Facts-2015.pdf.

44. Sherry Turkle, *Alone Together: Why We Expect More from Technology and Less from Each Other* (New York: Basic Books, 2012).

45. Dora L. Costa and Matthew E. Kahn, "Understanding the Decline in Social Capital, 1952–1998," *Working Paper* (National Bureau of Economic Research, May 2001), www.nber.org/papers/w8295.

46. Sara Green-Hamann, Kristen Campbell Eichhorn, and John C. Sherblom, "An Exploration of Why People Participate in Second Life Social Support Groups," *Journal of Computer-Mediated Communication 16* (2011): 465–91.

47. Ibid, 484.

48. Nick Yee, "The Demographics, Motivations, and Derived Experiences of Users of Massively Multi-user Online Graphical Environments," *Presence 15*, no. 3 (2006): 309–29..

49. See Bungie, *Halo: Reach* (2010); Winter Mason and Aaron Clauset, "Friends Ftw! Friendship and Competition in Halo: Reach," in *Proceedings of the 2013 Conference on Computer Supported Cooperative Work* (ACM, 2013), 375–86, dl.acm.org/citation.cfm?id=2441820.

50. Ibid.

51. Ibid.

52. Howard Rheingold, *The Virtual Community: Homesteading on the Virtual Frontier* (Addison-Wesley Longman Publishing Co., Inc., 1993).

53. See Elizabeth Reid, "Hierarchy and Power," in *Communities in Cyberspace,* ed. Marc A. Smith and Peter Kollock (London: Routledge, 1999), 107–33; Howard Rheingold, *The Virtual Community: Homesteading on the Virtual Frontier* (Addison-Wesley Longman Publishing Co., Inc., 1993).

54. Thierry Burger-Helmchen and Patrick Cohendet, "User Communities and Social Software in the Video Game Industry," *Long Range Planning 44*, no. 31 (2011): 317–43.

55. Ibid.

56. Ibid.

57. Ibid.

58. Sherry Turkle, *Life on the Screen: Identity in the Age of the Internet* (New York: Simon and Schuster, 1995).

59. Ibid.

60. Ibid, 215.

61. Ibid.

62. See Linden Lab, *Second Life* (2003); George Lucas, *Star Wars* (1977); Matthieu J. Guitton, "Living in the Hutt Space: Immersive Process in the Star Wars Role-Play Community of Second Life," *Computers in Human Behavior 28*, no. 5 (September 2012): 1681–91, doi: 10.1016/j.chb.2012.04.006.

63. Ibid.

64. Sherry Turkle, *Alone Together: Why We Expect More from Technology and Less from Each Other* (New York: Basic Books, 2012).

65. Ibid.

66. See Nick Yee and Jeremy Bailenson, "The Proteus Effect: The Effect of Transformed Self-representation on Behavior," *Human Communication Research 33*, no. 3 (2007): 271–90; Nick Yee, Jeremy N. Bailenson, and Nicolas Ducheneaut, "The Proteus Effect: Implications of Transformed Digital Self-representation on Online and Offline

Behavior," *Communication Research*, 2009, crx.sagepub.com/content/early/2009/01/22/0093650208330254.short.

67. Sherry Turkle, *Alone Together: Why We Expect More from Technology and Less from Each Other* (New York: Basic Books, 2012).

68. Nicolas Ducheneaut et al., "The Life and Death of Online Gaming Communities: A Look at Guilds in World of Warcraft," in *Proceedings of the SIGCHI Conference on Human Factors in Computing Systems* (ACM, 2007), 839–48, dl.acm.org/citation.cfm?id=1240750.

69. Nicolas Ducheneaut and Nicholas Yee, "Collective Solitude and Social Networks in World of Warcraft," in *Social Networking Communities and E-Dating Services: Concepts and Implications: Concepts and Implications*, ed. Celia Romm-Livermore and Kristina Setzekorn (Hershey, PA: Idea Group Publishing, 2008).

70. Ibid.

71. Sherry Turkle, *Alone Together: Why We Expect More from Technology and Less from Each Other* (New York: Basic Books, 2012).

72. Howard Rheingold, *The Virtual Community: Homesteading on the Virtual Frontier* (Addison-Wesley Longman Publishing Co., Inc., 1993).

73. Shira Chess and Adrienne Shaw, "A Conspiracy of Fishes, or, How We Learned to Stop Worrying About #GamerGate and Embrace Hegemonic Masculinity," *Journal of Broadcasting & Electronic Media* 59, no. 1 (January 2, 2015): 208–20, doi: 10.1080/08838151.2014.999917.

74. Ibid.

75. Ibid.

76. Monica Anderson, "Technology Device Ownership: 2015" (Pew Research Center, 2015), file:///C:/Users/Robert/Desktop/PI_2015-10-29_device-ownership_FINAL.pdf.

77. See Sony Online Entertainment, EverQuest (1999); Tanner Higgin, "Blackless Fantasy: The Disappearance of Race in Massively Multiplayer Online Role-playing Games," Games and Culture, 2009, gac.sagepub.com/content/early/2008/12/01/1555412008325477.short.

78. Tanner Higgin, "Blackless Fantasy: The Disappearance of Race in Massively Multiplayer Online Role-playing Games," Games and Culture, 2009, gac.sagepub.com/content/early/2008/12/01/1555412008325477.short.

79. See Sony Online Entertainment, EverQuest II (2004); Tanner Higgin, "Blackless Fantasy: The Disappearance of Race in Massively Multiplayer Online Role-playing Games," Games and Culture, 2009, gac.sagepub.com/content/early/2008/12/01/1555412008325477.short.

80. Lisa Nakamura, "It's a Nigger in Here! Kill the Nigger!," *The International Encyclopedia of Media Studies* (2012), onlinelibrary.wiley.com/doi/10.1002/9781444361506.wbiems159/full.

81. Ibid.

82. Mojang, *Minecraft*, 2011.

83. Mojang, "Home," *Minecraft*, accessed February 16, 2016, minecraft.net/, para. 1.

84. See Jessica D. Bayliss, "Teaching Game AI through Minecraft Mods," in *Games Innovation Conference (IGIC), 2012 IEEE International* (IEEE, 2012), 1–4, ieeexplore.ieee.org/xpls/abs_all.jsp?arnumber=6329841; Beth Bos et al., "Learning Mathematics through Minecraft," *Teaching Children Mathematics* 21, no. 1 (2014): 56–59; Sean C. Duncan, "Minecraft, Beyond Construction and Survival," *Well Played: A Journal on Video Games, Value and Meaning* 1, no. 1 (2011): 1–22; Daniel Short, "Teaching Scientific Concepts Using a Virtual world—Minecraft.," *Teaching Science-the Journal of the Australian Science Teachers Association* 58, no. 3 (2012): 55.

85. Greg Lastowka, "Minecraft as Web 2.0: Amateur Creativity & Digital Games," in *Amateur Media: Social, Cultural and Legal Perspectives* (2012): 18–19.

86. Mojang, "Home," *Minecraft*, accessed February 16, 2016, minecraft.net/.

87. Ibid.

88. Minebook, "Welcome to Minebook," *Minebook—Your Minecraft Social Site*, accessed February 16, 2016, minebook.me/.

89. The Minecraft Museum, "The Minecraft Museum," accessed February 16, 2016, minecraftmuseum.net/.

90. Toys"R"Us, "Minecraft Toys & Games for Kids," accessed February 16, 2016, www.toysrus.com/products/minecraft-toys.jsp.

91. Jeroen Jansz and Lonneke Martens, "Gaming at a LAN Event: The Social Context of Playing Video Games," *New Media & Society* 7, no. 3 (2005): 333–55.

92. Nintendo, "Nintendo Partners with Universal Parks & Resorts to Create World's First-ever Theme Park Attractions Based on Nintendo's Beloved Games and Characters—Nintendo Official Site," accessed February 16, 2016, www.nintendo.com/whatsnew/detail/vsMQJPFdvKCUCn-0T3D4eEAhoWb7jEEp.

93. Entertainment Software Association, "Essential Facts About Games and Violence" (Entertainment Software Association, 2015), www.theesa.com/wp-content/uploads/2015/04/ESA-Essential-Facts-2015.pdf.

94. Paul R. LaMonica, "Video Games Aren't Just for Antisocial Nerds!," *CNN Money*, October 16, 2015, money.cnn.com/2015/10/16/investing/electronic-arts-activision-video-games/.

95. See Christopher J. Ferguson, "The School Shooting/violent Video Game Link: Causal Relationship or Moral Panic?," *Journal of Investigative Psychology and Offender Profiling* 5, no. 1–2 (2008): 25–37; Christopher J. Ferguson, "Violent Video Games: Dogma, Fear and Pseudoscience," *Skeptical Inquirer* 33, no. 5 (2009): 38–54; Christopher J. Ferguson, "Blazing Angels or Resident Evil? Can Violent Video Games Be a Force for Good?," *Review of General Psychology* 14, no. 2 (2010): 68–81.

SEVENTEEN

Popular Culture, Pedagogy, and Dialoguing Difference

Starting Difficult Conversations in the Communication Classroom

Kristen L. McCauliff and Katherine J. Denker

In September 2015, college professors' Facebook and Twitter feeds were abuzz with a hotly debated *New York Times* article that asked "Are College Lectures Unfair?" Those of us that employ learner-centered, active engagement in the classroom were not surprised by the claim that this "specific cultural form . . . favors some people while discriminating against others, including women, minorities and low-income and first-generation college students. This is not a matter of instructor bias; it is the lecture format itself . . . that offers unfair advantages to an already privileged population."[1] Many professors noticed it lacked specific examples of what to put in the place of these lectures or what types of instructional supports would enhance a lecture-based course. We offer one such suggestion in this chapter. We argue that using popular culture examples in the classroom meets the demand that instructors find a way to provide "structure, feedback and interaction, prompting students to become participants in constructing their own knowledge rather than passive recipients."[2] For us, this active learning style is reminiscent of the literature on cultural literacy as using popular culture texts help students become critically literate in the classroom.

Critical literacy is defined as the ability not only to read and write, but also to assess texts in order to understand the relationships between power and domination that underlie and inform those texts.[3] The critically literate can understand the socially constructed meaning embedded in texts as well as the political and economic contexts of texts. Ultimately then, critical literacy can lead to an emancipated worldview and transform students.[4] Indeed, in this chapter, we argue that when instructors provide popular culture texts and encourage students to bring their own, the classroom transforms into a space that gives voice to more students and helps them work through controversial ideas. Additionally, the popular culture texts we use in class give legitimacy to subject positions other than the ones that we and many of our students occupy. In the following pages, we highlight two case studies from our own classes that demonstrate some possibilities in using popular culture texts to teach about race and sexuality.[5] Because we know that identity is always already intersectional, discussions of race and sexuality often include conversations about other identities such as class, gender, ethnicity and many more. So, while we discuss race and sexuality, we argue that readers will be able to transfer these suggestions to other identity politics discussions. In this chapter, we review the literature establishing the link between critical media literacy, learning, and student engagement. We pay particular attention to the great work being done by communication scholars that talk about the importance of popular culture and pedagogy as well as those writing about critical communication pedagogy. We then turn to a discussion of our experiences. We organize this discussion around two specific classes and identity categories. These specific experiences give way to a deductive argument that the strategy of using popular culture texts to discuss controversial issues can be used in other classrooms to discuss other issues. We hope, too, that while many of the examples we give here are mediated popular culture examples, we provide many ways to pull current, critical texts—such as books and current, popular speeches into classes.

CRITICAL LITERACY, AUTONOMY, AND LEARNING

As communication scholars we are, thankfully, not alone in noting the power of popular culture texts in the classroom. First and foremost, Deanna D. Sellnow and Barry Brummett have written useful textbooks directed toward communication professors eager to discuss and use popular culture in the classroom setting.[6] And as Sellnow reminds us, popular culture texts are powerful in influencing our take-for-granted beliefs and behaviors about how things ought to be as well as what is normal and desirable.[7] (See Sellnow chapter, this volume.) Thus, a pedagogy that uses popular culture is a critical pedagogy where students and instructors learn from and with one another while engaging in conversation centered on actual experiences. This focus on texts that highlight one's lived experiences gives way to an opportunity for students to attain critical literacy. Critical literacy encourages students to challenge the status quo in an effort to discover alternative paths for self and social development. This kind of literacy connects the political and the personal, the public and the private, the global and the local, the economic and the pedagogical, for rethinking our lives and for promoting justice in place of inequity.[8] We hope to make clear in this chapter that the classroom is a place to use and teach popular culture texts to encourage students and instructors to remake themselves and society.

We argue that using popular culture texts should be included in the robust discussion of critical communication pedagogy that is occurring in Communication Studies. Communication scholars Deanna L. Fassett and John T. Warren developed critical communication pedagogy as a framework for those scholars who incorporate critical pedagogy, focusing explicitly on how everyday communication helps to (re)produce and (de)construct dominant ideologies. Similar to critical pedagogy, critical communication depicts teachers as "transformative intellectuals who are located in a position to radically transform culture."[9] Critical communication pedagogy advocates a dialogic, reflexive approach to teaching and learning, where participants collaborate with one another to critique and transform traditional educational practices. In addition, critical communication pedagogy seeks to facilitate classrooms that are sites of resistance and empowerment, where students acquire their own critical perspectives and skills useful in other contexts. As Brenda Allen writes, "It invites instructors to specify higher education and the classroom as crucial sites of power dynamics" and as a place to examine the politics of the "real" world.[10]

There are a few reasons that using popular culture texts is in line with the critical communication pedagogy literature. It might be enough to remind readers that Warren and Fassett themselves say that critical communication pedagogy attends to the texts and technologies scholars use in their classrooms.[11] Several arguments bear fleshing out. First, using popular culture examples recognizes that our students and other popular figures are experts in their own right. Derek Greenfield argues that students may enter with more knowledge of popular culture than the instructor; thus, in sharing the authority in the classroom, we all can become co-learners.[12] Additionally, giving voice to experts outside of our textbooks shows that students and professors have much to learn from each other. Especially for those of us who are members of dominant identity groups, it is helpful to include other voices in the classroom space. As Bryant Keith Alexander writes, "Critical pedagogy is concerned with revealing, interrogating, and challenging those legitimated social forms and opening the space for additional voices."[13] When reflecting on their desire to make use of their digital native's expertise, Radhika Gajjala, Natalia Rybas, and Yahui Zhang created a participatory learning environment where, instead of being the expert imparting knowledge, they were critical pedagogues "become facilitators and learners at the same time."[14] This learning relationship—where both students and teachers are understood as living and situated beings with valuable insights—is in line with critical communication pedagogy.

Second, and related, it places the culture the students are often living within as front and center in the classroom space. As Andrew Herrmann notes, "popular culture helps us define who we are, what we believe, and influences whom we befriend."[15] To that end, then, popular culture also helps students discuss who they are and their influences. Popular culture examples provide a wonderful example of praxis in the classroom space. Critical communication pedagogy relies heavily on the work of Paolo Freire, who thought of liberatory education as a process where learners come to conscientization through praxis—the integration of critical theory with reflection.[16] This conscientization is key to developing and honing an awareness of one's social reality. Popular culture texts do just this. They give way to consideration of one's own bodies and experiences within the outside world. Bryant Keith Alexander elaborates, "teaching occurs at those intersections where sanctioned course content collides with lived experience—those moments when the 'unspeakable' is spoken and the reverberation of the social exchange ricochets and resonates in the classroom."[17]

The third connection to critical communication pedagogy is that using popular culture texts destabilizes the classroom space and helps faculty members acknowledge that they may be enacting domination and oppression in the classroom. As we cover later in the chapter, using popular culture examples ensures that diverse topics are talked about and they are done so in a way where we, white, middle-class, heterosexual women, are not positioning ourselves as experts. In sharing the authority in the classroom, all can become co-learners within the classroom space.[18] Since students will bring in popular culture texts that we are not familiar with and we employ popular culture readings from authors that do not come from traditional, academic sources, we are "self-reflexive regarding the power dynamics of how we 'manage' the classroom."[19] Not only does this inspire conversation, as we argue, it helps point the conversation in a productive way—often destabilizing narratives of oppression and domination. In short, turning over the classroom space to popular culture texts means that instructors are finding "ways to teach critically while also actively searching for ways to call privileged perspectives—including their own teacherly perspectives—into question with students."[20]

PUTTING IT INTO PRACTICE:
OUR EXPERIENCE(S) IN THE CLASSROOM

In this section, we both talk about our classes generally and then share specific examples of using popular culture texts in the classroom space to talk about identity politics issues. In our institution, discussions about race and sexuality are often difficult. While our struggles may be specific to the size, demographic make-up, and location, we have no doubt that we are not unique in the struggle to talk about race and sexuality or other controversial issues. In addition, we suspect we are not unique in our desire to trouble and counter the predominant academic voice, one that is typically white and privileged, in our classrooms. We use our experiences in the classroom with the hope that other educators will be able to use them in other contexts. Ellen D. Gagne, Carol Walker Yekovich, and Frank R. Yekovich argue that transfer is the application of knowledge learned in one setting or for one purpose to another setting or purpose.[21] Thus, we offer these narratives as a way to flesh out some of the possibilities of using popular culture in a communication classroom to give way to cultural literacy.

Taking Control of the Classroom Content by Adding Diverse Case Studies

My, Kristen's, large lecture popular culture class provides a real opportunity to engage in critical communication pedagogy. The course examines mediated, popular culture through a rhetorical theory and criticism lens. I state in my syllabus that the class will not be a semester long celebration or condemnation of the media and other cultural outlets. Instead, we take a look at the effects American popular culture has on race, class, gender, sexuality, class, and other areas of identity politics. I let students know that by the end of the semester I hope that all of us have a widened perspective of the power, potential, and problems of popular culture. Given the explicit focus on media and popular culture, a reader may assume that it was easy for me to integrate diverse voices and texts into my course. Unfortunately, it took several semesters of trial and error to find a pedagogically sound way of promoting cultural literacy. In this section, I share some information about my class and a few, specific practices that helped make my classroom space more critical. There are two interesting things about my classroom space. I mention these two aspects of my classroom because I want to encourage fellow instructors to think about how they can turn challenging classroom management issues into pedagogical opportunities. However, recognizing the challenges and the pedagogical implications of those challenges is an important first step in the classroom design process.

First, the diversity of my students' academic backgrounds makes for both a fruitful discussion and a difficult one. Because this class is an option for one of our university's core curriculum requirements, students from all over our university choose to enroll. It is populated mostly by students from the college that houses our department but even that community is widely disparate given that our college is made up of Journalism and our Telecommunications departments that both have a large focus on production and digital media. This provides an interesting challenge and opportunity in terms of content. Because the students are not all trained or skilled in the same areas, they are often more open to a variety of literature and sources as class readings. However, they do not have the same background knowledge. For example, I cannot assume that all of my students have had training in Marxist or feminist criticism or even have thought about academic criticism at all.

Next, given that the class is a popular culture course, many students view themselves as experts in the content despite their lack of training. Given that they may consume a lot of media—and even talk about it critically with friends and fellow students—they come into the classroom with a particular expectation of what the class will be and how they will perform on the graded exercises. While this presents a challenge in terms of metacognition, the ability to assess one's own ability and skill, it also provides an opportunity in terms of positioning the students as producers of course content and material. Because they feel confident talking about popular culture, it is fairly easy to break down typical power dynamics. Unfortunately, when I first started teaching this class, I did not realize this opportunity and did not always integrate student voices successfully.

When I first began using popular culture texts in my classroom, *I* selected ones that I believed supplemented the academic readings in the classroom. Often they were more interesting and timely than those talked about in our textbook and course reading packet but, upon reflection, they were not often more diverse. As someone who is white and came of age during the 1990s, my mediated examples often mimicked my subject position. And not only did I frequently get "the examples were so boring" on my teaching evaluations but I also got feedback from my students and teaching assistants that my examples were too white. I tried various ways to get students more involved in providing examples for lectures. I would give them time in class to brainstorm and then share out additional examples of shows they watched or commercials they had seen. However, the discussions never really went anywhere. And while I had surface level knowledge of other, more diverse shows, tracking down useful clips and being able to talk about them in class requires more than this surface level knowledge.

I knew that for real change to occur in my classroom, I needed to get my students involved in course design in a more planned, intentional way. I started capitalizing on my students' expertise and experience with media by requiring them to think about fitting examples outside of class.

Because my students were already keeping a class blog to record their reactions to the weekly readings, I was able to do an easy adjustment to have access to more diverse popular culture examples that were better integrated into the course. I started requiring that the students' blog posts provide an example (they could chose a television show, movie, commercial, artist, or work of literature) to illustrate the usefulness or not of the class material for the week. The students were required to post their examples early in the week and they were aware that I would use their examples in lecture and as examples on tests and quizzes. While students seemed hesitant to share at first, forcing them to do it before class rather than on the spot during lecture turned out to be revolutionary. I encouraged them to move from simple informative posts naming a television show to lengthier, more enriched posts that used clips, sample dialogue and clear ties to class material. I would highlight particularly useful blog posts in class and by mid-semester, the students really grasped not only how to do a helpful blog post but the pedagogical advantage to doing so.

The blog posts, while not graded for anything more than minimal participation points, became mediated hotbeds of examples. Over time the blog posts become less and less of a focus and, instead, I just automatically fold in the Youtube or Hulu videos posted on the blog posts. We use them as a way to extend our understanding of class readings. And, more often than not, we use them to critique things that are missing from our class reading. The critique is easy to do because of the focus of so many of the blog posts—on more racially diverse examples than what our class readings analyzed. So, while I started with the simple goal of having more timely and "cool" examples, I quickly realized that student-provided examples were a great way of troubling course content.

I had a wealth of popular culture examples at my fingertips during my first semester and it has grown every semester. So, now when I teach an article about television appropriating the girl power narratives of the 90s—an article that uses exclusively white examples—I have clips from shows that feature a diverse cast such as *That's So Raven* and *Everybody Hates Chris*. When we talk about sexuality and read articles that look at very prominent (white) lesbians such as Ellen DeGeneres, I now have examples that feature Laverne Cox, a trans woman of color, on Katie Couric and clips from *Jane The Virgin*, which features a Latina lead character. While I am familiar with all of these shows and people, the level of knowledge highlighted in the blog posts and the appropriateness of the clips surpasses my knowledge. Thus, the readily available examples make it easy to include these voices. The students and I can use the clips as a way to test out the theoretical ideas present in our class reading. So, for example, when the class reads an article about how DeGeneres was able to maintain her popularity as an "out" television star in the 1990s because her focus on the personal rather than the political made a heteronormative viewer feel comfortable, we talk about the differences that Cox offers us in terms of her own activism and her role on *Orange is the New Black*. An even more poignant example happened one semester during a unit on sports. That unit focuses on media coverage of athletes and the militaristic nature of sports. We watched a documentary that came out in 2010 and is critical of sports' homophobic tendencies. The students successfully brought in powerful articles about Michael Sam, the first openly gay, African American college football player to show just how homophobic sports culture continues to be more than five years later.

While I will never know for sure, I am fairly confident that these examples were successful precisely because they were student introduced and led. At a basic level, I have an ally in the student who blogged about the article to use in class discussion. So, I can count on at least one student to voice concerns, thoughts, and feelings that other students probably have as well. In addition, using examples from the students in the class provides an opportunity for the students to be experts—meaning they talk and think more because they are more invested in our learning community. While I have bursts of lecture throughout a seventy-five-minute class session, the class—even with over a hundred students—is predominately discussion based. My role as expert has been minimized and the students feel empowered to talk about class material using their own experience and examples as a starting point.

Over the years I have also tried to become more active during my course design process about selected academic articles that look at diverse texts. This is surprisingly difficult as many of the most accessible articles look at the most *white* of texts. In addition, I think there is pedagogical value in drawing upon student expertise. Using examples from the students gave way to the conscientization we mentioned above. Students not only used their experience with media to highlight and contradict class readings but they also reflected on their own relationship with media. So, the class turned into a space where they could talk about ESPN's homophobic coverage of Michael Sam and the impact of that coverage on their own attitudes toward gay athletes. For those students in the room who did not interact with diverse media, they were able to interrogate why and what impact that has on their conceptions of "normal." Students often wrote on student evaluations that they had "never thought popular culture was so important in the choices" they made as a consumer or reported they found the class "especially interesting and relevant" and that it "really opened their [my] eyes to new ideals." The power of using diverse popular culture examples can also be felt within my relationship with the students. No longer am I the only (white) expert in the room. Instead, I am one of over one hundred experts. We have all come together to talk about ideas and those ideas are enriched and challenged by all experiences and expertise.

Silencing the Dominant Textbook Voice with the Sex(y) Columnist

At times turning to pop culture offers a source of escape in the class-room. In this case study, instead of discussing a larger pedagogical shift, I, Kathy, offer details as to how the popular culture can enliven a course topic. I was searching to engage students in a more inclusive discussion about sexuality growing out of a frustration with the scientific serialization of the topic by our normally loved textbook authors in my upper-level interpersonal communication course. Though I work to incorporate popular culture into my classes in a variety of ways, I turn my attention to our use of pop culture for one week in my senior-level interpersonal class in order to best illustrate the choices that can be made in a class unit. This class, with a focus on the lifespan of a relationship, typically has around 25 students in it. As relationships start, we start the class with an understanding of self, interpersonal relationships, and attraction, and we move through the class, ending with relational termination. Teaching the course as a relational change perspective, we had one week to focus on sex and sexuality in relationships. In earlier semesters, this unit was often minimized and/or combined with the discussion of different topics due to both my limited expertise and the limited current content. However, in seeking to do something different, I spoke with colleagues, who led me to sex columnist Dan Savage.[22] Though I was excited to shift classroom authority from researchers to popular culture voices, I was also worried about students' reactions to the popular author, sex columnist and founder of the It Gets Better Project, but the use of popular culture in the classroom did open our dialogue, bring in new ideas, and illustrate missing perspectives.

At the beginning of the semester, after discussing the goals and objectives for the class, we spent time turning to the calendar as students reviewed details of the reading for the semester each week, often including a book chapter and an additional reading. Typically the additional reading comes in the form of a journal article as students learn to utilize original research. From the onset, students were able to see the additional readings including the option of Savage's chapter entitled "The GGG Spot" as part of our discussion for week nine on sex in relationships.[23]

When we came to the topic of sex in relationships, the use of popular culture examples also facilitated more open interactions. When discussing difficult subjects, there is a general concern about creating safe space and making students comfortable with the discussion. Stephanie Simon notes that often it is useful for professors who are about to lead a discussion on difficult topics to acknowledge this difficulty and center early engagement on this.[24] To open up the discussion of sexuality, the class first watched an Elite Daily video (a news source that calls itself the "voice of generation Y") that illustrated couples' first time talking about the number of people that they slept with, possibility a difficult conversation heightened by cameras and individuals who have avoided the conversation.[25] In seeing the discomforted in the video, this helped normalize the anxieties or hesitancy that the students might have had in talking more about sex in relationships, which then opened up a discussion of the question—as a culture, are we ready to talk about sex?

After recognizing the limitations that often surround discussions of sex, we next turned to a Ted Talk, focusing on the problems with how we talk about sex. In the video *Sex: Let's Talk*, sexual education teacher Al Vernacchio and entrepreneur Cindy Gallop address what we should be talking about in conversations of sex.[26] From the video, I have students engage in Think Pair Share conversations to first discuss the main takeaways from the video, allowing them to offer ideas on a difficult subject as a dyad instead of expecting individuals to be comfortable sharing in the larger group right away.[27] After pulling the class back together, we discuss their reactions further and look at the value judgments and framing of language around issues of sexuality in the videos.

After priming our discussion with videos, discussion about why this topic is difficult to discuss and then further focus on the need to examine and discuss sex in relationships, the class turned to Savage's chapter, "The GGG spot." Central to this chapter are concerns about partner care, mutual support and understanding, the impact of sex-negative culture, as well as communicating with your partner as the basis of sexual satisfaction, topics that are reflected in other research, yet become more engaging through Savage's conversational quality. As I led students through a discussion based on what points stood out to them, as well as what they appreicated and what they wanted to challenge, we maintained a dynamic discussion that hit on each of the key topics that Savage noted in the chapter.

Students had questions, pulled in other examples and challenged the ideas present in the chapter. One aspect of the chapter that helped offer legitimacy to Savage's perspective was his inclusion of research from the *Journal of Sex Research* that supports his claims.[28] Leland Spencer argues that having data to respond to student resistance is helpful in engaging in difficult discussions.[29] However, returning to the academic voice as Savage does in his chapter can be problematic as it works to re-stabilize the classroom experience, and once again return authority to the academic voice.

By offering popular culture and Dan Savage a place of legitimacy in the classroom, I am able to further destabilize the idea of traditional academic knowledge and authority, and also bring more diverse voices into focus in interpersonal relationships. Though textbooks have become more inclusive in depicting LGBTQ individuals in relationships, the information provided often is limited coverage offering a reductionist view of a spectrum of individuals. As students challenged Savage's arguments and delved into discussion quicker, it was clear that pop culture texts offered more access points for individuals into a space of real dialogue. Through this dialogue students seemed more comfortable offering arguments against the experts, creating a space of shared power, and becoming more aware of their relational reality.

Beyond utilizing popular culture examples selected by the instructor, all classes can benefit by the inclusion of more student-generated, popular culture examples in the classroom. Another way that I work to shift the power in the classroom in my interpersonal class is through the use of the media critique assignments. As one of the options in the syllabus, many students each semester sign up to both present and write on media framings of our course concepts. With this assignment, students present and describe the popular culture framing of our class content for the week, critique the source by discussing the aspects that were done well as well as the problems with the source and then finally envision how this source could be improved to offer consumers of the information a better understanding of interpersonal communication. This assignment not only allows the student the space to be the expert, but it has brought in material from the *Twilight* series to discuss attraction to *Ugly Betty* to highlight self-disclosure and coming out, examples that would otherwise not be part of the course dialogue.

CONCLUSION . . . OR NEW BEGINNINGS

In writing this chapter, we engaged in a variety of self-reflection. And, truthfully, we realized that we are only in the beginning stages of making our courses more diverse, inclusive and revolutionary. No matter how reflective and radical we are about our course design, teachers are marked with a particular expertise—that we often subconsciously embrace. Popular culture can facilitate growth in our teaching with adaptations that span the semester or focus on a particular week. We offer these brief exemplars of critical communication pedagogy that use popular culture examples as a way to inspire other faculty members to think through the possibilities of destabilizing traditional narratives in the classroom. We suggest that these examples function as more than just illustrations, destabilizing both traditional narrative and power structures in the classroom and offering a shift into a more dialogic view of education.[30] As individuals look for more inspiration for their teaching, there are plenty of other sources that focus on specific genres or even show specific ways to build in examples that will resonate with and challenge your students.[31] Part of "good" teaching means we impart content knowledge on to our students. But another large part is that we prepare students to navigate the complicated social and political world they occupy. Using popular culture texts is one way to do both. We hope this chapter serves as an invitation to join us in doing so!

NOTES

1. Annie Murphy Paul, "Are College Lectures Unfair?," *New York Times*, September 12, 2015, www.nytimes.com/2015/09/13/opinion/sunday/are-college-lectures-unfair.html?_r=0.

2. Ibid.

3. Glynda Hull, "Critical Literacy and Beyond: Lessons Learned From Students and Workers in a Vocational Program and on the Job," *Anthropology & Education Quarterly* 24, no. 4 (1993):373–396.

4. Paulo Freire, *The Pedagogy of the Oppressed* (New York: Continuum, 1970); Peter McLaren, *Life in Schools: An Introduction to Critical Pedagogy in the Foundation of Education* (Boston: Allyn and Bacon, 2003); Hull 1993.

5. Here we use Sellnow's definition of popular culture, which is "any set of interrelated written, oral, or visual signs and artifacts focused on everyday objects, actions, and events. Deanna D. Sellnow, *The Rhetorical Power of Popular Culture: Considering Mediated Texts* (Thousand Oaks, California: SAGE), 2014, 6.

6. Barry Brummett, *Rhetoric in Popular Culture, 4th ed* (Thousand Oaks, California: SAGE, 2015); Deanna D. Sellnow, *The Rhetorical Power of Popular Culture: Considering Mediated Texts* (Thousand Oaks, California: SAGE), 2014.

7. Sellnow, xi.

8. Ira Shore, "What is Critical Literacy," *The Journal of Pedagogy, Pluralism and Practice* 1, no. 4 (1999): n.p., Accessed September 23, 2015. www.lesley.edu/journal-pedagogy-pluralism-practice/ira-shor/critical-literacy/.

9. Jo Sprague, "Expanding the Research Agenda for Instructional Communication: Raising Some Unasked Questions," *Communication Education* 42, no. 2 (1992): 17. See also Brenda J. Allen, "Critical Communication Pedagogy as a Framework for Teaching Difference and Organizing" in *Reframing Difference in Organizational Communication Studies: Research, Pedagogy, Practice*, edited by Dennis K. Mumby, 103–125 (Thousand Oaks, California: Sage Publishing, 2010), 106.

10. Allen, 110.

11. John T. Warren and Deanna L. Fassett, "Critical Communication Pedagogy: Reframing the Field," in *The SAGE Handbook of Communication and Instruction*, edited by Deanna L. Fassett and John T. Warren, 283–291 (Thousand Oaks, California: Sage Publishing, 2010), 289.

12. Derek Greenfield, "What's the Deal With the White Middle-Aged Guy Teaching Hip-Hop? Lessons in Popular Culture, Positionality and Pedagogy" *Pedagogy, Culture & Society* 15, no. 2 (2007): 233.

13. Bryant Keith Alexander, "Performing Culture in the Classroom: An Instructional (Auto)Ethnography. *Text and Performance Quarterly* 19 (1999): 307.

14. Radhika Gajjala, Natalia Rybas, and Yahui Zhang, "Producing Digitally Mediated Environments as Sites for Critical Feminist Pedagogy," in *The SAGE Handbook of Communication and Instruction*, edited by Deanna L. Fassett and John T. Warren, 411–435 (Thousand Oaks, California: Sage Publishing, 2010), 415.

15. Andrew F. Herrmann, "Daniel Amos and Me: The Power of Pop Culture and Autoethnography," *The Popular Culture Studies Journal* 1, 1–2 (2013): 7.

16. Paulo Freire, *The Pedagogy of the Oppressed* (New York: Continuum, 1970). See also Brenda J. Allen, "Critical Communication Pedagogy as a Framework for Teaching Difference and Organizing" in *Reframing Difference in Organizational Communication Studies: Research, Pedagogy, Practice*, edited by Dennis K. Mumby, 103–125 (Thousand Oaks, California: Sage Publishing, 2010), 104.

17. Bryant Keith Alexander, "Embracing the Teachable Moment: The Black Gay Body in the Classroom as Embodied Text," in *Black Queer Studies: A Critical Anthology*, edited by E. Patrick Johnson and Mae G. Henderson, 249–265 (Durham, NC: Duke University Press, 2005), p. 253.

18. Derek Greenfield, "What's the Deal With the White Middle-Aged Guy Teaching Hip-Hop? Lessons in Popular Culture, Positionality and Pedagogy" *Pedagogy, Culture & Society 15*, no. 2 (2007): 233.

19. Brenda J. Allen, "Critical Communication Pedagogy as a Framework for Teaching Difference and Organizing" in *Reframing Difference in Organizational Communication Studies: Research, Pedagogy, Practice*, edited by Dennis K. Mumby, 103–125 (Thousand Oaks, California: Sage Publishing, 2010), 107.

20. Keith Nainby, John T. Warren, and Christopher Bollinger, "Articulating Contact in the Classroom: Towards a Constitutive Focus in Critical Pedagogy," *Language & Intercultural Communication 3*, no. 3 (2003), 199.

21. Ellen D. Gagne, Carol Walker Yekovich, and Frank R. Yekovich. *The Cognitive Psychology of School Learning* (New York: Harper Collins College, 1993), 235.

22. Thank you Jimmie Manning in guiding me back to this source and teaching idea.

23. Dan Savage, *American Savage: Insights, Slights, and Fights on Faith, Sex, Love, and Politics*. New York: Plume, 2013. Concerned with students' reading of the author's writing style (read frequent use of obscenities), I did post another reading as an alternative for that week and pulled it into class as well; however, discussion on this article was very limited and almost completely lacking in comparison.

24. Stephanie Simon, "'If you raised a boy in a pink room . . . ?' Thoughts on Teaching Geography and Gender," *Journal of Geography 108*, no.1 (2009):14–20.

25. Elite Daily, "Couples Reveal How Many People They've Had Sex With to Each Other" Posted March 10th, 2015. www.youtube.com/watch?v=hkxjuznXLP0. *Elite Daily*. Retrieved November 14, 2015. elitedaily.com/about/.

26. Thu-Huong Ha, "Sex: Let's talk." Posted on March 3rd, 2015. ideas.ted.com/sex-lets-talk/.

27. Stephen Brookfield, *The Skillful Teacher: On Technique, Trust, and Responsiveness in the Classroom* (Jossey Bass, 2006).

28. Savage, 63.

29. Leland G. Spencer, "Engaging Undergraduates in Feminist Classrooms: An Exploration of Professors' Practices," *Equity & Excellence in Education 48*, no. 2 (2015): 204.

30. Ronald C. Arnett, *Dialogic Education: Conversation about Ideas and Between Persons* (Southern Illinois University Press Carbondale, 1992).

31. Jennifer C. Dunn, Jimmie Manning, and Danielle M . Stern, *Lucky Strikes and a Three Martini Lunch: Thinking about Television's Mad Men (Second Edition)* (Cambridge, 2015). See also, Jodie A. Kreider and Meghan K. Winchell, *Buffy in the Classroom: Essays on Teaching with the Vampire Slayer* (Jefferson, NC: McFarland, 2010).

Bibliography

Abbott, Stacey, and David Lavery. *TV Goes to Hell: An Unofficial Road Map of* Supernatural. Toronto: ECW Press, 2011.

Acker, Joan. "Gender Capitalism and Globalization." *Critical Sociology* 30 (2004): 17–40. doi: 10.1163/156916304322981668.

Adams, Rachel. *Sideshow U.S.A.: Freaks and the American Cultural Imagination.* Chicago, IL: University of Chicago Press, 2001.

Adams, Tony E. *Narrating the Closet: An Autoethnography of Same-Sex Attraction.* Walnut Creek, CA: Left Coast Press, 2011.

Adams, Tony E., and Jimmie Manning. "Autoethnography and Family Research." *Journal of Family Theory & Review* 7 (2015): 350–66. doi: 10.1111/jftr.12116.

Adams, Tony E., Stacy Holman Jones, and Carolyn Ellis. *Autoethnography.* New York, NY: Oxford University Press, 2014.

Adorno, Theodor W. "Culture Industry Reconsidered." *New German Critique* 6 (1975): 12–9. doi: 10.2307/487650.

Ahmed, Sara. *Queer Phenomenology: Orientations, Objects, Others.* Durham, NC: Duke University Press, 2006.

Ahmed, Sara. *The Promise of Happiness.* Durham, NC: Duke University Press, 2010.

Alexander, Bryant Keith. "Embracing the Teachable Moment: The Black Gay Body in the Classroom as Embodied Text." In *Black Queer Studies: A Critical Anthology,* edited by E. Patrick Johnson and Mae G. Henderson, 249–65. Durham, NC: Duke University Press, 2005.

———. "Performing Culture in the Classroom: An Instructional (Auto)Ethnography." *Text and Performance Quarterly* 19 (1999): 307–31. doi: 10.1080/10462939909366272.

Alexander, Michelle. *The New Jim Crow: Mass Incarceration in the Age of Colorblindness.* New York, NY: The New Press, 2012.

Allen, Brenda J. "Critical Communication Pedagogy as a Framework for Teaching Difference and Organizing." In *Reframing Difference in Organizational Communication Studies: Research, Pedagogy, Practice,* edited by Dennis K. Mumby, 103–25. Thousand Oaks, CA: Sage, 2010.

Althusser, Louis. *Lenin and Philosophy and Other Essays.* New York, NY: Monthly Review Press, 2001.

Ames, Carol. "PR Goes to the Movies: The Image of Public Relations Improves from 1996 to 2008." *Public Relations Review* 36 (2010): 164–70. doi: 10.1016/j.pubrev.2009.08.016.

Anderson, Craig A., and Brad J. Bushman. "Effects of Violent Video Games on Aggressive Behavior, Aggressive Cognition, Aggressive Affect, Physiological Arousal, and Prosocial Behavior: A Meta-analytic Review of the Scientific Literature." *Psychological Science* 12 (2001): 353–9. doi: 10.1111/1467-9280.00366.

Anderson, Craig A., Douglas A. Gentile, and Katherine E. Buckley. *Violent Video Game Effects on Children and Adolescents.* New York, NY: Oxford University Press, 2007.

Anderson, Monica. "Technology Device Ownership: 2015." *Pew Research Center.* www.pewinternet.org/2015/10/29/technology-device-ownership-2015. (Accessed May 11, 2016).

Anderson, Rob, and Kenneth N. Cissna. *The Martin Buber-Carl Rogers Dialogue: A New Transcript with Commentary.* Albany, NY: SUNY Press, 1997.

Argyle, Michael. *Cooperation: The Basis of Sociability.* New York, NY: Routledge, 2013.

Arnett, Ronald C. *Dialogic Education: Conversation about Ideas and Between Persons.* Carbondale, IL: Southern Illinois University Press, 1992.

Arthurs, Jane. "Sex and the City and Consumer Culture: Remediating Postfeminist Drama." *Feminist Media Studies* 3 (2003): 83–8. doi: 10.1080/1468077032000080149.

Ashcraft, Karen Lee. "Resistance through Consent? Occupational Identity, Organizational Form, and the Maintenance of Masculinity among Commercial Airline Pilots." *Management Communication Quarterly* 19 (2005): 67–90. doi: 10.1177/0893318905276560.

Ashcraft, Karen Lee, and Lisa Flores. "'Slaves with White Collars': Persistent Performances of Masculinity in Crisis." *Text and Performance Quarterly* 23 (2003): 1–29. doi: 10.1080/10462930310001602020.

Ashcraft, Karen Lee, and Dennis K. Mumby. *Reworking Gender: A Feminist Communicology of Organization.* Thousand Oaks, CA: Sage, 2004.

Ashforth, Blake E., and Glen E. Kreiner. "'How Can You Do It?': Dirty Work and the Challenge of Constructing a Positive Identity." *Academy of Management Review* 24 (1999): 413–34. doi: 10.5465/AMR.1999.2202129.

Bailey, Cathryn. "Making Waves and Drawing Lines: The Politics of Defining the Vicissitudes of Feminism." *Hypatia* 12 (1997): 17–28. doi: 10.1111/j.1527-2001.1997.tb00003.x.

Bakhtin, Mikhail M. *Rabelais and His World,* translated by Helene Iswolsky. Bloomington, IN: Indiana University Press, 1984.

Banet-Weiser, Sarah. "What's Your Flava: Race and Postfeminism in Media Culture." In *The Media Studies Reader,* edited by Laurie Ouellette. New York, NY: Routledge, 2013.

Barker, Vanessa. *The Politics of Imprisonment: How the Democratic Process Shapes the Way America Punishes Offenders.* New York, NY: Oxford University Press, 2009.

Barnett, Jane, and Mark Coulson. "Virtually Real: A Psychological Perspective on Massively Multiplayer Online Games." *Review of General Psychology* 14 (2010): 167–79. doi: 10.1037/a0019442.

Bartesaghi, Mariaelena. "Coordination: Examining Weather as a Matter of Concern." *Communication Studies* 65 (2014): 535–57. doi: 10.1080/10510974.2014.957337.

Batchelor, Bob. *Cult Pop Culture: How the Fringe Became Mainstream.* Santa Barbara, CA: ABC-CLIO, 2011.

———. "Creating Public Intellectuals: Popular Culture's Move from Nicheto Mainstream in the Twenty-First Century." In *Popular Culture in the Twenty-First Century,* edited by Myc Wiatrowski and Corey Baker, 2–13. Newcastle upon Tyne: Cambridge Scholars Publishing, 2013.

———. "Editorial: What Is Pop Culture?" *Popular Culture Studies Journal* 1, no. 1 (2013): 1–5.

Baudrillard, Jean. *Simulacra and Simulation.* Translated by Sheila Faria Glaser. Ann Arbor, MI: University of Michigan Press, 1994.

Baxter, Leslie A. "Relationships as Dialogues." *Personal Relationships* 11 (2004): 1–22. doi: 10.1111/j.1475-6811.2004.00068.x.

———. *Voicing Relationships: A Dialogic Perspective.* Thousand Oaks, CA: Sage, 2011.

Bayliss, Jessica D. "Teaching Game AI through Minecraft Mods." *Games Innovation Conference (IGIC),* 2012: 1–4. ieeexplore.ieee.org/xpls/abs_all.jsp?arnumber=6329841. (Accessed May 11, 2016).

Baym, Nancy. *Tune In/Log On: Soaps, Fandom, and Online Community.* Thousand Oaks, CA: Sage, 2000.

Becker, Amy, Michael Xenos, and Don Waisanen. "Sizing Up The Daily Show: Audience Perceptions of Political Comedy Programming." *Atlantic Journal of Communication* 18 (2010): 144–57. doi: 10.1080/15456871003742112.

Beiner, Ronald. *Political Judgement.* New York, NY: Routledge, 2009.

Bennington, Barbara. "Crisis Communication: Sensemaking and Decision-making by the CDC under Conditions of Uncertainty and Ambiguity during the 2009–2010 H1N1 Pandemic." PhD diss., University of South Florida, 2014. ProQuest.

Berlant, Lauren. *Cruel Optimism*. Durham, NC: Duke University Press, 2011.

Berry, Gordon L. "Television and Afro-Americans: Past Legacy and Present Portrayals." In *Television and Social Behavior: Beyond Violence and Children*, edited by Stephen. B. Withey and Ronald P. Abeles, 231–47. London: Routledge, 1980.

Bjork, Daniel W. *B. F. Skinner: A Life*. New York, NY: Basic Books, 1993.

Bloodworth, John D. "Communication in the Youth Counter Culture: Music as Expression." *Communication Studies* 26 (1975): 304–9. doi: 10.1080/1080/10510977509367857.

Bochner, Arthur P., and Carolyn S. Ellis. "Autoethnography." In *Communication As . . . : Perspectives on Theory*, edited by Gregory Shepherd, Jeffrey St. John, and Ted Striphas, 110–22. Thousand Oaks, CA: Sage, 2006.

Bollhöfer, Björn. "'Screenscapes': Placing TV Series in their Contexts of Production, Meaning and Consumption." *Tijdschrift Voor Economische en Sociale Geografie* 98 (2007): 165–75. doi: 10.1111/j.1467-9663.2007.00389.x.

Bolling, Ben, and Matthew J. Smith, eds. *It Happens at Comic-Con: Ethnographic Essays on a Pop Culture Phenomenon*. Jefferson, NC: McFarland, 2014.

Bowen, Shannon A. "All Glamour, no Substance? How Public Relations Majors and Potential Majors in an Exemplar Program View the Industry and Function." *Public Relations Review* 35 (2009): 402–10. doi:10.1016/j.pubrev.2009.05.018.

———. "'I Thought it would be More Glamorous': Preconceptions and Misconceptions among Students in the Public Relations Principles Course." *Public Relations Review* 29 (2003): 199–214. doi:10.1016/S0363–8111(03)00012–2.

Bochantin, Jaime E. "'Morning Fog, Spider Webs, and Escaping from Alcatraz': Examining Metaphors Used by Public Safety Employees and their Families to Help Understand the Relationship between Work and Family." *Communication Monographs* 83 (2015): 1–25. doi: 10.1080/03637751.2015.1073853.

Boot, Adrian, and Chris Salewicz. *Punk: The Illustrated History of a Music Revolution*. New York, NY: Penguin, 1997.

Bos, Beth, Lucy Wilder, Marcelina Cook, and Ryan O'Donnell. "Learning Mathematics through Minecraft." *Teaching Children Mathematics* 21 (2014): 56–9. doi: 10.5951/teacchilmath.21.1.0056.

Boylorn, Robin. "As Seen on TV: An Autoethnographic Reflection on Race and Reality Television." *Critical Studies in Media Communication* 25 (2008): 413–33. doi: 10.1080/15295030802327758.

———. *Sweetwater: Black Women and Narratives of Resistance*. New York, NY: Peter Lang, 2013.

Bratich, Jack Z. "Spies Like Us: Secret Agency and Popular Occulture." In *Secret Agents: Beyond James Bond*, edited by Jeremy Packer, 111–32. New York, NY: Peter Lang, 2009.

Braun, Beth. "*The X-Files* and *Buffy the Vampire Slayer*: The Ambiguity of Evil in Supernatural Representations." *Journal of Popular Film and Television* 28 (2000): 88–94. doi: 10.1080/01956050009602827.

Brayton, Sean. "When Commodities Attack: Reading Narratives of the Great Recession and Late Capitalism in Contemporary Horror Films." *Studies in Media and Communication* 1 (2013): 150–61. redfame.com/journal/index.php/smc/article/view/234/239. (Accessed May 11, 2016).

Brewer, Rose M., and Nancy A. Heitzeg. "The Racialization of Crime and Punishment: Criminal Justice, Color-Blind Racism, and the Political Economy of the Prison Industrial Complex." *American Behavioral Scientist* 51 (2008): 625–44. doi: 10.1177/0002764207307745.

Brookfield, Stephen. *The Skillful Teacher: On Technique, Trust, and Responsiveness in the Classroom*. Hoboken, NJ: Jossey-Bass, 2006.

Brooks, Dwight E., and Walter R. Jacobs. "Black Men in the Margins: Space Traders and the Interpositional Strategy Against B(l)acklash." *Communication Studies* 47 (1996): 289–302. doi: 10.1080/10510979609368484.

Brooks, Meredith, and Shelly Peiken. "Bitch." Single. Capitol Records, 1997.

Bruhm, Steven, and Natasha Hurley. *Curiouser: On the Queerness of Children*. Minneapolis, MN: University of Minnesota Press, 2004.

Brummett, Barry. *Rhetoric in Popular Culture*, 4th ed. Thousand Oaks, CA: Sage, 2015.

———. *Uncovering Hidden Rhetorics: Social Issues in Disguise*. Thousand Oaks, CA: Sage, 2008.

Buckley, Tina. *The N.W.A. Handbook: Everything You Need to Know about N.W.A.* Queensland, Australia: Emereo Publishing, 2016.

Buerkel-Rothfuss, Nancy L., and Sandra Mayes. "Soap Opera Viewing: The Cultivation Effect." *Journal of Communication* 31 (1981): 108–15.

Buerkle, C. Wesley. "Metrosexuality Can Stuff It: Beef Consumption as (Heteromasculine) Fortification." *Text and Performance Quarterly* 29 (2009): 77–93. doi: 10.1080/10462930802514370.

Buhmann, Alexander, Lea Hellmueller, and Louis Bosshart, "Popular Culture and Communication Practice." *Communication Research Trends* 34, no. 3 (2015): 4–18.

Burger-Helmchen, Thierry, and Patrick Cohendet. "User Communities and Social Software in the Video Game Industry." *Long Range Planning* 44 (2011): 317–43. doi:10.1016/j.lrp.2011.09.003.

Burke, Kenneth. *The Philosophy of Literary Form: Studies in Symbolic Action*. Berkeley, CA: University of California Press, 1974.

Butler, Judith. "Gender as Performance." In *A Critical Sense: Interviews with Intellectuals*, edited by Peter Osborne, 109–25. New York, NY: Routledge, 1996.

Bush, George W. "War on Terror." *US Department of State Archive*, September 7, 2003. 2001-2009.state.gov/p/nea/rls/rm/23897.htm. (Accessed May 10, 2016).

Butsch, Richard. "Class and Gender in Four Decades of Television Situation Comedy: Plus Ça Change . . . " *Critical Studies in Media Communication* 9 (1992): 398–9. doi: 10.1080/15295039209366841.

Calka, Michelle. "Polymediation: The Relationship between Self and Media." In *Beyond New Media: Discourse and Critique in a Polymediated Age*, edited by Art Herbig, Andrew F. Herrmann, and Adam W. Tyma, 15–30. Lanham, MD: Lexington, 2015.

Callahan, Sara Dykins. "Academic Outings." *Symbolic Interaction* 31 (2008): 351–75. doi:10.1525/si.2008.31.4.351.

Campbell, Joseph. *The Hero with a Thousand Faces*, commemorative ed. Princeton, NJ: Princeton University Press, 2004.

Chan, Anne. "Bill Cosby: America's Father." In *Black Fathers: An Invisible Presence in America*, edited by Michael E. Connor and Joseph White, 125–43. London: Routledge, 2006.

Charles Rivers Editors. *Hollywood's Gangster Icons: The Lives and Careers of Humphrey Bogart, James Cagney, and Edward G. Robinson*. Boston, MA: Charles Rivers Editors, 2014.

Chelin, Pamela. "Exclusive: Rebecca Black Fighting Ark Music Factory Over 'Friday.'" *Rolling Stone*, April 1, 2011. www.rollingstone.com/music/news/exclusive-rebecca-black-fighting-ark-music-factory-over-friday-20110401#ixzz48EB2PJm3. (Accessed May 9, 2016).

Chess, Shira, and Adrienne Shaw. "A Conspiracy of Fishes, or, How We Learned to Stop Worrying About #GamerGate and Embrace Hegemonic Masculinity." *Journal of Broadcasting & Electronic Media* 59 (2015): 208–20. doi:10.1080/08838151.2014.999917.

Christ-Janer, Albert, Charles W. Hughes, and Carleton S. Smith. *American Hymns Old and New*. New York, NY: Columbia University Press, 1980.

Christian, David. *Maps of Time: An Introduction to Big History*. Berkeley, CA: University of California Press, 2004.

Christian, Johanna, and Shenique S. Thomas. "Examining the Intersections of Race, Gender, and Mass Imprisonment. *Journal of Ethnicity in Criminal Justice* 7 (2009): 72–3. doi: 10.1080/15377930802711797.

Cissna, Kenneth N., and Rob Anderson. *Moments of Meeting: Buber, Rogers, and the Potential for Public Dialogue*. Albany, NY: SUNY Press, 2002.

Collinson, David L. "Identities and Insecurities: Selves at Work." *Organization* 10 (2003): 527–47. doi: 10.1177/13505084030103010.

Cobb, Michael. *Single: Arguments for the Uncoupled*. New York, NY: New York University Press, 2012.

Cohen, Stanley. *Folk Devils and Moral Panics*. Oxford, UK: MacGibbon & Key, 1972.

Collins, Patricia Hill. *Black Feminist Thought: Knowledge, Consciousness, and the Politics of Empowerment*. New York, NY: Routledge, 2000.

Combs, Steven C. *The Dao of Rhetoric*. New York, NY: SUNY Press, 2005.

Compton, Josh. "More than Laughing? Survey of Political Humor Effects Research." In *Laughing Matters: Humor and American Politics in the Media Age*, edited by J. C. Baumgartner and J. S. Morris, 39–63. New York, NY: Routledge, 2008.

Contrara, Jessica. "Being Bad Luck Brian: When the Meme that Made You Famous Starts to Fade Sway." *The Washington Post*, January 5, 2015. www.washingtonpost. com/lifestyle/style/being-bad-luck-brian-when-the-meme-that-made-you-famous-starts-to-fade-away/2015/01/05/07cbf6ac-907c-11e4-a412-4b735edc7175_story.html. (Accessed May 16, 2016).

Cook, Betsy and Riley Vasold. "Team Ironman vs. Team Captain America." *The Talon*, May 13, 2016. thetalon.news/6062/features/team-iron-man-vs-team-captain-america. (Accessed May 14, 2016).

Cooper, Sandra. "Making Sense of Complex Failure: The Case of 9–11." PhD diss., University of South Florida, 2007. ProQuest.

Cooren, François. "Pragmatism as Ventriloquism: Creating a Dialogue Among Seven Traditions in the Study of Communication." *Language Under Discussion* 2 (2014): 1–26. ludjournal.org/index.php?journal=LUD&page=article&op=view&path[]=16&path[]=5.

Costa, Dora L., and Matthew E. Kahn. "Understanding the Decline in Social Capital, 1952–1998." *Working Paper*. National Bureau of Economic Research, May 2001. www.nber.org/papers/w8295. (Accessed May 14, 2016).

Craig, Robert T. "Communication Theory as a Field." *Communication Theory* 9 (1999): 119–61. doi: 10.1111/j.1468–2885.1999.tb00355.x.

Cragin, Becca. "Beyond the Feminine: Intersectionality and Hybridity in Talk Shows." *Women's Studies in Communication* 33 (2010): 154–72. doi: 10.1080/07491409.2010 .507585.

Creekmur, Corey, and Alexander Doty. *Out in Culture: Gay, Lesbian, and Queer Essays on Popular Culture*. Durham, NC: Duke University Press, 1995.

Crenshaw, Kimberlé. "Demarginalizing the Intersection of Race and Sex: A Black Feminist Critique of Antidiscrimination Doctrine, Feminist Theory and Antiracist Politics." *University of Chicago Legal Forum* 140 (1989): 139–67.

———. "Mapping the Margins: Intersectionality, Identity Politics, and Violence Against Women of Color." *Stanford Law Review* 43 (1991): 1241–99.

Cvetkovich, Ann. *Depression: A Public Feeling*. Durham, NC: Duke University Press, 2012.

Daniluk, Judith C. *Women's Sexuality Across the Life Span: Challenging Myths, Creating Meanings*. New York. NY: Guilford Press, 2003.

Davies, Stephen. "The Expression of Emotion in Music." *Mind* 89 (1980): 67–86. doi: 10.1093/mind/LXXXIX.353.67.

Day, Amber. "Shifting the Conversation: Colbert's Super PAC and the Measurement of Satirical Efficacy." *International Journal of Communication* 7 (2013): 414–29. ijoc.org/ index.php/ijoc/article/viewFile/1946/860. (Accessed May 12, 2016).

Deetz, Stanley, and Dennis Mumby. "Metaphors, Information, and Power." In *Information and Behavior*, edited by Brent D. Ruben, 369–86. Piscataway, NJ: Transaction, 1985.

DeFleur, Melvin L. *Mass Communication Theories: Explaining Origins, Processes, and Effects*. Boston, MA: Allyn & Bacon, 2010.

DeFleur, Melvin L., and Sandra Ball-Rokeach. *Theories of Mass Communication*. New York, NY: Pearson, 1989.

Demory, Pamela, and Christopher Pullen. *Queer Love in Film and Television: Critical Essays.* New York, NY: Palgrave Macmillan, 2013.

Denisoff, R. Serge. *Sing a Song of Social Significance,* second edition. Bowling Green, OH: Bowling Green State University Popular Press, 1983.

Denker, Katherine J. "Maintaining Gender During Work-Life Negotiations: Relational Maintenance and the Dark Side of Individual Marginalization." *Women & Language* 36 (2012): 11–34.

Denker, Katherine J., and Debbie Dougherty. "Corporate Colonization of Couples' Work-Life Negotiations: Rationalization, Emotion Management and Silencing Conflict." *Journal of Family Communication* 13 (2013): 242–62. doi: 10.1080/15267431.2013 .796946.

DeSalle, Rob, and Ian Tattersall. *Human Origins: What Bones and Genomes Tell Us about Ourselves.* College Station, TX: Texas A&M University Press, 2008.

Dewey, John. *Art as Experience.* New York, NY: Minton, Balch & Company, 1934.

Diliberto, John. "Zen & the Art of Fripp's Guitar." *Electronic Musician,* January 19, 2006. www.emusician.com/artists/1333/zen--the-art-of-fripps-guitar/36105. (Accessed May 1, 2016).

Dill, Bonnie Thornton, and Ruth Enid Zambrana. *Emerging Intersections: Race, Class, and Gender in Theory.* New Brunswick, NJ: Rutgers University Press, 2009.

Dooley, Patrick K. "Kuhn and Psychology: The Rogers-Skinner, Day-Giorgi Debates." *Journal for the Theory of Social Behaviour* 12 (1982): 275–90. doi: 10.1111/j.1468-5914.1982.tb00451.x.

Dornfeld, Barry. *Producing Public Television, Producing Public Culture.* Princeton, NJ: Princeton University Press, 1998.

Doty, Alexander. *Making Things Perfectly Queer: Interpreting Mass Culture.* Minneapolis: University of Minnesota Press, 1993.

Douglas, Susan. "The Turn Within: The Irony of Technology in a Globalized World." In *The Media Studies Reader,* edited by Laurie Ouellette. New York, NY: Routledge, 2013.

du Gay, Paul, Stuart Hall, Linda Janes, Anders Koed Madsen, Hugh Mackay, and Keith Negus. *Doing Cultural Studies: The Story of the Sony Walkman.* London, UK: Sage, 2013.

Ducheneaut, Nicolas, and Nicholas Yee. "Collective Solitude and Social Networks in World of Warcraft." In *Social Networking Communities and E-Dating Services: Concepts and Implications: Concepts and Implications,* edited by Celia Romm-Livermore and Kristina Setzekorn, 78–100. Hershey, PA: Idea Group Publishing, 2008.

Ducheneaut, Nicolas, Nicholas Yee, Eric Nickell, and Robert J. Moore. "The Life and Death of Online Gaming Communities: A Look at Guilds in World of Warcraft." In *Proceedings of the SIGCHI Conference on Human Factors in Computing Systems* (ACM, 2007), 839–48. dl.acm.org/citation.cfm?id=1240750. (Accessed May 9, 2016).

Duck, Steve. *Rethinking Relationships.* Thousand Oaks, CA: Sage, 2010.

Duncan, Sean C. "Minecraft, Beyond Construction and Survival." *Well Played: A Journal on Video Games, Value and Meaning* 1 (2011): 1–22.

Dunn, Jennifer C., Jimmie Manning, and Danielle M. Stern. *Lucky Strikes and a Three Martini Lunch: Thinking about Television's Mad Men,* second edition. Cambridge, UK: Cambridge Scholars Publishing, 2015.

Dunn, Robert Andrew. "Polyreality." In *Beyond New Media: Discourse and Critique in a Polymediated Age,* edited by Art Herbig, Andrew F. Herrmann, and Adam Tyma, 109–24. Lantham, MD: Lexington, 2015.

Dyer, W. Gibb, and Wendy Handler. "Entrepreneurship and Family Business: Exploring the Connections." *Entrepreneurship Theory and Practice* 19 (1994): 71–83.

Edelman, Murray J. *From Art to Politics: How Artistic Creations Shape Political Conceptions.* Chicago, IL: University of Chicago Press, 1995.

Eisenberg, Eric M. "Building a Mystery: Toward a New Theory of Communication and Identity." *Journal of Communication* 51 (2001): 534–52. doi: 10.1111/ j.1460–2466.2001.tb02895.x.

———. "Jamming: Transcendence through Organizing." *Communication Research* 17 (1990): 139–64. doi: 10.1177/009365090017002001.

Eisenberg, Eric M., Zachary Johnson, and Willem Pieterson. "Leveraging Social Networks for Strategic Success." *International Journal of Business Communication* 52 (2015): 143–54. doi: 10.1177/2329488414560283.

Eisikovits, Zvi, and Chaya Koren. "Approaches to and Outcomes of Dyadic Interview Analysis." *Qualitative Health Research* 20 (2010): 1642–55. doi:10.1177/1049732310376520.

Eisler, Riane. *The Chalice and the Blade: Our History, Our Future.* San Francisco, CA: Harper & Row, 1988.

El-Nasr, Magy Seif, Bardia Aghabeigi, David Milam, Mona Erfani, Beth Lameman, Hamid Maygoli, and Sang Mah. "Understanding and Evaluating Cooperative Games." In *Proceedings of the SIGCHI Conference on Human Factors in Computing Systems* (2010): 253–62. dl.acm.org/citation.cfm?id=1753363.

Elite Daily. "Couples Reveal How Many People They've Had Sex With to Each Other." *Elite Daily*, March 10, 2015. www.youtube.com/watch?v=hkxjuznXLP0. (Accessed on November 14, 2015).

Ellis, Carolyn. "Seeking My Brother's Voice: Holding onto Long-term Grief through Photographs, Stories, and Reflections." In *Stories of Complicated Grief: A Critical Anthology*, edited by Eric D. Miller, 3–29. Washington, DC: National Association of Social Workers, 2014.

Enck, Suzanne M., and Megan E. Morrissey. "If *Orange is the New Black*, I Must Be Color Blind: Comic Framing of Post-Racism in the Prison-Industrial Complex." *Critical Studies in Media Communication* 32 (2015): 303–17 doi: 10.1080/15295036.2015.1086489.

Enright, Michael. "The Birth of Punk." *Rewind with Michael Enright.* April 21, 2016, CBC-Radio Canada. www.cbc.ca/radio/rewind/the-birth-of-punk-1.3541039. (Accessed May 14, 2016).

Erhart, Julia. "Donor Conception in Lesbian and Non-lesbian and Television Families." In *Queer Love in Film and Television: Critical Essays*, edited by Pamela Demory and Christopher Pullen, 83–93. New York, NY: Palgrave Macmillan, 2013.

Everett, Anna. "Scandalicious: *Scandal*, Social Media, and Shonda Rhimes' Auteurist Juggernaut." *The Black Scholar* 45 (2015): 34–43. doi: 10.1080/00064246.2014.997602.

Ewen, Stuart. *PR! A Social History of Spin.* New York, NY: Perseus Books Group, 1996.

Ewoldsen, David R., Cassie A. Eno, Bradley M. Okdie, John A. Velez, Rosanna E. Guadagno, and Jamie DeCoster. "Effect of Playing Violent Video Games Cooperatively or Competitively on Subsequent Cooperative Behavior." *Cyberpsychology, Behavior, and Social Networking* 15 (2012): 277–80. doi:10.1089/cyber.2011.0308.

Faraci, Devin. "Fandom Is Broken: Controversies and Entitlement Shine a Light on a Deeply Troubling Side of Fandom." *Birth. Movies. Death.* May 30, 2016. birthmoviesdeath.com/2016/05/30/fandom-is-broken. (Accessed June 8, 2015).

Federal Bureau of Investigation. "The Crime of 'Swatting'Fake 9–1–1 Calls Have Real Consequences." September 3, 2013. www.fbi.gov/news/stories/2013/september/the-crime-of-swatting-fake-9-1-1-calls-have-real-consequences. (Accessed May 19, 2016).

Feil, Ken. "'Fearless Vulgarity': Camp Love as Queer Love for Jackie Susan and *Valley of the Dolls*." In *Queer Love in Film and Television: Critical Essays*, edited by Pamela Demory and Christopher Pullen, 141–51. New York, NY: Palgrave Macmillan, 2013.

Feldman, Lauren. "Cloudy with a Chance of Heat Balls: The Portrayal of Global Warming on The Daily Show and The Colbert Report." *International Journal of Communication* 7 (2013): 430–51. ijoc.org/index.php/ijoc/article/view/1940/861. (Accessed May 12, 2016).

Feng, Hairong, Hui-Ching Chang, and Richard Holt. "Examining Chinese Gift-Giving Behavior from the Politeness Theory Perspective." *Asian Journal of Communication* 21 (2011): 301–17. doi:10.1080/01292986.2011.559257.

Ferguson, Christopher J. "Blazing Angels or Resident Evil? Can Violent Video Games Be a Force for Good?" *Review of General Psychology* 14 (2010): 68–81. doi: 10.1037/a0018941.

———. "Evidence for Publication Bias in Video Game Violence Effects Literature: A Meta-analytic Review." *Aggression and Violent Behavior* 12 (2007): 470–82. doi:10.1016/j.avb.2007.01.001.

———. "The Good, the Bad and the Ugly: A Meta-analytic Review of Positive and Negative Effects of Violent Video Games." *Psychiatric Quarterly* 78 (2007): 309–16. doi: 10.1007/s11126–007–9056–9.

———. "The School Shooting/violent Video Game Link: Causal Relationship or Moral Panic?" *Journal of Investigative Psychology and Offender Profiling* 5 (2008): 25–37. doi: 10.1002/jip.76.

———. "Video Games and Youth Violence: A Prospective Analysis in Adolescents." *Journal of Youth and Adolescence* 40 (2011): 377–91. doi: 10.1007/s10964–010–9610–x.

Ferguson, Christopher J., Stephanie M. Rueda, Amanda M. Cruz, Diana E. Ferguson, Stacey Fritz, and Shawn M. Smith. "Violent Video Games and Aggression Causal Relationship or Byproduct of Family Violence and Intrinsic Violence Motivation?" *Criminal Justice and Behavior* 35 (2008): 311–32. doi: 10.1177/0093854807311719.

Fine, Marlene G. "Soap Opera Conversations: The Talk that Binds." *Journal of Communication* 31 (1981): 97–107.

Finnegan, Cara A. *Picturing Poverty: Print Culture and FSA Photographs.* Washington, DC: Smithsonian Books, 2003.

Fisher, Walter R. "Narration as a Human Communication Paradigm: The Case of Public Moral Argument." *Communication Monographs* 51 (1984): 1–22. doi: 10.1080/03637758409390180.

Fiske, John. *Television Culture.* London: Methuen, 1987.

———. *Understanding Popular Culture,* 2nd ed. London, UK: Routledge, 2010.

Fitch, Kate. "Promoting the Vampire Rights Amendment: Public Relations, Postfeminism and *True Blood.*" *Public Relations Review* 41 (2014): 607–14. doi:10.1016/j.pubrev.2014.02.029.

Fitzgerald, F. Scott. *The Great Gatsby.* New York, NY: Cambridge University Press, 1991.

Foley, Megyn. "Sound Bites: Rethinking the Circulation of Speech from Fragment to Fetish." *Rhetoric & Public Affairs* 15, no. 4 (2012): 613–22.

Follett, Mary Parker. *Creative Experience.* New York, NY: Longmans, Green & Company, 1951.

Foucault, Michel. *The Archaeology of Knowledge & the Discourse on Language.* Translated by A. M. Sheridan Smith. New York: Pantheon Books, 1972.

———. *Discipline and Punish: The Birth of the Prison.* Translated by Alan Sheridan. New York, NY: Vintage Books, 1995.

Foss, Susan K., and Cindy L. Griffin. "A Feminist Perspective on Rhetorical Theory: Toward a Clarification of Boundaries." *Western Journal of Communication,* 56 (1992): 330–49. doi: 10.1080/10570319209374422.

Fraser, Jill Andresky. *White-Collar Sweatshop.* New York, NY: Norton, 2001.

Freire, Paulo. *The Pedagogy of the Oppressed.* New York, NY: Continuum, 1970.

Gagne, Ellen D., Carol Walker Yekovich, and Frank R. Yekovich. *The Cognitive Psychology of School Learning.* New York, NY: Harper Collins, 1993.

Gajjala, Radhika, Natalia Rybas, and Yahui Zhang. "Producing Digitally Mediated Environments as Sites for Critical Feminist Pedagogy." In *The SAGE Handbook of Communication and Instruction,* edited by Deanna L. Fassett and John T. Warren, 411–35. Thousand Oaks, CA: Sage Publishing, 2010.

Gamble, Sera, and Lou Bollo. "Are You There, God? It's Me, Dean Winchester." *Supernatural.* Burbank, CA: Warner Brothers, 2008.

Gentile, Douglas A., Craig A. Anderson, Shintaro Yukawa, Nobuko Ihori, Muniba Saleem, Lim Kam Ming, Akiko Shibuya, Albert K. Liau, Angeline Khoo, Brad J. Bushman, L. Rowell Huesmann, and Akira Sakamoto. "The Effects of Prosocial

Video Games on Prosocial Behaviors: International Evidence From Correlational, Longitudinal, and Experimental Studies." *Personality and Social Psychology Bulletin* 36 (2009): 752–63. doi: 10.1177/0146167209333045.

Gentile, Douglas A., and William Stone. "Violent Video Game Effects on Children and Adolescents. A Review of the Literature." *Minerva Pediatrica* 57 (2005): 337–58.

Glass, Adam. "Sharp Teeth." *Supernatural*. Burbank, CA: Warner Brothers, 2014.

Goffman, Erving. *Frame Analysis: An Essay on the Organization of Experience*. London: Harper and Row, 1972.

———. *The Presentation of Self in Everyday Life*. New York, NY: Doubleday, 1959.

———. *Stigma: Notes on the Management of Spoiled Identity*. New York, NY: Prentice Hall, 1963.

Golden, Annis G., and Cheryl Geisler. "Work–life Boundary Management and the Personal Digital Assistant." *Human Relations* 60 (2007): 519–51. doi: 10.1177/0018726707076698.

Goltz, Dustin Bradley. *Queer Temporalities in Gay Male Representation*. New York, NY: Routledge, 2010.

Gonzalez, Alberto, and John J. Makay. "Rhetorical Ascription and the Gospel According to Dylan." *Quarterly Journal of Speech* 69.1 (1983): 1–14. doi: 10.1080/00335638309383630.

Goodale, Greg. *Sonic Persuasion: Reading Sound in the Recorded Age*. Urbana, IL: University of Illinois Press, 2011.

Grabe, Maria Elizabeth, and Erik Page Bucy. *Image Bite Politics: News and the Visual Framing of Elections*. New York, NY: Oxford University Press, 2009.

Gramsci, Antonio. *Selections from The Prison Notebooks of Antonio Gramsci*. New York, NY: International Publishers, 1995.

Granic, Isabela, Adam Lobel, and C. M. E. "The Benefits of Playing Video Games." *American Psychologist* 69 (2014): 66–78. doi:10.1037/a0034857.

Green-Hamann, Sara, Kristen Campbell Eichhorn, and John C. Sherblom. "An Exploration of Why People Participate in Second Life Social Support Groups." *Journal of Computer-Mediated Communication* 16 (2011): 465–91. doi: 10.1111/j.1083-6101.2011.01543.x.

Greenberg, Bradley S., and Kimberly Neuendorf. "Black Family Interactions on Television." In *Life on Television: Content Analyses of U.S. TV Drama*, edited by Bradley S. Greenberg, 173–81. Norwood, NJ: Ablex, 1980.

Greenfield, Derek. "What's the Deal with the White Middle-Aged Guy Teaching Hip-Hop? Lessons in Popular Culture, Positionality and Pedagogy." *Pedagogy, Culture & Society* 15 (2007): 229–43. doi: 10.1080/14681360701403789.

Greenwald, Ted. "Q&A: Ridley Scott Has Finally Created the *Bladerunner* He Always Imagined." *Wired*, September 26, 2007. www.wired.com/2007/09/ff-bladerunner. (Accessed May 14, 2016).

Gregg, Melissa, and Gregory J. Seigworth. *The Affect Theory Reader*. Durham, NC: Duke University Press, 2010.

Greitemeyer, Tobias, and Christopher Cox. "There's No 'I' in Team: Effects of Cooperative Video Games on Cooperative Behavior." *European Journal of Social Psychology* 43 (2013): 224–28. doi: 10.1002/ejsp.1940.

Grossberg, Lawrence. *Caught in the Crossfire: Kids, Politics, and America's Future*. Boulder, CO: Paradigm Publishers, 2005.

———. *Cultural Studies in the Future Tense*. Durham. NC: Duke University Press, 2010.

———. *Dancing in Spite of Myself: Essays on Popular Culture*. Durham, NC: Duke University Press, 1997.

———. "On Postmodernism and Articulation. An Interview with Stuart Hall." *Journal of Communication* 45 (1986): 45–60. doi: 10.1177/019685998601000204.

———. "Rock, Territorialization and Power." *Cultural Studies* 5 (1991): 358–67. doi: 10.1080/ 09502389100490301.

———. "Some Preliminary Conjunctural Thoughts on Countercultures." *Journal of Gender and Power* 1 (2014): 13–23.

————. *We All Want to Change the World: The Paradox of the U.S. Left (A Polemic)*. London, UK: Lawrence & Wishart, 2015. www.lwbooks.co.uk/book/we-all-want-change-world. (Accessed May 12, 2016).

————. *We Gotta Get Out of This Place: Popular Conservatism and Postmodern Culture*. New York, NY: Routledge, 1992.

Grovitz, Gordon. "FBI vs. Apple Isn't Over." *The Wall Street Journal*, March 27, 2016. www.wsj.com/articles/fbi-vs-apple-isnt-over-1459116064. (Accessed May 22, 2016).

Guitton, Matthieu J. "Living in the Hutt Space: Immersive Process in the Star Wars Role-Play Community of Second Life." *Computers in Human Behavior* 28 (2012): 1681–91. doi:10.1016/j.chb.2012.04.006.

Gulla, Bob. *The Greenwood Encyclopedia of Rock History: The Grunge and Post-grunge Years, 1991–2005*. Westport, CT: Greenwood Press, 2006.

Ha, Thu-Huong. "Sex: Let's Talk." ideas.ted.com/sex-lets-talk. (Accessed March 3, 2015).

Haggins, Bambi. "Afterword: Television in the Age of Digital: New Frontier and Brave New World." *Emergences: Journal for the Study of Media and Composite Cultures* 11 (2001): 175–9. doi: 10.1080/10457220120044729.

Halberstam, Judith. *The Queer Art of Failure*. Durham, NC: Duke University Press, 2011.

Hall, Elizabeth. "Will Success Spoil B. F. Skinner?" *Psychology Today*, November 1972.

Hall, Stuart. "The Centrality of Culture: Notes on the Cultural Revolutions of our Time." In *Media and Cultural Regulation*, edited by Kenneth Thompson, 208–38. London: Sage, 1997.

————. "Cultural Studies and Its Theoretical Legacies." In *Stuart Hall: Critical Dialogues in Cultural Studies*, edited by Kuan-Hsing Chen and David Morley, 262–75. New York: Routledge, 1996.

————. "Encoding/Decoding." In *Culture, Media, Language: Working Papers in Cultural Studies, 1972–9*, edited by Stuart Hall, 128–38. London: Routledge, 1980.

————. "What is this 'Black' in Black Popular Culture." *Social Justice* 20 (1993): 104–14.

Hall, Stuart, Jessica Evans, and Sean Nixon. *Representation*. London, UK: Sage, 2013.

Hammond, Scott C., Rob Anderson, and Kenneth N. Cissna. "Problematics of Dialogue and Power." In *Communication Yearbook 27*, edited by Pamela J. Kalbfleisch, 125–57. Mahwah, NJ: Erlbaum, 2003.

Hardwick, Chris, and a Many Headed Beast. *The Nerdist* (blog). January 5, 2016, nerdist.com. (Accessed June 13, 2016).

Hare, Breeanna. "Twice as much TV? How Networks are Adapting to the Second Screen." *CNN*. September 15, 2012. www.cnn.com/2012/09/15/showbiz/tv/second-screen-tv-our-mobile-society/. (Accessed June 8, 2015).

Hariman, Robert and John Louis Lucaites. *No Caption Needed: Iconic Photographs, Public Culture, and Liberal Democracy*. Chicago, IL: University of Chicago Press, 2007.

Harris, Anita. "Young Women, Late Modern Politics, and the Participatory Possibilities of Online Cultures." *Journal of Youth Studies* 11 (2008): 481–95. doi: 10.1080/13676260802282950.

Harris, Anne M. "Ghost-child." In *On (Writing) Families: Autoethnographies of Presence and Absence, Love and Loss*, edited by Jonathan Wyatt and Tony E. Adams, 69–75. Rotterdam, The Netherlands: Sense Publishers, 2014.

Hart, Roderick P., and E. Johanna Hartelius. "The Political Sins of Jon Stewart." *Critical Studies in Media Communication* 24 (2007): 263–72. doi: 10.1080/07393180701520991.

Hawken, Paul. *Blessed Unrest* . New York, NY: Viking Press, 2007.

Herbig, Art and Aaron Hess. "Convergent Critical Rhetoric at the 'Rally to Restore Sanity': Exploring the Intersection of Rhetoric, Ethnography, and Documentary Production." *Communication Studies* 63, no. 3 (2012): 269–289. doi:10.1080/10510974.2012.674617.

Herbig, Art, Alix Watson, and Aaron Hess. *Never Forget: Public Memory & 9/11*. Living-Text Productions, 2015.

Herbig, Art, and Andrew F. Herrmann. "Polymediated Narrative: The Case of *Supernatural*'s 'Fan Fiction.'" *International Journal of Communication* 10 (2016): 748–65. ijoc.org/index.php/ijoc/article/view/4397/1560. (Accessed May 10, 2016).

Herbig, Art, Andrew F. Herrmann, and Adam W. Tyma, eds. *Beyond New Media: Discourse and Critique in a Polymediated Age*. Lanham, MD: Lexington Books.

Herrmann, Andrew F. "'C-can We Rest Now?': Foucault and the Multiple Discursive Subjectivities of Spike. *Slayage: The Journal of the Whedon Studies Association* 10 (2013). slayageonline.com/essays/slayage35/Herrmann.pdf. (Accessed May 12. 2016).

———. "Communicating, Sensemaking, and (Dis)organizing: Theorizing the Complexity of Polymediation." In *Beyond New Media: Discourse and Critique in a Polymediated Age*, edited by Art Herbig, Andrew F. Herrmann, and Adam W. Tyma, 61–82. Lanham, MD: Lexington Books, 2015.

———. "'Criteria Against Ourselves?': Embracing the Opportunities of Qualitative Inquiry." *International Review of Qualitative Research* 5 (2012): 135–52.

———. Daniel Amos and Me: The Power of Pop Culture and Autoethnography. *Popular Culture Studies Journal* 1 (2013): 6–17. mpcaaca.org/wp-content/uploads/2013/10/PCSJ-V1-N12-Herrmann-Daniel-Amos-and-Me.pdf. (Accessed May 12, 2016).

———. "Ghosts, Vampires, Zombies, and Us: The Undead as Autoethnographic Bridges." *International Review of Qualitative Research* 7 (2013): 327–41.

———. "Narrative as an Organizing Process: Identity and Story in a New Nonprofit." *Qualitative Research in Organizations and Management: An International Journal* 6 (2011): 246–64. doi: 10.1108/17465641111188411.

———. "*Re-discovering Kolchak and Twin Peaks: Elevating the Influence of the First Television Supernatural Dramas.*" Paper presented at Central States Communication Association Convention, Minneapolis, MN, 2014.

Herrmann, Andrew F., and Art Herbig. "'All Too Human': Xander Harris and the Embodiment of the Fully Human." *Popular Culture Studies Journal* 3 (2015): 84–112. mpcaaca.org/wp-content/uploads/2015/10/pcsj_vol3_no1-2.pdf. (Accessed May 12, 2016).

Hewett, Ivan. "Is it Time to End the Distinction between High and Low Art?" *The Telegraph*. January 30, 2015. www.telegraph.co.uk/culture/11378145/Is-it-time-to-end-the-distinction-between-high-and-low-art.html. (Accessed May 14, 2016).

Heywood, Leslie, and Jennifer Drake. *Third Wave Agenda: Being Feminist, Doing Feminism*. Minneapolis, MN: University of Minnesota Press, 1997.

Higgin, Tanner. "Blackless Fantasy: The Disappearance of Race in Massively Multiplayer Online Role-playing Games." *Games and Culture* 4 (2008): 3–26: doi: 10.1177/1555412008325477.

Hill, Jeffrey, Maria Ferris, and Vjollca Märtinson. "Does It Matter Where You Work? A Comparison of How Three Work Venues (Traditional Office, Virtual Office, and Home Office) Influence Aspects of Work and Personal/Family Life." *Journal of Vocational Behavior* 63 (2003): 220–41. doi: 10.1016/S0001–8791(03)00042–3.

Hitchens, Christopher. "Ohio's Odd Numbers." *Vanity Fair*. October 17, 2006. www.vanityfair.com/news/2005/03/hitchens200503. (Accessed May 10, 2016).

Hochschild, Arlie. *The Time Bind: When Work Becomes Home and Home Becomes Work*. New York, NY: Metropolitan Books, 1997.

Hodson, Tom. "Documentary Filmmakers Discuss the Making of 'Creative Abundance.'" *WOUB*, September 8, 2015, woub.org/2015/09/08/documentary-filmmakers-discuss-making-creative-abundance/. (Accessed June 13, 2016).

Hoffman, Lindsay H., and Dannagal G Young. "Satire, Punch Lines, and the Nightly News: Untangling Media Effects on Political Participation." *Communication Research Reports* 28 (2011): 159–68. doi: 10.1080/08824096.2011.565278.

Holbert, R. Lance. "A Typology for the Study of Entertainment Television and Politics." *American Behavioral Scientist* 49 (2005): 436–53. doi:10.1177/0002764205279419.

Holbert, R. Lance, David A. Tschida, Maria Dixon, Kristin Cherry, Keli Steuber, and David Airne. "The West Wing and Depictions of the American Presidency: Expanding the Domains of Framing in Political Communication." *Communication Quarterly* 53 (2005): 505–22. doi:10.1080/01463370500102228.

Holman Jones, Stacy, and Tony E. Adams. "Undoing the Alphabet: A Queer Fugue on Grief and Forgiveness." *Cultural Studies* ↔ *Critical Methodologies* 14 (2014): 102–10. doi:10.1177/1532708613512260.

Holmes, Linda, ed. "Pop Culture Happy Hour (podcast)." *Monkey See: Pop-Culture News and Analysis from NPR* (blog), January 5, 2016, www.npr.org/sections/monkeysee/129472378/pop-culture-happy-hour/. (Accessed June 13, 2016).

Horkheimer, Max, and Theodor W. Adorno. *Dialectic of Enlightenment: Philosophical Fragments*, edited by Gunzelin Schmid Noerr. translated by Edmund Jephcott. Stanford, CA: Stanford University Press, 2002.

Huff, Richard M. *Reality Television*. New York: Praeger, 2006.

Hull, Glynda. "Critical Literacy and Beyond: Lessons Learned From Students and Workers in a Vocational Program and on the Job." *Anthropology & Education Quarterly* 24 (1993): 373–96. doi: 0.1525/aeq.1993.24.4.04x0066n.

Holman Jones, Stacy, and Tony E. Adams. "Undoing the Alphabet: A Queer Fugue on Grief and Forgiveness." *Cultural Studies* ↔ *Critical Methodologies* 14 (2014): 102–10. doi: 10.1177/1532708613512260.

Huynh, Kim-Phong, Si-Wei Lim, and Marko M. Skoric. "Stepping Out of the Magic Circle: Regulation of Play/Life Boundary in MMO-Mediated Romantic Relationship." *Journal of Computer-Mediated Communication* 18 (2013): 251–64. doi:10.1111/jcc4.12011.

Iommi, Tony, Ozzy Osbourne, Geezer Butler, and Bill Ward. "Iron Man." Single. Burbank, CA: Warner Brothers, 1971.

Irvine, James R., and Walter G. Kirkpatrick. "The Musical Form in Rhetorical Exchange: Theoretical Considerations." *Quarterly Journal of Speech* 58 (1972): 272–84. doi: 10.1080/00335637209383124.

Isaac, Alicia R., Lettie L. Lockhart, and Larry Williams. "Violence Against African American Women in Prisons and Jails." *Journal of Human Behavior in the Social Environment*, 4 (2001): 129–53. doi: 10.1300/J137v04n02_07.

Iwamoto, Derek. "Tupac Shakur: Understanding the Identity Formation of Hyper-Masculinity of a Popular Hip-Hop Artist." *The Black Scholar* 33 (2003): 44–9. doi: 10.1080/00064246.2003.11413215.

Jackson, Michael, and Lionel Ritchie. "Feed the World." Single. Los Angeles, CA: Columbia, 1985.

Jansz, Jeroen, and Lonneke Martens. "Gaming at a LAN Event: The Social Context of Playing Video Games." *New Media & Society* 7 (2005): 333–55. doi: 10.1177/1461444805052280.

Jenkins, Henry. *Confessions of an Aca-Fan: The Official Weblog of Henry Jenkins* (blog), December 22, 2015, henryjenkins.org/. (Accessed June 13, 2016).

———. *Convergence Culture: Where Old and New Media Collide*. New York: New York University Press, 2006.

Jenkins, Henry, Sam Ford, and Joshua Green. *Spreadable Media: Creating Value and Meaning in a Networked Culture*. New York, NY: NYU Press, 2013.

Jensen, Jeff. "Firefly: 'Browncoats Unite' Reunion Tonight: Why Joss Whedon's Cult Classic has Endured for a Decade." *Entertainment Weekly*, November 11, 2012. www.ew.com/article/2012/11/11/firefly-browncoats-reunion-joss-whedon. (Accessed May 7, 2016).

Jerabeck, Jessica M., and Christopher J. Ferguson. "The Influence of Solitary and Cooperative Violent Video Game Play on Aggressive and Prosocial Behavior." *Computers in Human Behavior* 29 (2013): 2573–78. doi:10.1016/j.chb.2013.06.034.

Johnston, Jane. "Girls on Screen: How Film and Television Depict Women in Public Relations." *PRism* 7 (2010). www.prismjournal.org. (Accessed May 12, 2016).

Jones, Bethan. "Buffy vs. Bella: Gender, Relationships and the Modern Vampire." In *The Modern Vampire and Human Identity*, edited by Deborah Mutch, 37–54. London, UK: Palgrave McMillan, 2013.

Jones, Ryessia, Johnny Jones, and Siobhan E. Smith. "From 90s Girl to Hiphop Wife: An Analysis of the Portrayal of Tiny as Black Mother in Reality Television." In *Black Women Are Loud! A Critical Analysis of Black Women's Portrayals on Reality Television,* edited by Donnetrice Allison, 39–61. Lanham, Maryland: Lexington Books, 2016.

Jorgenson, Jane. "Engineering Selves: Negotiating Gender and Identity in Technical Work." *Management Communication Quarterly* 15 (2002): 350–80. doi: 10.1177/0893318902153002.

Juul, Matt. "Why the Music of 'Jaws' is Still Terrifying." *Boston Globe,* June 15, 2015. www.boston.com/culture/entertainment/2015/06/16/why-the-music-of-jaws-is-still-terrifying. (Accessed October 30, 2015).

Kaulingsfreks, Ruud, Geoff Lightfoot, and Hugo Letiche. "The Man in the Black Hat." *Culture and Organization* 15 (2009): 151–65. doi: 10.1080/14759550902925328.

Keeley, Michael. *A Social Contract Theory of Organizations.* Notre Dame, IN: University of Notre Dame Press, 1988.

Keller, Jessalyn Marie. "Virtual Feminisms." *Information, Communication & Society* 15 (2012), 429–47. doi: 10.1080/1369118X.2011.64289.

Kellner, Douglas. *Media Culture: Cultural Studies, Identity Politics Between the Modern and the Post-Modern.* London: Routledge, 1995.

Kerman, Piper. *Orange is the New Black: My Year in a Women's Prison.* New York, NY: Spiegel & Grau, 2011.

King, Darryn. "Ermahgerddon: The Untold Story of the Ermahgerd Girl." *Vanity Fair,* October 15, 2015. www.vanityfair.com/culture/2015/10/ermahgerd-girl-true-story. (Accessed May 10, 2016).

Kinsky, Emily and Coy Callison. "PR in the News: How a Sample of Network Newscasts Framed Public Relations." *Public Relations Journal* 3 (2009): 1–17.

Kirschenbaum, Howard, and Valerie Land Henderson, eds. *Carl Rogers: Dialogues.* Boston, MA: Houghton Mifflin, 1989.

Kivy, Peter. *Authenticities: Philosophical Reflections of Musical Performance.* Ithaca, NY: Cornell University Press, 1995.

Korten, David. *The Great Turning.* West Hartford, CT: Kumarian Press, 2007.

Krakowiak, K. Maja, and Mina Tsay-Vogel. "What Makes Characters Bad Behavior Acceptable? The Effects of Character Motivation and Outcome on Perception, Character Liking, and Moral Disengagement." *Mass Communication and Society* 16 (2013): 179–99. doi: 10.1080/15205436.2012.690926.

Krasner, Leonard. "The Future and the Past in the Behaviorism-Humanism Dialogue." *American Psychologist* 33 (1978): 799–804.

Kreber, Carolyn. *The University and its Disciplines: Teaching and Learning within and beyond Disciplinary Boundaries.* New York, NY: Routledge, 2010.

Kreider, Jodie A. and Meghan K. Winchell. *Buffy in the Classroom: Essays on Teaching with the Vampire Slayer.* Jefferson, NC: McFarland, 2010.

Krizek, Robert L. "Lessons: What the Hell are we Teaching the Next Generation Anyway?" In *Fiction and Social Research: By Ice or Fire,* edited by Anna Banks and Stephen P. Banks, 89–114. Walnut Creek, CA: AltaMira Press, 1998.

Kunz, William M. "Prime-Time Television Program Ownership in a Post-Fin/Syn World." *Journal of Broadcasting & Electronic Media* 53 (2009): 636–51. doi: 10.1080/08838150903327181.

Lacan, Jacques. "The Mirror Stage as Formative of the *I* Function as Revealed in Psychoanalytic Experience." In *Ecrits: The First Complete Edition in English,* translated by Bruce Fink. New York, NY: W.W. Norton and Company, 2006.

Lacayo, Richard. "All-TIME 100 Novels." *Time,* January 6, 2010. entertainment.time.com/2005/10/16/all-time-100-novels. (Accessed May 12, 2016).

Ladipo, David. "The Rise of America's Prison Industrial Complex." *New Left Review* 7 (2001): 109–23.

Lambert, Cheryl A. "Fed up with Filmmakers Stereotypes of Public Relations?" *Public Relations Society of America ComPRehension,* October 14, 2013. comprehension.prsa.org/?p=5571. (Accessed May 12, 2016).

Lambert, Cheryl A., and Candace White. "Feminization of the Film? Occupational Roles of Public Relations Characters in Movies." *Public Relations Journal* 6 (2012). test.prsa.org/Intelligence/PRJournal/Documents/2012LambertWhite.pdf. (Accessed June 5, 2016).

Lametti, Daniel, Aisha Harris, Natasha Geiling, and Natalie Matthews-Ramo. "Which Pop Culture Property Do Academics Study the Most?" *Slate,* June 11, 2012. www.slate.com/blogs/browbeat/2012/06/11/pop_culture_studies_why_do_academics_study_buffy_the_vampire_slayer_more_than_the_wire_the_matrix_alien_and_the_simpsons_.html. (Accessed May 14, 2016).

LaMonica, Paul R. "Video Games Aren't Just for Antisocial Nerds!" *CNN Money,* October 16, 2015. money.cnn.com/2015/10/16/investing/electronic-arts-activision-video-games. (Accessed May 12, 2016).

Langer, Suzanne K. *Feeling and Form.* New York, NY: Charles Scribner's Sons, 1953.

———. *Philosophy in a New Key,* third edition. Cambridge, MA: Harvard University Press, 1957.

Lapidus, Lenora, Namita Luthra, Anjuli Verma, Deborah Small, Patricia Allard, and Kirsten Levingston. "Caught in the Net: The Impact of Drug Policies on Women and Families." *American Civil Liberties Union,* 2005. www.aclu.org/files/images/asset_upload_file431_23513.pdf. (Accessed March 27, 2016).

Lastowka, Greg. "Minecraft as Web 2.0: Amateur Creativity & Digital Games." In *Amateur Media: Social, Cultural and Legal Perspectives,* edited by Dan Hunter, Ramon Lobato, Megan Richardson, and Jillian Thomas, 153–69. New York, NY: Routledge, 2012.

Lea, James W. "What Is a Family Business? More Than You Think." *Triangle Business Journal* 1 (1998). www.bizjournals.com/triangle/stories/1998/11/02/smallb3. (Accessed May 10, 2014).

Leavy, Patricia. *Blue.* Rotterdam, Netherlands: Sense Publishers, 2016.

———. *Low-Fat Love.* Rotterdam, Netherlands: Sense Publishers, 2011.

Ledbetter, Andrew. "'Why Don't We See What's on TV?:' Shared TV Viewing, Relational Maintenance Behavior, and Romanticism as Predictors of Romantic Relationship Quality." Paper presentation, Central States Communication Association Annual Convention, Grand Rapids, MI, April 16, 2016.

Lee, Mordecai. "Flicks of Government Flacks: The Sequel." *Public Relations Review* 35 (2009): 159–61. doi:10.1016/j.pubrev.2008.09.017.

———. "The Image of the Government Flack: Movie Depictions of Public Relations in Public Administration." *Public Relations Review* 27 (2001): 297–315. doi: 10.1016/S0363-8111(01)00088-1.

Levin, Jack, and Jack McDevitt. Hate *Crimes Revisited: America's War on those Who Are Different.* Cambridge, MA: Westview Press, 2002.

Levine, Elana. *Cupcakes, Pinterest, and Ladyporn: Feminized Popular Culture in the Early Twenty-First Century.* Urbana, IL: University of Illinois Press, 2015.

Litvak, Joseph. "Glad to be Unhappy." *South Atlantic Quarterly* 106 (2007): 523–31. doi: 10.1215/00382876-2007-011.

LivingText Productions' Facebook Page, www.facebook.com/LivingText/. (Accessed June 16, 2016).

Lloyd, Will "Five Mistakes Single Women Make in Trying to Date a Man." *Singles Scene by It's Just Lunch* (blog). www.itsjustlunchblog.com/2015/10/the-3-biggest-dating-mistakes-women-make-with-tips-for-how-to-avoid-them.html. (Accessed October 25, 2015).

Lotz, Amanda. "Communicating Third-Wave Feminism and New Social Movements: Challenges for the Next Century of Feminist Endeavor." *Women and Language* 26 (2003): 2–9.

Lukitsch, Courtney. "How to Fix the Misrepresentation of PR Pros in the Media." *PR Newser.* January 29, 2016. www.adweek.com/prnewser/how-to-fix-the-misrepresentation-of-pr-pros-within-the-global-media/120937. (Accessed March 15, 2016).

Mack, Oliver, Anshuman Khare, Andreas Kramer, and Thomas Burgartz. *Managing in a VUCA World*. New York, NY: Springer, 2015.

Madianou, Mirca, and Daniel Miller. "Polymedia: Towards a New Theory of Digital Media in Interpersonal Communication." *International Journal of Cultural Studies* 16 (2012): 169–87. doi: 10.1177/1367877912452486.

Malone-Colon, Linda, and Alex Roberts. *Marriage and the Well-Being of African American Boys*. Institute for American Values: Center for Marriage and Families (2006): 1–6. americanvalues.org/catalog/pdfs/researchbrief2.pdf. (Accessed May 13, 2016).

Manning, Jimmie. "Because the Personal *Is* the Political: Politics and the Unpacking the Rhetoric of (Queer) Relationships." In *Queer Identities/Political Realities*, edited by Kathleen German and Bruce Dreshel, 1–12. Newcastle, UK: Cambridge Scholars, 2009.

———. "A Constitutive Approach to Interpersonal Communication Studies." *Communication Studies* 65 (2014): 432–40. doi: 10.1080/10510974.2014.927294.

———. "Exploring Family Discourses about Purity Pledges: Connecting Relationships and Popular Culture." *Qualitative Research Reports in Communication* 15 (2014): 92–99. doi:10.1080/17459435.2014.955597.

———. "Finding Yourself in *Mad Men*." In *Lucky Strikes and a Three-Martini Lunch: Thinking about Television's Mad Men*, edited by Danielle S. Stern, Jimmie Manning, and Jennifer C. Dunn, 89–96. Newcastle, UK: Cambridge Scholars, 2012.

———. "Ipsedixitism, Ipseity, and Ipsilateral Identity: The Fear of Finding Ourselves in the Fissures between Phishing and *Catfish*." In *Beyond New Media: Discourse and Critique in a Polymediated Age*, edited by Art Herbig, Andrew F. Herrmann, and Adam Tyma, 83–107. Lanham, MD: Lexington Books, 2015.

———. "Paradoxes of (Im)purity: Affirming Heteronormativity and Queering Heterosexuality in Family Discourses of Purity Pledges." *Women's Studies in Communication* 38.1 (2015): 99–117. doi: 10.1080/07491409.2014.954687.

———. "The Rhetorical Function of Laugh Tracks in Situation Comedies: Examining Queer Shame in Will & Grace and Roseanne." *Relevant Rhetoric* 6 (2015): 1–16. commons.lib.niu.edu/bitstream/handle/10843/13679/RR%20Will%20Grace%20Roseanne%202015.pdf?sequence=1. (Accessed May 13, 2016).

Manning, Jimmie, and Tony E. Adams. "Popular Culture Studies and Autoethnography: An Essay on Method." *The Popular Culture Studies Journal* 3 (2015): 187–221. mpcaaca.org/the-popular-culture-studies-journal/volume-3. (Accessed May 13, 2016).

Manning, Jimmie, and Katherine J. Denker. "Doing Feminist Interpersonal Communication Studies: A Call for Action, Two Methodological Approaches, and Theoretical Potentials." *Women & Language* 38 (2015): 133–42.

Manning, Jimmie, and Adrianne Kunkel. "Qualitative Approaches to Dyadic Data Analyses in Family Communication Research: An Invited Essay." *Journal of Family Communication* 15 (2015) 185–92. doi:10.1080/15267431.2015.1043434.

Manson, Michael. "Interview." In Micheal Moore. [Director]. *Bowling for Columbine*. Los Angeles, CA: United Artists, 2002.

Mastro, Dana E., and Susannah R. Stern. "Representations of Race in Television Commercials: A Content Analysis of Prime-Time Advertising." *Journal of Broadcasting and Electronic Media* 47 (2003): 638–47. doi:10.1207/s15506878jobem4704_9.

Masunaga, Jennifer. "Comic Reflections on Academic Work," *LMU/LA Library News*, November 5, 2014, lmulibrary.typepad.com/lmu-library-news/2014/11/comic-reflections-on-academic-work.html. (Accessed June 13, 2016).

Mathews, David. *Politics and People: Finding a Responsible Public Voice*, second edition. Urbana, IL: University of Illinois Press, 1999.

Matthews, Stephen and Sally Mallam. "Pre-Axial Thought: Paleolithic Beginnings." *The Human Journey*. The Institute for the Study of Human Knowledge. www.humanjourney.us/PaleolithicBeginnings.html. (Accessed May 14, 2016).

Marx, Karl, and Freidrich Engels. *The Marx-Engels Reader, second edition.* Edited by Robert C. Tucker. New York, NY: W.W. Norton and Company, 1978.

Mason, Winter and Aaron Clauset. "Friends Ftw! Friendship and Competition in Halo: Reach." In *Proceedings of the 2013 Conference on Computer Supported Cooperative Work* (ACM, 2013), 375–86. dl.acm.org/citation.cfm?id=2441820. (Accessed May 13, 2016).

Mauer, Marc. *Race to Incarcerate.* New York, NY: The New Press, 1999.

McCluskey, Michael, and Young Mie Kim. "Moderatism or Polarization? Representation of Advocacy Groups' Ideology in Newspapers." *Journalism and Mass Communication Quarterly* 89 (2012): 565–84. doi:10.1177/1077699012455385.

McGee, Michael C. "Text, Context, and the Fragmentation of Contemporary Culture." *Western Journal of Speech Communication* 54 (1990): 274–89. doi: 10.1080/10570319009374343.

McKerrow, Raymie E. "Critical Rhetoric: Theory and Praxis." *Communication Monographs* 56 (1989): 91–111. doi: 10.1080/03637758909390253.

———. "Critical Rhetoric and the Possibility of the Subject." In *The Critical Turn: Rhetoric and Philosophy in Postmodern Discourse,* edited by Ian Angus and Lenore Langsdorf, 51–67. Carbondale, IL: Southern Illinois University Press, 1993.

———. "Critical Rhetoric in a Postmodern World." *Quarterly Journal of Speech* 77, no. 1 (1991): 75–8. doi: 10.1080/00335639109383945.

———. "Criticism is as Criticism Does." *Western Journal of Communication* 77, no. 5 (2013): 546–9. doi: 10.1080/10570314.2013.799284.

———. "Foucault's Relationship to Rhetoric." *The Review of Communication* 11, no. 4 (2011): 253–71. doi: 10.1080/15358593.2011.602103.

———. "Research in Rhetoric: A Glance at our Recent Past, Present, and Potential Future." *The Review of Communication* 10, no. 3 (2010): 197–210. doi: 10.1080/15358590903536478.

———. "'Research in Rhetoric' Revisited." *Quarterly Journal of Speech* 101, no. 1 (2015): 151–61. doi: 10.1080/15358590903536478.

McKerrow, Raymie E. and Jeffrey St. John. "Critical Rhetoric and Continual Critique." In *Rhetorical Criticism: Perspectives in Action,* edited by Jim A. Kuypers, 321–40. Lanham, MD: Lexington Books, 2009.

McKinnon, Sara L., Robert Asen, Karma R. Chávez, and Robert Glenn Howard, eds. *Text + Field: Innovations in Rhetorical Method.* University Park, PN: Penn State University Press, 2016.

McLaren, Peter. *Life in Schools: An Introduction to Critical Pedagogy in the Foundation of Education.* Boston, MA: Allyn and Bacon, 2003.

McLaughlin, Terence. *Music and Communication.* New York, NY: St. Martin's Press, 1970.

McLuhan, Marshall. *Understanding Media: The Extensions of Man.* New York, NY: McGraw-Hill, 1964.

McRobbie, Angela. *The Aftermath of Feminism: Gender, Culture, and Social Change.* London: Sage, 2009.

Meizel, Katherine. "Making the Dream a Reality (Show): The Celebration of Failure in American Idol." *Popular Music and Society* 32 (2009): 475–88. doi:10.1080/03007760802217725.

Merritt, Bishetta, and Carolyn A. Stroman. "Black Family Imagery and Interactions on Television." *Journal of Black Studies* 23 (1993): 492–9. doi: 10.1177/002193479302300404.

Meyer, Michaela D. E. "'I'm Just Trying to Find My Way Like Most Kids': Bisexuality, Adolescence and the Drama of *One Tree Hill.*" *Sexuality and Culture* 13 (2009): 237–51. doi: 10.1007/s12119-009-9056-z.

———. "'It's Me. I'm It.': Defining Adolescent Sexual Identity through Relational Dialectics in *Dawson's Creek.*" *Communication Quarterly* 51 (2003): 262–76. doi: 10.1080/01463370309370156.

———. "The "Other" Woman in Contemporary Television Drama: Analyzing Intersectional Representation on *Bones.*" *Sexuality & Culture* 19 (2015): 900–15. doi: 10.1007/s12119-015-9296-z.

Meyer, Michaela D. E., Linda M. Waldron, and Danielle M. Stern. "Relational Aggression on Film: An Intersectional Analysis of Mean Girls." *Popular Culture Studies Journal* 2 (2014): 5–34. mpcaaca.org/wp-content/uploads/2014/11/B02-Meyer-Waldron-and-Stern-Relational-Aggression.pdf. (Accessed May 13, 2016).

Meisenbach, Rebecca J. "Stigma Management Communication: A Theory and Agenda for Applied Research on How Individuals Manage Moments of Stigmatized Identity." *Journal of Applied Communication Research* 38 (2010): 268–92. doi: 10.1080/00909882.2010.490841.

Middleton, Michael, Aaron Hess, Danielle Endres, and Samantha Senda-Cook, eds. *Participatory Critical Rhetoric: Theoretical and Methodological Foundations for Studying Rhetoric in Situ.* Lanham, MD: Lexington Books, 2015.

Milbauer, Ron, and Terri Hughes Burton. "Windego." *Supernatural.* Burbank, CA: Warner Brothers, 2005.

Miller, Karen S. "Public Relations in Film and Fiction: 1930–1995." *Journal of Public Relations Research* 11 (1999): 3–28. doi: 10.1207/s1532754xjprr1101_01.

Mills, C. Wright. "Mass Society and Liberal Education." In *Power, Politics, and People: The Collected Essays of C. Wright Mills,* edited by Irving Louis Horowitz, 353–73. New York, NY: Ballantine Books, 1963.

Mittell, Jason. *Complex TV: The Poetics of Contemporary Television Storytelling.* New York, NY: New York University Press, 2015.

Molina, Brett. "AMC Ditches Plan to Allow Texting in Theaters." *USA Today,* April 15, 2016. www.usatoday.com/story/tech/news/2016/04/15/amc-ditches-plan-allow-texting-theaters/83074118/. (Accessed June 8, 2016).

Mukerji, Chandra and Michael Schudson. "Introduction: Rethinking Popular Culture." In *Rethinking Popular Culture: Contemporary Perspectives in Cultural Studies,* edited by Chandra Mukerji and Michael Schudson, 1–61. Berkeley: University of California Press, 1991.

Mulvey, Laura. "Visual Pleasure and Narrative Cinema." *Screen* 16 (1975): 6–18.

Munford, Rebecca, and Melanie Waters. *Feminism & Popular Culture: Investigating the Postfeminist Mystique.* London: IB Tauris, 2014.

Murphy, B. Keith. "A Rhetorical and Cultural Analysis of the Protest Rock Movement, 1964–1971." Ph.D. diss., Ohio University, 1988. ProQuest.

Murray, Keat. "Surviving Survivor: Reading Mark Burnett's Field Guide and De-naturalizing Social Darwinism as Entertainment." *Journal of American & Comparative Cultures* 24 (2001): 43–54. doi: 10.1111/j.1537-4726.2001.2403_43.x.

Mutz, Diana C., and Lilach Nir. "Not Necessarily the News: Does Fictional Television Influence Real-World Policy Preferences?" *Mass Communication and Society* 13 (2010): 196–217. doi: 10.1080/15205430902813856.

Nabi, Robin L., Emily Moyer-Gusé, and Sahara Byrne. "All Joking Aside: A Serious Investigation into the Persuasive Effect of Funny Social Issue Messages." *Communication Monographs* 74 (2007): 29–54. doi: 10.1080/03637750701196896.

Nainby, Keith, John T. Warren, and Christopher Bollinger. "Articulating Contact in the Classroom: Towards a Constitutive Focus in Critical Pedagogy." *Language & Intercultural Communication* 3 (2003): 198–212.

Nakamura, Lisa. "It's a Nigger in Here! Kill the Nigger!" In *The International Encyclopedia of Media Studies, Volume VI: Media Studies Futures,* edited by Kelly Gates, 1–14. New York: NY: Blackwell Publishing, 2012.

Neal, Mark A. *New Black Man.* New York: Routledge, 2006.

Newcomb, Horace, and Paul M. Hirsch. "Television as a Cultural Forum: Implications for Research." *Quarterly Review of Film and Video* 8 (1983): 45–55. doi: 10.1080/10509208309361170.

Northouse, Peter. *Leadership: Theory and Practice.* Thousand Oaks, CA: Sage, 2012.

Norton, Anne. *95 Theses on Politics, Culture, and Method*. New Haven, CT: Yale University Press, 2004.

O'Donohue, William, and Kyle E. Ferguson. *The Psychology of B. F. Skinner*. Thousand Oaks, CA: Sage, 2001.

O'Rourke, Sean Patrick. "Circulation and Noncirculation of Photographic Texts in the Civil Rights Movement: A Case Study of the Rhetoric of Control." *Rhetoric & Public Affairs* 15, no. 4 (2012): 685–94.

Olson, Christopher J. and CarrieLynn D. Reinhard, "About the Podcast." *The Pop Culture Lens* (podcast), January 5, 2016, thepopculturelens.podbean.com/p/about-the-podcast/. (Accessed June 13, 2016).

Ong, Walter J. *Orality and Literacy: The Technologizing of the Word*. London: Routledge, 1982.

Opam, Kwame. "*Orange is the New Black* is Getting Three More Seasons." *The Verge*, February 5, 2016. www.theverge.com/2016/2/5/10922190/orange-is-the-new-black-netflix-three-season-renewal. (Accessed May 13, 2016).

Orbe, Mark P. "Constructions of Reality on MTV's 'The Real Word': An Analysis of the Restrictive Coding of Black Masculinity." *Southern Communication Journal* 64 (1998): 32–47. doi: 10.1080/10417949809373116.

Orr, Catherine. "Charting the Currents of the Third Wave." *Hypatia* 12 (1997): 29–45. doi: 10.1111/j.1527-2001.1997.tb00004.x.

Osteen, Mark. *The Question of the Gift: Essays across Disciplines*. New York, NY: Routledge, 2013.

Othman, Nafishah, Shafiz A. M. Yusof, and R. S. Osman. "A Conflict between Professional vs. Domestic Life? Understanding the Use of ICT in Teleworking for Balance in Work and Family Units." *Computer and Information Science* 2 (2009). doi: 10.5539/cis.v2n2p3. (Accessed May 13, 2016).

Pacanowski, Michael, and Nick O'Donnell Trujillo. "Communication and Organizational Cultures." *Western Journal of Communication* 46 (1982): 115–30. doi: 10.1080/10570318209374072.

Parry-Giles, Trevor, and Shawn J Parry-Giles. *The Prime-Time Presidency: The West Wing and U.S. Nationalism*. Urbana, IL: University of Illinois Press, 2006.

Paskin, Willa. "Network TV is Broken. So How Does Shonda Rhimes Keep Making Hits?" *The New York Times Magazine*, May 9, 2013. www.nytimes.com/2013/05/12/magazine/shonda-rhimes.html?ref=magazine&_r=0&pagewanted=all. (Accessed May 13, 2016).

Patterson, Shawn, Joshua Bartholomew, Lisa Harriton, Andy Samberg, Akiva Schaffer, and Jorma Taccone. "Everything is AWESOME!!!" Single. Burbank, CA: Water-Tower, 2014.

Paul, Annie Murphy. "Are College Lectures Unfair?" *New York Times*, September 12, 2015. www.nytimes.com/2015/09/13/opinion/sunday/are-college-lectures-unfair.html?_r=0. (Accessed May 16, 2016).

Pauly, John J. "Is Journalism Interested in Resolution, or Only in Conflict? *Marquette Law Review* 93 (2009): 7–23.

Paxton, Blake. "Queerly Conversing with the Dead: Re-membering Mom." *Cultural Studies ↔ Critical Methodologies* 14 (2014): 164–73. doi: 10.1177/1532708613512273.

Payne, Chris. "Rage Against the Machine, Public Enemy & Cypress Hill Members form Supergroup Prophets of Rage: Sources." *Billboard.com*, May 18, 2016. www.billboard.com/articles/news/7377487/rage-against-machine-public-enemy-cypress-hill-prophets-rage. (Accessed May 22, 2016).

Pehlke II, Timothy Allen, Charles B. Hennon, M. Elise Radina, and Katherine A. Kuvalanka. "Does Father Still Know Best? An Inductive Thematic Analysis of Popular TV Sitcoms." *Fathering* 7 (2009): 114–39.

Peng, Wei, and Gary Hsieh. "The Influence of Competition, Cooperation, and Player Relationship in a Motor Performance Centered Computer Game." *Computers in Human Behavior* 28 (2012): 2100–6. doi:10.1016/j.chb.2012.06.014.

Pickering, Michael. *Research Methods for Cultural Studies*. Edinburgh, UK: Edinburgh University Press, 2008.

Pitts, Carl E. "Twelve Years Later: A Reply to Carl Rogers." *Journal of Humanistic Psychology* 13 (1973): 75–81. doi: 10.1177/002216787301300109.

Plato. *The Republic*, translated by Richard W. Sterling and William C. Scott. New York, NY: W.W. Norton.

Powell, Mark Allan. *Encyclopedia of Contemporary Christian Music*. Peabody, MA: Hendrickson Publishers, 2002.

Pozner, Jennifer. "The 'Big Lie': False Feminist Death Syndrome, Profit, and the Media." In *Catching a Wave: Reclaiming Feminism for the 21st Century*, edited by Rory Dicker and Alison Piepmeier, 41–56. Boston, MA: Northeastern University Press, 2003.

Pratt, Carroll C. *The Meaning of Music*. New York: McGraw-Hill, 1931.

Press, Andrea. "Feminism and Feminist Media in the Post-feminist Era: What to Make of the 'Feminist' in Feminist Media Studies." *Feminist Media Studies* 11 (2011): 107–13. doi: 10.1080/14680777.2011.537039.

Public Relations Society of America. "Public Relations Society of America (PRSA) Member Code of Ethics." www.prsa.org/AboutPRSA/Ethics/CodeEnglish/index. html#.VrZ-OfldUuc. (Accessed February 6, 2016).

Pullen, John P. "6 Times People Died While Taking Selfies." *Time*, March 14, 2016, time.com/4257429/selfie-deaths. (Accessed May 22, 2016).

Radner, Hilary. *Neo-Feminist Cinema: Girly Films, Chick Flicks, and Consumer Culture*. London, UK: Routledge, 2010.

Radway, Janice. *Reading the Romance: Women, Patriarchy, and Popular Culture*. Chapel Hill, NC: University of North Carolina Press, 1984.

Rand, Erin J. *Reclaiming Queer: Activist & Academic Rhetorics of Resistance*. Tuscaloosa, AL: University of Alabama Press, 2014.

Raney, Arthur A. "Expanding Disposition Theory: Reconsidering Character Liking, Moral Evaluations, and Enjoyment." *Communication Theory* 14 (2004): 348–69. doi: 10.1111/j.1468-2885.2004.tb00319.x.

Rasmussen, Karen. Transcendence in Leonard Bernstein's *Kaddish Symphony*. *Quarterly Journal of Speech* 80 (1994): 150–73. doi: 10.1080/00335639409384065.

Reagan, Ronald. "Farewell Speech." *WGBH - American Experience*, nd. www.pbs.org/wgbh/americanexperience/features/primary-resources/reagan-farewell. (Accessed May 16, 2016).

Rehn, Alf. "Pop (Culture) Goes the Organization: On Highbrow, Lowbrow and Hybrids in Studying Popular Culture Within Organization Studies." *Organization* 15 (2008): 765–83. doi: 10.1177/1350508408093652.

Reid, Elizabeth. "Hierarchy and Power." In *Communities in Cyberspace*, edited by Marc A. Smith and Peter Kollock, 107–33. London, UK: Routledge, 1999.

Reinhard, CarrieLynn D. and Christopher J. Olson, eds. *Making Sense of Cinema: Empirical Studies into Film Spectators and Spectatorship*. New York: Bloomsbury Academic, 2016.

Rheingold, Howard. *The Virtual Community: Homesteading on the Virtual Frontier*. New York, NY: Addison-Wesley, 1993.

Ringrose, Jessica. "Are You Sexy, Flirty, Or A Slut? Exploring 'Sexualisation' and How Teen Girls Perform/Negotiate Digital Sexual Identity on Social Networking Sites." In *New Femininities Postfeminism, Neoliberalism and Subjectivity*, edited by Rosalind Gill and Christina Scharff, 99–116. London: Palgrave MacMillan, 2011.

Riordan, Ellen. "Commodified Agents and Empowered Girls: Consuming and Producing Feminism." *Journal of Communication Inquiry* 25 (2001): 279–97. doi: 10.1177/0196859901025003006.

Roberts, Brad. "Superman's Song." Single. Los Angeles, CA: BMG/Arista, 1991.

Rodnitzky, Jerome. *Minstrels of the Dawn: The Folk-protest Singer as a Cultural Hero*. Chicago, IL: Nelson-Hall, 1976.

Rogers, Carl R. *The Carl R. Rogers Collection.* Collections of the Manuscript Division, Library of Congress.

―――. "In Retrospect: Forty-six Years." *American Psychologist* 29 (1974): 115–123.

―――. *On Becoming a Person.* Boston, MA: Houghton Mifflin, 1961.

Rogers, Carl R., and B. F. Skinner. "Some Issues Concerning the Control of Human Behavior: A Symposium." *Science* 124 (1956): 1057–66.

Rogers, Carl R., and B. F. Skinner. *Rogers/Skinner Dialogue: A Dialogue on Education and the Control of Human Behavior.* Edited by Gerald A. Gladstein. New York, NY: Psychology Today Library Cassettes, 1975.

Rollins, Peter. *Hollywood's White House.* University Press of Kentucky, 2005.

Rosenbloom, Stephanie. "A Simple Show of Hands," *New York Times,* October 5, 2006. www.nytimes.com/2006/10/05/fashion/05hands.html?pagewanted=all&_r=0. (Accessed September 15, 2015).

Roszak, Theodore. *The Making of a Counterculture* . Berkeley, CA: University of California Press, 1969.

Rottinghaus, Brandon, Kenton Bird, Travis Ridout, and Rebecca Self. "'It's Better than Being Informed': College-Aged Viewers of The Daily Show." In *Laughing Matters: Humor and American Politics in the Media Age,* edited by Jody C. Baumgartner and Jonathan S. Morris, 279–94. New York, NY: Routledge, 2008.

Saltzman, Joe. "The Image of the Public Relations Practitioner in Movies and Television, 1901–2011." *The IJPC Journal* 3 (2012): 1–50.

Samuels, Allison. "Black Women Seize Center Stage at Last." *The Daily Beast,* July 17, 2013. www.thedailybeast.com/articles/2013/07/17/black-women-seize-center-stage-at-last.html. (Accessed May 16, 2016).

Santoro, Patrick. "Lather, Rinse, Reclaim: Cultural (Re)conditioning of the Gay (Bear) Body." In *Critical Autoethnography: Intersecting Cultural Identities in Everyday Life,* edited by Robin M. Boylorn and Mark P. Orbe, 159–75. Walnut Creek, CA: Left Coast Press, 2014.

Savage, Dan. *American Savage: Insights, Slights, and Fights on Faith, Sex, Love, and Politics.* New York, NY: Plume, 2013.

Scaruffi, Piero. *A History of Popular Music before Rock Music: Blues, Country, Cabaret, Ragtime, Film Music, Soul, European, Latin, Jamaican, African, Arab, Indian….* USA: Piero Scaruffi, 2007.

Schiano, Diane J., Bonnie Nardi, Thomas Debeauvais, Nicolas Ducheneaut, and Nicholas Yee. "The 'Lonely Gamer' Revisited." *Entertainment Computing* 5 (2014): 65–70. doi: 10.1016/j.entcom.2013.08.002.

Schlitz, Don, and Steve Seskin. "I Think About You." Single. New York, NY: Epic Records, 1996.

Schlosser, Eric. "The Prison-Industrial Complex." *The Atlantic,* December, 1998. www.theatlantic.com/magazine/archive/1998/12/the-prison-industrial-complex/304669. (Accessed February 16, 2016).

Sedgwick, Eve Kosofsky. "How to Bring Your Kids Up Gay." In *Fear of a Queer Planet: Queer Politics and Social Theory,* edited by Michael Warner, 69–81. Minneapolis, MN: University of Minnesota Press, 1993.

Seifert, Christine. "Bite Me (Or Don't)." *Bitch Media,* December 15, 2008. bitchmedia.org/article/bite-me-or-dont. (Accessed May 22, 2016).

Sellnow, Deanna D. "Music as Persuasion: Refuting Hegemonic Masculinity in 'He Thinks He'll Keep Her.'" *Women's Studies in Communication* 22 (1999): 66–81. doi: 10.1080/07491409.1999.10162562.

―――. "Music as a Unifying Social Force for Neo-Nazi Skinheads: Skrewdriver's *White Ryder* as a Case Study." Paper presented at the annual conference of the Speech Communication Association, New Orleans, LA, November 19–22, 1994.

―――. *The Rhetorical Power of Popular Culture: Considering Mediated Texts.* Thousand Oaks, CA: Sage, 2014.

———. "Teaching Peace: A Rhetorical Analysis of Contemporary Children's Music." Paper presented at the annual conference of the Central States Communication Association, Cleveland, OH, April 9–12, 1992.

Sellnow, Deanna D., and Timothy L. Sellnow. "The 'Illusion of Life' Rhetorical Perspective: An Integrated Approach to the Study of Music as Communication." *Critical Studies in Media Communication* 18 (2001): 395–415. doi: 10.1080/07393180128090.

Sellnow, Timothy L., and Deanna D. Sellnow. "The Appeal of the Tragic Rhythm: Bruce Springsteen as a Case Study." *Speaker and Gavel* 27 (1990): 38–49.

Shaddix, Jacoby. "Last Resort." Single. Recorded by Papa Roach. Beverly Hills, CA, Dreamworks, 2000.

Shanahan, James, and Michael Morgan. *Television and Its Viewers: Cultivation Theory and Research*. Cambridge, UK: Cambridge University Press, 1999.

Sharma, Pramodita. "An Overview of the Field of Family Business Studies: Current Status and Directions for the Future." *Family Business Review* 17: (2004): 1–36. doi: 10.1111/j.1741-6248.2004.00001.x.

Sheeler, Kristina Horn, and Karrin Vasby Anderson. *Woman President: Confronting Postfeminist Political Culture*. College Station, TX: Texas A&M University Press, 2013.

Sherry, John L. "The Effects of Violent Video Games on Aggression." *Human Communication Research* 27 (2001): 409–31. doi: 10.1111/j.1468-2958.2001.tb00787.x.

Shore, Ira. "What is Critical Literacy." *The Journal of Pedagogy, Pluralism and Practice* 1 (1999): n.p. www.lesley.edu/journal-pedagogy-pluralism-practice/ira-shor/critical-literacy. (Accessed September 23, 2015).

Short, Daniel. "Teaching Scientific Concepts Using a Virtual world—Minecraft." *Teaching Science-The Journal of the Australian Science Teachers Association* 58 (2012): 55–8.

Silva, Alyssa. "Dean Winchester: An Existentialist Hero?" *Sesión no Numerada: Revista de Letras y Ficción Audiovisual* 2 (2012): 67–83.

Silvestri, Lisa. "A Rhetorical Forecast." *The Review of Communication* 13, no. 2 (2013): 127–142. doi: 10.1080/15358593.2013.789121.

Simon, Stephanie. "'If you raised a boy in a pink room . . . ?' Thoughts on Teaching Geography and Gender." *Journal of Geography* 108 (2009): 14–20. doi: 10.1080/00221340902758443.

Simons, Nele. "Audience Reception of Cross- and Transmedia TV Drama in the Age of Convergence." *International Journal of Communication*, 8 (2014): 2220–39. ijoc.org/index.php/ijoc/article/view/2598/1207. (Accessed June 8, 2016).

Skinner, B. F. *Beyond Freedom and Dignity*. New York, NY: Knopf, 1971.

———. *Burrhus Frederic Skinner Papers*. Harvard Archives, Pusey Library, Harvard University.

———. "Comment on Rogers." *American Psychologist* 29 (1974): 640. doi: 10.1037/h0038169.

———. *Science and Human Behavior*. New York, NY: Macmillan, 1953.

———. *Walden Two*. New York, NY: Macmillan, 1948.

Smith, Debra C. "Critiquing Reality-Based Televisual Black Fatherhood: A Critical Analysis of *Run's House* and *Snoop Dogg's Father Hood*." *Critical Studies in Media Communication* 25 (2008): 393–412. doi: 10.1080/15295030802328020.

Smith, Marc A., and Peter Kollock. *Communities in Cyberspace*. London, UK: Routledge, 1999.

Smith, Matthew J. "Introduction: The Pilgrimage to Comic-Con." In *It Happens at Comic-Con: Ethnographic Essays on a Pop Culture Phenomenon*, edited by Ben Bolling and Matthew J. Smith, 9–14. Jefferson, NC: McFarland & Company, 2014.

Smith, Ruth C., and Eric M. Eisenberg, "Conflict at Disneyland: A Root Metaphor Analysis." *Communication Monographs* 54 (1987): 367–380. doi: 10.1080/03637758709390239.

Spencer, Leland G. "Engaging Undergraduates in Feminist Classrooms: An Exploration of Professors' Practices." *Equity & Excellence in Education* 48 (2015): 195–211. doi: 10.1080/10665684.2015.1022909.

Sprague, Jo. "Expanding the Research Agenda for Instructional Communication: Raising Some Unasked Questions." *Communication Education* 42 (1992): 1–25. doi: 10.1080/03634529209378867.

Springsteen, Bruce. "Born to Run." Single. Los Angeles, CA: Columbia Records, 1975.

Steinkuehler, Constance A., and Dmitri Williams. "Where Everybody Knows Your (Screen) Name: Online Games as 'Third Places.'" *Journal of Computer-Mediated Communication* 11 (2006): 885–909. doi:10.1111/j.1083–6101.2006.00300.x.

Stern, Danielle M. "It Takes a Classless, Heteronormative Utopian Village: Gilmore Girls and the Problem of Postfeminism." *The Communication Review* 15 (2012): 167–86. doi: 10.1080/10714421.2012.702005.

Stern, Danielle M., and Chelsea Henderson. "Hashtagging Feminism: Tetradic Polymediated Activism." In *Beyond New Media: Discourse and Critique in a Polymediated Age*, edited by Art Herbig, Andrew F. Herrmann, and Adam W. Tyma, 125–41. Lanham, MD: Lexington, 2015.

Stewart, Charles J., Craig A. Smith, and Robert E. Denton, Jr. *Persuasion and Social Movements*, sixth edition. Long Grove, IL: Waveland, 2012.

Stewart, Ian. *White Ryder*. Album. Performed by *Skrewdriver*. Bruh, West Germany: Rock-o-Rama Records, 1987.

Stravinsky, Igor. *Expositions and Developments*. New York, NY: Doubleday, 1962.

Street, John. *Politics and Popular Culture*. Philadelphia: Temple University Press, 1997.

Stuckey, Mary. "On Rhetorical Circulation." *Rhetoric & Public Affairs* 15, no. 4 (2012): 609–612.

Sturken, Marita. *Tangled Memories: The Vietnam War, The AIDS Epidemic, and the Politics of Remembering*. Berkeley, CA: University of California Press, 1997.

———. *Tourists of History: Memory, Kitsch, and Consumerism from Oklahoma City to Ground Zero*. Durham, NC: Duke University Press, 2007.

Supiano, Beckie. "How Liberal-Arts Majors Fare Over the Long Haul." *The Chronicle of Higher Education*, January 22, 2014, chronicle.com/article/How-Liberal-Arts-Majors-Fare/144133/. (Accessed June 13, 2016).

Szatsmary, David P. *Rockin' in Time: A Social History of Rock and Roll*. Englewood Cliffs, NJ: Prentice-Hall, 1987.

Talvi, Silja J. A. "On the Inside with the American Correctional Association." In *Prison Profiteers: Who Makes Money from Mass Incarceration*, edited by Tara Herival and Paul Wright, 119–27. New York, NY: The New Press, 2007.

Tracy, Sarah J., and Angela Trethewey. "Fracturing the Real-Self↔Fake-Self Dichotomy: Moving Toward 'Crystallized' Organizational Discourses and Identities." *Communication Theory* 15 (2005): 168–95. doi: 10.1111/j.1468–2885.2005.tb00331.x.

Tucker, Ken. "'Watchmen': Why Rush Limbaugh Isn't Gonna like It." *Entertainment Weekly*, March 8, 2008. www.ew.com/article/2009/03/08/watchmen-rush-l. (Accessed May 14, 2016).

Turkle, Sherry. *Life on the Screen: Identity in the Age of the Age of Internet*. New York, NY: Simon and Schuster, 1995.

———. *Alone Together: Why We Expect More from Technology and Less from Each Other*. New York, NY: Basic Books, 2012.

Tyma, Adam W. "The Stories They Tell—A Technophobic Narrative Analysis of Three Popular Films: *Blade Runner, Terminator, The Matrix*." *Communication & Theater Association of Minnesota Journal* 31 (2004): 51–68.

———. "I am you and you are we and we are all… me? Understanding Media and/as Context (The Road to Polymediation)." In *Beyond New Media: Discourse and Critique in a Polymediated Age*, edited by Art Herbig, Andrew F. Herrmann & Adam W. Tyma, 1–14. Lanham, MD: Lexington Books, 2015.

Tyma, Adam W., Andrew F. Herrmann, and Art Herbig. "Introduction: The beginnings: #WeNeedaWord." In *Beyond New Media: Discourse and Critique in a Polymediated Age*, edited by Art Herbig, Andrew F. Herrmann & Adam W. Tyma, ix–xxiv. Lanham, MD: Lexington Books, 2015.

Valenti, Jessica. "Punching Gloria Steinem: Inside the Bizarre World of Anti-feminist Women." *The Guardian,* July 7, 2014. www.theguardian.com/commentisfree/2014/jul/07/anti-feminist-women-hobby-lobby-decision-great. (Accessed May 12, 2016).

Valenzano III, Joseph M., and Erika Engstrom. "Homilies and Horsemen: Revelation in the CW's *Supernatural.*" *Journal of Communication & Religion* 36 (2013): 50–72.

Vega, Tanzina. "A Show Makes Friends and History: 'Scandal' on ABC Is Breaking Barriers." *The New York Times,* January 6, 2013. www.nytimes.com/2013/01/17/arts/television/scandal-on-abc-is-breaking-barriers.html?_r=0. (Accessed May 12, 2016).

Verschelde, Tom. "New Approaches to Theory in Interpersonal Communication: Incorporating Media Perspectives." Paper presented at the Central States Communication Association Annual Convention, Kansas City, MO, April 6, 2013.

Waisanen, Don J., and Amy B. Becker. "The Problem with Being Joe Biden: Political Comedy and Circulating Personae." *Critical Studies in Media Communication* 32 (2015): 256–71. doi: 10.1080/15295036.2015.1057516.

Walker, Rebecca. *To Be Real: Telling the Truth and Changing the Face of Feminism.* New York, NY: Anchor, 1995.

Wallace, Aurora. "Better Here Than There: Prison Narratives in Reality." In *Punishment in Popular Culture,* edited by Charles J. Ogletree, Jr. and Austin Sarat, 55–78. New York: New York University Press, 2015.

Wander, Phillip. "Contiguous Fields of Study." *Text and Performance Quarterly* 34, no. 1 (2014): 99–101. doi: 10.1080/10462937.2013.848465.

Ward, Morgan K., and Susan M. Broniarczyk. "It's Not Me, It's You: How Gift Giving Creates Giver Identity Threat as a Function of Social Closeness." *Journal of Consumer Research* 38 (2011): 164–81. doi: 10.1086/658166.

Warner, Michael. *Publics and Counterpublics.* New York, NY: Zone Books, 2005.

Warren, John T., and Deanna L. Fassett. "Critical Communication Pedagogy: Reframing the Field." In *The SAGE Handbook of Communication and Instruction,* edited by Deanna L. Fassett and John T. Warren, 283–91. Thousand Oaks, CA: Sage Publishing, 2010.

Watson, Elwood, and Marc W. Shaw. *Performing American Masculinities: The 21st-century Man in Popular Culture* . Bloomington, IN: Indiana State University Press, 2011.

Weick, Karl E. *Sensemaking in Organizations.* Thousand Oaks, CA: Sage, 1995.

Wheatley, Margaret. *Leadership and the New Science.* San Francisco, CA: Berrett-Koehler, 2006.

Wilcox, Kirstin R. "How to Advocate for the Liberal Arts: The State-University Edition." *The Chronicle of Higher Education,* June 8, 2015, chronicle.com/article/How-to-Advocate-for-the/230743/. (Accessed June 13, 2016).

Wilde, Oscar. *The Decay of Lying: And Other Essays.* London: Penguin, 2010.

Williams, Jeffrey J. *How to Be An Intellectual: Essays on Criticism, Culture, and the University.* New York, NY: Fordham University Press, 2014.

———. "Long Island Intellectual." In *The Critical Pulse: Thirty-Six Credos by Contemporary Critics,* edited by Jeffrey J. Williams and Heather Steffen, 30–8. New York, NY: Columbia University Press, 2012.

Williams, Raymond. "Base and Superstructure in Marxist Cultural Theory." In *Rethinking Popular Culture: Contemporary Perspectives in Cultural Studies,* edited by Chandra Mukerji and Michael Schudson, 407–23. Berkeley, CA: University of California Press, 1991.

Wilson, Meredith. "Chicken Fat." Single. President's Council on Physical Fitness/Capitol Records, 1961.

Wood, Peter. "Lily Bart vs. Lady Gaga." *The Chronicle of Higher Education,* March 1, 2011. chronicle.com/blogs/innovations/lily-bart-vs-lady-gaga/28742. (Accessed May 14, 2016).

Woodward, William R. "Introduction: Skinner and Behaviorism as Cultural Icons: From Local Knowledge to Reader Reception." In *B. F. Skinner and Behaviorism in American Culture,* edited by Laurence D. Smith and William R. Woodward, 7–29. Bethlehem, PA: Lehigh University Press, 1996.

Wright, Paul. "The Cultural Commodification of Prisons." *Social Justice* 27 (2000), 15–21.

Wright, Robin Redmon, and Jennifer A. Sandlin. "You are What You Eat!?: Television Cooking Shows, Consumption, and Lifestyle Practices as Adult Learning." *Adult Education Research Conference,* paper 70, May 28, 2009. newprairiepress.org/aerc/2009/papers/70. (Accessed May 10, 2016).

Wyatt, Jonathan. "What Kind of Mourning? Autoethnographic Fragments." *International Review of Qualitative Research* 2 (2010): 499–512.

Xavier, Robina, Amisha Mehta, and Ingrid Larkin. "Destination Public Relations: Understanding the Sources that Influence Course Selection for and Career Preferences of Postgraduate Students." *PRism* 5 (2007/8): www.prismjournal.org/fileadmin/Praxis/Files/Journal_Files/Xavier_Mehta_Larkin.pdf. (Accessed May 13, 2016).

Yagoda, Ben. "The Strange 1960s Gym-class Anthem in Apple's New iPhone Commercial." *Slate,* June 13, 2014. www.slate.com/blogs/browbeat/2014/06/13/chicken_fat_song_apple_iphone_5s_commercial_uses_kennedy_era_exercise_anthem.html. (Accessed October 31, 2015).

Yee, Nick. "The Demographics, Motivations, and Derived Experiences of Users of Massively Multi-user Online Graphical Environments." *Presence* 15 (2006): 309–29. doi: 10.1162/pres.15.3.309.

———. "Motivations for Play in Online Games." *CyberPsychology & Behavior* 9 (2006): 772–75. doi:10.1089/cpb.2006.9.772.

———. "The Psychology of Massively Multi-user Online Role-playing Games: Motivations, Emotional Investment, Relationships and Problematic Usage." In *Avatars at Work and Play: Collaboration and Interaction in Shared Virtual Environments,* edited by Ralph Schroeder and Ann-Sofie Axelsson, 187–207. The Netherlands: Springer, 2006.

Yee, Nick, and Jeremy Bailenson. "The Proteus Effect: The Effect of Transformed Self-representation on Behavior." *Human Communication Research* 33 (2007): 271–90. doi:10.1111/j.1468–2958.2007.00299.x.

Yee, Nick, Jeremy N. Bailenson, and Nicolas Ducheneaut. "The Proteus Effect: Implications of Transformed Digital Self-representation on Online and Offline Behavior." *Communication Research* 38 (2009): 285–312. doi: 10.1177/0093650208330254.

Yep, Gust A. "The Violence of Heteronormativity in Communication Studies: Notes on Injury, Healing, and Queer World-Making." *Journal of Homosexuality* 45 (2003): 11–59. doi: 10.1300/J082v45n02_02.

Yoon, Youngmin, and Heather Black. "Learning about Public Relations from Television: How is the Profession Portrayed?" *Communication Science* 28 (2011): 85–106.

Yoshino, Kenji. *Covering: The Hidden Assault on Our Civil Rights.* New York: Random House, 2006.

Young, Iris Marion. "Communication and the Other: Beyond Deliberative Democracy." In *Democracy and Difference: Contesting the Boundaries of the Political,* edited by Seyla Benhabib, 120–35. Princeton, NJ: Princeton University Press, 1996.

Young, James E. *At Memory's Edge: After-Images of the Holocaust in Contemporary Art and Architecture.* New Haven, CT: Yale University Press, 2000.

———. *The Texture of Memory: Holocaust Memorials and Meaning.* New Haven, CT: Yale University Press, 1993.

Young, Jun, and Kirsten Foot. "Corporate E-cruiting: The Construction of Work in Fortune 500 Recruiting Web Sites." *Journal of Computer-Mediated Communication,* 11 (2005). doi: 10.1111/j.1083-6101.2006.tb00303.x. jcmc.indiana.edu/vol11/issue1/young.html. (Accessed May 13, 2016).

Yuko, Elizabeth. "Op-ed: Why *The Golden Girls* Never Lost Its Luster." *Advocate,* September 8, 2015. www.advocate.com/commentary/2015/09/08/op-ed-why-golden-girls-never-lost-its-luster. (Accessed September 15, 2015).

Zakaria, Fareed. *In Defense of a Liberal Education.* New York, NY: W. W. Norton, 2015.

Zarefsky, David. "Institutional and Social Goals for Rhetoric." *Rhetoric Society Quarterly* 34, no. 3 (2004), 36–7. doi: 10.1080/02773940409391288.

Zelizer, Barbie. "Reading the Past Against the Grain: The Shape of Memory Studies." *Critical Studies in Mass Communication* 12, no. 2 (1995): 214–39. doi:10.1080/15295039509366932.

———. *Remembering to Forget: Holocaust Memory through the Camera's Eye.* Chicago, IL: University of Chicago Press, 2000.

Zweig, Michael. *The Working Class Majority: America's Best-Kept Secret.* Ithaca, NY: Cornell University Press, 2000.

Index

blog, xvi, 97, 106, 109, 129, 130, 131, 134, 212
Blue Bloods, 40
Blue Valentine, 7
Bochco, Steven, 41
Bogart, Humphrey, xi
Bolger, Niall, 161
Bolling, Ben, 155
borderland, 32
Boston Legal, 40
Boston Marathon, 89
boundaries, 22, 27, 30–31, 200
Bowen, Shannon A., 97
Boylorn, Robin, 5
Brooks, Meredith, 71
Brooks, Dwight E., 49
brother(s), 3, 28, 29, 30–31, 94, 121, 156, 157
Browne, Ray B., 22
Brummett, Barry, 208
Buerkle, C. Wesley, 33
Budweiser, 66
Buffy the Vampire Slayer, xviii, 28, 32, 104
Burger-Helmchen, Thierry, 197
Burke, Kenneth, 86
Bush, George H. W., 96
Bush, George W., 81, 82, 84, 85, 148
business, 25–33, 167, 182, 187; family, 28–29, 94, 187

Cagney, James, xi
Calka, Michelle, xiv, 129
Campbell, Karlyn Kohrs, 108
capitalism, 124, 141, 144, 145
career, 22, 29, 41, 97, 120, 187
Carpenter, John, 57
Cartwright, Veronica, 55
Casablanca, 26
catfish, xv, xvi, xviii
celebrity, 16, 19, 20, 129, 168, 169
character, xiii, xviii, 5–6, 41–42, 53, 54, 77, 80, 81, 82, 84–85, 92–94, 95, 115, 118, 120, 124–125, 158, 182
Cherry, Kristin, 78
children, 6, 15, 68, 71, 72, 91, 94, 156, 164n10, 181, 182, 183, 184, 185, 186–190, 193
Christian Right, 133

Chrysler, 66
Chuck D, xi
civilization, 20
Civilization(video game), 26
civil rights, 63, 95
The Clash, xi
Clauset, Aaron, 65
Clerks, 26
Coca-cola, 19
coercion, 38, 52, 55, 93, 164n17
Cohendet, Patrick, 197
Colbert, Stephen, x
Cold War, 43, 81, 82, 83, 141, 144
collaboration, 38, 46, 108, 168, 193, 194
Collins, Patricia Hill, 118, 125, 186
comics, xi, xii, xx, 26, 41, 81, 105, 201; and graphic novels, xi, xx, 79–81, 86; DC, 81; Marvel, xi
Comic-Con International, x, xviii, 155
commercial, 17, 66, 181, 187, 189, 213
communication, x, xii, xiii, xvi, xviii, xix, xxiii, 31, 38, 44, 61–65, 84, 105, 110, 157, 159, 162, 176, 197; aesthetic, 63; dialogic, 168, 174, 176; familial, 30, 195–196; indexical, 66; individual, 63, 64; interpersonal, 154, 156, 217; leadership and, 25, 37–46; mass, 28, 211; organizational, 25–28, 33; and polymedia, xi, xvi, xviii–xix, xxvn41, 33, 107, 108, 129–130, 131, 132, 133–134, 136, 138; superior-subordinate, 27
communication pedagogy, 207, 209–210, 211, 217
competition, 7, 26, 38, 40
Comprehensive Crime Control Act, 116
computer, 18, 50, 51, 52, 53, 54, 62, 108, 129, 138, 196, 200
Confessions of an Aca-Fan, 106
Confucius, 61
conscientization, 210, 214
consciousness, ix, 19, 69, 115, 146, 148, 190
consumer, xvi, xvii–xviii, xxvn41, 14, 16, 17, 19, 21, 77, 108, 130, 131, 132, 157, 214, 217
convergence, xii, 106, 129
Cooper, Sandra, 43

About the Contributors

Tony E. Adams (tony.e.adams@gmail.com) is an Associate Professor and Chair of the Department of Communication, Media and Theatre at Northeastern Illinois University. He is the author of *Narrating the Closet: An Autoethnography of Same Sex Desire* (2011) and coauthor, with Stacy Holman Jones and Carolyn Ellis, of *Autoethnography* (2015). He also coedited, with Stacy and Carolyn, the *Handbook of Autoethnography* (2013), and coedited, with Jonathan Wyatt, *On (Writing) Families: Autoethnographies of Presence and Absence, Love and Loss* (2014).

Rob Anderson (PhD, University of Missouri), an emeritus professor of communication and an award-winning teacher at Saint Louis University, explores dialogue in everyday relations and media institutions. Most of his eleven books—several written or edited with Ken Cissna—focus on challenges of public dialogue, including *The Conversation of Journalism, Dialogue: Theorizing Difference in Communication Studies, The Martin Buber-Carl Rogers Dialogue: A New Transcript with Commentary, Moments of Meeting, Questions of Communication*, and *The Reach of Dialogue*. Rob continues to learn and write since retiring, while nursing along his vintage turntables, exercising two lively labs, studying the varied moods of Lake Michigan, and savoring quiet dinners with Dona. You might contact him by emailing robertjport@gmail.com, or maybe by driving through downtown Jacksonport, Wisconsin, and yelling his name out the window.

Bob Batchelor (PhD, University of South Florida) writes about contemporary American culture and teaches strategic communications at Miami University. His books include *Mad Men: A Cultural History* (2016), *Gatsby: The Cultural History of the Great American Novel* (2013), and *Updike: A Critical Biography* (2013). Batchelor is the founding editor of the *Popular Culture Studies Journal* and edits five book series for Rowman & Littlefield. For more information, please visit www.bobbatchelor.com.

Krista J. Catalfamo (BA, Christopher Newport University) is a recent graduate from Christopher Newport University with a degree in Communication. Krista recently moved to Chicago, where she is studying at The Second City as she pursues a career in Comedy. She got a concussion working in retail. The full story will be told in her upcoming autobiography "Concussed and Confused."

Kenneth N. Cissna (PhD, University of Denver) is emeritus professor of communication at the University of South Florida. He served as editor of the *Journal of Applied Communication Research*, the *Southern Communication Journal*, and *Qualitative Communication Research*. In addition to his work on dialogue published with Rob Anderson, his books include *The Routledge Handbook of Applied Communication Research* (with Larry Frey) and *Applied Communication in the 21st Century*. Among other awards, he received the 2008 Gerald M. Phillips Award for Distinguished Applied Communication Scholarship from the National Communication Association and the 2013 Distinguished Service Award from the University of South Florida. In retirement, he enjoys hiking in the north Georgia mountains and playing with his rescue dog, Artie. He (Ken, not Artie) responds well to email directed to kcissna@usf.edu.

Katherine J. Denker is an Associate Professor and Basic Course Director at Ball State University where she explore issues of power and voice in instructional and interpersonal communication. Her recent work has been published in both book chapters as well as journals including *Communication Teacher, Communication Reports, Journal of Computer Assisted Learning, Journal of Family Communication*, and *Women & Language*.

Robert Andrew Dunn (PhD, University of Alabama) is an associate professor of mass communication at East Tennessee State University and head of the journalism program. He teaches both journalism and mass communication courses. His research focuses on avatars, virtual identity, mediated identity, media psychology, media effects, fandom, and communication technology. He also has a strong interest in journalism and media convergence. Academically, Dunn holds a PhD in mass communication from the University of Alabama. Professionally, Dunn worked in newspapers for nearly a decade. He is an avid gamer, dedicated sports fanatic, expert comic collector, enthusiastic sci-fi/fantasy devotee, and frequent fan convention attendee.

Eric M. Eisenberg is Professor of Communication and Dean of the College of Arts and Sciences at the University of South Florida. Eisenberg graduated Phi Beta Kappa from Rutgers University and received his doctorate in Organizational Communication from Michigan State University. Dr. Eisenberg twice received the National Communication Association award for outstanding research publication in organizational communication, as well as the Burlington Foundation award for excellence in teaching. Dr. Eisenberg is the author of over seventy articles, chapters, and books on the subjects of organizational communication, health communication, and communication theory. He is an internationally recognized researcher, teacher, and consultant specializing in the strategic use of communication to promote positive organizational change.

Lawrence Grossberg is the Morris Davis Distinguished Professor of Communication and Cultural Studies, at the University of North Carolina Chapel Hill. He has authored seven books including *We Gotta Get out of this Place, Caught in the Crossfire,* and most recently, *Cultural Studies in the Future Tense* and *We All Want to Change the World.* He has coedited a dozen books, and published over 200 essays, and his work has been translated into over a dozen languages. He has edited the international journal *Cultural Studies* for twenty-five years. He is currently completing a sympathetic critique of the speculative/ontological turn.

Art Herbig (PhD, University of Maryland, 2011) is the Associate Professor of Media Production at Indiana University–Purdue University, Fort Wayne. His research spans the areas of criticism, method, and theory. He has coedited books, written chapters and articles, as well as produced and directed films. Ultimately, the three works he is most proud of to date are this volume, his coedited book *Beyond New Media: Discourse and Critique in a Polymediated Age* which he worked on with Andrew F. Herrmann and Adam W. Tyma, and the film *Never Forget: Public Memory & 9/11* which he directed alongside Alix Watson and Aaron Hess. He may be contacted at artherbig@gmail.com.

Andrew F. Herrmann (PhD, University of South Florida) is an Assistant Professor of Communication Studies at East Tennessee State University. His communication research examines power and personal identity at the intersections of organizational, occupational, familial, and mediated contexts. He coedited *Beyond New Media: Discourse and Critique in a Polymediated Age* with Art Herbig and Adam W. Tyma (2015). His recent research appears in *Departures in Critical Qualitative Research, Popular Culture Studies Journal, International Journal of Communication, IRQR,* and *Qualitative Inquiry.* He drinks too much coffee, collects too many comic books, and binge-watches too much television. He may be contacted at andrew.f.herrmann@gmail.com and @ComDoc_H via Twitter.

Will P. Howell is a doctoral student at the University of Maryland, College Park, studying Rhetoric and Political Culture. He graduated from Macalester College in 2008 with a BA in political science and worked for roughly five years on a variety of political campaigns and advocacy efforts in Minnesota and Oregon. He studies how entertainment—particularly, humor—engages US citizens' sense of empowerment, identity, and efficacy. He can be reached at will.p.howell@gmail.com.

Johnny Jones (MFA, California Institute of the Arts) is an Assistant Professor of Theatre Arts at University of Louisville. His creative writing and performance studies research examines black masculinities within contemporary black performance and American culture contexts. Recent work appeared in *NORMA: International Journal for Masculinity Studies*. He watches *Mad Men* obsessively and enjoys all things hip-hop studies. Most proudly and unapologetically, he incorporates Prince Rogers Nelson into daily conversations, office meetings, scholarship, and pedagogy. Hence, his public mourning of the celebrity artist's transition is truly a personal, creative, and intellectual thing. He may be contacted at johnny. jones@louisville.edu.

Ryessia Jones (MA, University of Louisville) is a doctoral candidate at The University of Texas at Austin in the Department of Communication Studies with a focus on Rhetorical and Language Studies. Her research interests include portrayals of African Americans in reality television, specifically in the areas of Black fatherhood, Black motherhood, and masculinity. Furthermore, she has taken an interest in examining media representations of police brutality victims, specifically Black males. In her free time, she steeps tea and watches Netflix on her ex-boyfriend's account. She may be contacted at ryessiaj@gmail.com.

Michelle Kelsey Kearl (PhD, Arizona State University) is an Assistant Professor of Communication at Indiana University Purdue University— Fort Wayne. Michelle's work is grounded in critical rhetoric and intersectional orientations and is interested in unpacking the discourses that emerge when intersectional conflicts erupt. She has published in *Communication and Critical/Cultural Studies* on the intersectional discourses of social movements, but her current research focuses on instances of cultural controversy around power, identity, and difference.

Cheryl Ann Lambert (PhD, University of Tennessee) is an assistant professor at Kent State University. Her scholarship in the areas of media representations of public relations and journalism norms have been informed by seven years in corporate public relations at Sears, Roebuck and Co., and five years at Chilton Publishing. Her work has been published in the *Journal of Media Ethics*, *Public Relations Inquiry*, *Health Marketing Quarterly*, and *PRism Online PR Journal*. Her quest to explore representations includes academic conference participation and a healthy diet of television and film. She can be reached at clambe17@kent.edu or @PRProfLamb on Twitter.

Jimmie Manning (PhD, University of Kansas) is Associate Professor of Communication at Northern Illinois University. His research areas include relational communication, sexuality, health, and technology. This research has accrued over 70 publications including articles in *Communication Monographs* and *Journal of Computer-Mediated Communication* and the coauthored book *Researching Interpersonal Relationships: Qualitative Methods, Research, and Analysis* (Sage Publications). Professor Manning is the Executive Director for the Central States Communication Association and serves in several other national and international leadership positions. He is also the recipient of the prestigious Teaching Award from the International Association for Relationship Research.

Kristen L. McCauliff (PhD, University of Georgia) is an Associate Professor of Communication Studies at Ball State University. Her research examines the intersections of feminism, citizenship and media. Her recent work can be found in *Communication Studies, Rhetoric Society Quarterly and Teaching Media Quarterly.* Her coauthored book entitled *(Feminist) Rhetorical Strategies of Conservative Women* is set to be released in Fall 2016. She can be reached at klmccauliff@bsu.edu and on twitter @klmccauliff.

Trevor Parry-Giles is a professor in the Department of Communication at the University of Maryland and the Director for Academic & Professional Affairs at the National Communication Association (NCA). His primary research interests are in the areas of political and legal rhetoric; Dr. Parry-Giles is the author of *The Character of Justice: Rhetoric, Law, and Politics in the Supreme Court Confirmation Process* (2006), which received the Kohrs-Campbell Prize in Rhetorical Criticism as well as NCA's Diamond Anniversary Book Award, and the coauthor of *The Prime-Time Presidency: The West Wing and U.S. Nationalism* (2006).

Devin Scott is a doctoral student at the University of Maryland, College Park, studying Rhetoric and Political Culture. He graduated from Truman State University in 2010 with a BA in Communication. His research areas are political rhetoric and new media, with an emphasis on ethnographic approaches. He can be reached at dss094@umd.edu.

Deanna Sellnow (PhD, University of North Dakota) is a research professor of strategic communication in the Nicholson School of Communication at the University of Central Florida. Dr. Sellnow conducts research in two major areas. The first focuses on strategic instructional communication in a variety of contexts (e.g., risk, crisis, health). The second focuses on rhetorical studies of popular culture. She has conducted funded research for the USGS, USDA, Department of Homeland Security, and CDC. Her work is published in refereed national and international journals, and she has authored or coauthored several books including *Effective Speaking in a Digital Age, Communicate!, Communicate!,* and *The Rhetorical Power of Popular Culture.*

Siobhan E. Smith (PhD, University of Missouri) is an Assistant Professor in the Department of Communication at the University of Louisville. She teaches courses in mass media, race, and culture, including one on Reality Television. She has presented her research at several conferences and in peer reviewed journals, such as the *Western Journal of Black Studies*. Her research interests include media literacy and cultural diversity. She loves watching (trashy!) reality television, reading and watching sci-fi/fantasy/ horror texts, and eating chocolate. She can be reached at siobhan. smith@louisville.edu.

Danielle M. Stern (PhD, Ohio University) is an associate professor in Christopher Newport University's Department of Communication. Her research engages the role of feminism in transforming popular culture and pedagogy. She is coeditor of *Lucky Strikes and a Three-Martini Lunch: Thinking about Television's Mad Men*. Her nearly 20 scholarly articles have been published in *Text and Performance Quarterly, The Communication Review, Women's Studies in Communication, Sexuality & Culture, The Popular Culture Studies Journal*, and *Women & Language*, as well as in various edited books. To survive academia, Danielle is an avid yogi and dog lover.

Jessalynn Strauss (PhD, University of Oregon) is an assistant professor at Elon University in Elon, NC. Her research addresses corporate social responsibility and public relations in the casino industry, particularly in the city of Las Vegas, Nevada, where she also researches the history of public relations and tourism marketing. Her book *Challenging Corporate Social Responsibility: Lessons for Public Relations from the Casino Industry* was published by Routledge in 2015. She can be reached at jstrauss2@elon.edu or on Twitter at @jrstrauss.

Natalie T. J. Tindall (PhD, University of Maryland, 2007) is an associate professor in the Department of Communication at Lamar University. Her research focuses on diversity in organizations, specifically the public relations function, and the situational theory of publics and intersectionality. She can be reached through her website (natalietjtindall.com) and via Twitter at @dr_tindall.

Adam W. Tyma (PhD, North Dakota State University) is an associate professor of critical media studies and graduate program chair in the School of Communication at the University of Nebraska at Omaha, fellow for the UNO Center for Collaborative Science, cofounder of the UNO Social Media Lab, and coordinator for the Visual Communication and Culture minor. Dr. Tyma has published work in the *Journal of Communication Inquiry, The Popular Culture Studies Journal, International Journal of Communication, Communication Teacher*, and *Basic Communication Course*

Best Practices: A Training Manual for Instructors (edited volume), amongst others. He is also coeditor and contributor to *Beyond New Media*. In addition to publishing, Dr. Tyma has developed the Media Literacy Education Project (MLEP), a service-learning program that creates curriculum for after-school programs at the 5th to 8th grade level.